FOURTH EDITION

COMPUTER SCIENCE

AN OVERVIEW

FOURTH EDITION

COMPUTER SCIENCE

AN OVERVIEW

J. Glenn Brookshear
Marquette University

The Benjamin/Cummings Publishing Company, Inc.

Redwood City, California • Menlo Park, California
Reading, Massachusetts • New York • Don Mills, Ontario • Wokingham, U.K.
Amsterdam • Bonn • Sydney • Tokyo • Madrid • Spain

To my parents
Garland and Reba Brookshear

Sponsoring Editor: Carter Shanklin
Editorial Assistant: Melissa Standen
Production Coordinator: Andy Marinkovich
Cover Design: Yvo Riezebos
Copyeditor: Barbara Conway
Proofreader: Holly Mclean-Aldis
Artists: Ben Turner Graphics
Composition: Graphic World

Library of Congress Cataloging-in-Publication Data
Brookshear, J. Glenn.
    Computer science : an overview / J. Glenn Brookshear. — 4th ed.
      p.   cm.
    Includes bibliographical references and index.
    ISBN 0-8053-4627-9
    1. Computer science.   I. Title.
QA76.B743   1993   93-24520
004 — dc20   CIP

12345678910-DOCR-97 96 95 94 93

The Benjamin/Cummings Publishing Company, Inc.
390 Bridge Parkway
Redwood City, CA 94065

PREFACE

I wrote this book to provide a comprehensive overview of computer science, one that presents a thought-provoking introduction to the key issues and concepts throughout the field. I have done this with two primary audiences in mind.

Computer Science Majors

The first audience consists of computer science majors and minors in the early stages of their college careers. Students at this stage tend to equate computer science with programming because that is essentially all they have seen. Yet computer science is much more than programming. In turn, beginning computer science students need to be exposed to the breadth of the subject in which they are planning to major. Providing this exposure is the purpose of this book. It gives students an overview of computer science — a foundation from which they can understand the relevance and interrelationships of future courses. Without such a perspective, students easily become immersed in the details of specialized courses and never understand the true scope and dynamics of the field. In short, this book represents the application of top-down methodologies, as taught within the curriculum, to the computer science curriculum itself.

A lot has happened since the first edition of this book. Today, the computer-science-is-much-more-than-programming philosophy is widely endorsed, as witnessed by the famous Denning Report and, more recently, the report of the ACM/IEEE-CS Joint Curriculum Task Force. Those who subscribe to this movement will be pleased that this fourth edition continues the tradition of the preceding ones in that its content conforms closely to the subject areas of computer science as identified in these reports. This text provides students of computer science with an accessible introduction to the breadth of their subject, all within a single volume.

Students of Other Disciplines

I also designed this book with majors of others fields in mind. Too often, these students are channelled into courses that teach them merely how to use some software packages or provide an elementary introduction to programming. Unfortunately, the subject matter of these courses is often time-sensitive, limited in portability, or not developed to a depth to be useful outside the classroom. Any benefits from such courses dissipate quickly after the semester is over.

I believe that these students are seeking "computer literacy," which I loosely define as the ability to distinguish between computer science and science fiction. Providing this level of "literacy" in their respective fields is the purpose of such courses as general chemistry, biology, and physics. Students do not take these courses to develop specific skills. Rather, the major goal is to develop an understanding of the discipline — including its scope, major results and consequences, research techniques, and the current status of the field. The fact that a student might be required to develop certain skills while taking the course is merely a temporary consequence. The true benefit of the course — obtaining an overall picture of the subject — survives long after these specific items have been forgotten.

Why, then, do we insist that a computer science course for nonmajors emphasize skills? The goal should be to present an overall picture of the science, which is exactly what I have designed this book to provide. After taking a course based on this text, a student will have obtained an understanding of the science behind today's computerized society. This understanding will remain long after the details and skills "memorized" during the semester have dissipated. Indeed, the student will have been educated rather than trained.

The Fourth Edition

In addition to numerous minor changes designed to update, correct, or generally improve the text, this fourth edition differs from the third in the following, more significant ways.

- The role of abstraction and abstract tools is explicitly presenting as a recurring theme.
- Ties to social, ethical, and professional issues have been expanded.
- The material on networks in Chapter 3 has been expanded to include an introduction to the OSI reference model and its significance.
- The material on parallel computing has been expanded, including a new section on parallel programming using the Linda primitives in Chapter 5.
- A new section in Chapter 6 discusses the role of metrics in software engineering.
- The object-oriented paradigm has been given additional emphasis by means of specific examples using Ada and C++ in Chapter 7 and a new section on object-oriented databases in Chapter 9.
- Significantly more exercises have been added.
- Manuals for closed laboratories are now available in the languages Pascal and C.

Pedagogical Features

This text is the product of many years of teaching the material. As a result, it is rich in pedagogical aids. Paramount in this regard is the abundance of problems to enhance the student's participation. Each section within a chapter closes with several Questions/Exercises to challenge students to think independently. They review the material just discussed, extend the previous discussion, or hint at related topics to be covered later. These questions are answered in Appendix F.

Each chapter concludes with a collection of Chapter Review Problems. These problems are designed to serve as "homework" problems in that they call for specific answers, can be solved in a short period of time, and are not answered in the text.

Following the Chapter Review Problems are Problems for the Programmer. These problems are designed for students who already have a programming background and serve to enhance the student's problem-solving/program-development skills as well as provide additional insights into the material in the chapter. If desired, many of these problems can be expanded into programming projects. These problems are an excellent resource when the book is used as a text for a course following the traditional introductory programming course.

Another pedagogical aid is the use of optional sections. These sections are marked in the table of contents. The fact that a section is declared optional does not mean that its material is necessarily more difficult or should be skipped. It merely means that the material in later (nonoptional) sections does not rely on these sections. The purpose of identifying these sections is to allow students to reach later portions of the text more quickly than would otherwise be possible. For example, many instructors may wish to skip or postpone much of the material on machine architecture and operating systems in order to spend more time on algorithm development and representation as discussed in chapters 4 and 5. The use of optional sections allows for this change yet leaves the material available for the more inquisitive students or courses with different goals.

Laboratory Materials

Supplementary laboratory manuals that are coordinated with the text are available for courses with an introductory-level programming component. These manuals, one for the language Pascal and the other for C, are designed for a closed laboratory that meets once a week for approximately two hours. Each manual contains material for 16 laboratory sessions (many are optional) that teach the rudiments of the particular programming language and provide experiments that reinforce material in the parent text.

Each laboratory session consists of explanatory material, activities for the student that are presented in a true experiment format that encourages investigation, and post-laboratory problems that ask students to apply their knowledge outside the closed laboratory environment.

The laboratory manuals are supported by software that is available from The Benjamin/Cummings Publishing Company via the Internet using ftp. The address is bc.aw.com. When asked for a name, respond by typing anonymous; when asked for a password, respond with your own address. From the directory in which you will be placed, the software is two directories down along the path bc/brookshear. (For non-UNIX readers, you get to this directory by typing cd bc/brookshear.) For more details, consult the 00README file in the brookshear directory. (Again, for the non-UNIX crowd, type get 00README to download this file to your local environment and type bye to terminate the connection.)

Acknowledgments

With each new edition, the list of those who have contributed through their suggestions and comments continues to grow. Today this list includes J. M. Adams, D. C. S. Allison, P. Bankston, M. Barnard, K. Bowyer, P. W. Brashear, C. M. Brown, B. Calloni, M. Clancy, D. H. Cooley, F. Deek, M. J. Duncan, N. E. Gibbs, J. D. Harris, D. Hascom, P. Henderson, L. Hunt, L. A. Jehn, K. Korb, G. Krenz, T. J. Long, C. May, S. J. Merrill, J. C. Moyer, J. Paul Myers, Jr., G. Rice, N. Richert, J. B. Rogers, J. C. Simms, M. C. Slattery, J. Slimick, D. Smith, J. Solderitsch, L. Steinberg, J. Talburt, P. Tromovitch, and M. Ziegler. To these individuals I give my sincere thanks. A special thank you goes to Phil Bender and Jody Jung for writing the laboratory manuals.

As in the case of the earlier editions, I also thank my family, Earlene and Cheryl, for their support. They have seen how the development of a manuscript can expand to dominate an author's time. I thank them for their understanding and patience.

J.G.B.

CONTENTS

* Sections marked by an asterisk are optional in that they provide additional depth of coverage that is not required for an understanding of future chapters.

INTRODUCTION

Computer science is the discipline that seeks to build a scientific foundation for a variety of topics, including computer design, computer programming, information processing, algorithmic solutions of problems, and the algorithmic process itself. In turn, it is the science that provides the underpinnings for today's computer applications as well as the foundations on which tomorrow's applications will be based. It follows that we cannot become knowledgeable in computer science by studying only a few topics as isolated subjects or by merely learning how to use the computing tools of today. Rather, to understand the science of computing we must grasp the scope and dynamics of a wide range of topics.

This book is designed to provide such a background. It presents computer science through an integrated introduction of the subjects that constitute a typical university computer science curriculum. The book can therefore serve as a foundation for beginning computer science students or as an accessible source for other students seeking an introduction to the science behind today's computer-oriented society.

0-1 The Study of Algorithms

We begin with the most fundamental concept of computer science—that of an algorithm. Informally, an algorithm is a set of instructions that directs the execution of a task.[1] For example, there are algorithms for constructing model airplanes (expressed in the form of instruction sheets), for operating washing machines (usually

---

[1]More precisely, an algorithm is a finite set of unambiguous, executable instructions that directs a terminating activity. These details are discussed in Chapter 4.

displayed on the inside of the washer's lid), for playing music (expressed in the form of sheet music), and for performing magic tricks (Figure 0-1).

In the domain of computing machinery, algorithms are represented as programs within computers. (These programs are collectively called software in contrast to the machinery itself, which is hardware.) To get a machine to perform a task, an algorithm for performing that task must first be discovered and programmed into the machine. As a result, the study of algorithms plays a central role in computer science.

The study of algorithms began as a subject in mathematics. In fact, the search for algorithms was a significant activity of mathematicians long before the development of today's computers. The major goal of that search was to find a single set of directions that described how any problem of a particular type could be solved. One

Figure 0-1 An algorithm for a magic trick

Effect: The performer places some cards from a normal deck of playing cards face down on a table and mixes them thoroughly while spreading them out on the table. Then, as the audience requests either red or black cards, the performer turns over cards of the requested color.

Secret and Patter:

1. From a normal deck of cards, select ten red cards and ten black cards. Deal these cards face up in two piles on the table according to color.

2. Announce that you have selected some red cards and some black cards.

3. Pick up the red cards. Under the pretense of aligning them into a small deck, hold them face down in your left hand and, with the thumb and first finger of your right hand, pull back on each end of the deck so that each card is given a slightly backward curve. Then place the deck of red cards face down on the table as you say, "Here are the red cards in this stack."

4. Pick up the black cards. In a manner similar to that in step 3, give these cards a slight forward curve. Then return these cards to the table in a face-down deck as you say, "And here are the black cards in this stack."

5. Immediately after returning the black cards to the table, use both hands to mix the red and black cards (still face down) as you spread them out on the tabletop. Explain that you are thoroughly mixing the cards.

6. As long as there are face-down cards on the table, repeatedly execute the following steps:

    6.1. Ask the audience to request either a red card or a black card.

    6.2. If the color requested is red and there is a face-down card with a concave appearance, turn over such a card while saying, "Here is a red card."

    6.3. If the color requested is black and there is a face-down card with a convex appearance, turn over such a card while saying, "Here is a black card."

    6.4. Otherwise, state that there are no more cards of the requested color and turn over the remaining cards to prove your claim.

Figure 0-2 The Euclidean algorithm for finding the greatest common divisor of two positive integers

Description: This algorithm assumes that its input consists of two positive integers and proceeds to compute the greatest common divisor of these two values.

Procedure:

1. Assign M and N the value of the larger and smaller of the two input values, respectively.

2. Divide M by N, and call the remainder R.

3. If R is not 0, then assign M the value of N,
          assign N the value of R, and
          return to step 2;
          otherwise, the greatest common divisor is the value currently assigned to N.

of the best-known consequences of this early search for algorithms (and one of the more elementary examples of it) is the long division algorithm for finding the quotient of two multiple-digit numbers. Another example is the Euclidean algorithm (discovered by the ancient Greek mathematician Euclid) for finding the greatest common divisor of two positive integers (Figure 0-2).

Once an algorithm for performing a task has been found, the performance of that task no longer requires an understanding of the principles on which the algorithm is based. Instead, the performance of the task is reduced to the process of merely following directions. (One can follow the long division algorithm to find a quotient or the Euclidean algorithm to find a greatest common divisor without understanding why the algorithm works.) In a sense, the intelligence required to perform the task is encoded in the algorithm.

It is through this ability to capture and convey intelligence by means of algorithms that we are able to build machines that display intelligent behavior. Consequently, the level of intelligence displayed by machines is limited by the intelligence that can be conveyed through algorithms. If we can find an algorithm that directs the performance of a task, then we can construct a machine to perform that task (provided technology has advanced far enough). Conversely, if no algorithm exists for performing a task, then the performance of that task lies beyond the capabilities of machines.

A major undertaking throughout the computing field, then, is the development of algorithms, and consequently a significant part of computer science is concerned with issues relating to that task. In turn, we can gain an understanding of the breadth of computer science by considering some of these issues. One such issue deals with the question of how algorithms are discovered in the first place—a question that is closely related to that of problem solving in general. (To discover an algorithm for solving a problem is essentially to discover a solution for the problem.) It follows that studies in this branch of computer science draw heavily from such areas as the psychology of human problem solving and theories of education. We consider some of these ideas in Chapters 4 and 6.

Once an algorithm for solving a problem has been discovered, the next step is to represent the algorithm so it can be communicated to a machine or to other humans. This means that we must transform the conceptual algorithm into a clear set of instructions and represent these instructions in an unambiguous manner. Studies emerging from these concerns draw from our knowledge of language and grammar and have led to an abundance of algorithm representation schemes (known as programming languages) based on a variety of approaches to the programming process (known as programming paradigms). We consider some of these in Chapter 5.

In many instances, such as in business environments, the development of programs does not require the discovery of radically new algorithms. Rather, the major obstacle in these cases is to identify what automated systems are needed and how these new systems will interact with existing ones. (Will the new employee benefits system blend with the existing personnel records system?) In such cases, the task of program development is seen as a small part of the overall business management process. Combining this insight with the realization that the algorithmic structure of large automated systems must be engineered in much the same way as the machines themselves has led to the branch of computer science known as software engineering. Today, research in this field is providing automated organization and planning systems that allow nonprogrammers to develop the systems they need without technical assistance. We study software engineering in Chapter 6.

Still another important branch of computer science deals with the design and construction of machines. We consider these topics later in this introduction as well as in Chapters 1 and 2. Although our study of computer architecture incorporates some discussions of technological issues, our goal is not to master the details of how today's architecture is implemented in electronic circuitry. That would lead us too far into the subject of electrical engineering. Moreover, just as yesterday's gear-driven calculators gave way to electronic devices, today's electronics may soon be replaced by other technologies, a prime candidate being optics. Our goal is to understand just enough of today's technology so that we can appreciate its ramifications in today's machines as well as its influence on the development of computer science.

Ideally, we would like the architecture of computers to be a consequence solely of our knowledge of algorithmic processes and not limited by the capabilities of technology. That is, rather than allowing the dictates of technology to determine machine design and thus the way we represent algorithms, we would like our knowledge of algorithms to be the driving force behind modern machine architecture. As technology advances, this dream is becoming more of a reality. Today, it is possible to construct machines that allow algorithms to be represented as multiple sequences of instructions that are executed simultaneously (Chapter 2) or as patterns of connections between numerous processing units, in much the same way that our minds represent information as links between neurons (Chapters 2 and 10).

Another context in which we study computer architecture relates to data storage and retrieval. Here the internal features of a machine are often reflected in the machine's external characteristics. We consider these features and ways of avoiding their undesirable effects in Chapters 1, 7, 8, and 9.

Closely related to the design of computing machinery is the design of a machine's interface with the outside world. How, for example, will algorithms be inserted into a machine, and how will the machine be told which algorithm to execute? Resolving such problems in an environment in which the machine is expected to provide a variety of services requires the solution to many problems involving coordination of activities and resource allocation. We investigate some of these solutions in our discussion of operating systems in Chapter 3.

As machines have been asked to perform more and more intelligent tasks, computer science has turned to the study of human intelligence for leadership. The hope is that by understanding how our own minds reason and perceive, we will be able to design algorithms that mimic these processes and thus transfer these capabilities to machines. The result is the area of computer science known as artificial intelligence, which leans heavily on research in such areas as psychology, biology, and linguistics. We discuss some of these topics in artificial intelligence in Chapter 10.

The search for algorithms to direct increasingly complex tasks also leads to questions regarding the ultimate limitations of algorithmic processes. Remember, if no algorithm exists for performing a task, then that task cannot be performed by a machine. We say that a task that can be described by an algorithm is algorithmic. In short, then, machines are only capable of performing algorithmic tasks.

The realization that there are nonalgorithmic tasks surfaced as a subject in mathematics in the early 1900s with the publication of Kurt Gödel's incompleteness theorem. This theorem essentially states that in any mathematical theory encompassing our traditional arithmetic system, there are statements that can be neither proved nor disproved. In short, any complete study of our simple arithmetic system lies beyond the capabilities of algorithmic activities.

The desire to study the limitations of algorithmic methods that followed Gödel's discovery led mathematicians to design abstract machines for executing algorithms (this was before technology was able to provide actual machines for investigation) and to study the theoretical powers of such hypothetical machines. Today, this study of algorithms and machines forms the theoretical backbone of computer science. We discuss some of these topics in this area in Chapter 11.

0-2 The Development of Algorithmic Machines

The abstract machines hypothesized by mathematicians in the early 1900s form an important part of the family tree for today's computers. However, other branches of the tree extend much further back in time. Indeed, the quest for machines that perform algorithmic tasks (which we will call algorithmic machines) has had a long history.

One of the first computing devices was the abacus. Its history has been traced as far back as the ancient Greek and Roman civilizations, and it is still used today. The machine is quite simple, consisting of beads strung on rods that are in turn mounted in a rectangular frame. As the beads are moved back and forth on the rods, their positions represent stored values. It is in the positions of the beads that this "computer" represents and stores data. Data input is accomplished by a human who positions the beads; data output consists of observing the bead positions. For control of an algorithm's execution, the machine relies on the human operator. Thus, the abacus alone is merely a data storage system; it must be combined with a human to create a complete algorithmic machine.

In more recent years, the design of computing machines was based on the technology of gears. Among the inventors were Blaise Pascal (1623–1662) of France, Gottfried Wilhelm Leibniz (1646–1716) of Germany, and Charles Babbage (1792–1871) of England. With these machines, data were represented by the positions of gears, with data being input mechanically to establish gear positions (Figure 0-3). Output from Pascal's and Leibniz's machines was achieved by observing the final gear positions in much the same way that we read the numbers on a car's odometer. Babbage, on the other hand, envisioned a machine that would print output values on paper so that the possibility of errors in transcribing would be eliminated.

Figure 0-3 A prototype of Babbage's difference engine (Courtesy of International Business Machines Corporation)

As for the ability to follow an algorithm, we can see a progression of flexibility in the machines. Pascal's machine was built to follow only the addition algorithm. Consequently, the appropriate sequence of steps was embedded into the structure of the machine itself. In a similar manner, Leibniz's machine had its algorithms firmly embedded in its architecture, although it offered a variety of arithmetic operations from which the operator could select. Finally, Babbage's machine was designed so that the sequence of steps the machine was to perform could be communicated to the machine in the form of holes in paper cards.

This idea of communicating an algorithm via holes in paper was not originated by Babbage. In 1801, Joseph Jacquard had applied a similar technique to control weaving looms in France (Figure 0-4). In particular, he developed a loom in which the steps to be performed during the weaving process were determined by patterns of holes in paper cards. In this manner the algorithm followed by the machine could be easily changed to produce different woven designs.

The weaving looms of Jacquard are as much the forerunners of modern computers as are the machines previously mentioned. The only reason the looms are sometimes overlooked is that some historians have recorded the history of computers as the history of numeric calculators rather than that of algorithmic machines. This

Figure 0-4 Jacquard's loom (Courtesy of International Business Machines Corporation)

is a narrow and unfortunate point of view. In reality, a significant number (probably the majority) of computer applications today are nonnumeric. Moreover, it was the programmable weaving loom and not the more complex gear-driven calculators that the technology of the time was able to reproduce, and it was therefore these looms that raised the population's anxiety in ways similar to those caused by the computers of today. Indeed, many people lost their jobs to these weaving machines.

The technology of the time was unable to provide the precision required to popularize the complex gear-driven calculators of Pascal, Leibniz, and Babbage. It was not until electronics began to supplement mechanical devices that technology was able to support the theoretical developments taking place in the embryonic science of computing. Examples of this advance include the electromechanical machine of George Stibitz, completed in 1940 at Bell Laboratories, and the Mark I that was completed in 1944 at Harvard University by Howard Aiken and a group of IBM engineers (Figure 0-5). These machines made heavy use of electronically controlled mechanical relays. In this sense they were obsolete almost as soon as they were built, because other researchers were applying the technology of vacuum tubes to construct totally electronic digital computers. The first of these machines was apparently the Atanasoff-Berry machine, constructed during the period from 1937 to 1941 at Iowa State College (now Iowa State University) by John Atanasoff and his assistant, Clifford Berry. Another was a machine called COLOSSUS, built in England to decode German messages during the latter part of World War II. Other, more flexible machines such

Figure 0-5 The Mark I (Courtesy of Cruft Photo Laboratory, Harvard University)

as the ENIAC (electronic numerical integrator and calculator) developed by John Mauchly and J. Presper Eckert at the Moore School of Electrical Engineering, University of Pennsylvania soon followed.

From that point on, the history of algorithmic machines is one of advancing technology, the most notable steps being the invention of transistors and the subsequent development of integrated circuits, which today allow machines with significantly more power than the machines of the 1940s to be placed on a desk top.

0-3 Modern Machine Architecture

History gives Charles Babbage credit for isolating the components necessary for an algorithmic machine. Thus, "modern" machine architecture dates back to the 1800s. On the other hand, one look at a piece of today's equipment quickly reveals that a lot has happened since Babbage in the way these components are implemented. In this section, we discuss the composition of today's computers in terms of their roles in algorithm execution.

We begin with data storage. Here we find that gear positions have been replaced by tiny electronic circuits, each of which is capable of storing a single digit of information called a bit (for binary digit). Large numbers of these circuits are collected into the unit of the machine called the main memory. Through coding systems, in which information is represented as patterns of bit values, both data and algorithms are stored in this main memory.

To perform algorithm execution, another unit called the central processing unit (CPU) is attached to the machine's main memory. This unit is actually responsible for two activities: the manipulation of data as requested by the algorithm and the coordination of the algorithmic steps. Thus, the CPU fetches instructions from main memory and executes them, while the execution of these instructions causes the CPU to retrieve data from main memory, manipulate the data, and possibly return results to main memory for storage.

In many respects, the CPU–main memory combination constitutes what we call "the computer." However, a computer consisting of only a CPU and main memory would prove highly restricted. In particular, without the assistance of today's peripheral devices, such as terminals, printers, disk drives, and voice synthesizers, a machine would lack the ability to communicate with its environment. It would therefore be more accurate to consider a complete computer as consisting of a CPU, main memory, and peripheral devices, as represented in Figure 0-6 (on the following page), where the close association between the CPU and main memory is shown by enclosing their respective rectangles within yet another rectangle, which is then connected to peripheral devices.

The vast collection of peripheral devices can be divided into two categories: mass storage devices and input/output (I/O) devices. The first category is designed mainly

Figure 0-6 A conceptual structure of a computer system

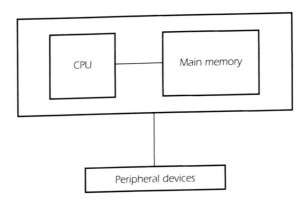

to extend the machine's data storage capabilities beyond the capability of its main memory. A primary example consists of disk storage devices in which information is recorded magnetically on the surface of flat spinning disks. The higher-capacity units use rigid disks, called hard disks, mounted one above the other on a spindle. Lower-capacity systems use single flexible disks, called diskettes or floppy disks, mounted in paper or plastic sleeves.

The category of I/O devices seems to expand every day. Those most common today are keyboards for data input and monitors, using cathode ray tubes (CRTs), for output. A keyboard combined with a monitor is called a terminal or sometimes a video display terminal (VDT). Another popular input device is the mouse. This is a small handheld device whose movement across a flat surface is communicated to the computer. In turn, the mouse can be used to indicate positions or to draw lines on the monitor screen.

Output devices using CRTs are called soft-copy devices because the output they produce does not appear in a permanent form. In contrast are the hard-copy devices, such as printers, that range in technology from typewriterlike mechanisms operating as slow as 15 characters per second to laser printers that can produce combinations of high-resolution graphics and text. Other I/O devices are based on such technologies as magnetic ink character recognition (MICR), optical character recognition (OCR), and audio input and output in the form of voice recognition and voice synthesis devices. This short list, however, does not begin to exhaust the scope of I/O devices in use today. Indeed, devices exist that sense and control building temperature, monitor a patient's vital signs, and detect the speed of aircraft.

The peripheral devices we have been discussing are not normally connected directly to the CPU–main memory combination but rather are usually connected to a controller that is in turn connected to "the computer" through a connection called a port (Figure 0-7). A controller is actually a small computer and is charged with

Figure 0-7 A computer system using controllers to coordinate peripheral activity

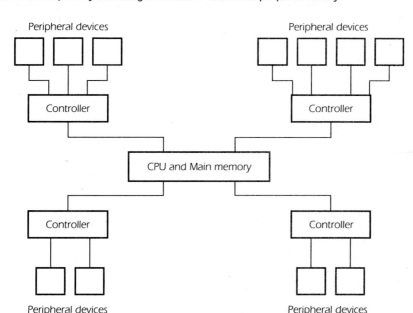

coordinating the activities of the devices attached to it as well as with dealing with each device's idiosyncrasies. Such a design relieves the CPU from the time-consuming chores of communicating with peripheral devices and allows it to concentrate on the major system activities while the potential interruptions of peripheral devices are handled by the controllers. This delegation of duties does not stop here, however. In particular, it is efficient to assign peripheral devices to controllers according to device type. One controller might handle the system's disk drives, while another might specialize in printers. (This is why a new disk controller is required when a hard disk is added to a microcomputer system and why a new graphics adapter is installed along with the installation of a new, more advanced monitor.)

The physical characteristics of computers today cover the spectrum from very small machines used in such home appliances as microwave ovens and vacuum cleaners, where both CPU and main memory are contained on a single chip no larger than a fingernail, to massive machines that occupy large rooms and require special cooling systems to counteract the heat generated by their circuitry. For our purposes, it is advantageous to consider two examples on this spectrum: the microcomputer and the supercomputer.

The typical microcomputer (often called a personal computer or PC) is small enough to fit on a desk top and is used by one person at a time. Most manufacturers combine the CPU and main memory of a microcomputer in the same case along with some peripheral devices, such as one or more floppy-disk drives and a hard-disk system. Other devices, such as a keyboard and a monitor, are provided as separate components so they can be positioned for the convenience of the user.

Supercomputers represent the most powerful machines on the computer spectrum. They are designed for applications that tax the capabilities of today's technology, such as global weather forecasting, simulations of nuclear reactions, and analysis of geological data. The CPU and main memory of these machines are housed in large cabinets designed to minimize the distance between related units of circuitry while allowing space for cooling fluid to be pumped between the machine's components. These machines, together with their mass storage devices, usually occupy a large room with raised flooring under which connecting cables are placed.

Users of supercomputers rarely come into direct contact with these machines. Instead, communication with supercomputers is normally handled through remote workstations that range from simple terminals to small computer systems. These workstations may be in the next room or located in distant cities.

0-4 The Evolution of Computer Science

Such conditions as limited data storage capabilities and detailed, time-consuming programming procedures restricted the complexity of the algorithms to which early machines were applied. However, as these limitations began to disappear, machines were applied to increasingly larger and more complex tasks. Because attempts to express the composition of these tasks in algorithmic form began to tax the abilities of the human mind, more and more research efforts were directed toward the study of algorithms and the programming process.

It was in this context that the theoretical work of mathematicians began to pay dividends. Indeed, as a consequence of Gödel's incompleteness theorem, mathema-

Figure 0-8 The central role of algorithms in computer science

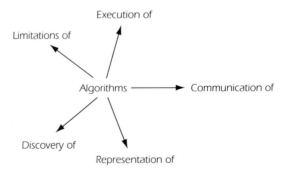

ticians had already been investigating those questions regarding algorithmic processes that began to be raised by advancing technology. Thus, the stage was set for the emergence of a new discipline known as computer science.

Today, this new discipline has established itself as the science of algorithms. As we have seen, the scope of this science is broad, drawing from such diverse subjects as mathematics, engineering, psychology, biology, business administration, linguistics, and others. In the following chapters we discuss many of the topics of this science. In each case our goal is to introduce the central ideas in the subject, the current topics of research, and some of the techniques being applied to advance knowledge in the area. For example, our discussion of programming is not geared toward developing programming skills but concentrates on the principles behind the programming tools of today, how these tools have evolved, and the problems current research is trying to overcome.

As we progress through this study of topics, it is easy to lose track of the overall picture. We therefore close this introduction by identifying some questions that define the science of computing and provide the focus for its study.

- Which problems can be solved by algorithmic processes?
- How can the discovery of algorithms be made easier?
- How can the techniques of representing and communicating algorithms be improved?
- How can our knowledge of algorithms and technology be applied to provide better algorithmic machines?

Note that the theme common to all of these questions is the study of algorithms (Figure 0-8).

Additional Reading

Dewdney, A. K. *The Turing Omnibus*. Rockville, Md.: Computer Science Press, 1989.

Forester, T. and Morrison, P. *Computer Ethics: Cautionary Tales and Ethical Dilemmas*. Cambridge, Mass.: MIT Press, 1990.

Goldstine, H. H. *The Computer from Pascal to von Neumann*. Princeton, N.J.: Princeton University Press, 1972.

Harel, D. *Algorithmics: The Spirit of Computing*, 2nd ed. Reading, Mass.: Addison-Wesley, 1992.

Mollenhoff, C. R. *Atanasoff: Forgotten Father of the Computer*. Ames, Iowa: Iowa State University Press, 1988.

Randell, B. *The Origins of Digital Computers*. New York: Springer-Verlag, 1973.

Shurkin, J. *Engines of the Mind*. New York: W. W. Norton and Company, 1984.

PART ONE

MACHINE ARCHITECTURE

A major process in the development of a science is the construction of theories that are confirmed or rejected by experimentation. In some cases, these theories lie dormant for extended periods, waiting for technology to develop to the point that they can be tested. (Many theories about our solar system are only now being tested, while others will remain untestable for years to come.) In other cases, the capabilities of current technology influence the concerns of the science. (The reality of space travel has generated research on the effects of weightlessness as well as on ways to build better spacecraft.)

Computer science has developed, and continues to develop, along both of these avenues. We have already seen that the science itself grew from theories that originated well before technology could produce the machines envisioned by early researchers. Even today, our advancing knowledge of algorithmic processes is leading to new machine designs that challenge the limits of technology. In contrast, other subjects in the science are rooted in the application of today's technology. Thus, computer science is a blend of theoretical research and advancing technology, each influencing the other in a mutually beneficial relationship.

It follows that to appreciate the role of various subjects within computer science, one should understand the basics of today's technology and how it influences the design and implementation of today's computers. Providing this foundation is the purpose of the following two chapters. In Chapter 1, we discuss techniques by which information is represented and stored inside computers. In Chapter 2, we discuss ways in which today's machines manipulate data.

CHAPTER ONE

DATA STORAGE

*Sections marked by an asterisk are optional in that they provide additional depth of coverage that is not required for an understanding of future chapters.

If we were to build a machine for executing algorithms, a major concern would involve the internal representation of data. Over the years, many technologies have been used to accomplish this (for example, beads on rods, gear positions, and electromagnetic relays). Theoretically, the technology used for data storage has no effect on which problems the machine can ultimately solve. In reality, however, the technology applied and the techniques used in its implementation have an enormous impact on the issues of practicality and are repeatedly reflected in the external characteristics of the system. Thus, just as a knowledge of anatomy is essential in the practice of medicine, a familiarity with a machine's internal storage techniques pays dividends throughout the study of computer science. We begin our study, then, by acquiring this beneficial background.

1-1 Main Memory

Fundamental to the storage of data within today's algorithmic machines is the concept of a *bit* (short for *binary digit*), which can be represented by a device that can exist in one of two states, such as on or off (a switch), open or closed (a relay), or even raised or lowered (a flag on a flagpole). Of course, the actual technology used for bit storage in machines varies as new and more cost-effective techniques are devised. Because it might be helpful to have a particular device in mind as you read the following sections, we will take a brief look at a popular technology for bit representation in computers today: the capacitor.

Storage of Bits
Suppose two metal plates are placed parallel to one another with a short distance separating them, as shown in Figure 1-1. If we connect these plates to opposite terminals of a battery, we find that the positive and negative charges from the battery distribute themselves over the plates to which each terminal is connected. If we then disconnect the battery, the plates are left holding these charges. In this charged condition, the plate combination behaves as a power source similar to the battery. In particular, if the plates are connected either directly or indirectly through an electronic circuit, an electric current flows through the connection until the charges on the plates are neutralized. A capacitor is nothing more than such a system of plates and can be made so small that several million capacitors can be assembled on a single wafer (called a *chip*) no larger than a dime.

The significance of a capacitor from our point of view is that it is an electronic device that can be placed in one of two states (in this case, charged or discharged) and thus a capacitor is suitable for representing a bit within an electronic computer. In reality, we seldom use the terms *charged* and *discharged* when referring to the status of a bit in a machine, because not all bits are represented with capacitor technology.

Figure 1-1 The charging and discharging of a capacitor

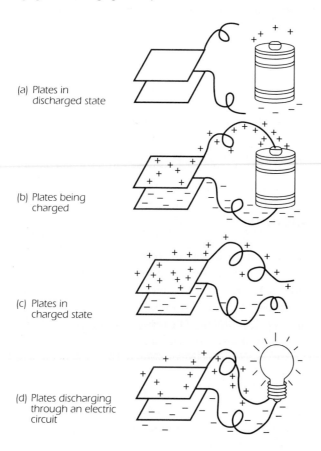

(a) Plates in
    discharged state

(b) Plates being
    charged

(c) Plates in
    charged state

(d) Plates discharging
    through an electric
    circuit

Instead, it is more common to use the terms *one* and *zero*. (Other popular terms frequently used in place of *one* are *true, set, on,* and *high*. Moreover, each of these has its corresponding substitute for *zero*, which is *false, reset* (or *clear*), *off,* and *low,* respectively.)

Main Memory Organization

It is clear that little information can be stored in a circuit that can represent only 1 bit. Thus, information is represented by means of a coding system in which different bit patterns are used to represent different symbols, such as the letters of the alphabet, digits, or punctuation. For this reason, we find that a computer's **main memory** (in contrast to the machine's mass storage, or secondary memory, discussed in the next section) consists of a large collection of circuits capable of storing numerous bits. For reasons of practicality, this bit reservoir is divided into manageable units called *cells*

Figure 1-2 An eight-bit memory cell containing the pattern 10100100

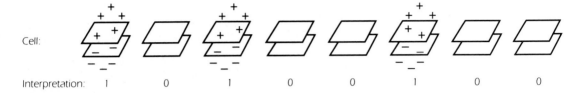

Cell:

Interpretation: 1   0   1   0   0   1   0   0

(or words), with a typical cell size being 8 bits (Figure 1-2). In fact, bit collections of size 8 have become so popular that the term **byte** is now widely used in reference to bit collections of that size.

A tremendous variation exists in the number of cells appearing in the memories of different machines. For instance, the small computers used in such household devices as microwave ovens may have memory sizes measured in hundreds of cells or fewer, whereas large computers used to store and manipulate extensive amounts of data can have billions of cells in their main memories. The size of a machine's main memory is often measured in terms of 1,048,576-cell units. (The value 1,048,576 is a power of two, namely 2^{20}, so it is more natural as a unit of measure within a computer than an even 1,000,000.) The term *mega* (sometimes shortened to *meg*) is used to indicate this unit of measure. The abbreviation Mb is often used for the term *megabyte*. Thus, a memory of 4Mb contains 4,192,304 (which is $4 \times 1,048,576$) cells, each of which is 1 byte in size. Other units of measuring memory size are kilobyte (abbreviated as Kb), which is equal to 1024 bytes (2^{10} bytes), and gigabyte (abbreviated as Gb), which is equal to 1024Mb, or 2^{30} bytes.

To identify individual cells in a machine's main memory, each cell is assigned a unique name, called its **address.** The system is analogous to, and uses the same terminology as, the technique of identifying houses in a city by addresses. In the case of memory cells, however, the addresses used are entirely numeric since there are no street names involved. To be more precise, one envisions all the cells being placed in a single row and numbered in this order starting with the value 0. Thus, the cells in a machine with a 4Mb memory would be addressed as 0, 1, 2, . . . , 4192303. Note that such an addressing system not only gives us a way of uniquely identifying each cell but also associates an order to the cells (Figure 1-3). Thus, phrases such as "the next cell" or "the previous cell" make sense.

To complete the main memory of a machine, the circuitry that actually holds the bits is combined with the circuitry required to allow other circuits to store and retrieve data from the memory cells. Thus, other circuits can get data from the memory by electronically asking for the contents of a certain address (called a read operation), or they can record information in the memory by requesting that a certain bit pattern be placed in the cell at a particular address (called a write operation).

Figure 1-3 Memory cells arranged by address

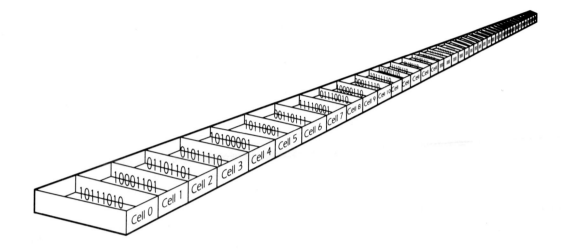

A common analogy to a main memory's organization is the collection of mailboxes at a post office, where you find numerous boxes (cells) consecutively numbered on the outside (addresses). This analogy breaks down, however, when we consider the insertion and removal of data. First, a mailbox does not have a well-established capacity. (It seems that one more envelope can always be squeezed into it.) On the other hand, a memory cell can retain only a fixed amount of data. If more information is stored, the old information is lost. Second, when material is extracted from a mailbox, the box becomes empty. In contrast, when a bit pattern is retrieved from a memory cell, a copy of that pattern remains behind. Thus, the same pattern can be extracted over and over.

An important consequence of organizing a machine's main memory as small, addressable cells is that each cell can be referenced, accessed, and modified individually. A memory cell with a low address is just as accessible as one with a high address. In turn, data stored in a machine's main memory can be processed in any order desired, and thus a machine's main memory is often referred to as random access memory (RAM). This random access of small data units is in stark contrast to the mass storage systems that we will discuss in the next section, in which long strings of bits must be manipulated as a block.

Organization Within a Cell

Returning now to the memory cells themselves, we should note that the bits found there are not merely "thrown in a pile" but are arranged in a sequential order similar to the arrangement of the cells. Thus, a memory cell is conceptually like an egg carton, except that instead of containing two rows of eggs, a cell contains a single row of bits.

Figure 1-4 *The organization of a byte-size memory cell*

We call one end of this row the **high-order** end and the other the **low-order** end. Although there is no left or right within a machine, we imagine the bits arranged in a row from left to right with the high-order end on the left. The bit at this end is often called either the high-order bit or the **most significant** bit; similarly, the bit at the other end is referred to as the low-order bit or the **least significant** bit. Thus, we may represent the contents of a byte-size cell as shown in Figure 1-4.

An important consequence of the ordering of both the cells and the bits within each cell is that the entire collection of bits within a machine's main memory is essentially ordered in one long row. Thus, pieces of this long row can be used to store bit patterns that may be longer than the length of a single cell. In particular, if the memory is divided into byte-size cells, one can still store a string of 16 bits merely by using two consecutive memory cells.

Hexadecimal Notation

At this point, it would probably not be difficult to convince you that anyone dealing with the internal characteristics of a computer might spend a lot of time looking at strings of bits and that such a job could be extremely tedious and error prone. It is

Figure 1-5 *A hexadecimal table*

Bit pattern	Hexadecimal representation
0000	0
0001	1
0010	2
0011	3
0100	4
0101	5
0110	6
0111	7
1000	8
1001	9
1010	A
1011	B
1100	C
1101	D
1110	E
1111	F

not surprising then that shorthand notations have been developed for expressing strings of bits. The most popular of these, and the one we use in this book, is known as *hexadecimal notation.* This technique groups the string that is to be represented into a sequence of short 4-bit blocks and then represents each of these blocks with a single symbol. Note that a block might contain only 1 of 16 different patterns. These patterns, along with the symbols used to represent them, are shown in Figure 1-5.

Using this system, the 8-bit pattern 01011010 can be represented by the condensed pattern 5A, and the 32-bit pattern 10100100011000001110101100010011 reduces to the more palatable form of A460EB13.

Questions/Exercises

1. If the memory cell whose address is 5 contains the value 8, what is the difference between writing the value 5 into cell number 6 and moving the contents of cell number 5 into cell number 6?
2. Suppose you want to interchange the values stored in memory cells 2 and 3. What is wrong with the following sequence of steps:
    Step 1. Move the contents of cell number 2 to cell number 3.
    Step 2. Move the contents of cell number 3 to cell number 2.
    Design a sequence of steps that correctly interchanges the contents of these cells.
3. How many bits would be in the memory of a computer with a 4Kb memory?
4. Using a square to represent the pattern 00, a triangle to represent 01, a circle for 10, and a diamond for 11, represent the bit pattern 01001011111001.
5. Use hexadecimal notation to represent the following bit patterns:
    a. 0110101011110010   b.   1110100001010100010111
    c. 01001000
6. What bit patterns are represented by the following hexadecimal patterns:
    a. 5FD97   b.   610A   c.   ABCD   d.   0100

1-2 Mass Storage

Limitations of technology, economic concerns, and the necessity of maintaining backup copies of sensitive data dictate that the main memory of a computer rarely fills the needs of all the machine's applications. Thus, most machines are provided with a *mass storage* system (also called *secondary memory*) in addition to their main memory. As we will see, these mass storage systems have both advantages and disadvantages. Paramount among the disadvantages is that secondary storage systems typically require mechanical motion; therefore, the process of either storing or retrieving data with such systems is relatively slow compared with the machine's main memory. Among the advantages is that, in many cases, the medium on which the data are recorded in mass storage can be removed from the machinery and stored elsewhere for backup purposes or shipped to another location where it may be needed.

You will hear the terms *on-line* and *off-line* in relation to devices that can be either attached to or detached from a machine. On-line means that the device or information is connected and readily available to the machine without human intervention. In contrast, off-line means that human intervention is required before the device or information can be accessed by the machine. This may be because the device must be turned on or the medium holding the information must be inserted into some mechanism.

Disk Storage

The most common form of mass storage in use today is disk storage, in which a thin spinning disk with magnetic coating is used to hold the data. Read/write heads are placed above and/or below the disk so that as the disk spins, the heads traverse a circle, called a *track,* around the disk's upper and/or lower surface. Since each track can contain more information than we would normally want to process at any one time, tracks are divided into arcs called *sectors* on which information is recorded as a continuous string of bits (Figure 1-6). (Tracks and sectors are not a permanent part of a disk's physical structure. Instead, they are recorded magnetically through a process called formatting (or initializing) the disk. Thus, before a new, blank disk can be used for data storage, it must be formatted.)

By moving a read/write head closer to the center of the disk or farther out to the edge, we can quickly change to sectors on other tracks. The entire disk can therefore be thought of as a collection of short segments that can be quickly and individually selected. Thus, the information on a sector can be retrieved or updated without disturbing the data on the other sectors.

The time required to move the read/write head from one track to another is known as seek time. Other measures of a disk system's performance include rotation delay or latency time (half the time required for the disk to make a complete rotation, which is the average amount of time required for the desired data to rotate around to the read/write head once the head has been positioned over the desired track),

Figure 1-6 A disk storage system

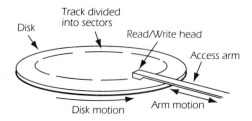

access time (the sum of seek time and rotation delay), and transfer rate (the rate at which data can be transfered to or from the disk system).

Traditionally, a disk system has several disks mounted on a spindle, one on top of the other, with enough space for read/write heads to slip between the platters. Such an arrangement might consist of 5 disks providing a total of 10 surfaces for data storage. Such a disk system might have a maximum capacity of several gigabytes and be able to transfer the characters at the rate of several million per second. For microcomputers, it is common to find disk systems with capacities of several hundred megabytes, with larger capacities available if required.

Another form of disk storage uses a single plastic disk known as a diskette or, since the disk is quite flexible, by the less prestigious title of floppy disk. (In contrast, the rigid disks previously discussed are often called hard disks.) Such diskettes are available in diameters of 8, 5¼, and 3½ inches. (The 3½-inch varieties, being housed in rigid plastic cases, do not constitute as flexible a package as the larger versions that are housed in paper sleeves.) Although capacities of diskettes tend to be limited to a few megabytes, they are easily inserted and removed from their corresponding read/write units and are easily mailable. As a consequence, diskettes provide a good medium for long-term data storage and transportation.

On the other hand, the fact that diskettes are removable from their read/write devices means that such systems have less precision than the permanently mounted hard disk systems. For instance, a permanently mounted hard-disk system can be constructed so that the read/write head does not touch the disk surface but instead floats slightly above it. This alleviates friction between the head and disk that is present in a floppy-disk system and allows for much faster rotation speeds. Hard-disk systems rotate at speeds on the order of 3000 to 4000 revolutions per minute, whereas floppy systems are in the 300-revolutions-per-minute range. In turn, hard-disk systems have shorter access times, averaging 10 to 30 milliseconds, compared to floppy systems with access times of approximately 300 milliseconds. The result is that data transfer rates for hard-disk systems are much higher than for floppy systems, so hard-disk systems are more popular for storing on-line information.

Due to the ease of handling and portability, floppy disks have become the medium of choice for distributing software for personal computers. However, an original distribution disk purchased from a software company can be duplicated easily, resulting in software piracy, a romantic reference to the unauthorized attainment and use of commercial software.

An early attempt to counter this problem used diskettes on which a particular sector had been recorded using a weaker than normal recording signal. This resulted in what were called weak bits, that is, bits represented by weaker than normal magnetic fields. The goal was to produce a sector that would present a different bit pattern each time it was read. If the disk were copied using normal equipment, the supposedly weak sector on the new disk would be written using normal recording signals and would no longer be composed of weak bits. Thus, software could detect the presence of the original disk by simply reading the supposedly weak sector twice; if the same pattern was retrieved both times, the software could conclude that the disk being used was a copy of the original.

Unfortunately, disk units in many computer systems were too accurate for weak bits to be effective. They tended to read the weak bits correctly every time, resulting in software products that would not execute properly even in the presence of the original distribution disk. Moreover, most applications today require that purchased software be transferred onto the system's hard disk and that the floppy disk, on which the software was shipped, be stored off-line for backup purposes. Hence, the use of weak bits was short lived.

Software piracy remains a major problem for commercial software developers. Large numbers of software users continue to rationalize the legitimacy of making unauthorized copies of software ("The software is too expensive," "I'm only going to use it for a short time," "It doesn't hurt anyone," or "I don't think restricting the use of software is reasonable"), which places a strain on the development of better software for the future.

Compact Disks

The technology of mass storage devices is continually evolving. Although devices based on the technology of magnetic media dominate the scene today, optical systems are appearing on the market that may challenge the popularity of magnetic devices in the near future. Most prominent among these systems is the compact disk (CD), which closely resembles its cousin in the music industry.

These disks, approximately 5 inches in diameter, consist of reflective material covered with a clear protective coating. Information is recorded on them by creating variations in their reflective surfaces. This information can then be retrieved by monitoring these irregularities with a laser beam as the disk spins. The exact recording format varies among manufacturers. Such inconsistencies, however, should disappear under standardization efforts by the International Standards Organization (ISO) and the American National Standards Institute (ANSI).

Today, the most common use of compact disk storage devices is in the context of read-only devices called CD-ROM (compact disk read-only memory). These disks are purchased with information already recorded on them. Due to their enormous storage capacities, these disks provide an excellent way of making information available to a computer system. Disks on the market today contain such things as complete literary works of major authors, government regulations, highly detailed national maps, abstracts of publications on various subjects, and entire encyclopedias that include sound and video of various entries such as historical events.

CD systems in which stored data can be altered are also available. For example, systems using magneto-optical drives record information by effectively melting the

CD's reflective surface with a laser beam and then rearranging it by magnetic fields before it cools again. The fact that more than 100Mb of data can be stored on a single disk surface with this process testifies to the precision of these devices.

Tape Storage

An older form of mass storage device uses magnetic tape (Figure 1-7). Here information is recorded on the magnetic coating of a thin plastic tape that is in turn wound on a reel for storage. To access the data, this tape is mounted in a device called a tape drive that typically can read, write, and rewind the tape under control of the computer. Tape drives range in size from small cartridge units, called streaming tape units, that use tape similar in appearance to that in stereo systems to older, large reel-to-reel units. Although the capacity of these devices depends on the format used, a typical cartridge can hold well over 100Mb.

Recording information on older tape systems involved starting the tape moving, waiting for it to reach the proper speed, transferring the data to the tape, and stopping the tape. This start-and-stop process resulted in blank sections of tape, called *inter-record gaps,* between the blocks. These gaps consisted of the length of tape that passed by the read/write head while the tape was starting and stopping between consecutive write commands. Such gaps, on the order of $\frac{1}{2}$ to 1 inch in length, could result in inefficient use of tape. For example, if separate blocks no larger than 3000 characters each were written on a tape that held 6250 characters per inch (a typical value for the larger tape units), then two-thirds of the tape would remain blank and therefore wasted since each $\frac{1}{2}$-inch block of data would be followed by a one-inch inter-record gap.

A second disadvantage of older tape systems was that the data recorded on a tape inherited the sequential order of the tape itself. To retrieve data stored at the end of the tape, the tape drive had to scan past all of the earlier data on the tape.

Contemporary streaming tape units apply several techniques to overcome the problems of their ancestors. One is to write reference markers along the tape through

Figure 1-7 A tape storage mechanism

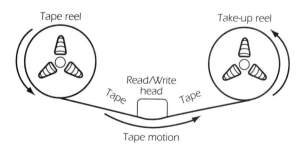

a formatting process similar to that used in disk storage systems. This has the effect of dividing a long tape into segments that can be identified by the tape drive.

These systems also allow data to be recorded in both forward and backward directions on the tape. For this purpose, the tape is divided into tracks running lengthwise along the tape. Some tracks are designated for data recorded in one direction, while others are designated for data recorded in the opposite direction. Thus, each segment on a tape actually consists of several track segments. In turn, a file can be recorded on a single track from one segment to another or back and forth within a single segment.

The data on a track within a segment are normally divided into blocks separated by short spaces. However, these gaps are not the result of starting and stopping the tape as in older systems, because modern tape drives are capable of recording and reading consecutive blocks at high speeds without stopping the tape. Instead, these gaps represent the need to divide the data on the tape into manageable, uniform-size units that can be processed individually. In turn, each block on a track is accompanied by synchronization signals and identification markers so it can be manipulated separately from the other blocks on the tape. Thus, these tape systems can access a single block in much the same way that a disk system can access an individual sector.

Even with these improvements over older designs, today's tape storage systems have much longer data access times than disk systems that can shift from one track to another merely by moving their read/write heads a few millimeters. Thus, disk systems are popular for on-line data storage, while tape systems are used mainly in off-line, backup storage applications. Indeed, streaming tape units are rapidly becoming the de facto standard for backup storage on small computer systems.

Logical Versus Physical Records

Whereas data in a machine's main memory can be referenced by individual byte-size cells, the physical properties of mass storage devices dictate that data stored on these systems be manipulated in multiple byte units. For example, each sector on a disk must be handled as one long string of bits. A typical sector size is 1024 bytes. A block of data conforming to the physical characteristics of a storage device is called a *physical record.*

In contrast to the division of data into physical records whose sizes are determined by machine characteristics, the information being represented usually has natural divisions. For example, the information maintained by a company regarding its employees is conveniently divided into a block of information for each employee. Such natural occurring blocks of data are called *logical records.*

Logical record sizes rarely match the physical record size dictated by a mass storage device. In turn, one may find several logical records residing within a single physical record and perhaps a logical record split between two or more physical

Figure 1-8 *Logical records versus physical records on a disk*

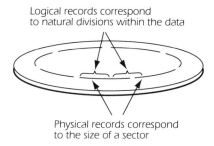

Logical records correspond
to natural divisions within the data

Physical records correspond
to the size of a sector

records (Figure 1-8). The result is that a certain amount of unscrambling is associated with retrieving data from mass storage systems. We return to this problem in Chapter 3.

Questions/Exercises

1. What advantage does a hard-disk system gain from the fact that its disks spin faster than those in a floppy-disk system?
2. When only one side of a disk is used for storing data, it is called single-sided. When both surfaces are used, we say it is double-sided. Drives for double-sided disks are provided with two read/write heads (one for each side) that are mechanically linked so that they move as a single unit and always traverse tracks directly opposite each other on the two surfaces. When recording data on a double-sided disk, should we fill a complete side before starting the other or alternate between the surfaces by filling each opposing track pair before moving to the next pair?
3. Why should the data in a reservation system that is constantly being updated be stored on a disk instead of on tape?
4. a. When using a streaming tape unit, what is an advantage of storing blocks of data in one direction along a single track rather than back and forth within a single segment?
   b. When using a streaming tape system, what is an advantage of storing blocks of data back and forth within a single segment rather than in one direction along a single track?

1-3 Coding Information for Storage

It is time now to take a closer look at the techniques used for representing information in terms of bit patterns.

Symbol Representation

As alluded to earlier, one popular procedure for representing symbols within a machine is to design a code in which different symbols (such as the letters of the alphabet or punctuation marks) are assigned unique bit patterns and to store the information as coded sentences in main memory or on mass storage media. Unfortunately, over the years, many such codes have been designed and used in connection with different pieces of equipment, producing a corresponding proliferation of communication problems. To alleviate this situation, the American National Standards Institute has adopted what is known as the **American Standard Code for Information Interchange** (**ASCII,** pronounced "as'—kee"), which has become extremely popular. This code, part of which appears in Appendix A, uses 7 bits to represent each symbol. For convenience, however, each symbol represented in ASCII is normally stored in an individual byte-size memory cell, with the extra bit in each cell being ignored or used to extend the code for some special purpose. In Appendix A, you can see that ASCII includes codes for upper- and lowercase letters, digits, punctuation marks, and a space. It also includes bit patterns for representing printing commands, such as carriage return, line feed, form feed, and tab.

As an example, Figure 1-9 shows that the bit pattern

100100011010010100000101001111101011001010101110

represents the sentence "Hi Sue."

Although ASCII is probably the most common code in use today, others continue to be used, and you should be aware of their existence. One such code is Extended Binary Coded Decimal Interchange Code (EBCDIC). This is an 8-bit code adopted by IBM, and as with ASCII, it includes both uppercase and lowercase characters (Appendix A).

Representing Numeric Values

Although the method of storing information as coded characters is quite popular, it is extremely inefficient when the data being recorded is purely numeric. To see why, suppose we want to store the number 25. If we insist on storing it as coded symbols in ASCII using 1 byte per symbol, we need a total of 16 bits. Moreover, the largest number we can store using 16 bits is 99. A more efficient approach is to store the value in its base two, or binary, representation. To see why, let us first investigate the base two (binary) system.

Figure 1-9 The message "Hi Sue." in ASCII

Consider a car's odometer. When the car is new the odometer reads

00000000

Each 0 is actually painted on a wheel, and on each wheel are also painted the digits 1, 2, 3, 4, 5, 6, 7, 8, and 9. As the car is driven, the rightmost wheel (the low-order wheel) begins to turn, causing the digits painted on it to appear in the correct sequence until the odometer has the following appearance:

00000009

At this point, as the rightmost wheel continues to turn, it hooks the wheel next to it and pulls it over one notch. The result is that as the rightmost wheel cycles back to its original 0 position, the wheel next to it is rotated one notch to expose the 1 painted on it. The odometer now appears as follows:

00000010

As the car continues to be driven, the rightmost wheel continues to rotate alone until its 9 is again showing. At this point, the adjacent wheel once more rotates as the rightmost wheel returns to its 0 position. Thus, the odometer changes from

00000019

to

00000020

Counting in base two is the same process, except that each wheel has only two digits, 0 and 1, painted on it, and the adjacent wheel rotates every time the 1 rotates over to expose the 0 instead of the 9 rotating to expose the 0. If cars had base two odometers, the sequence of odometer readings would appear, as in Figure 1-10, as a new car was driven for its first few miles.

Thus, Figure 1-10 represents the symbols obtained when counting from zero to six in base two. If moving from 00000011 to 00000100 bothers you, think again about what the car odometer does when it moves from 00000099 to 00000100 and remember that changing a digit from 9 to 0 on the odometer coincides with changing a digit from 1 to 0 when counting in base two.

Figure 1-10 Binary odometer readings starting from zero

```
00000000
00000001
00000010
00000011
00000100
00000101
00000110
```

This counting technique not only provides a down-to-earth introduction to binary notation but also constitutes a brute force system for converting back and forth between the binary and decimal notations. In the case of large values in which counting becomes impractical, a more efficient technique exists that we discuss in Section 1-4. In reality, however, learning the binary system is much like learning a foreign language or foreign currency system. Once you use it for a while, you overcome the need to translate back into your original notation.

Recall now our original problem of storing numeric data. Using binary notation, we see that in one byte we can store any integer between 0 and 255 (00000000 to 11111111), and given 2 bytes, we can store the integers from 0 to 65535. This is a drastic improvement over the ability to store only the integers from 0 to 99 when coding characters using one ASCII pattern per byte.

For this and other reasons, it is far more common to store numeric information in a form of binary notation rather than in coded symbols. We say "a form of binary notation" because, in reality, the straightforward binary system just described is only the basis for several numeric storage techniques used within machines. Some of these variations of the binary system are discussed later in this chapter. For now, we merely note that a system called *two's complement notation* is common for storing whole numbers because it provides a convenient method for representing negative numbers as well as positive. For representing numbers with fractional parts such as 4½ or ¾, another technique, called *floating-point notation,* is used. Thus, a particular value (such as 25) may be represented by several different bit patterns (coded characters, two's complement notation, or in floating-point notation as 25%); conversely, a particular bit pattern may be given several interpretations.

At this point, we should mention a significant problem with numeric storage systems that we deal with in more depth later. Regardless of the pattern size that a machine might allocate for the storage of numeric values, there will still be values too large or fractions too small to be stored in the space allotted. The result is the constant potential for errors such as *overflow* (values too large) and *round-off* (fractions too small) that must be dealt with, or an unsuspecting computer user can soon be faced with a multitude of erroneous data.

Questions/Exercises

1. Here is a message coded in ASCII. What does it say?

   1000011 1101111 1101101 1110000 1110101 1110100
   1100101 1110010 0100000 1010011 1100011 1101001
   1100101 1101110 1100011 1100101

2. In the ASCII code, what is the relationship between the codes for an uppercase letter and the same letter in lowercase?

3. Code these sentences in ASCII:
   a.   I like milk.
   b.   Where are you?
   c.   "How?" Cheryl asked.
   d.   2 + 3 = 5.
4. Describe a device from everyday life that can be in either of two states, such as a flag on a flagpole that is either up or down. Assign the symbol 1 to one of the states, 0 to the other, and show how the ASCII representation for the letter b would appear when stored with such bits.
5. Convert each of the following binary representations to its equivalent decimal form:
   a.   0101   b.   1001   c.   1011   d.   0110
   e.   10000   f.   10010
6. Convert each of the following decimal representations to its equivalent binary form:
   a.   6   b.   13   c.   11   d.   18   e.   27   f.   4
7. What is the largest numeric value that could be represented with 3 bytes if each digit were coded using one ASCII pattern per byte? What if binary notation were used?

1-4 The Binary System

We now take a closer look at numeric storage techniques with the goal of better understanding the role of each and the problems of overflow and round-off mentioned earlier. We begin this pursuit with a more thorough treatment of the base two representation system.

In a base two representation of a number, each bit position is assigned a quantity (often called a weight) according to its position within the pattern. These quantities are specified from right to left as 1, 2, 4, 8, and so on. The rule is that the quantity assigned each position is twice that of the position to its right. Thus, the 1 in the binary representation 10000 is in the position assigned the quantity 16.

To decode a binary representation, you merely multiply each position's quantity by the value of the bit at that position and then add these results. For example, the binary number 100101 is found to be equivalent to 37 in our usual base ten notation (Figure 1-11, on the following page). (The technique of multiplying each bit value by the corresponding position quantity is based on a general procedure for converting representations from other bases as well. For those who wish the utmost in simplicity, the effect of this process in the binary case is merely to add the quantities of those positions occupied by 1s.)

Figure 1-11 Decoding the binary representation 100101

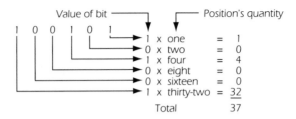

Binary Addition

You will note that the assignment of quantities to the digit position is common to other base systems as well. In particular, our more common base ten system uses the same concept, except that the quantity assigned to each position is ten times that to its right instead of two times. This common approach allows us to use the same addition process in base two as that used in the base ten system to which we are accustomed. Thus, to add two values represented in binary notation we begin, just as we did with base ten in elementary school, by memorizing the addition facts (Figure 1-12).

The binary facts are used to add two strings of bits in the same way the decimal facts are used to add two strings of decimal digits. That is, add the digits in the right-hand column, write the least significant digit of this sum under the column, carry the more significant digit of the sum (if there is one) to the next column to the left, and proceed by adding that column. Thus, to solve the following problem,

$$00111010$$
$$+00011011$$

we begin by adding the rightmost 0 and 1; we obtain 1, which we write below the column. Now we add the 1 and 1 from the next column, obtaining 10. We write the 0 from this 10 under the column and carry the 1 to the top of the next column. At this point, our solution looks like this:

$$1$$
$$00111010$$
$$+00011011$$
$$01$$

We add the 1, 0, and 0 in the next column, obtain 1, and write the 1 under this column. The 1 and 1 from the next column total 10; we write the 0 under the column and carry the 1 to the next column. Now our solution looks like this:

$$1$$
$$00111010$$
$$+00011011$$
$$0101$$

Figure 1-12 *The binary addition facts*

$$
\begin{array}{cccc}
0 & 1 & 0 & 1 \\
+0 & +0 & +1 & +1 \\
\hline
0 & 1 & 1 & 10
\end{array}
$$

The 1, 1, and 1 in the next column total 11; we write the low order 1 under the column and carry the other 1 to the top of the next column. We add that 1 to the 1 and 0 already in that column to obtain 10. Again, we record the low order 0 and carry the 1 to the next column. We now have this:

$$
\begin{array}{r}
1 \\
00111010 \\
+\,00011011 \\
\hline
010101
\end{array}
$$

Now we add the 1, 0, and 0 from the next to the last column, obtaining 1, which we record below the column with nothing to carry. Finally, we add the last column, which yields 0, and record this under the column. Our final solution is this:

$$
\begin{array}{r}
00111010 \\
+\,00011011 \\
\hline
01010101
\end{array}
$$

Fractions in Binary

To extend binary notation to accommodate fractional values, we use a *radix point* in the same role as the decimal point in decimal notation. That is, the digits to the left of the point represent the integer part of the value and are interpreted as in the binary system discussed previously. The digits to its right represent the fractional part of the value and are interpreted in a manner similar to the other bits, except their positions are assigned fractional quantities. That is, the first position to the right of the radix is assigned the quantity $\frac{1}{2}$, the next position the quantity $\frac{1}{4}$, the next $\frac{1}{8}$, and so on. Note that this is merely a continuation of the rule stated previously: Each position is assigned a quantity twice the size of the one to its right. With these quantities assigned to the bit positions, decoding a binary representation containing a radix point requires the same procedure as used without a radix point. In particular, we multiply each bit value by the quantity assigned to that bit's position in the representation. Thus, the binary representation 101.101 decodes to $5\frac{5}{8}$, as shown in Figure 1-13 on the following page.

Again, when it comes to addition, the techniques applied in the base ten system are also applicable in binary. That is, to add two binary representations having radix points, we merely align the radix points and apply the same addition process as before. Thus, 10.011 added to 100.11 produces 111.001, as shown here:

$$
\begin{array}{r}
10.011 \\
+\,100.11 \\
\hline
111.001
\end{array}
$$

Figure 1-13 Decoding the binary representation 101.101

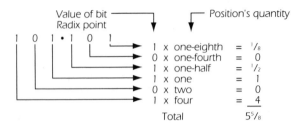

Questions/Exercises

1. Convert each of the following binary representations to its equivalent decimal form:
   a. 101010   b. 100001   c. 10111   d. 0110   e. 11111

2. Convert each of the following decimal representations to its equivalent binary form:
   a. 32   b. 64   c. 96   d. 15   e. 27

3. Convert each of the following binary representations to its equivalent base ten form:
   a. 11.01   b. 101.111   c. 10.1   d. 110.011   e. 0.101

4. Express the following values in binary notation:
   a. 4½   b. 2¾   c. 1⅛   d. ⁵⁄₁₆   e. 5⅝

5. Perform the following additions in binary notation:

   a.   11011   b.   1010.001   c.   11111   d.   111.11
       + 1100   +   1.101   +   1   +   .01

1-5 Storing Integers

When searching for an efficient technique for representing whole numbers as bit patterns, we might try the binary notation presented in Section 1-4, except that we often need to store negative values as well as positive ones. Thus, we need a notational system that encompasses both positive and negative integers. Mathematicians have long been interested in numeric notational systems, and many of their ideas have turned out to be very compatible with the design of electronic circuitry and thus are used extensively in computing equipment. In this section we consider two of these notational systems, excess notation and two's complement. Then we consider a major limitation of these systems as it is reflected in the problem of overflow.

Figure 1-14 An excess eight conversion table

Bit pattern	Value represented
1111	7
1110	6
1101	5
1100	4
1011	3
1010	2
1001	1
1000	0
0111	−1
0110	−2
0101	−3
0100	−4
0011	−5
0010	−6
0001	−7
0000	−8

Excess Notation

One method of representing integer values that is often used in floating-point systems (Section 1-6), is *excess notation.* Each of the values in an excess notation system is represented by a bit pattern of the same length. Thus, to establish an excess system, we first select the pattern length to be used, and then we write down all the different bit patterns of that length in the order they would appear if we were counting in binary. Next, we observe that the first pattern with a 1 as its most significant bit appears approximately halfway through the list. We pick this pattern to represent zero; the patterns following this are used to represent 1, 2, 3, . . . ; and the patterns preceding it are used for −1, −2, −3, ... The resulting code, when using patterns of length four, is shown in Figure 1-14. There we see that the value 5 is represented by the pattern 1101 and −5 is represented by 0011.

Note that it is easy to distinguish the patterns in an excess notation system that represent negative values from those that do not. Those that represent negative values have a 0 as their most significant bit, and those that do not represent negative values have a 1 as their most significant bit. The most significant bit is often called the *sign bit.* In excess notation, a sign bit equal to 0 indicates a negative value, and a sign bit equal to 1 indicates a positive or zero value.

The system represented in Figure 1-14 is known as excess eight notation. To understand why, first interpret each of the patterns in the code using the traditional binary system and then compare these results to the values represented in the excess code. In each case, you will find that the binary interpretation exceeds the excess code interpreted by the value 8.

Figure 1-15 *An excess notation system using bit patterns of length three*

Bit pattern	Value represented
111	3
110	2
101	1
100	0
011	−1
010	−2
001	−3
000	−4

For example, the pattern 1100 normally represents the value 12, but in our excess system it represents 4; 0000 normally represents 0, but in the excess system it represents −8. In a similar manner, an excess system based on patterns of length five would be called excess 16 notation, because the pattern 10000, for instance, would be used to represent 0 rather than representing its usual value of 16. Likewise, you may want to confirm that the 3-bit excess system would be known as excess four notation (Figure 1-15).

Based on these observations, we obtain a quick method of coding values when using excess notation. To code a value using excess eight, we need to add 8 to the value, write the result in base two, and then add leading 0s (if required) to obtain a pattern of 4 bits. For example, to code the value 5 using excess eight notation, we would first add 8, giving us the value 13, and then write this value in binary to obtain 1101, which is the desired pattern. To find the pattern representing −5, we would add 8 to obtain the value 3, which in binary is 11, so the 4-bit pattern we desire is 0011.

Two's Complement Notation

The most popular system for representing integers within today's computers is *two's complement notation.* Like excess notation, this system uses a fixed number of bits to represent each of the values in the system. Figure 1-16 shows two's complement systems based on bit patterns of length three and four. Note that in a two's complement system, a sign bit of 0 indicates either a positive or zero value, whereas a sign bit of 1 indicates a negative value.

For discussion purposes, let us consider the system using 4 bits per value. First observe that the value zero as well as the positive values in the system are represented simply by their base two representations, where 0s have been added to the left of the pattern to produce a total of 4 bits. The value 3, whose binary representation is 11,

Figure 1-16 Two's complement notation systems

Using patterns of length three		Using patterns of length four	
Bit pattern	Value represented	Bit pattern	Value represented
011	3	0111	7
010	2	0110	6
001	1	0101	5
000	0	0100	4
111	−1	0011	3
110	−2	0010	2
101	−3	0001	1
100	−4	0000	0
		1111	−1
		1110	−2
		1101	−3
		1100	−4
		1011	−5
		1010	−6
		1001	−7
		1000	−8

is represented by the 4-bit pattern 0011; and the value 5, whose binary representation is 101, is represented by 0101.

There are several methods of determining the pattern that represents a negative value. One is to subtract the magnitude of the value (represented in binary) from the binary representation 10000 (which is 1 followed by a string of 0s whose length is that of the final bit pattern desired—in our case four). Thus, to represent −3, we would subtract 11 (which is 3 in binary) from 10000 to obtain 1101. Likewise, −5 would be represented by 10000 − 101, which is 1011.

Other techniques for finding the two's complement representation for a negative value are based on the operation of forming the *complement* of a bit pattern. This is the process of changing all the 0s to 1s and the 1s to 0s. For example, the complement of 1011 is 0100, and the complement of 1000 is 0111.

Using the complement concept, we can find the two's complement representation for a negative value by first writing down the representation for the corresponding positive value, finding the first 1 from the low-order end of that pattern, and then complementing the part of the pattern to the left of that 1 (Figure 1-17, on the following page). Because 2 is represented by 0010, −2 is represent by 1110; and because 5 is represented by 0101, −5 is represented by 1011.

Still another method of finding the representation for a negative value is to write down the representation for the corresponding positive value, complement the entire

Figure 1-17 Coding the value −6 in two's complement notation using 4 bits

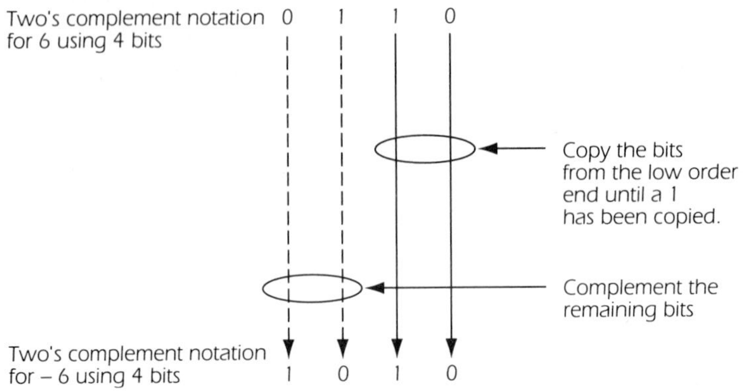

Two's complement notation   0   1   1   0
for 6 using 4 bits

Copy the bits
from the low order
end until a 1
has been copied.

Complement the
remaining bits

Two's complement notation
for − 6 using 4 bits   1   0   1   0

pattern, and then add 1 to the result. Figure 1-18 demonstrates this technique for a two's complement system using bit patterns of length eight.

Note that all three of these techniques work in reverse. That is, given the bit pattern representing a negative value (except for the most negative value in the system), we can produce the pattern representing the corresponding positive value by either subtracting the given pattern from 10000, complementing the bits to the left of the least significant 1 in the given pattern, or complementing the entire pattern and then adding 1. In fact, the ease in which patterns can be converted back and forth between corresponding positive and negative values is one reason for the popularity of two's complement notation.

This ease of conversion also makes it easy to decode two's complement patterns. If the sign bit is 0, we merely decode the pattern as though it were a normal binary representation. If the sign bit is 1, we first convert the pattern to its associated positive pattern and then read that pattern as a binary representation, obtaining the magnitude

Figure 1-18 Coding −5 in two's complement notation using 8 bits

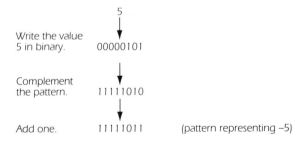

Write the value
5 in binary.   00000101

Complement
the pattern.   11111010

Add one.   11111011   (pattern representing −5)

of the value represented by the original pattern. Thus, to decode the two's complement pattern 1010, we would first convert it to its associated positive pattern 0110, recognize this to be the binary representation for 6, and conclude that the original pattern represented -6.

Addition in Two's Complement Notation

The source of popularity for two's complement notation lies in the simplicity and scope of the addition process used in conjunction with it. To understand this, we first note that adding values represented in two's complement notation is the same process as the binary addition previously described, except that all bit patterns, including the answer, are the same length. This means that when adding in a two's complement system, any extra bit generated on the left of the answer by a final carry must be truncated. Thus, "adding" 0101 and 0010 produces 0111, and "adding" 0111 and 1011 results in 0010 (0111 + 1011 = 10010, which is truncated to 0010).

With this understanding, consider the three addition problems in Figure 1-19. In each case, we have translated the problem into two's complement notation (using four bits), performed the addition process previously described, and decoded the result back into our usual decimal notation.

Observe that if we were to use the traditional techniques taught in elementary school, the third problem would require an entirely different process (subtraction) than the previous problems. On the other hand, by translating the problems into two's complement notation, we can compute the correct answer in all cases by applying the same computational process. This, then, is the advantage of two's complement notation: Addition of any combination of signed numbers can be accomplished using the same process.

In contrast to elementary schoolchildren, who must first learn to add and later to subtract, a machine using two's complement notation needs to know only how to add. For example, the subtraction problem $7 - 5$ is the same as the addition problem

Figure 1-19 Addition problems converted to two's complement notation

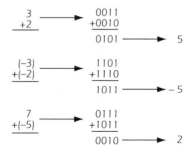

$7 + (-5)$. Consequently, if a machine were asked to subtract 5 (stored as 0101) from 7 (stored as 0111), it would first change the 5 to -5 (represented as 1011) and then perform the addition process of $0111 + 1011$ to obtain 0010, which represents 2 as shown below:

$$
\begin{array}{ccccc}
7 & & 0111 & & 0111 \\
\underline{-5} & \rightarrow & \underline{-0101} & \rightarrow & \underline{+1011} \\
& & & & 0010 \quad \rightarrow \quad 2
\end{array}
$$

Consequently, if we build a circuit to negate values (which with two's complement is little more than a complementing circuit) and another to perform the above addition process, these two circuits provide the ability to solve both addition and subtraction problems. The benefits do not stop there, however. Multiplication is merely repeated addition, and division is repeated subtraction ($6/2$ is the number of times 2 can be subtracted from 6 without getting a negative result). Thus, we can ultimately get all four of the standard arithmetic operations of addition, subtraction, multiplication, and division from these two circuits.

The Problem of Overflow

One problem we have avoided in the preceding examples is that in any of the numeric systems we have introduced, there is a limit to the size of the values that can be represented. When using two's complement with patterns of 4 bits, the value 9 has no pattern associated with it. Thus, we could not hope to obtain the correct answer to the problem $5 + 4$. In fact, the result would appear as -7. A similar problem arises if patterns of 5 bits are used and we try to represent the value 17. Such an error is called *overflow*. When using two's complement notation, this might occur when adding two positive values or when adding two negative values. In either case, the condition can be detected by checking the sign bit of the answer. That is, an overflow is indicated if the addition of two positive values results in the pattern for a negative value or if the sum of two negative values appears to be positive.

The point is that contrary to public belief, computers can make mistakes. So, the person using the machine must be aware of the dangers involved. Of course, because most machines manipulate longer bit patterns than we have used here, larger values can be computed without causing an overflow. For example, many machines use patterns of 32 bits for storing values in two's complement notation, allowing for positive values as large as 2,147,483,647 to accumulate before overflow occurs. If still larger values are needed, the technique called *double precision* is often used. This means that the length of the patterns used is increased from that which the machine normally uses. Another approach to the problem is to change the units of measure. For instance, finding a solution in terms of miles instead of inches results in smaller numbers being used and still provides the accuracy required.

Questions/Exercises

1. Convert each of the following excess eight representations to its equivalent decimal form without referring to the table in the text:

     a.   1110   b.   0111   c.   1000
     d.   0010   e.   0000   f.   1001

2. Convert each of the following decimal representations to its equivalent excess eight form without referring to the table in the text:

     a.   5   b.   −5   c.   3   d.   0   e.   7   f.   −8

3. Can the value 9 be represented in excess eight notation? What about representing 6 in excess four notation? Explain your answer.

4. Convert each of the following two's complement representations to its equivalent decimal form:

     a.   00011   b.   01111   c.   11100
     d.   11010   e.   00000   f.   10000

5. Convert each of the following decimal representations to its equivalent two's complement form using patterns of eight bits:

     a.   6   b.   −6   c.   −17   d.   13   e.   −1   f.   0

6. Suppose the following bit patterns represent values stored in two's complement notation. Find the two's complement representation of the negative of each value:

     a.   00000001   b.   01010101   c.   11111100
     d.   11111110   e.   00000000   f.   01111111

7. Suppose a machine stores numbers in two's complement notation. What are the largest and smallest numbers that could be stored if the machine uses bit patterns of the following lengths?

     a.   four   b.   six   c.   eight

8. In the following problems, each bit pattern represents a value stored in two's complement notation. Find the answer to each problem in two's complement notation by performing the addition process described in the text. Then check your work by translating the problem and your answer into decimal notation.

     a.   0101   b.   0011   c.   0101   d.   1110   e.   1010
          +0010   +0001   +1010   +0011   +1110

9. Solve each of the following problems in two's complement notation, but this time watch for overflow and indicate which answers are incorrect because of this phenomenon.

     a.   0101   b.   0101   c.   1010   d.   1010   e.   0111
          +0011   +0110   +1010   +0111   +0001

10. Translate each of the following problems from decimal notation into two's complement notation using bit patterns of length four, then convert each problem to an equivalent addition problem (as a machine might do), and finally

perform the addition. Check your answers by converting them back to decimal notation.

a.   6   b.   3   c.   4   d.   2   e.   1
    +1   −2   −6   +4   −5

11. Can overflow ever occur when adding values in two's complement notation when one value is positive and the other is negative? Explain your answer.

1-6 Storing Fractions

In contrast to the storage of integers, the storage of a value with a fractional part requires that we store not only the pattern of 0s and 1s representing its binary representation but also the position of the radix point. A popular way of doing this is based on scientific notation and is called *floating-point notation.*

Floating-Point Notation

Let us explain floating-point notation with an example using only one byte of storage. (Although machines normally use much longer patterns, this example is representative of actual systems and serves to demonstrate the important concepts without the clutter of long bit patterns.) We first designate the high-order bit of the byte as the sign bit. Once again, a 0 in the sign bit will mean that the value stored is nonnegative, and a 1 will mean that the value is negative. Next, we divide the remaining 7 bits of the byte into two groups, or fields, called the *exponent field* and the *mantissa field.* Let us designate the 3 bits following the sign bit as the exponent field and the remaining 4 bits as the mantissa field. The byte is therefore divided as shown in Figure 1-20.

We can explain the meaning of the fields by considering the following example. Suppose a byte contains the bit pattern 01101011. Analyzing this pattern with the preceding format, we see that the sign bit is 0, the exponent is 110, and the mantissa is 1011. To decode the byte, we first extract the mantissa and place a radix point on its left side, obtaining

.1011

Next, we extract the contents of the exponent field (110) and interpret it as an integer stored using the 3-bit excess method. Thus, the pattern in the exponent field

Figure 1-20 Floating-point notation components

Field
Sign bit
Exponent
Mantissa

in our example represents a positive 2 (see Figure 1-15). This tells us to move the radix in our solution to the right by two bits. (A negative exponent would mean to move the radix to the left.) Consequently, we obtain

$$10.11$$

which represents 2¾. Next, we note that the sign bit in our example is 0; the value represented is thus nonnegative. We conclude that the byte 01101011 represents 2¾.

As another example, consider the byte 10111100. We extract the mantissa to obtain

$$.1100$$

and move the radix one bit to the left, since the exponent field (011) represents the value −1. We therefore have

$$.01100$$

which represents ⅜. Since the sign bit in the original pattern is 1, the value stored is negative. We conclude that the pattern 10111100 represents −⅜.

To store a value using floating-point notation, we reverse the above process. For example, to code 1⅛, first we express it in binary notation and obtain 1.001. Next, we copy the bit pattern into the mantissa field from left to right, starting with the first nonzero bit in the binary representation. At this point, the byte looks like this:

$$\_\ \_\ \_\ \_\ \underline{1\ 0\ 0\ 1}$$

We must now fill in the exponent field. To this end, we imagine the contents of the mantissa field with a radix point at its left and determine the number of bits and the direction the radix must be moved to obtain the original binary number. In our example, we see that the radix in .1001 must be moved one bit to the right to obtain 1.001. Because the exponent should therefore be a positive 1, we place 101 (which is positive 1 in excess four notation) in the exponent field. Finally, we fill the sign bit with 0 because the value being stored is nonnegative. The finished byte looks like this:

$$\underline{0\ 1\ 0\ 1\ 1\ 0\ 0\ 1}$$

Before moving on, we should discuss why excess notation is used for representing the exponent in floating-point systems. It reduces the task of comparing the relative size of two values to the process of scanning their representations from left to right, looking for the first bit in which the two patterns differ. For example, if both sign bits are 0, the larger of the two values being compared is the one containing a 1 in the first bit position from the left in which the two patterns differ. Thus, if 00101010 and 00011001 were floating-point representations, we could conclude that the former represents a larger value without first determining what the values involved actually are.

Figure 1-21 Coding the value 2⅝

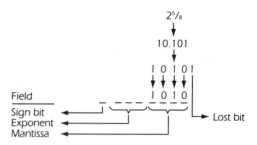

Round-Off Errors

Let us consider the annoying problem that occurs if we try to store 2⅝ with our 1-byte floating-point system. We first write 2⅝ in binary, which gives us 10.101. But now when we copy this into the mantissa field, we run out of room, and the last 1 (which represents the last ⅛) is lost (Figure 1-21). If we ignore this problem for now and continue by filling in the exponent field and the sign bit, we end up with the bit pattern 01101010, which represents 2½ instead of 2⅝. What has occurred is called a *round-off error,* and in this case it was caused by the fact that our mantissa field contains only 4 bits, whereas 5 were required for accuracy. This suggests the solution of lengthening this field, which is exactly what is done on real machines. As with integer storage, it is common to use at least 32 bits for storing floating-point notation instead of the 8 we have used here. This approach also allows for a longer exponent field at the same time. Even with these longer formats, however, there are still times when more accuracy is required. Again we find the concept of *double precision* being applied when extreme precision is required.

Another source of round-off errors is a phenomenon that you are already accustomed to in decimal notation. This is the problem of nonterminating expansions, such as those found when trying to express ⅓ in decimal form. Some values cannot be accurately expressed regardless of how many digits we use.

The difference between our normal decimal notation and binary notation is that more values have nonterminating representations in binary than in decimal notation. For example, the value one-tenth is nonterminating when expressed in binary. (Imagine the problems this might cause the unwary person using floating-point notation to store and manipulate dollars and cents. In particular, if the dollar is used as the unit of measure, the value of a dime could not be stored accurately. A solution in this case is to manipulate the data in units of pennies so that all values are integers that can be accurately stored using a method such as two's complement.)

Round-off errors and their related problems are an everyday concern for people working in the area of numerical analysis. This branch of mathematics deals with the problems involved when doing actual computations that are often massive and require significant accuracy.

We close this section with an example of a general rule of thumb that would warm the heart of any numerical analyst. Suppose we are asked to add the following three values using our 1-byte floating-point notation defined previously:

$$2\frac{1}{2} + \frac{1}{8} + \frac{1}{8}$$

If we add the values in the order listed, we first add 2½ to ⅛ and obtain 2⅝, which in binary is 10.101. Unfortunately, because this value cannot be stored accurately (as seen previously), the result of our first step ends up being stored as 2½ (which is the same as one of the values we were adding). The next step is to add this result to the last ⅛. Here again a round-off error occurs, and our final result turns out to be the incorrect answer 2½.

Now let us add the values in the opposite order. We first add ⅛ to ⅛ to obtain ¼. In binary this is .01; so the result of our first step is stored in a byte as 00111000, which is accurate. We now add this ¼ to the next value in the list, 2½, and obtain 2¾, which we can accurately store in a byte as 01101011. The result this time is the correct answer.

In summary, when adding values in floating-point notation, the order in which they are added can be extremely important. The general rule is to always add the smaller values together first; however, even this does not guarantee accuracy.

Questions/Exercises

1. Decode the following bit patterns using the floating-point format discussed in the text:
    a. 01001010   b.   01101101   c.   00111001
    d. 11011100   e.   10101011
2. Code the following values into the floating-point format discussed in the text. Indicate the occurrence of round-off errors.
    a. 2¾   b.   5¼   c.   ¾   d.   −3½   e.   −4⅜
3. In terms of the floating-point format discussed in the text, which of the patterns 01001001 and 00111101 represents the larger value? Describe a simple procedure for determining which of two patterns represents the larger value.
4. When using the floating-point format discussed in the text, what is the largest value that can be represented? What is the smallest positive value that can be represented?

1-7 Communication Errors

When information is transferred back and forth among the various parts of a computer, transmitted from the earth to the moon and back, or, for that matter, merely left in storage, a chance exists that the bit pattern finally retrieved may not be identical to the original one. For instance, particles of dirt or grease on a magnetic recording surface or a malfunctioning circuit may cause data to be incorrectly recorded or read. Moreover, in the case of some technologies, background radiation can alter patterns stored in a machine's main memory.

Of course, today's technology allows us to build extremely reliable devices. A disk drive, for example, may have an error rate of no more than one error per million bits. However, when considered in an application, this error rate translates into one possible error for every 30 pages of a novel. Thus, if the material were transferred often, the error rate could easily become intolerable.

To resolve this problem, a variety of coding techniques have been developed to allow the detection and even the correction of errors. Today, because these techniques are largely built into the internal components of a computer system, they are not apparent to the personnel using the machine. Nonetheless, their presence is important and represents a significant contribution to scientific research. In fact, many of these techniques are prime examples of the contributions made by theoretical mathematics, often scorned as too abstract to be applicable. It is fitting, therefore, for us to investigate some of these techniques that lie behind the reliability of today's equipment.

Parity Bits

A simple method of detecting errors is based on the principle that if each bit pattern being manipulated has an odd number of 1s and a pattern is found with an even number of 1s, an error must have occurred.

To use this principle, we need a system in which each pattern contains an odd number of 1s. This is easily obtained by first adding an additional bit, called the *parity bit,* to each pattern in a system already available (usually at the high order end). (Thus, the 7-bit ASCII code becomes an 8-bit code, or a 16-bit pattern representing a value in two's complement notation becomes a 17-bit pattern.) In each case, we assign the value 1 or 0 to this new bit so that the resulting pattern has an odd number of 1s. Thus,

Figure 1-22 *The ASCII codes for A and I adjusted for odd parity*

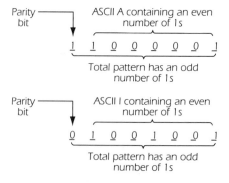

as Figure 1-22 shows, the ASCII code for A becomes 11000001 (parity bit 1), and the ASCII for I becomes 01001001 (parity bit 0). Although the 7-bit pattern for A has an even number of 1s in it and the 7-bit pattern for I has an odd number of 1s, both the 8-bit patterns have an odd number of 1s. Once our coding system has been modified in this way, a pattern with an even number of 1s indicates an error has occurred and the pattern being manipulated is incorrect.

The particular parity system just described is called *odd parity,* because we designed our system so that each pattern would contain an odd number of 1s. Another technique is to use *even parity.* In such a system, each pattern is designed to contain an even number of 1s, and thus an error is signaled by the occurrence of a pattern with an odd number of 1s.

Today, it is not unusual to find parity bits being used in a microcomputer's main memory. Thus, whereas we envision these machines having memory cells of 8 bits, in reality they may have 9-bit cells, 1 bit of which is used as a parity bit. Each time an 8-bit pattern is given to the memory circuitry for storage, the circuitry adds a parity bit and stores the resulting 9-bit pattern. When the pattern is later retrieved, the circuitry checks the parity of the 9-bit pattern. If this does not indicate an error, the memory removes the parity bit and confidently returns the remaining 8-bit pattern. Otherwise, the memory returns the 8 data bits with a warning that the pattern being returned may not be the same pattern that was originally entrusted to memory.

Error-Correcting Codes

Although the use of a parity bit allows the detection of an error, it does not provide the information needed to correct the error. Many people are surprised that codes, known as *error-correcting codes,* can be designed so that errors can be not only detected but also corrected. After all, intuition says that we cannot correct errors in a received message unless we already know the information in the message. However, a simple code with such a corrective property is presented in Figure 1-23.

To understand how this code works, we first define the *Hamming distance* (named after R. W. Hamming, who pioneered the search for error-correcting codes

Figure 1-23 An error-correcting code

Symbol	Code
A	000000
B	001111
C	010011
D	011100
E	100110
F	101001
G	110101
H	111010

Figure 1-24 Decoding the pattern 010100 using the code in Figure 1-23

Character	Distance between the received pattern and the character being considered
A	2
B	4
C	3
D	1 (Smallest distance)
E	3
F	5
G	2
H	4

after becoming frustrated with the lack of reliability of the early relay machines of the 1940s) between two patterns to be the number of bits in which the two differ. Thus, the Hamming distance between A and B in the code in Figure 1-23 is four, and the Hamming distance between B and C is three. The important feature of the code is that any two patterns are separated by a Hamming distance of at least three. If a single bit is modified by a malfunctioning device, the error can be detected since the result will not be a legal pattern. (We must change at least 3 bits in any pattern before it will look like another legal pattern.)

If a single error has occurred in a pattern from Figure 1-23, we can also figure out what the original pattern was. Indeed, the modified pattern will be a Hamming distance of only one from its original form but at least two from any of the other legal patterns. Thus, to decode a message, we simply compare each received pattern with the patterns in the code until we find one that is within a distance of one from the received pattern. This we consider to be the correct symbol for decoding. For example, suppose we receive the bit pattern 010100. If we compare this pattern to the patterns in the code, we obtain the table in Figure 1-24. Thus we can conclude that the character transmitted must be a D because this is the closest match.

You will observe that using this technique with the code in Figure 1-23 actually allows us to detect up to two errors per pattern and to correct one error. If we designed the code so that each pattern was a Hamming distance of at least five from each of the others, we would be able to detect up to four errors per pattern and correct up to two. Of course, the design of efficient codes associated with large Hamming distances is not a straightforward task. In fact, it constitutes a part of the branch of mathematics called algebraic coding theory.

Issues of Application

As mentioned earlier, the use of parity bits or error-correcting codes today is almost always a concern handled within the equipment itself and is rarely visible to the person using the machine. The average computer user may be concerned with these concepts only when it is necessary to connect two pieces of equipment, such as a printer and a computer. In such cases, most devices have switches whose settings determine the communication technique to be used. Under these circumstances, it is the user's responsibility to adjust the switches so that both pieces of equipment are set for the same technique. For instance, you could imagine that little would be accomplished if a computer sent characters with odd parity to a printer that was expecting even parity.

The decision whether to use parity checks, an error-correcting code, or some other error-handling system depends on the application at hand and to what extent one is willing to go for the added reliability. As already mentioned, parity systems are used in many small computer memory systems. Error-correcting codes are often used by high-capacity disk units, where the need for accuracy exceeds the costs introduced by the added complexity.

Of course, no error-handling system is foolproof. Parity systems cannot detect the occurrence of an even number of errors, and too many errors in a single pattern of an error-correcting code can produce another valid but incorrect pattern.

Questions/Exercises

1. The following bytes were originally coded using odd parity. In which of them do you know that an error has occurred?
   a. 10101101   b. 10000001   c. 00000000
   d. 11100000   e. 11111111
2. Could errors have occurred in a byte from question 1 without your knowing it? Explain your answer.
3. How would your answers to questions 1 and 2 change if you were told that even parity had been used instead of odd?
4. Code these sentences in ASCII using odd parity by adding a parity bit at the high-order end of each character code:
   a. I like milk.
   b. Where are you?
   c. "How?" Cheryl asked.
   d. 2 + 3 = 5.
5. Using the error-correcting code presented in Figure 1-24, decode the following messages:
   a. 001111 100100 001100
   b. 010001 000000 001011
   c. 011010 110110 100000 011100
6. Construct a code for the characters A, B, C, and D using bit patterns of length five so that the Hamming distance between any two patterns is at least three.

Chapter 1 Review Problems

(Asterisked problems are associated with optional sections.)

1. The following table represents (using hexadecimal notation) the addresses and contents of some cells in a machine's main memory. Starting with this memory arrangement, follow the sequence of instructions below and record the final contents of each of these memory cells:

Address	Contents
00	AB
01	53
02	D6
03	02

   Step 1. Move the contents of the cell whose address is 03 to the cell at address 00.

   Step 2. Move the value 01 into the cell at address 02.

   Step 3. Move the value stored at address 01 into the cell at address 03.

2. How many cells can be in a computer's main memory if each cell's address can be represented by three hexadecimal digits?

3. What bit patterns are represented by the following hexadecimal notations:
   a. BC   b. 67   c. 9A   d. 10   e. 3F

4. What is the value of the most significant bit in the bit patterns represented by the following hexadecimal notations:
   a. FF   b. 7F   c. 8F   d. 1F

5. Express the following bit patterns in hexadecimal notation:
   a. 101010101010
   b. 110010110111
   c. 000011101011

6. Suppose a monitor screen displayed 24 rows containing 80 text characters each. If the image on the screen were stored in memory by representing each character by its ASCII code (one character per byte), how many bytes of the machine's memory would be required to hold the entire screen image?

7. Suppose a graph is represented on a monitor screen by a rectangular array containing 1024 columns and 768 rows of small dots (called pixels, short for picture elements). If 8 bits are required to code the color and intensity of each pixel, how many byte-size memory cells are required to hold the entire graph?

8. a. Identify two advantages that a machine's main memory has over disk storage.
   b. Identify two advantages that disk storage has over a machine's main memory.

9. Suppose you are about to use your personal computer to write a term paper that you estimate will be 40 double-spaced typed pages. Your machine has a disk drive for 5¼-inch floppy disks with a capacity of 1.2Mb per disk. Will your completed term paper fit on one of these disks? If so, how many such papers can be stored on one disk? If not, will it fit on a 3½-inch disk with a capacity of 1.44Mb?

10. Suppose the hard drive on your personal computer has a capacity of 40Mb, of which 30Mb is allocated for storing the programs you have purchased, and that you use your machine merely for writing personal correspondence. If you write two letters a day, each approximately 2Kb in size, and keep each letter on your hard drive, how long will it take for the hard drive to fill up?

11. Suppose that only 5Mb of your personal computer's 40Mb hard disk drive is empty and you are about to replace that drive with a 120Mb drive. You want to save all the information stored on the hard drive on 3¼ inch floppy disks while the conversion is made. How many floppy disks are required if each has a capacity of 1.44Mb?

12. If each sector on a disk contained 512 bytes, how many sectors are required to store a single double-spaced typed page?

13. Suppose a 5¼-inch floppy disk contained 40 tracks, each of which is divided into sectors capable of holding 256 characters. How many characters will the disk hold if each track is divided into 10 sectors? What if each track contains 16 sectors? How do these capacities compare to the size of a 400-page novel in which each page contains 3500 characters?

14. If the 16-sectored floppy disk in problem 13 were spinning at the rate of 300 revolutions per minute, at approximately what rate, measured in characters per second, will the data pass by the read/write head?

15. If the microcomputer using the floppy disk in problem 14 executed ten instructions every microsecond (millionths of a second), how many instructions can it execute in the time between consecutive characters passing the read/write head?

16. If a floppy disk is rotating at 300 revolutions per minute and the machine can execute ten instructions in a microsecond (millionths of a second), how many instructions can the machine perform during the disk's latency time?

17. Compare the latency time of the typical floppy disk in problem 16 with that of a typical hard-disk drive spinning at 60 revolutions per second.

18. What is the average access time for a hard disk spinning at 60 revolutions per second with a seek time of 10 milliseconds?

19. Approximately how many 350-page novels with approximately 3300 characters per page can be recorded on a disk drive with a 80Mb capacity? What if the storage device is a CD-ROM with a capacity of 500Mb?

20. Here is a message in ASCII. What does it say?
1010111 1101000 1100001 1110100 0100000
1100100 1101111 1100101 1110011 0100000
1101001 1110100 0100000 1110011 1100001
1111001 0111111

21. The following is a message coded in ASCII using 1 byte per character and then represented in hexadecimal notation. What is the message?
        68657861646563696D616C

22. List the binary representations of the integers from 6 to 16.

23. a. Write the number 13 by representing the 1 and 3 in ASCII.
    b. Write the number 13 in binary representation.

24. Code the following sentences in ASCII using 1 byte per character. In each byte, use the least significant 7 bits for the ASCII pattern and place a 0 in the most significant bit.
    a. 100/5 = 20
    b. To be or not to be?
    c. The total cost is $7.25.

25. Express your answers to problem 24 in hexadecimal notation.

*26. Code the following sentences in ASCII using 1 byte per character. Use the most significant bit of each byte as a (odd) parity bit.

a. 100/5 = 20
b. To be or not to be?
c. The total cost is $7.25.

*27. The following message was originally transmitted with odd parity in each short bit string. In which strings have errors definitely occurred?
11011 01011 10110 00000 11111 10101 10001 00100 01110

*28. Suppose a 21-bit code is generated by representing each symbol by three consecutive copies of its ASCII representation (for example, the symbol A is represented by the bit string 100000110000011000001). What error-correcting properties does this new code have?

*29. Using the error-correcting code described in Figure 1-23, decode the following words:
    a. 111010 110110
    b. 101000 100110 001100
    c. 011101 000110 000000 010100
    d. 010010 001000 001110 101111
        000000 110111 100110
    e. 010011 000000 101001 100110

*30. Convert each of the following binary representations to its equivalent decimal form:
    a. 111   b. 0001   c. 11101
    d. 10001   e. 10111   f. 000000
    g. 100   h. 1000   i. 10000
    j. 11001   k. 11010   l. 11011

*31. Convert each of the following decimal representations to its equivalent binary form:
    a. 7   b. 12   c. 16   d. 15   e. 33

*32. Convert each of the following excess 16 representations to its equivalent decimal form:
    a. 100007   b. 10011   c. 01101
    d. 01111   e. 10111

*33. Convert each of the following decimal representations to its equivalent excess four form:
    a. 0   b. 3   c. −3   d. −1   e. 1

*34. Convert each of the following two's complement representations to its equivalent decimal form:
    a. 10000   b. 10011   c. 01101
    d. 01111   e. 10111

*35. Convert each of the following decimal representations to its equivalent two's complement form using patterns of 7 bits:
    a. 12   b. −12   c. −1   d. 0   e. 8

*36. Perform each of the following additions assuming the bit strings represent values in two's complement notation. Identify each case in which the answer is incorrect because of overflow.

a. 00101 b. 01111 c. 11111
   +01000   +00001   +00001

d. 10111 e. 00111 f. 00111
   +11010   +00111   +01100

g. 11111 h. 01010 i. 01000
   +11111   +10101   +01000

j. 01010
   +00011

*37. Solve each of the following problems by translating the values into two's complement notation (using patterns of 5 bits), converting any subtraction problem to an equivalent addition problem, and performing that addition. Check your work by converting your answer to decimal notation. (Watch out for overflow.)

a. 7 b. 7 c. 12
   +1   − 1   − 4

d. 8 e. 12 f. 4
   −7   + 4   − 11

*38. Convert each of the following binary representations into its equivalent base ten form:
a. 11.001 b. 100.1101 c. .0101
d. 1.0 e. 10.01

*39. Express each of the following values in binary notation:
a. 5¾ b. ¹⁄₁₆ c. 7⅞
d. 1¼ e. 6⅝

*40. Decode the following bit patterns using the floating-point format discussed in this chapter:
a. 01011100 b. 11001000
c. 00101010 d. 10111001

*41. Code the following values using the floating-point format discussed in this chapter. Indicate each case in which a round-off error occurs.
a. ½ b. 7½ c. −3¾
d. ³⁄₃₂ e. ³¹⁄₃₂

*42. What is the best approximation to the square root of 2 that can be expressed in the floating-point format described in Section 1-6? What value is actually obtained if this approximation is squared by a machine using this floating-point format?

*43. In each of the following addition problems, interpret the bit patterns using the floating-point format discussed in Section 1-6, add the values

represented, and code the answer in the same floating-point format. Indicate those cases in which round-off errors occur.

a. 01011100 b. 01101010
   +01101000   +00111000

c. 01111000 d. 01011000
   +00011000   +01011000

*44. One of the bit patterns 01011 and 11011 represents a value stored in excess 16 notation and the other represents the same value stored in two's complement notation.
a. What can be determined about this common value?
b. What is the relationship between a pattern representing a value stored in two's complement notation and the pattern representing the same value stored in excess notation using the same bit pattern length?

*45. The three bit patterns 01101000, 10000010, and 00000010 are representations of the same value in two's complement, excess, and the floating-point notation discussed in this chapter, but not necessarily in that order. What is the common value, and which pattern is in which notation?

*46. In each of the following cases the different bit strings represent the same value but in different numeric coding systems that we have discussed. Identify each value and the coding systems used to represent it.
a. 11111010 0011 1011
b. 11111101 01111101 11101100
c. 1010 0010 01101000

*47. Which of the following bit patterns are not valid representations in an excess 16 notation system?
01001 101 010101 00000 1000 000000 1111

*48. Which of the following values cannot be represented accurately in the floating-point format introduced in Section 1-6?
a. 6½ b. 9 c. 1³⁄₁₆ d. ¹⁷⁄₃₂ e. ¹⁵⁄₁₆

*49. If you doubled the length of the bit strings being used to represent integers in binary from 4 bits to 8 bits, what change would be made in the value of the largest integer you could represent? What if you were using two's complement notation?

*50. What would be the hexadecimal representation of the largest memory address in a memory consisting of 4Mb if each cell had a 1-byte capacity?

Problems for the Programmer

1. What is the largest integer your language/machine combination can conveniently handle? As an experiment, write a loop that initializes an integer at 1 and repeatedly multiplies by 2 seventy times while printing the result at each step. Explain the results.

2. What statements does your programming language provide for identifying how the various data items in your programs are to be coded by the machine?

3. Does your programming language provide a convenient technique for handling overflow?

4. Write a program that requests two integers as input, adds them, and displays the result. What happens if the values entered are very large? Can you modify your program so that it prints the message "overflow occurred" when such is the case?

5. What statements in your programming language allow access to data

a. in main memory?
b. in mass storage?

6. Write a loop that initializes a real variable at 0.01 and repeatedly increments it by 0.01 up to the value 1, printing its value at each step. Does it print the correct values? Why would you suspect that it may not? Experiment with different initial values and step sizes.

7. Does your programming language allow you to mix data types in the same instruction? For example, can you add an integer value to a floating-point value and place the result in a floating-point field? How about placing the result in an integer field? What activities must be done by the language/machine system to accomplish such a procedure?

8. Write a program to convert binary numerals into Roman numerals. (Recall that $1 = I$, $5 = V$, $10 = X$, $50 = L$, $100 = C$, $500 = D$, and $1000 = M$.)

Additional Reading

Buchanan, J. L. and Turner, P. R. *Numerical Methods and Analysis.* New York: McGraw-Hill, 1992.

Burden, L. B. and Faires, J. D. *Numerical Analysis,* 5th ed. Boston, Mass.: Prindle, Weber, and Schmidt, 1993.

Dejoie, D.; Fowler, G.; and Paradice, D. *Ethical Issues in Information Systems.* Boston, Mass.: Boyd and Fraser, 1991.

Knuth, D. E. *The Art of Computer Programming,* Vol. 2, 2nd ed. Reading, Mass.: Addison-Wesley, 1981.

Levy, H. M. and Eckhouse, R. H., Jr. *Computer Programming and Architecture.* Bedford, Mass.: Digital Equipment Corp., 1980.

Tanenbaum, A. S. *Structured Computer Organization,* 3rd ed. Englewood Cliffs, N.J.: Prentice-Hall, 1990.

Waser, S. and Flynn, Michael J. *Introduction to Arithmetic for Digital Systems Designers.* New York: Holt, Rinehart, and Winston, 1982.

CHAPTER TWO

DATA MANIPULATION

*Sections marked by an asterisk are optional in that they provide additional depth of coverage that is not required for an understanding of future chapters.

In Chapter 1, we studied the concepts relating to the storage of data and a computer's memory. In addition to being able to store data, an algorithmic machine must be able to manipulate the data as directed by an algorithm. Thus, the machine must have the mechanism for performing operations on data and coordinating the sequence of these operations. In today's typical machine, this mechanism is called the central processing unit. This unit is conceptually divided into two smaller units: one that coordinates the machine's activities and one that performs the requested operations. It is the study of these units and related topics on which this chapter concentrates.

2-1 The Central Processing Unit

The circuitry in a typical computer that performs operations (such as addition and subtraction) on data is not directly connected to the storage cells in the machine's main memory. Instead, this circuitry is isolated in an area of the computer called the *central processing unit,* or *CPU.* This unit is actually charged with two conceptually different tasks, because the execution of an algorithm requires not only that operations be performed on data but also that the execution of these operations be coordinated. Consequently, the CPU consists of two parts: the *arithmetic/logic unit,* which contains the circuitry that performs data manipulation and the *control unit,* which contains the circuitry for coordinating the machine's activities.

Registers

Since the CPU is a separate device from the machine's memory, it contains special memory cells, called *registers,* that are used as temporary holding places for data being manipulated. In particular, these registers hold the inputs to the arithmetic/logic unit's circuitry and provide a storage place for the result. When an operation is to be performed on data, it is the control unit's responsibility to see that the data are placed in the registers, to inform the arithmetic/logic unit as to which registers hold the data, to activate the appropriate operation circuitry in the arithmetic/logic unit, and to tell the arithmetic/logic unit which register should hold the result.

It is instructive to consider registers in the context of a machine's overall memory facilities. Registers are used to hold the data immediately applicable to the operation at hand; main memory is used to hold the data that will be needed in the near future; and mass storage is used to hold data that will likely not be needed in the near future. (In many machines, an additional level, called cache memory, is added to this hierarchy. Cache memory is merely a section of high-speed memory with response times similar to that of the CPU's registers, often located within the CPU itself. In this special memory area, the machine attempts to keep a copy of that portion of main memory that is of current interest. In this setting, data transfers that normally would be made between registers and main memory are made between registers and cache memory. These changes are then transferred collectively to main memory at a more opportune time.)

Figure 2-1 A CPU/main memory architecture

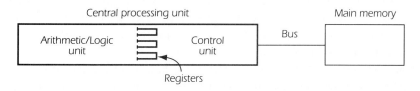

CPU/Memory Interface

To perform an operation on data stored in memory, the data first must be copied from memory into the registers in the CPU. Moreover, it is highly likely that we will want the result of the operation stored somewhere in memory. To facilitate this data transfer, the CPU is connected to main memory by a collection of wires called a *bus* (Figure 2-1). In most machines, this bus also is equipped with numerous sockets through which additional circuitry such as a disk controller can be attached. Through this bus, the CPU is able to extract, or read, data from main memory by supplying the address of the pertinent memory cell along with a read signal. In a similar manner, the CPU can place, or write, data in memory by providing the address of the destination cell and the data to be stored together with a write signal.

With this mechanism in mind, we see that performing an operation such as addition on data stored in main memory involves more than the mere execution of the addition operation itself. The process involves the combined efforts of both the control unit, which coordinates the transfer of information between the registers and main memory, and the arithmetic/logic unit, which performs the operation of addition when instructed to do so by the control unit. The complete process of adding two values stored in memory might be broken down into the steps listed in Figure 2-2.

Machine Instructions

Let us now take a brief look at the types of instructions that a typical machine might be able to execute (a more in-depth discussion appears later in the chapter). You may be surprised to learn that the list is really quite short. One of the fascinating aspects

Figure 2-2 Adding values stored in memory

Step 1. Get one of the values to be added from memory and place it in a register.
Step 2. Get the other value to be added from memory and place it in another register.
Step 3. Activate the addition circuitry with the registers used in steps 1 and 2 as inputs and another register designated to hold the result.
Step 4. Store the result in memory.
Step 5. Stop.

of computer science is that once a machine can perform certain elementary but well-chosen tasks, adding more features does not increase the machine's theoretical capabilities. In other words, beyond a certain point, additional features may increase such things as convenience and speed but add nothing to the machine's basic abilities. We discuss these ideas further in Chapter 11.

When discussing the instructions in a machine's repertoire, it is helpful to recognize that they can be classified into three categories: the data transfer group, the arithmetic/logic group, and the control group.

Data Transfer

The first group consists of instructions that request the movement of data from one location to another. Steps 1, 2, and 4 in Figure 2-2 fall into this category. As in the case of main memory, it is unusual for the data being transferred from any location in a machine to be erased from its original location. The process involved in a transfer instruction is more like copying the data into another location rather than moving it. In this sense, the popular *transfer* or *move* terminology is actually a misnomer, with more descriptive terms being *copy* or *clone*. While on the subject of terminology, we should mention that special terms are used when referring to the transfer of data between the CPU and main memory. A request to fill a register with the contents of a memory cell is commonly referred to as a LOAD instruction; conversely, a request to transfer the contents of a register to a memory cell is called a STORE instruction. Thus, steps 1 and 2 in Figure 2-2 are LOAD instructions, while step 4 is a STORE instruction.

An important group of instructions within the data transfer category consists of the commands for communicating with devices outside the CPU-main memory context. Since these instructions handle the input/output (I/O) activities of the machine, they are classified as the I/O instructions and are sometimes considered as a category in their own right. On the other hand, Section 2-6 describes how these I/O activities are often handled by the same instructions that request data transfers between the CPU and main memory, and placing them in a separate category therefore would be somewhat misleading.

Arithmetic/Logic

The arithmetic/logic group consists of the instructions that tell the control unit to request an activity within the arithmetic/logic unit. Step 3 in Figure 2-2 falls into this group. As its name suggests, the arithmetic/logic unit is capable of performing operations other than the basic arithmetic operations. Some of these additional operations are the common logic operations AND, OR, and EXCLUSIVE OR, which we discuss later. For now, we merely mention that these operations are often used for manipulating individual bits within a register without disturbing the rest of the register. Another collection of operations available within most arithmetic/logic units

Figure 2-3 Dividing values stored in memory

Step 1. LOAD a register with a value from memory.
Step 2. LOAD another register with another value from memory.
Step 3. If this second value is zero, jump to step 6.
Step 4. Divide the contents of the first register by the second register and leave the result in the accumulator.
Step 5. STORE the contents of the accumulator in memory.
Step 6. Stop.

allows the contents of registers to be moved to the right or the left within the register. These operations are known as either SHIFT or ROTATE operations, depending on whether the bits that "fall off the end" of the register when its contents are moved are merely discarded (SHIFT) or are used to fill the holes left at the other end (ROTATE).

Control

The control group consists of those instructions that direct the execution of the program rather than the manipulation of data. Step 5 in Figure 2-2 falls into this category, although it is an extremely elementary example. This group contains many of the more interesting instructions in a machine's repertoire, such as the family of JUMP (or BRANCH) instructions used to direct the control unit to execute an instruction other than the next one in the list. These JUMP instructions appear in two varieties: unconditional jumps and conditional jumps. An example of the former would be the instruction "skip to step number 5"; an example of the latter would be "If the value obtained is 0, then skip to step number 5." Thus, the distinction is that a conditional jump results in a "change of venue" only if a certain condition is satisfied. As an example, Figure 2-3 displays a sequence of instructions for dividing two values where Step 3 is a conditional jump that protects against the possibility of division by zero.

Questions/Exercises

1. What sequence of events do you think would be required in a machine to move the contents of one memory cell to another?

2. What information must the CPU supply to the main memory circuitry to write a value into a memory cell?

3. Why might the term *move* be considered an incorrect name for the operation of moving data from one location in a machine to another?

4. In the text, JUMP instructions were expressed by identifying the destination explicitly by stating the name (or step number) of the destination within the JUMP instruction (for example, "Jump to step 6"). This technique's drawback is that if an instruction name (number) is later changed, we must be sure to find all jumps to that instruction and change that name also. Describe another way of expressing a JUMP instruction so that the name of the destination is not explicitly stated.

5. Is the instruction "If 0 equals 0, then jump to step 7" a conditional or unconditional jump? Explain your answer.

2-2 The Stored-Program Concept

Early computing devices were not known for their flexibility, as the program that each device executed tended to be built into the control unit as a part of the machine. Such a system is analogous to a music box that always plays the same tune when what is needed is the flexibility of a CD changer. One approach used to gain this flexibility in early electronic computers was to design the control units so they could be conveniently rewired. This flexibility was accomplished by means of a pegboard arrangement similar to old telephone switchboards in which the ends of jumper wires were plugged into holes.

Instructions as Bit Patterns

A breakthrough (credited, perhaps incorrectly,[1] to John von Neumann) came with the realization that a program, just like data, can be coded and stored in main memory. If the control unit is designed to extract the program from memory, decode the instructions, and execute them, a computer's program can be changed merely by changing the contents of the computer's memory instead of rewiring the control unit. (This technique even allows the machine to change its own program.) This stored-program concept has become the standard approach used today. To apply it, a machine is designed to recognize certain bit patterns as representing certain instructions. This collection of instructions along with the coding system is called the *machine language* because it defines the means by which we communicate algorithms to the machine.

The coded version of a machine instruction typically consists of two parts: the *op-code* (short for operation code) field and the *operand* field. The bit pattern appearing in the op-code field indicates which of the elementary operations, such as STORE, SHIFT, EXCLUSIVE OR, and JUMP, is requested by the instruction. The bit patterns found in the operand field provide more detailed information about the operation specified by the op-code. For example, in the case of a STORE operation, the information in the operand field indicates which register contains the data to be stored and which memory cell is to receive the data.

The concept of storing a program in memory is not difficult at all. What made it difficult to think of originally was that everyone thought of programs and data as different entities: Data were stored in memory; programs were part of the control unit.

---

[1]Some people claim that this idea was originally developed by J. P. Eckert, Jr., at the Moore School but that his ideas became a part of a group effort and were ultimately misattributed to von Neumann.

The result was a prime example of not being able to see the forest for the trees. It is easy to be caught in such ruts, and the development of computer science might well remain in many of them today without our knowing it. Indeed, part of the excitement of the science is that new insights are constantly opening doors to new theories and applications.

A Typical Machine Language

Let us see how the instructions of a typical machine might be coded. The machine that we will use for our discussion is described in Appendix B and summarized in Figure 2-4. It has 16 registers, named R0 through R15 (R0 through RF in hexadecimal). Moreover, the machine has 256 cells in its main memory. Consequently, each memory cell is uniquely addressed, or identified, by an integer in the range from 0 to 255. As we mentioned earlier, memory cells containing 8 bits are quite popular, so let us pretend that the memory cells in our machine are that size. Since the registers are used to hold data from memory cells on a temporary basis, it makes sense to have each register also consist of 8 bits.

Op-Codes

Referring to the machine language listing in Appendix B, you find that each instruction is coded with a total of 16 bits, represented in the listing by four hexadecimal digits (Figure 2-5, on the following page). The op-code for each instruction consists of the first four bits or, equivalently, the first hexadecimal digit. The entire instruction list

Figure 2-4 The architecture of the machine of Appendix B

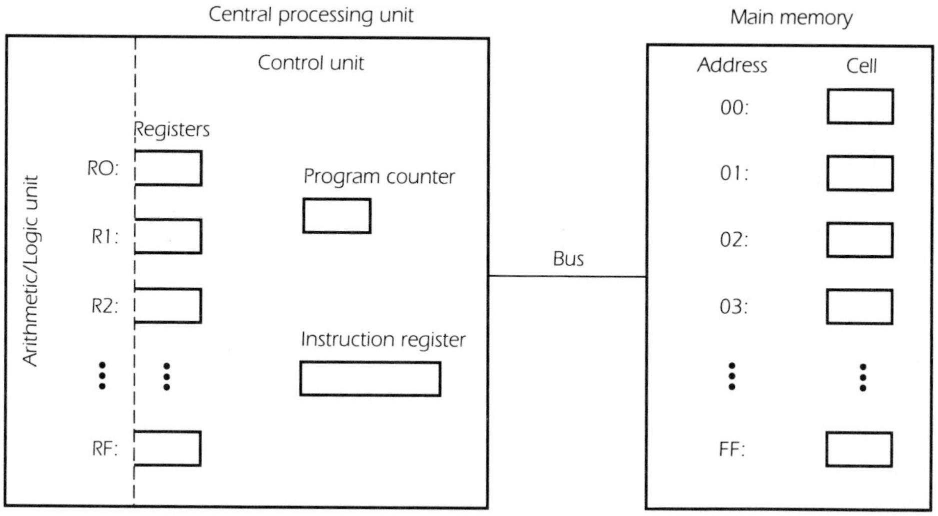

Figure 2-5 The format of a machine instruction

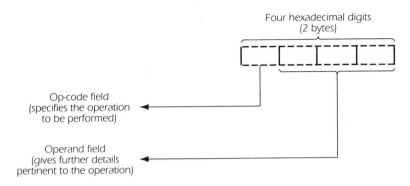

Four hexadecimal digits
(2 bytes)

Op-code field
(specifies the operation
to be performed)

Operand field
(gives further details
pertinent to the operation)

consists of only 12 basic instructions whose op-codes are represented by the hexadecimal digits 1 through C. Thus, any instruction code starting with the bit pattern 0011 (hexadecimal 3) refers to a STORE instruction, and any instruction code starting with 1010 (hexadecimal A) refers to a ROTATE instruction.

The machine has two ADD instructions: one for adding two's complement representations and one for adding floating-point representations. This distinction results from the fact that adding bit patterns that represent values coded in binary notation requires different activities within the arithmetic/logic unit than when adding floating-point notation.

Operands

Now we take a look at the operand field. It consists of 12 bits, or three hexadecimal digits, and in each case (except for the HALT instruction, which needs no further refinement) clarifies the general instruction given by the op-code. For example, if the first 4 bits of an instruction were 0001 (the op-code for loading from memory), the next 4 bits of the instruction would indicate which register is to be loaded, and the last 8 bits would indicate which memory cell is to provide the data. Thus, the instruction 1347 translates to the statement "LOAD register R3 with the contents of the memory cell at address 47." In the case of the op-code hexadecimal 7, which requests that the contents of two registers be ORed, the next 4 bits indicate where the result should be placed, while the last 8 bits of the operand field are used to indicate which two registers are to be ORed. Thus, the instruction 70C5 translates to the statement "OR the contents of R12 (C in hexadecimal is 12 in decimal) with the contents of R5 and leave the result in register R0."

A subtle distinction exists between our machine's two LOAD instructions. Here we see that the op-code 0001 (hexadecimal 1) refers to the instruction that loads a register with the contents of a memory cell, whereas the op-code 0010 (hexadecimal 2) refers to the instruction that loads a register with a particular value. The difference is that the operand field in an instruction of the first type contains an address, whereas in the second type it contains the bit pattern to be loaded.

An interesting situation occurs in the case of the JUMP instruction (op-code hexadecimal B). The first 4 bits of the operand field indicate which register is to be compared with register R0. If this register contains the same pattern as R0, the machine jumps to the instruction at the address indicated by the last 8 bits of the operand. Otherwise, the execution of the program continues as usual. In general, this provides a conditional jump. However, if the first 4 bits of the operand field are 0000 (hexadecimal 0), the instruction requests that R0 be compared with R0. Since a register is always equal to itself, the jump is always taken. Consequently, any instruction whose code starts with the hexadecimal digits B0 translates to an unconditional jump.

A Program Example

We close this section with the following coded version of the steps in Figure 2-2. We have assumed that the values to be added are stored in two's complement notation at memory addresses 6C and 6D and the sum is to be placed in memory at address 6E.

Step 1.   156C
Step 2.   166D
Step 3.   5056
Step 4.   306E
Step 5.   C000

Questions/Exercises

1.   The following are instructions written in the machine language described in Appendix B. Rewrite them in English.
     a.   368A   b.   BADE   c.   803C   d.   40F4
2.   What is the difference between the instructions 15AB and 25AB in the machine language of Appendix B?
3.   Here are some instructions in English. Translate each of them into the machine language of Appendix B.
     a.   LOAD register number 3 with the hexadecimal value 56.
     b.   ROTATE register number 5 three bits to the right.
     c.   JUMP to the instruction at location F3 if the contents of register number 7 are equal to the contents of R0.
     d.   AND the contents of register number 10 (hexadecimal A) with the contents of register number 5 and leave the result in register number 0.

2-3 Program Execution

A computer follows a program stored in its memory by moving the instructions from memory to the control unit as needed. Once in the control unit, each instruction is decoded and obeyed. The order in which the instructions are fetched from memory corresponds to the order in which the instructions are stored in memory unless otherwise specified by a JUMP instruction. To understand how the overall execution process takes place, it is necessary to take a closer look at the control unit inside the CPU. Within this unit are two special-purpose registers called the *program counter* and the *instruction register* (Figure 2-4). The program counter contains the address of the next instruction to be executed, thereby serving as the machine's way of keeping track of where it is in the program. The instruction register is used to hold the instruction being executed.

The control unit performs its job by continually repeating what is called the *machine cycle,* which consists of three steps: fetch, decode, and execute (Figure 2-6). During the fetch step, the control unit requests that main memory provide it with the next instruction to be executed. The unit knows where the next instruction is in memory because its address is kept in the program counter. The control unit places the instruction received from memory in its instruction register and then increments the program counter so that the counter contains the address of the next instruction.

With the instruction now in the instruction register, the control unit begins the decode phase of the machine cycle. At this time, it analyzes the op-code and operand fields to determine what action the instruction is requesting.

Figure 2-6 The machine cycle

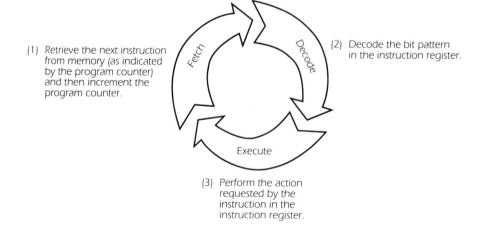

(1) Retrieve the next instruction from memory (as indicated by the program counter) and then increment the program counter.

Fetch

Decode

(2) Decode the bit pattern in the instruction register.

Execute

(3) Perform the action requested by the instruction in the instruction register.

Having decoded the instruction, the control unit enters the execute phase, during which it activates the correct circuitry to perform the requested task. For example, if the instruction is a load from memory, the control unit causes the load to occur; if the instruction is for an arithmetic operation, the control unit activates the appropriate circuitry in the arithmetic/logic unit with the correct registers as inputs.

When the instruction has been executed, the control unit again begins the machine cycle with the fetch phase. Observe that since the program counter was incremented at the end of the previous fetch phase, it again provides the control unit with the correct instruction address.

A somewhat special case is the execution of a JUMP instruction. Consider, for example, the instruction B258, which translates into "JUMP to the instruction at address 58 if the contents of R2 is the same as that of R0." In this case the execute phase of the machine cycle begins with the comparison of registers R2 and R0. If they are different, the execute phase terminates and the next fetch phase begins. If, however, the contents of these registers are equal, the machine places the value 58 in its program counter before completing the execute phase. In this case, then, the next fetch phase finds 58 in the program counter, so the instruction at that address is the next instruction executed.

An Example of Program Execution

Let us follow this process through the program we coded at the end of Section 2-2. We first need to put the coded program somewhere in memory. For our example, suppose the program is stored in consecutive addresses, starting at address A0 hexadecimal. A table representing the contents of this area of memory appears in Figure 2-7. With the program stored in this manner, we can cause the machine to execute it by placing the address (A0) of the first instruction in the program counter and starting the machine.

Figure 2-7 Our "add" program stored in memory starting at address A0

Address	Contents
A0	15
A1	6C
A2	16
A3	6D
A4	50
A5	56
A6	30
A7	6E
A8	C0
A9	00

The control unit begins its fetch phase by extracting the instruction at location A0 and placing this instruction (156C) in its instruction register. Notice that, in our machine, instructions are 16 bits (2 bytes) long. Thus, the instruction register in our example CPU is twice the size of the other registers we have mentioned. This instruction size also means that each instruction occupies two memory cells. The control unit is designed to take this into account so that it knows to retrieve the contents of both cells. It then adds 2 to the program counter so that this register contains the address of the next instruction. Thus, at the end of the fetch phase of the first machine cycle, the program counter and instruction register contain the following data:

Program Counter: A2
Instruction Register: 156C

Next, the control unit analyzes the instruction in its instruction register and concludes that it is to load register R5 with the contents of the memory cell at address 6C. This load activity is performed during the execution phase, and the control unit then returns to the fetch phase of the machine cycle.

During this fetch phase, the control unit obtains the instruction 166D from the two memory cells starting at address A2, places this instruction in its instruction register, and increments the program counter to A4. The values in the program counter and instruction register therefore become the following:

Program Counter: A4
Instruction Register: 166D

Now the control unit decodes the instruction 166D and determines that it is to load register R6 with the contents of memory address 6D. It then enters the execute phase, during which register R6 is actually loaded.

Since the program counter now contains A4, the control unit extracts the next instruction starting at this address. The result is that 5056 is placed in the instruction register, and the program counter is incremented to A6. The control unit now decodes the contents of its instruction register and enters the execution phase by activating the two's complement addition circuitry with the inputs R5 and R6.

During this execution phase, the arithmetic/logic unit performs the requested addition, leaves the result in R0 (as requested by the control unit), and reports to the control unit that it has finished. The control unit then begins another fetch phase of the machine cycle. Once again, with the aid of the program counter, it fetches the next instruction (306E) from the two memory cells starting at memory location A6 and increments the program counter to A8. This instruction is decoded during the next decode phase and executed during the next execute phase. At this point, the sum is placed at memory location 6E.

The next instruction is fetched starting from memory location A8, and the program counter is incremented to AA. The contents of the instruction register

(C000) are now decoded as the halt instruction. Consequently, the machine stops during the next execute phase of the machine cycle, and the program is completed.

In summary, we see that the execution of a program stored in memory involves nothing mysterious. In fact, the process is similar to the process you and I might use if we needed to follow a detailed list of instructions. Whereas we might keep our place by checking the instructions off as we do them, the computer keeps its place by using the program counter. After determining which instruction to execute next, we would read the instruction and extract its meaning just as the machine decodes its instructions. Finally, we would perform the task requested and return to the list for the next instruction in the same manner that the machine executes its instructions during the execute phase and then continues with another fetch.

The significant differences between humans and machines when following such a list of instructions are accuracy and speed. The control unit faithfully repeats the machine cycle again and again without any tendency or desire to cut corners and, thus, without errors. Humans, on the other hand, quickly become bored, think they see what is to be done, and hurry to do it without giving each instruction its fair attention. The result is that the bolts we have left to attach the swing to the chain are the ones that were supposed to connect the ladder to the swingset.

As for speed, technology continues to amaze us with faster and faster equipment. Today it is not unusual to find machine speeds measured in units of a million instructions per second (MIPS), with common speeds in the 10-MIPS to 100-MIPS range. There are signs, however, that there will be a limit to the speed with which machines can execute instructions, and technology is already turning toward alternatives. This is the subject of Section 2-4.

Programs Versus Data

Many programs can be stored simultaneously in a computer's main memory, so long as they occupy different locations. Which program will be run when the machine is started can then be determined merely by setting the program counter appropriately.

One must keep in mind, however, that data are also contained in memory, and since it is also coded in terms of 0s and 1s, the machine alone has no way of knowing what is data and what is program. If the program counter is assigned the address of data instead of the address of the desired program, the computer, not knowing any better, extracts the data bit patterns as though they were instructions and executes them. The final result depends on the data involved.

Care must be taken at this point not to assume that this feature is all bad. Once again, the concept of programs and data being completely different entities can be severely limiting. In reality, providing programs and data with a common appearance in a machine's memory has proven a useful attribute because it allows one program to manipulate other programs (or even itself) as it would data. Indeed, we will see that what may be data to one program often turns out to be another program.

Questions/Exercises

1. Suppose the memory cells from addresses 00 to 05 in the machine described in Appendix B contain the (hexadecimal) bit patterns given in the following table:

Address	Contents
00	14
01	02
02	34
03	17
04	C0
05	00

If we start the machine with its program counter containing 00, what bit pattern is in the memory cell whose address is hexadecimal 17 when the machine halts?

2. Suppose the memory cells at addresses B0 to B8 in the machine described in Appendix B contained the (hexadecimal) bit patterns given in the following table:

Address	Contents
B0	13
B1	B8
B2	A3
B3	02
B4	33
B5	B8
B6	C0
B7	00
B8	0F

a. If the program counter starts at B0, what bit pattern is in register number 3 after the first instruction has been executed?

b. What bit pattern is in memory cell B8 when the halt instruction is executed?

3. Suppose the memory cells at addresses A4 to B1 in the machine described in Appendix B contain the (hexadecimal) bit patterns given in the following table:

Address	Contents
A4	20
A5	00
A6	21
A7	03
A8	22
A9	01
AA	B1
AB	B0
AC	50
AD	02
AE	B0
AF	AA
B0	C0
B1	00

Answer the following questions assuming that the machine is started with its program counter containing A4:

    a. What is in register 0 the first time the instruction at address AA is executed?

    b. What is in register 0 the second time the instruction at address AA is executed?

    c. How many times is the instruction at address AA executed before the machine halts?

4. Suppose the memory cells at addresses F0 to F9 in the machine described in Appendix B contain the (hexadecimal) bit patterns described in the following table:

Address	Contents
F0	20
F1	C0
F2	30
F3	F8
F4	20
F5	00
F6	30
F7	F9
F8	FF
F9	FF

If we start the machine with its program counter containing F0, what does the machine do when it reaches the instruction at address F8?

2-4 Other Architectures

To broaden our perspective, let us consider some alternatives to the machine architecture of the previous sections.

CISC Versus RISC Architectures

The design of a machine's language involves numerous decisions, one of which is whether to build a complex machine that is able to decode and execute a wide variety of instructions or a simpler machine that has a limited instruction set. The former results in what is called a complex instruction set computer, or CISC; the latter produces a reduced instruction set computer, or RISC. The more complex machine is easier to program because a single instruction can be used to accomplish a task that requires a multi-instruction sequence in the simpler machine. However, the complex machine is harder and more costly to build and perhaps costs more to operate. Moreover, many of the complex instructions can find limited applications and thus tend merely to increase overhead. On the one hand we are encouraged to build a CPU with an extensive instruction set, and on the other hand we desire a machine with a restricted instruction repertoire.

One method of implementing a CISC design with a minimum amount of circuitry is to build a two-tiered machine in which each machine instruction is actually executed as a sequence of simpler instructions. In such designs, the CPU contains a block of memory cells, known as micromemory, where a program, called the microprogram, is stored. This program is expressed in simple instructions, known as microinstructions, and directs the activities of the CPU. In a sense, the CPU contains a small, simple computer that controls the CPU by executing the microprogram.

In a microprogrammed machine, then, a "machine-language" instruction fetched from main memory does not activate a circuit specifically designed for that instruction, but instead identifies which part of the microprogram is to be executed. In turn, the CPU need contain only those circuits required to execute the simple microinstructions.

As an example, if we were to construct the machine in Appendix B using a microprogrammed architecture, each instruction described in Appendix B would be implemented in the form of a sequence of simpler microinstructions rather than by a unique maze of electronic circuitry.

The microprogrammed approach has the advantage of providing a CISC architecture without the complex circuitry that would otherwise be required to support the elaborate instruction repertoire. It also has the advantage of allowing a single machine design to be customized to include special machine-language instructions by merely changing its microprogram. However, proponents of RISC architecture argue that these benefits do not outweigh the overhead associated with the microprogram. They argue that a better approach is to design a simple machine with a small, well-designed instruction set, which is then presented as the machine language. This approach removes the complexity involved with a micromemory and results in a simpler CPU design. On the other hand, it means that programs represented in the machine's language must be longer than those in a CISC architecture, because several instructions are required to perform the complex operations represented by single instructions in a CISC architecture.

We conclude that both sides of the CISC versus RISC debate have pros and cons. Currently, both architectures are commercially available.

Pipelining

In Section 2-3, we indicated that a barrier exists to the development of increasingly faster machines. This occurs because data and control signals are transferred electronically within a computer and electric pulses travel through a wire no faster than the speed of light. (Optical machines are a current subject of research, but these machines also suffer from the speed-of-light limitation.) Since light travels approximately 1 foot in a nanosecond (one billionth of a second), it requires at least 2 nanoseconds for the control unit in the CPU to fetch an instruction from a memory cell that is 1 foot away. (The read request must be sent to memory, requiring at least 1 nanosecond, and the instruction must be sent back to the control unit, requiring at least another nanosecond.) Consequently, to fetch, decode, and execute an instruction in such a machine requires several nanoseconds. Thus, increasing the execution speed of a machine ultimately becomes a miniaturization problem, and although fantastic advances have been made in this area, there appears to be a limit.

In an effort to solve this dilemma, computer scientists have turned to the concept of *throughput* rather than execution speed. Throughput refers to the total amount of work the machine can accomplish in a given amount of time rather than to how long it takes to do one task. One example of how a machine's throughput can be increased without requiring an increase in execution speed is the technique called *pipelining.* This term comes from the analogy of pushing objects—in our case instructions—into a pipe at one end and having them emerge from the other. At any given time, several instructions are in the pipe, each at a different stage of being processed. In particular, while one instruction is being executed, another instruction is being decoded, while still another is being fetched.

With such a system, although each instruction requires the same amount of time to be fetched, decoded, and executed, the total throughput of the machine is increased by a factor of three because three instructions are processed at once. (In reality, an increase of a factor of three is seldom achieved because of the occurrence of JUMP instructions. For example, if an instruction is a jump, the pipe must be emptied because the instructions in it are not the ones needed after all. Thus, any gain that would have been obtained by prefetching is not realized.)

Multiprocessor Machines

Other approaches to increasing throughput fall under the classification of *parallel processing,* in which more than one processing unit is applied to the task at hand. One argument in favor of such an approach looks to the human mind as a model. Today's technology is approaching the ability to construct electronic circuitry with roughly as many switching circuits as there are neurons in the human brain (neurons are believed to be nature's switching circuits), yet the capabilities of today's machines still fall far short of those of the human mind. This, so it is claimed, is a result of the inefficient use of a machine's components as dictated by its architecture. After all, if a machine is constructed with a lot of memory circuits but only a single CPU, then most of its circuitry is destined to be idle most of the time. In contrast, much of the human mind can be active at any given moment. Thus, the proponents of parallel processing argue in favor of a machine with many processing units. This, they argue, results in a configuration with the potential of a much higher utilization factor.

A variety of machines today are designed with this idea in mind. One approach is to attach several processing units, each resembling the CPU in a single processor machine, to the same main memory. In this configuration, the processors are able to proceed independently of each other yet coordinate their efforts by leaving messages to one another in their common memory cells. For instance, when one processor is faced with a large task, it can store a program for part of that task in the common memory and then request another processor to execute it.

A variation of this multiple processor architecture is to link the processors together so that they execute the same sequence of instructions in unison. Such machines are known as array processors and are useful in applications in which the same task must be applied to each item within a large block of data.

Another approach to the parallel processing concept is to construct large machines as conglomerates of smaller machines, each with its own memory and CPU. Within such an architecture, each of the small machines is coupled to its neighbors so that tasks assigned to the whole system can be divided among the individual machines. Thus, if a task assigned to one of the internal machines can be broken into independent subtasks, that machine can ask its neighbors to perform these subtasks concurrently. Consequently, the original task can be completed in much less time than would be required by a single processor machine.

Still another machine architecture based on the multiprocessor concept is the artificial neural network, whose design is based on our understanding of the human brain. These machines consist of many elementary processors called processing units, each of whose output is merely a simple reaction to its combined inputs. These simple processors are linked to form a network in which the outputs of some processors are used as inputs to others. Such a machine is programmed by adjusting the extent to which each processor's output is allowed to influence the reaction of the other processors to which it is connected. This simulates the way in which we believe our brains learn. Apparently, biological neural networks learn to produce a particular reaction to a given stimulus by adjusting the chemical composition of the junctions (synapses) between neurons, which in turn adjusts the ability of one neuron to affect the action of others. We consider neural networks more thoroughly in Chapter 10.

Questions/Exercises

1. Why does the CPU in a microprogrammed machine require two program counters and two instruction registers?
2. Referring back to question 3 of Section 2-3, if the machine used the pipeline technique discussed in the text, what will be in "the pipe" when the instruction at address AA is executed? Under what conditions would the pipelining technique not be beneficial at this point in the program?
3. What conflicts must be resolved when running the program in question 4 of Section 2-3 on a pipeline machine?
4. Suppose there were two "central" processing units attached to the same memory and executing different programs. Furthermore, suppose that one of these

processors needs to add one to the contents of a memory cell at roughly the same time that the other needs to subtract one from the same cell. (Thus, the net effect should be that the cell ends up with the same value with which it started.)

a. Describe a sequence in which these activities could occur that would result in the cell's ending up with a value one less than its starting value.

b. Describe a sequence in which these activities could occur that would result in the cell's ending up with a value one greater than its starting value.

2-5 Arithmetic/Logic Instructions

As previewed earlier in the chapter, the class of arithmetic/logic instructions consists of instructions requesting arithmetic, logical, or shift operations. We have already discussed several issues of arithmetic in Chapter 1. In many ways, this early introduction to arithmetic is unfortunate because it tends to give these operations an air of priority over the other members of the class of arithmetic/logic instructions. The fact is the majority of computer applications today are not numeric but deal with the manipulation of strings of characters such as names and addresses. For this reason, we now emphasize the nonnumeric operations by beginning our presentation of the arithmetic/logic instructions with them.

Logical Operations

Three popular operations within the group of logical operations are AND, OR, and EXCLUSIVE OR. They are similar to addition and subtraction in that each accepts two operands (or inputs) and produces a single result. (In contrast, consider an operation that finds the values that, when squared, produce a given positive number. It accepts one operand and produces two results; for example, given the operand 4, it produces the outputs 2 and −2.) We therefore introduce these operations, as we did binary addition, by first looking at the results they produce when both operands are single bits and then extending them to more complex operands.

The AND Operation

Figure 2-8 shows a table indicating the results of the AND operation when applied to single-bit operands. Note that the only way the result can be 1 is for both operands to be 1. That is, both the first *and* the second operands must be 1 for the result to be 1.

Figure 2-8 The AND operation

1	1	0	0
AND 1	AND 0	AND 1	AND 0
1	0	0	0

In contrast to the addition operation for which operands of single bits can produce a multiple-bit output, all such results from the AND operation are single bits. Consequently, extending the table in Figure 2-8 to include cases where the operands are strings of bits involves nothing more than applying the basic rules to each individual column without any interplay between columns. For example, ANDing the bytes 10011010 and 11001001 results in:

$$
\begin{array}{r}
10011010 \\
\text{AND } \underline{11001001} \\
10001000
\end{array}
$$

One of the major uses of the AND operation is for placing 0s in one part of a bit pattern while not disturbing the other part. Consider, for example, what happens if the byte 00001111 is the first operand of an AND operation. Without knowing the contents of the second operand, we still can conclude that the four most significant bits of the result are 0s. Moreover, the four least significant bits of the result are a copy of that part of the second operand, as shown in the following example:

$$
\begin{array}{r}
00001111 \\
\text{AND } \underline{10101010} \\
00001010
\end{array}
$$

This use of the AND operation is an example of the process called **masking.** Here one operand, called the **mask,** is used to determine which part of the other operand will affect the result. In the case of the AND operation, masking is used to produce a result that is a partial replica of one of the operands, with 0s occupying the nonduplicated positions.

Such an operation is useful when manipulating bit maps, which are strings of bits in which each bit represents the presence or absence of a particular object. For example, a string of 52 bits, in which each bit is associated with a particular playing card, can be used to represent a poker hand by assigning 1s to those 5 bits associated with the cards in the hand and 0s to all the others. Likewise, a bit map of 52 bits, of which 13 are 1s, can be used to represent a hand of bridge, or a bit map of 32 bits can be used to represent which of 32 ice cream flavors are available.

Suppose, then, that an 8-bit memory cell is being used as a bit map, and we want to find out if the object associated with the third bit from the high-order end is present. We merely need to AND the entire byte with the mask 00100000, which produces a byte of all 0s if and only if the third bit from the high-order end of the bit map is itself 0. A program can then act accordingly by following the AND operation with a conditional branch instruction. Moreover, if the third bit from the high-order end of the bit map is a 1, and we want to change it to a 0 without disturbing the other bits, we can AND the bit map with the mask 11011111 and then store the result in place of the original bit map.

Figure 2-9 The OR operation

```
    1        1        0        0
 OR 1     OR 0     OR 1     OR 0
 ----     ----     ----     ----
    1        1        1        0
```

The OR Operation

Now let us take a look at the OR operation. Its basic rules are shown in Figure 2-9. Note in this case that the only way the result can be 0 is for both operands to be 0. That is, if either the first operand *or* the second operand is 1, the result is 1.

Again, the basic rules can be expanded to strings of bits by applying the operation to the individual columns, as shown by the following:

```
       10011010
 OR    11001001
       --------
       11011011
```

Where the AND operation can be used to duplicate a part of a string while placing 0s in the nonduplicated part, the OR operation can be used to duplicate a part of a bit string while putting 1s in the nonduplicated part. For this we again use a mask, but this time we indicate the bit positions to be duplicated with 0s and use 1s to indicate the nonduplicated positions. For example, ORing any byte with 11110000 produces a result with 1s in its most significant 4 bits while its remaining bits contain a copy of the least significant 4 bits of the other operand, as demonstrated by the following example:

```
       11110000
 OR    10101010
       --------
       11111010
```

Consequently, just as the AND operation and the mask 11011111 can be used to force a 0 in the third bit from the high-order end of an 8-bit bit map, the OR operation and the mask 00100000 can be used to force a 1 in that position.

The EXCLUSIVE OR Operation

The basic rules for the EXCLUSIVE OR (XOR) operation are shown in Figure 2-10 on the following page. In this case, to obtain a 1 for the result, exactly one of the operands must be 1. That is, one operand *or* the other must be 1, *exclusive* of the other. As before, the result of EXCLUSIVE ORing two strings together can be calculated by applying these rules to each column, as seen by the following example:

```
       10011010
 XOR   11001001
       --------
       01010011
```

Figure 2-10 The EXCLUSIVE OR operation

$$\begin{array}{cccc}
1 & 1 & 0 & 0 \\
\underline{XOR\ 1} & \underline{XOR\ 0} & \underline{XOR\ 1} & \underline{XOR\ 0} \\
0 & 1 & 1 & 0
\end{array}$$

A major use of this operation is in forming the complement of a bit string. For example, note the relationship between the second operand and the result in the following example:

$$\begin{array}{r}
11111111 \\
\underline{XOR\ 10101010} \\
01010101
\end{array}$$

EXCLUSIVE ORing any byte with a byte of 1s produces the complement of the first byte.

Rotation and Shift Operations

The operations in the class of rotation and shift operations provide a means for the movement of bits within a register and are often used in solving alignment problems, such as preparing a byte for future use in masking operations or manipulating the mantissa of floating-point representations. These operations are classified as to the direction of motion (right or left) and as to whether or not the process is circular. Within these classification guidelines are numerous variations with mixed terminology. Let us take a quick look at the ideas involved.

If we consider starting with a byte of bits and shifting its contents 1 bit to the right or the left, we might imagine the bit on one end falling off the edge and a hole appearing at the other end. What happens with this extra bit and the hole is the distinguishing feature among the various shift operations. One technique is to place the extra bit in the hole at the other end. The result is a circular shift, or a rotation. Thus, if we perform a right circular shift on a byte eight times, we obtain the same bit pattern we started with, and seven right circular shifts are equivalent to a single left circular shift.

Another technique is to discard the bit that falls off the edge and always fill the hole with a 0. The term *logical shift* is often used to refer to these operations. Such shifts to the left can be used for multiplying two's complement representations by 2. After all, shifting binary digits to the left corresponds to multiplication by 2, just as a similar shift of decimal digits corresponds to multiplication by 10. Moreover, division by 2 can be accomplished by shifting the binary string to the right. In either shift, care must be taken to preserve the sign bit when using certain notational systems. Thus, we often find right shifts that always fill the hole (which occurs at the sign bit position) with its original value. Shifts that leave the sign bit unchanged are sometimes called *arithmetic shifts.*

Arithmetic Operations

Although we have already mentioned the arithmetic operations of add, subtract, multiply, and divide, a few loose ends must still be connected. First, as we have mentioned, this collection of operations can often be generated from the single add operation and a negation process. For this reason, some small computers are designed with only the add or perhaps only the add and subtract instructions.

We should also mention that for each arithmetic operation, numerous variations exist. We have already alluded to this in relation to the add operations available on our machine in Appendix B. In the case of addition, for example, if the values to be added are stored in two's complement notation, the addition process must be performed as a straightforward binary add. However, if the operands are stored as floating-point values, the addition process must extract the mantissa of each, shift them right or left according to the exponent fields, check the sign bits, perform the addition, and translate the result into floating-point notation. We see, then, that although both operations are considered addition, the action of the machine is not the same. As far as the machine is concerned, the two operations may have no relationship at all. Consequently, it is common to find machines with a variety of add instructions.

Questions/Exercises

1. Perform the indicated operations.

   a.   01001011   b.   10000011   c.   11111111
       AND 10101011   AND 11101100   AND 00101101

   d.   01001011   e.   10000011   f.   11111111
        OR 10101011   OR 11101100   OR 00101101

   g.   01001011   h.   10000011   i.   11111111
       XOR 10101011   XOR 11101100   XOR 00101101

2. Suppose you want to isolate the middle 3 bits of a 7-bit string by placing 0s in the other 4 bits without disturbing the middle 3 bits. What mask must you use together with what operation?

3. Suppose you want to complement the 3 middle bits of a 7-bit string while leaving the other 4 bits undisturbed. What mask must you use together with what operation?

4. a. Suppose you EXCLUSIVE OR the first 2 bits of a string of bits and then continue down the string by successively EXCLUSIVE ORing each result with the next bit in the string. How is your result related to the number of 1s appearing in the string?

   b. How does this problem relate to determining what the appropriate parity bit should be when coding a message?

5. It is often convenient to use a logical operation in place of a numeric one. For example, the logical operation AND combines 2 bits in the same manner as multiplication. Which logical operation is almost the same as adding 2 bits, and what goes wrong in this case?

6. What logical operation together with what mask can you use to change ASCII codes of lowercase letters to uppercase? What about uppercase to lowercase?

7. What is the result of performing a 3-bit right circular shift on the following bit strings:
   a.   01101010   b.   00001111   c.   01111111

8. What is the result of performing a 1-bit left circular shift on the following bytes represented in hexadecimal notation? Give your answer in hexadecimal form.
   a.   AB   b.   5C   c.   B7   d.   35

9. A right circular shift of 3 bits on a string of 8 bits is equivalent to a left circular shift of how many bits?

10. What bit pattern represents the sum of 01101010 and 11001100 if the patterns represent values stored in two's complement notation? What if the patterns represent values stored in the floating-point format discussed in Chapter 1?

11. Using the machine language of Appendix B, write a program that places a 1 in the most significant bit of the memory cell whose address is A7 without modifying the remaining bits in the cell.

12. Using the machine language of Appendix B, write a program that copies the middle 4 bits from memory cell E0 into the least significant 4 bits of memory cell E1, while placing 0s in the most significant 4 bits of that same cell.

2-6 Computer/Peripheral Communication

In this section, we discuss the communication between a machine's CPU and its peripheral devices. This communication is carried out through a variety of plugs normally found on the back of the machine. Although there are numerous technical issues associated with these connections, our purposes allow us to consider them as merely locations through which data can enter and/or leave the machine. In fact, this perspective is the reason these connections are called *ports.*

Communication Through Ports

With respect to the control unit within the CPU, the ports are identified by port numbers, just as memory cells are identified by addresses. In fact, in many machines, ports are actually disguised as memory cells occupying certain addresses in memory. In other words, the port replaces the memory cell in such a way that when the CPU writes a bit pattern to that location in memory (as in a STORE instruction), the bit pattern is really transferred to the port. In a similar fashion, if the CPU tries to read data from that memory location (as in a LOAD instruction), what it really gets is the bit pattern that has arrived at the port from a peripheral device. Such a system is called **memory mapped I/O** and is represented conceptually by Figure 2-11. It has the advantage of not requiring special machine-language instructions for I/O purposes because the regular LOAD and STORE instructions fill the bill. On the other hand, it has the disadvantage of reducing the actual size of a machine's memory.

To transfer data in and out of ports in machines not using memory mapped I/O, extra instructions called I/O instructions are provided in the machine's language. These instructions are classified in the data transfer group. In such cases, we might find an instruction that transfers the contents of a register to a port, with the port number indicated in the instruction's operand field. Likewise, an instruction might load a register with the data from a port, again with the port identified in the operand field.

Figure 2-11 A conceptual representation of memory mapped I/O

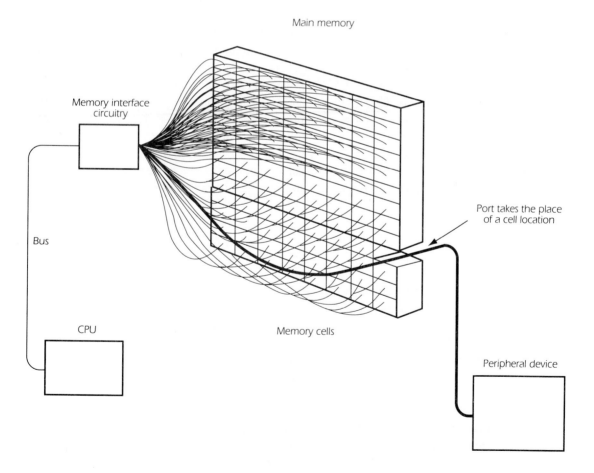

We should point out here that more information than merely the data being transferred is passed through a port. This is due to the communication required between the peripheral device and the machine. For example, in most cases, the machine can produce characters to be printed much faster than a printing device can print them. Consequently, without additional communication between the machine and the printer, the printer would quickly fall behind.

To rectify such problems, most systems allow a two-way communication, called *handshaking,* to take place between the peripheral device and the machine in addition to allowing the passing of data. In our printing example, the printer not only would have the circuitry and mechanisms to receive and print characters but also would have the circuitry required to transmit the printer's status in a coded form back to the computer. With these provisions, a program can be designed so that the machine waits for the appropriate status information from the printer before a character is transmitted through the port.

We see, then, that two-way communication is often taking place between a computer and a peripheral device, even though it may appear to the casual observer that information is flowing in only one direction. In turn, most communication lines between computers and peripheral devices employ two-way *(duplex)* systems rather than one-way *(simplex)* systems. There are, however, two ways of implementing duplex systems: one called *half duplex* and the other called *full duplex.* Half-duplex systems allow for two-way communication but allow only one direction at a time. Full-duplex systems allow communication in both directions at the same time. Telephone systems are based on full-duplex communication (except in the case of some very long distance calls that are actually half duplex, although the system is implemented so subtly that the callers seldom notice the difference). In contrast, the communication between a CPU and memory is half duplex, because data can be transferred in either direction but not simultaneously.

Controllers

At times it is necessary to connect several devices to a computer at the same port. You can imagine that such an arrangement increases the communication's complexity, because it becomes necessary to coordinate the activities of the various devices competing for the use of the port. In such cases, we normally find additional circuitry, called a *controller* (or by the less generic term of *channel*), positioned at the junction of the device cables and the port. This circuitry coordinates the devices attached to it and often takes the form of a small computer in itself.

To increase efficiency, it is common to connect controllers to a machine's main memory in the same fashion as the CPU. That is, the controller takes the form of another CPU connected to the same main memory as the original CPU. In this case, the controller is said to have *direct memory access (DMA).* In such systems, the CPU can prepare a complete line of text in memory and direct the controller to send the line to a particular printer. Thus, the controller handles the character-by-character communication with the printer as it extracts the character codes from memory, and the CPU is free to begin preparing the next line in another area of memory. The controller plays a similar role in the case of data entering the system from a peripheral device. In particular, the controller takes care of the communication with the device until the incoming bit patterns have been received and placed in main memory. Then it informs the CPU that the patterns have been read and are ready for processing.

Such delegation of device communication to controllers has proven to be so effective that many computer systems use the technique even though only one device may be connected to a port. One common use of this delegation occurs in the case of communication with mass storage devices, in which the controller is assigned the duty of moving the physical records back and forth between main memory and the secondary memory device. All the CPU must do is send the directions to the controller (through the port), telling it what physical record is to be read and where in memory the record is to be placed. In the case of sending data to mass storage, the CPU merely places the data in a block of main memory cells and requests the controller to copy that block into mass storage.

The area of memory used for the transfer of data between the CPU and the controller as just described is called a **buffer.** In a more general sense, a buffer is any location where one system can leave data to be picked up later by another system. Thus, the registers in a CPU serve as buffers between the control unit and the arithmetic/logic unit or between the CPU as a whole and the main memory. The process of moving data from one system to another through a buffer is called **buffering.**

Parallel and Serial Communication

Before leaving this section on computer/peripheral communication, we should say a few words about parallel versus serial communication. These terms refer to the manner in which the bit patterns are transferred with respect to time. With **parallel communication,** all the bits in a bit pattern are transferred at the same time, each on a separate line. Such a technique is capable of transferring data rapidly but requires a relatively complex communication path, which results in the use of large multiwire cables. In contrast, **serial communication** is based on transmitting only 1 bit at a time. This technique tends to be slower but requires a simpler data path because the bits of a character's code are transferred over the same line as a sequence of bits.

The simpler data path required for serial communication allows computer data transfers to take place over existing communication systems that were originally developed for other purposes. One common example of this is the use of telephone lines where the digital data is converted into audio signals by a **modem** (short for modulator-demodulator), serially transferred via the existing telephone system, and converted back into digital form when it is received. Such communication would not be feasible using parallel techniques because of the inherent properties of the existing telephone system.

The speed of serial communication is measured in bits per second *(bps)* with common speeds ranging from a few hundred bits per second to several million bps. Another common (but often misused) measure is **baud rate,** which refers to the rate at which the communication line transfers states. Let us clarify this with an example. If we apply a tone at one end of a telephone connection, the tone can be detected at the other end. Consequently, we can send messages over the phone system by agreeing that a certain note represents a 0 and another note represents a 1. In such a system, the communication line can be in one of two states: carrying one of the notes or carrying the other. Since each state represents a single bit, the rate in which states are communicated is the same as the rate in which bits are communicated; thus, the baud rate is the same as the bits per second. However, if we change our protocol to include four possible states (notes), each state can represent two bits. For example, we might agree to use a low pitch to represent the bits 00, a higher pitch to represent the bits 01, a still higher pitch to represent the bits 10, and the highest pitch to represent the bits 11. In this system, the rate at which bits are transferred is twice the rate that states (or notes) are transferred because each state represents 2 bits. Thus, the bits per second is twice the baud rate.

In reality, the simple technique of representing different bit patterns by tones of different frequencies (known as frequency-shift keying) is used only for low-speed communication. To construct modems with data transfer rates of 2400 bps, 9600 bps, and higher, the different states used to represent bit patterns are created by combining changes in tone frequency, amplitude (volume), and phase (the degree to which the transmission of the tone is delayed). But the general theme remains the same; by representing several bits with a single state, the rate in which bits are transferred (measured in bits per second) can significantly exceed the rate in which states are transferred (the baud rate).

Questions/Exercises

1. Suppose a serial communication system is capable of transmitting and receiving eight different states. If bit patterns are assigned to each of the eight states so that each state represents a total of 3 bits, how does the baud rate of the system compare to the measure of bits per second?

2. Give examples of simplex, half-duplex, and full-duplex communication occurring in situations outside the computer field.

3. Suppose the computer described in Appendix B uses memory mapped I/O without the added advantage of a controller, and a printer is connected to the port represented by memory location FA (hexadecimal).

   a. Assuming that the ASCII code for a character is currently in register number 5, what machine-language instruction causes this character to be printed at the printer?

b. If the machine executes a million instructions per second, how many times can this character be sent to the printer in one second?

c. Can a printer capable of printing five traditional pages of text per minute keep up with the characters being sent to it in part b?

4. What are some status messages that a printer might send to the computer?

Chapter 2 Review Problems

(Asterisked problems are associated with optional sections.)

1. Give a brief definition of each of the following:
    a. register   b. cache memory
    c. main memory   d. mass storage

2. Suppose a block of data is stored in the memory cells of the machine described in Appendix B from address B9 to C1, inclusive. How many memory cells are in this block? List their addresses.

3. What is the value of the program counter in the machine described in Appendix B immediately after executing the instruction B0BA?

4. Suppose the memory cells at addresses 00 through 05 in the machine described in Appendix B contain the following (hexadecimal) bit patterns:

Address	Contents
00	21
01	04
02	31
03	00
04	C0
05	00

Assuming that the program counter initially contained 00, record the contents of the program counter, instruction register, and memory cell at address 00 at the end of each fetch phase of the machine cycle until the machine halts.

5. Suppose three values (x, y, and z) are stored in a machine's memory. Describe the sequence of events (loading registers from memory, saving values in memory, and so on) that lead to the computation of $x + y - z$. How about $(2x) + y$?

6. The following are instructions written in the machine language described in Appendix B. Translate them into English.
    a. 407E   b. 9028   c. A302
    d. B3AD   e. 2835

7. Suppose a machine language is designed with an op-code field of 4 bits. How many different instruction types can the language contain? What if the op-code field is increased to 8 bits?

8. Translate the following instructions from English into the machine language described in Appendix B.
    a. Load register R8 with the contents of memory cell 55.
    b. Load register R8 with the hexadecimal value 55.
    c. Rotate register R4 three bits to the right.
    d. AND the contents of registers RF and R2 leaving the result in register R0.
    e. Jump to the instruction at memory location 31 if the contents of register R0 equals the value in register RB.

9. Classify each of the following instructions (in the machine language of Appendix B) in terms of whether its execution changes the contents of the memory cell at location 3B, retrieves the contents of the memory cell at location 3B, or is independent of the contents of the memory cell at location 3B.
    a. 153B   b. 253B   c. 353B
    d. 3B3B   e. 403B

10. Suppose the memory cells at addresses 00 through 03 in the machine described in Appendix B contain the following (hexadecimal) bit patterns:

Address	Contents
00	23
01	02
02	C0
03	00

a. Translate the first instruction into English.
b. If the machine is started with its program counter containing 00, what bit pattern is in register R3 when the machine halts?

11. Suppose the memory cells at addresses 00 through 05 in the machine described in Appendix B contain the following (hexadecimal) bit patterns:

Address	Contents
00	10
01	04
02	30
03	45
04	C0
05	00

Answer the following questions assuming that the machine starts with its program counter equal to 00:
a. Translate the instructions that are executed into English.
b. What bit pattern is in the memory cell at address 45 when the machine stops?
c. What bit pattern is in the program counter when the machine stops?

12. Suppose the memory cells at addresses F0 through FD in the machine described in Appendix B contain the following (hexadecimal) bit patterns:

Address	Contents
F0	20
F1	00
F2	21
F3	01
F4	23
F5	05
F6	B3
F7	FC
F8	50
F9	01
FA	B0
FB	F6
FC	C0
FD	00

If we start the machine with its program counter equal to F0, what is the value in register R0 when the machine finally executes the halt instruction at location FC?

13. If the machine in Appendix B executes an instruction every microsecond (a millionth of a second), how long does it take to complete the program in problem 12?

14. Suppose the memory cells at addresses 00 through 05 in the machine described in Appendix B contain the following (hexadecimal) bit patterns:

Address	Contents
00	25
01	B0
02	35
03	04
04	C0
05	00

If we start the machine with its program counter equal to 00, when does the machine halt?

15. In each of the following cases, write a short program in the machine language described in Appendix B to perform the requested activities. Assume that each of your programs is placed in memory starting at address 00.
a. Move the value at memory location 8D to memory location B3.
b. Interchange the values stored at memory locations 8D and B3.
c. If the value stored in memory location 45 is 00, then place the value CC in memory location 88; otherwise, put the value DD in memory location 88.

16. A popular game among computer hobbyists is core wars—a variation of battleship. (The term *core* originates from an early memory technology in which 0s and 1s were represented as magnetic fields in little rings of magnetic material.) The game is played between two opposing programs, each stored in different locations of the same computer's memory. The computer is assumed to alternate between the two programs, executing an instruction from one followed by an instruction from the other. The goal of each program is to destroy the other by writing extraneous data on top of it; however, neither program knows the location of the other.
a. Write a program in the machine language of Appendix B that approaches the game in a defensive manner by being as small as possible.
b. Write a program in the language of Appendix B that tries to avoid any attacks from the opposing program by moving to different locations. More precisely, write your program to start at location 00, copy itself to location 70, and then jump to this new copy.

c. Extend the program in part b to continue relocating to new memory locations. In particular, make your program move to location 70, then to E0 (70 + 70), then to 60 (70 + 70 + 70), etc.

17. Write a program in the machine language of Appendix B to compute the sum of the binary values stored at memory locations A1, A2, A3, and A4. Your program should store the total at memory location A5.

18. Suppose the memory cells at addresses 00 through 05 in the machine described in Appendix B contain the following (hexadecimal) bit patterns:

Address	Contents
00	10
01	C0
02	20
03	04
04	00
05	00

What happens if we start the machine with its program counter equal to 00?

19. What happens if the memory cells at addresses 06 and 07 of the machine described in Appendix B contain the bit patterns B0 and 06, respectively, and the machine is started with its program counter containing the value 06?

20. Suppose you are given 32 processors, each capable of finding the sum of two multidigit numbers in a millionth of a second. Describe how concurrent processing techniques can be applied to find the sum of 64 numbers in only six-millionths of a second. How much time does a single processor require to find this same sum?

21. Summarize the difference between a CISC architecture and a RISC architecture.

22. Summarize the distinction between main memory and micromemory.

23. Identify two approaches to increasing throughput.

24. Describe how the average of a collection of numbers can be computed more rapidly with a multiprocessor machine than a single processor machine.

*25. Suppose the registers R4 and R5 in the machine described in Appendix B contain the bit patterns 3C and C8, respectively. What bit pattern is left in register R0 after executing each of the following instructions:
  a. 5045   b. 6045   c. 7045
  d. 8045   e. 9045

*26. Using the machine language described in Appendix B, write programs to perform each of the following tasks:
  a. Copy the bit pattern stored in memory location 66 into memory location BB.
  b. Change the least significant 4 bits in the memory cell at location 34 to 0s while leaving the other bits undisturbed.
  c. Copy the least significant 4 bits from memory location A5 into the least significant 4 bits of location A6 while leaving the other bits at location A6 undisturbed.
  d. Copy the least significant 4 bits from memory location A5 into the most significant 4 bits of A5. (Thus, the first 4 bits in A5 will be the same as the last 4 bits.)

*27. Perform the indicated operations:

a.   111000
   AND 101001

b.   000100
   AND 101010

c.   000100
   AND 010101

d.   111011
   AND 110101

e.   111000
   OR 101001

f.   000100
   OR 101010

g.   000100
   OR 010101

h.   111011
   OR 110101

i.   111000
   XOR 101001

j.   000100
   XOR 101010

k.   000100
   XOR 010101

l.   111011
   XOR 110101

*28. Identify both the mask and the logical operation needed to accomplish each of the following objectives:
  a. Put 0s in the middle 4 bits of an 8-bit pattern without disturbing the other bits.
  b. Complement a pattern of 8 bits.
  c. Complement the most significant bit of an 8-bit pattern without changing the other bits.
  d. Put a 1 in the most significant bit of an 8-bit pattern without disturbing the other bits.
  e. Put 1s in all but the most significant bit of an 8-bit pattern without disturbing the most significant bit.

*29. Identify a logical operation (along with a corresponding mask) that, when applied to an input string of 8 bits, produces an output string of all 0s if and only if the input string is 10000001.

*30. Describe a sequence of logical operations (along with their corresponding masks) that, when applied to an input string of 8 bits, produces an output byte of all 0s if the input string both begins and ends with 1s. Otherwise, the output should contain at least one 1.

*31. What would be the result of performing a 4-bit left circular shift on the following bit patterns:
a. 10101   b. 11110000   c. 001
d. 101000   e. 00001

*32. What would be the result of performing a 1-bit right circular shift on the following bytes represented in hexadecimal notation (give your answers in hexadecimal notation):
a. 3F   b. 0D   c. FF   d. 77

*33. Write a program in the machine language of Appendix B that reverses the contents of the memory cell at address 8C.

*34. List the symbols +, (, [, m, 5, $, and G in the "alphabetical" order they inherit by means of being coded in ASCII.

*35. Can a printer, printing 40 characters per second, keep up with a string of ASCII characters (each with a parity bit) arriving serially at the rate of 300 bps? What about 1200 bps?

*36. Suppose a person is typing 30 words per minute at a keyboard. (A word is considered to be five characters.) If a machine executes one instruction every microsecond (millionth of a second), how many instructions does the machine execute during the time between the typing of two consecutive characters?

*37. How many bits per second must a keyboard transmit to keep up with a typist typing 30 words per minute? (Assume each character is coded in ASCII along with a parity bit and each word consists of five characters.)

*38. A communication system capable of transmitting any sequence of eight different states at the rate of at most 300 states per second could be used to transfer information at what rate in bits per second?

*39. Suppose the machine described in Appendix B communicates with a printer using the technique of memory mapped I/O. Suppose also that address FF is used to send characters to the printer, and address FE is used to receive information about the printer's status. In particular, suppose the least significant bit at the address FE indicates whether or not the printer is ready to receive another character (with a 0 indicating "not ready" and a 1 indicating "ready"). Starting at address 00, write a machine-language routine that waits until the printer is ready for another character and then send the character represented by the bit pattern in register R5 to the printer.

*40. Write a program in the machine language described in Appendix B that places 0s in all the memory cells from address A0 through C0 but is small enough to fit in the memory cells from address 00 through 13 (hexadecimal).

Problems for the Programmer

1. Even though the programming language you may know may not be a machine-level language, does it still use a structure similar to the op-code/operand system found in machine languages? That is, does it use a few basic statement forms, identified perhaps by a key word, that have numerous variations depending on the specifics of the rest of the statement?

2. Which statements in your programming language are straightforward applications of the traditional machine-language operations discussed in this chapter? Which are not?

3. Pick a simple statement in a programming language you know and translate it into the machine language of Appendix B.

4. What notation does your programming language use to indicate arithmetic addition? What determines whether this addition ultimately is performed by the machine's floating-point instruction or by its integer instruction?

5. Write a program to simulate the machine in Appendix B.

Additional Reading

Almasi, G. S., and Gottlieb, A. *Highly Parallel Computing,* 2nd ed. Redwood City, Calif.: Benjamin/Cummings, 1994.

Brink, J., and Spillman, R. T. *Computer Architecture and VAX Assembly Language Programming.* Redwood City, Calif.: Benjamin/Cummings, 1986.

Hennessy, J. L., and Patterson, D. A. *Computer Organization and Design: The Hardware/Software Interface.* San Mateo, Calif.: Morgan Kaufmann, 1993.

Hillis, W. D. *The Connection Machine.* Cambridge, Mass.: MIT Press, 1985.

Hwang, K. *Advanced Computer Architecture: Parallelism, Scalability, Programmability.* New York: McGraw-Hill, 1993.

Knuth, D. E. *The Art of Computer Programming,* Vol. 1, 2nd ed. Reading, Mass.: Addison-Wesley, 1973.

Levy, H. M., and Eckhouse, R. H., Jr. *Computer Programming and Architecture.* Bedford, Mass.: Digital Equipment Corp., 1980.

Sebesta, R. W. *VAX-11 Structured Assembly Language Programming.* Redwood City, Calif.: Benjamin/Cummings, 1984.

Stallings, W. *Computer Organization and Architecture,* 3rd ed. New York: Macmillan, 1993.

Stone, H. S. *High-Performance Computer Architecture,* 2nd ed. Reading, Mass.: Addison-Wesley, 1990.

Tabak, D. *RISC Architecture.* New York: John Wiley and Sons, 1987.

PART TWO

SOFTWARE

In Part One, we discussed the major components from which a computer is constructed. These components, which are tangible, are classified as hardware. In contrast, the programs that the hardware executes are intangible and are classified as software. In Part Two, we turn our attention to topics associated with software, which leads us to the core of computer science—the study of algorithms. In particular, we will investigate the discovery, representation, and communication of algorithms.

We begin by discussing operating systems in Chapter 3. These systems are traditionally large, complex software packages that control the overall activities of a machine as well as establish the basic communication paths between a machine and the people using it. In Chapter 4, we study algorithms, with an emphasis on how algorithms are discovered and represented. In Chapter 5, we turn to the topic of how algorithms are communicated to machines through the programming process and investigate properties of popular programming languages. Finally, in Chapter 6, we look at the entire software development process in the context of software engineering.

CHAPTER THREE

OPERATING SYSTEMS

*Sections marked by an asterisk are optional in that they provide additional depth of coverage that is not required for an understanding of future chapters.

The previous chapters have concentrated on the equipment making up a computer system. The collection of such tangible equipment, including the computer itself, printers, printer paper, disk drives, and so on, is classified as **hardware.** Hardware alone is of little use, because without programs to control it, the equipment does little more than occupy space. Consequently, the intangible programs called *software* are just as important to a computer installation as the hardware.

This chapter discusses a major software unit called the operating system, including its role in a variety of computer systems, some of the problems involved, and a look at how some of these problems might be resolved.

3-1 Functions of Operating Systems

Let us first say a few words about the terminology. A program is the intangible logic, normally expressed as a sequence of instructions, that a machine follows to perform a task. Although we recognize that it is the hardware that actually performs the task, it is common to give credit to the controlling software in our terminology. For example, we may say that a program sorts a list of names, whereas in reality it is the machine that actually sorts the list by executing the program.

With this understanding, we turn our attention to operating systems and what they do. Suppose you had access to a computer's monitor, keyboard, and mouse. How would you get the computer to do something for you? The answer is that the computer automatically begins executing a program called the *operating system* when it is first turned on. This program accepts input from the keyboard and mouse and compares this input to the commands it is designed to obey. Such a command might be to execute an application program (such as a spreadsheet, word processor, or database system) or to perform a "housekeeping" chore (such as formatting a new floppy disk or copying information from one disk to another). If the operating system finds that the input constitutes a legal command, it performs the requested action. Otherwise, it sends an appropriate response to the monitor screen (or perhaps produces a beeping sound) and continues to watch for other commands.

An operating system therefore contains the algorithms that define how the computer is to interact with the outside world. These algorithms are often referred to collectively as the operating system's shell. This shell, however, is only a small part of the overall operating system. Beneath the shell is a large collection of additional algorithms for controlling the activities of the machine. The task of many of these fall under the classification of resource management.

Here we are using the term *resource* in a broad sense, including such things as peripheral devices, data stored on these devices, space in main memory, and the CPU itself. Let us consider each of these individually.

The management of peripheral devices occurs in two contexts: One involves the problem of allocating the available devices to the various tasks at hand. In this context, an operating system must coordinate the allocation of devices among the tasks that are competing for resources. For example, if two users of a machine are allowed to use a printer at the same time, the output is intertwined and worthless to both.

The other context in which an operating system must manage peripheral devices deals with the efficient use of the devices. In this context, operating systems provide prewritten routines that shield the users of the machine from the complexities and idiosyncrasies of the various peripheral devices. For example, many operating systems allow the output of a program to be directed to a printer, monitor screen, or mass storage device without alterations to the program itself. Thus, from the program's point of view, these devices appear equivalent even though their characteristics are very different.

In addition to managing peripheral devices, an operating system is charged with managing the data stored on those devices in the machine's mass storage system. These data are stored in collections called *files*. Most operating systems maintain a record of the files held in mass storage in the form of a hierarchical directory system. Many operating systems also provide a security system by which access to each file is controlled.

Another resource managed by the operating system is the machine's main memory. Most operating systems are given the task of determining where programs are placed in memory, where data retrieved from mass storage devices are placed in memory, and which areas of memory are accessible by the various tasks being performed. In turn, the operating system must contain algorithms for allocating portions of main memory to the tasks at hand, retrieving memory areas that are no longer being used, and maintaining records of those areas of main memory that are available.

Still another resource managed by an operating system is the CPU itself. When a machine has several activities to perform, it is the task of the operating system to coordinate the execution of these activities. In a sense, these activities compete for access to the CPU. Thus, the CPU is essentially a resource to which the operating system controls access. As we see in Section 3-5, some operating systems can distribute access to a single CPU so that it appears that all the activities are being performed at the same time.

Another important function of operating systems is to standardize the human/machine interface across the entire computer industry. For example, even though two machines might be significantly different in terms of their internal design and construction, their operating systems can be constructed so that their dialogues with a user are essentially the same. Thus, if a person is trained to communicate with one piece of equipment through the use of a universal operating system, that training can be applied to other equipment as well.

The first application of this standardizing effect was implemented by IBM with the System/360 series of machines introduced in the 1960s. This series consisted of a variety of machines ranging from designs for small-business applications to large machines for businesses with significant needs. These machines were all supplied with operating systems that made them communicate with their environments in essentially the same manner. Thus, as a business grew, it could change to a larger machine in the 360 series without major reprogramming and retraining efforts.

Today, such uniformity bridges the boundaries between the equipment of different manufacturers. The operating system UNIX® (developed at Bell Laboratories) is now available on numerous machines, including both large machines and microcomputers. Among the avalanche of microcomputers on the market today, one finds the human/machine interface often standardized through the use of MS-DOS® (an operating system developed by Microsoft Corporation), which has gained popularity because of its adoption by IBM for use in its early line of personal computers. Another example is the Macintosh® operating system used by Apple Computer, Inc., for its entire line of Macintosh® microcomputers.

Accompanying the benefits of a standardized interface are a multitude of legal controversies, one of which is the question of who owns an interface. This question becomes particularly significant when an interface designed by a particular company becomes popular. It then becomes advantageous for competing companies to design their systems to look like the well-known one. In particular, if a competitor designs its system to communicate with the user by means of the same screen layouts, key strokes, and mouse movements as the original well-known system, then users of the well-known system can convert to the competitor's system with no additional training, even though the interior designs of the two systems remained different. Of course, the designer of the original system claims ownership of the "look and feel" of the original system, just as he or she claims ownership to the design of the system itself. How the courts ultimately rule in "look and feel" cases remains an open question.

Questions/Exercises

1. Describe an analogy to the distinction between hardware and software in the following settings:
    a. musical recordings   b. television   c. novels

2. Which of the activities of an operating system presented in the text are least prominent in a microcomputer system?

3. Which of the operating system activities identified in this section are required when a user requests that a previously saved document be displayed on the monitor screen?

3-2 Virtual Characteristics and Abstraction

The common thread running throughout Section 3-1 is that the role of the operating system is to make the machine more compatible with its environment. Although the actual hardware responds only to its machine-language instructions and "thinks" in terms of bits, with the addition of an operating system the machine can respond intelligently to requests such as to retrieve and execute programs stored in mass storage, to make copies of files, or to list the names of the files currently in mass storage.

Thus, the operating system alters the machine's characteristics so that one gets the illusion of dealing with a different and usually more application-oriented piece of equipment than is actually present. Through the operating system, the machine is given the ability to understand commands stated in a human-compatible form, whereas the hardware alone only "understands" the machine language. By restricting unauthorized access to data in mass storage, the operating system creates the illusion of containing only a single user's data, whereas in reality the machine's mass storage might contain data belonging to a multitude of users. Through its file-management routines, the operating system creates the illusion of data being stored in units of logical records, whereas the information is actually stored in physical blocks compatible with the particular storage device being used.

We use the term *virtual* to refer to a characteristic whose existence is simulated with software rather than actually existing within hardware (Figure 3-1). Thus, the illusionary, more application-oriented machine created by an operating system is called a virtual machine. In general, a machine with the same characteristics could be

Figure 3-1 Virtual versus real characteristics

Virtual Characteristics	Real Characteristics
Data stored in logical blocks	Data stored in physical blocks
Presence of only data pertinent to a single user	Presence of data belonging to all users
Ability to "understand" commands in human-compatible form	Ability to "understand" only machine language
Same internal characteristics as other machines	Significantly different internal characteristics from other machines

constructed entirely by hardware, although the result would be a more rigid, more expensive, and less practical device than its virtual counterpart.

The term *virtual* is important enough for us to consider the following analogy. Consider a family-owned-and-operated mail-order business that operates out of a converted garage where two family members fill each day's orders. The business obtains orders by running large, impressive magazine advertisements. It is incorporated, has its own letterhead, and handles all its sales through the mail. With this arrangement, a customer's image of the business is likely to be quite different from reality. The advertisements, letterheads, and so on are designed to create an image (a virtual business) for the customer consisting of a large warehouse, various departments, and numerous employees. The fact that this virtual business is not the same as the actual one is not important so long as the system continues to function like the virtual business from the customer's point of view. If, however, a customer is trying to resolve a problem of an incorrectly filled order, it might well be advantageous to know more about the actual business structure involved.

Such is the case with computer systems. The operating system creates the illusion of a machine (a virtual machine) that communicates more conveniently with its environment than does the actual hardware and relieves the user from the burden of understanding the technical details of the hardware activities. The fact that this illusion does not accurately reflect the true internal characteristics of the machine is an asset so long as the virtual machine is faithfully simulated. With the correct operating system, a person can use a computer without any knowledge of the internal functions. On the other hand, just as when dealing with the mail-order business, an understanding of the activities behind the scene can often increase one's ability to use the system efficiently or to resolve problems that might occur.

The creation of virtual machines by means of software is a specific instance of the general theme of abstraction that is found throughout computer science. In general, *abstraction* is the separation of a concept from the details of its implementation.

Abstraction is an important simplification device with which our society has created a lifestyle that would otherwise be impossible. Few of us understand how the various conveniences of daily life are actually implemented. We eat food and wear clothes that we ourselves cannot produce. We use electrical devices without understanding the underlying technology. We use the services of others without knowing the details of their activities. With each new advancement, a small part of society chooses to specialize in its implementation, while the rest of society learns to use the results in their abstract forms. Thus, society's warehouse of tools expands and society's ability to advance further increases.

So it is with computer science, as well as any science. Progress is made by first solving small problems, then using the solutions of these small problems as tools (called abstract tools) for solving larger problems. The result is a hierarchy of solutions, each level providing additional abstraction that simplifies the problems at the next level.

In our study of computer science, abstraction will be a recurring theme. We have already seen that it is by means of abstraction that operating systems create convenient virtual machines from complex, technical hardware. Later we will see abstraction applied as a general problem-solving methodology (Chapters 4 and 6), witness its role in the evolution of programming languages (Chapter 5), and see it applied to the problem of information storage (Chapters 7, 8, and 9).

Questions/Exercises

1. Describe an analogy (other than the mail-order business in the text) of a virtual entity.
2. In what ways is the distinction between virtual and real characteristics important to a computer user?
3. Identify a hierarchy of abstractions in our society.
4. Give two examples of abstract tools provided by an operating system.

3-3 The Evolution of Operating Systems

The algorithmic machines of the 1940s and 1950s were not extremely flexible or efficient. The execution of a program required significant preparation of the equipment in terms of mounting tapes, placing punched cards in the card reader, setting switches, and so on. Thus, the execution of each program (also called a job) was handled as an isolated entity. When several programmers were required to share the same machine, sign-up sheets on which the various users could reserve the machine for particular blocks of time were common. During the time period allocated to a programmer, the machine was totally under that programmer's control. The session usually began with program setup, followed by short periods of program execution, and was often completed in a hurried effort to do just one more thing ("It will take only a minute") while the next programmer was impatiently starting to set up.

Batch Processing

Operating systems began as systems for simplifying program setup and for streamlining the transitions between jobs. One early development in this direction was the separation of programmers and equipment to eliminate the physical transition of people in and out of the computer room. For this purpose a computer operator was hired to perform the actual operation of the machine. Anyone wanting a program run was required to submit it (along with any required data and special directions about the program's requirements) to the operator and return later for the results. The operator in turn loaded these materials into the machine's mass storage where the operating system could access them for execution. This was the beginning of *batch processing,* which refers to the execution of jobs by first collecting them and their associated data in a single batch in mass storage and then executing them without further interaction with the user.

To further streamline the operation, operating systems were designed to allow the operator to insert jobs into mass storage as they were submitted. Thus, several jobs could be waiting in mass storage at any one time. Each time the job being executed terminated, the operating system automatically selected another job from mass storage according to some selection process and started it. Such a process resulted in a job storage system, called a *job queue,* in which jobs waited before being executed (Figure 3-2).

A queue is a collection of objects (in our case, jobs) ordered in a *first-in-first-out (FIFO)* fashion. That is, the objects are removed from the queue in the order in which they arrive. Most job queues do not rigorously follow the FIFO structure (and thus the term *queue* is a misnomer in the literal sense) since most operating systems provide for consideration of job priorities. As a result, it is possible for a job waiting in the job queue to be bumped by a higher-priority job.

In early batch processing systems, any instructions pertaining to the requirements of a program being submitted for execution (such as which tapes must be mounted in the machine's tape drives) had to be communicated to the operator, because the person making the request was not present when the program ran. However, with a job queue, the operating system determined when the program was actually run; this, in turn, complicated the operator's task of associating instructions with jobs. Thus, a coding system, called a *job control language (JCL),* was designed by which these special instructions were stored with the job in the queue. When the job was finally selected for execution, the operating system printed these instructions at a printer where they could be read and followed by the operator.

Figure 3-2 Batch processing

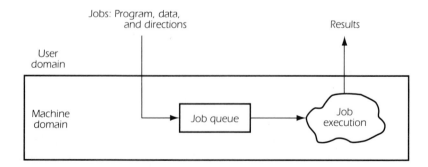

The development of job control languages meant that a user could code instructions to the operator and submit them as part of the job. This meant that a person-to-person meeting between the operator and the user was no longer necessary. In turn, users were provided with input devices such as card readers by which they could submit their jobs and instructions directly into the job queue rather than indirectly through the operator. As the sophistication of operating systems developed, more and more of these instructions could be obeyed by the operating system without the aid of the operator. Today, job control languages are used more for sending instructions to the operating system than to the computer operator.

Interactive Processing

The major drawback to a batch processing system is that the program and its data cannot be altered once they are in the job queue. This system is acceptable for such applications as processing payroll or performing scientific calculations, because in these cases, all the data and decisions about how it is to be manipulated are made before the execution of the program. On the other hand, transaction processing applications exist in which the data that the program is to manipulate is not available until the program is running and thus cannot be submitted with the program into the job queue. One example consists of data retrieval and update applications such as a reservation system in which the program must interact with a person by means of a terminal to report vacancies or record reservations as they occur. Another example is the process of program development, in which it is convenient to stop, modify, and restart new programs to correct errors. In such cases, it is inherent in the application that the computer user be allowed to interact with the machine during program execution.

To accommodate these needs, new operating systems were developed to provide *interactive processing* rather than batch processing (Figure 3-3). These systems were

Figure 3-3 Interactive processing

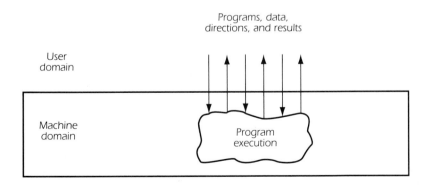

designed to carry on a dialogue with the user and to allow user access to the machine (through remote workstations) during program execution. Instead of requests to the system being placed in a queue for later attention, they were acted on immediately, and the result or an appropriate error message was returned to the requester in a conversational fashion.

Interactive processing is closely associated with another concept called *real-time processing,* which refers to the requirement that the software coordinate its activities with those of its environment. When controlling the flight of an aircraft, it is not sufficient merely to raise and lower the landing gear; major consideration must be given to the actual (or real) time frame in which this action is performed. Likewise, a reservation system must respond to the agent requesting service in a reasonable amount of time or the system becomes ineffective. Today, interactive real-time systems dominate the scene, with batch processing mainly relegated to processing large managerial record-keeping projects.

Time-Sharing Systems

Recall that one of the major issues in the origins of batch processing systems was the need to coordinate the requirements of several users competing for the same machine. If an interactive system is to be used in a similar environment, it too must be able to coordinate the needs of several users. Early batch processing systems achieved this coordination by postponing requested activities (by placing them in the job queue) until time was available. In an interactive environment, however, each request from the various users must be acted upon at the time of the request.

This requirement of interactive multiuser machines was met by means of *time-sharing,* which we discuss later in more detail. For now we simply note that time-sharing is a technique by which the attention of a single CPU alternates among the various tasks in such a way that the CPU appears to be performing the tasks simultaneously. In particular, the time available is divided into short periods called time slices that are awarded to the various tasks in an alternating fashion. Thus, using time-sharing techniques, interactive operating systems appear to serve different users at the same time.

Although we have introduced time-sharing as a way of implementing multiuser operating systems, it has major applications in single-user systems as well. Consider, for example, a user of a small, single-user, interactive computer system. The user wants the machine to print a copy of a document. While that is being done, the user wants to begin typing another document. This document, however, requires the results of several time-consuming calculations that the user wants the machine to perform while the earlier parts of the document are being prepared. In short, the user wants the operating system to coordinate the execution of several tasks at the same time, in much the same way that it would if each task had been requested by different users.

Such needs are satisfied by time-sharing techniques that result in operating systems known as multitasking operating systems. These systems allow a user to request the execution of more than one task at the same time. Today, multitasking interactive systems are becoming quite popular on personal computers.

Note that interactive and batch processing are contrasting ways of handling the machine/user interface. Time-sharing, on the other hand, is a technique for performing several activities at the "same time." Thus, time-sharing can be applied within batch processing systems as well as interactive ones.

In fact, the technique of time-sharing often improves the total throughput of a batch processing system because the operating system can remove several jobs from the job queue and allow them to share time in hopes of obtaining a mix of jobs that will make judicious use of the machine's resources. For example, if one job requires significant use of a disk drive, and another job consists mainly of manipulating data in main memory, the second job can be running during those time intervals in which the first job is waiting for data to arrive from the disk. In such cases, the two jobs together will be completed in much less time than if they had been executed separately because, through time-sharing, the execution of one program is allowed to proceed while the other is waiting for an I/O device to perform a task.

Networks

Time-sharing was not a viable solution to the problem of competition among users of the early machines largely because the machines of that period were not capable of the execution speeds and storage capacities required for multiuser applications. The irony is that now that technology has provided equipment capable of efficient multiuser applications, it has also removed much of the need for such systems. The price and size of equipment have decreased to the point that competition among users can often be resolved by merely supplying each user with a different machine running its own single-user interactive operating system.

In a sense, the irony is twofold. As more and more users acquire their own machines, there seems to be more and more desire to link the machines for the exchange of information. Thus, coupled computer systems called *networks* are becoming extremely common. Today, the concept of a large central machine serving many users is giving way to the concept of many small machines connected via a network in which users share the resources in the system. Such resources may include printing capabilities, software packages, and data storage facilities. This sharing of resources often conforms to the client/server model in which the machine containing the resource (the server) responds to requests from the other machines (the clients). In other cases, such as in a distributed data system, each machine contains a portion of the total resource, and the machines communicate on more equal terms. In either case, the need to coordinate network activities is creating new research directions in operating system design, and hence the field of operating systems continues to evolve.

Computer networks are classified as either local area networks (LANs) or wide area networks (WANs). A LAN consists of a collection of computers in a single building or building complex that is usually managed by one company. For example, the computers used on a university campus or those used in a manufacturing plant might be connected by a local area network. In contrast, a WAN links machines that may be on opposite sides of a city or the world. Examples include BITNET, an international network connecting universities and research centers, and the Internet, a worldwide collection of networks that are also heavily involved with academic traffic.

Another dichotomy of networks is based on whether the network is comprised of hardware and software from a single vendor or implemented as a conglomerate of products from different manufacturers. Networks of the former type are sometimes called closed networks (or proprietary networks), whereas networks of the latter variety are known as open networks. (Actually, the term *open* refers to the fact that the specifications for the network components are open to the public, which leads to compatibility among the products of different vendors and thus indirectly implies that the network consists of equipment and software from competing sources.)

Instances of closed networks are most common among LANs because in these cases a single organization is usually in charge of the entire network. In contrast, wide area networks tend to be open networks because they often involve different organizations, each with their own equipment, or else the distances encompassed make the purchase of equipment from a single vendor either inconvenient or impossible.

The Internet is an open network. It consists of a "backbone" network consisting of high-speed, high-capacity communication paths that span the United States. To this backbone, other more centrally located networks connect at designated machines, known as gateways. These networks, in turn, connect through other gateways to other networks. In this manner, an international network of hundreds of thousands of machines has evolved and continues to evolve on a daily basis.

The demand for open networks has generated a need for published standards with which various manufacturers can build equipment that can function properly with products from other vendors. One standard that has resulted is the Open System Interconnection (OSI) reference model published by the International Standards Organization (ISO), of which the American National Standards Institute is a member. Although this standard has not been widely implemented, it has become an often-quoted model because it identifies the activities required for network communication, classifies these activities into well-defined layers of abstraction, and carries the authority of the International Standards Organization. We discuss this model in more detail in Section 3-8.

Multiprocessor Systems

Computer networks represent only one example of the multiprocessor systems in use today. Whereas a network produces a multiprocessor system by combining many individual machines, each of which may contain only a single CPU, many multiprocessor systems are designed as single machines containing more than one processor. In this environment, the appearance of several activities being performed at the same time is reality, not a virtual characteristic simulated by time-sharing. An operating system for such a machine must not only coordinate the competition between the various activities that are actually executing simultaneously but also control the assignment of activities to the processors in the machine. Thus, as new activities are requested, the operating system must decide which processor should execute that activity so that the total throughput of the machine is maximized.

In turn, the development of multiprocessor machines has added new dimensions to operating system research and design, and the field promises to remain active for years to come.

Questions/Exercises

1. What are some examples of queues in everyday life? In each example, indicate any situations in which the strict queue structure (FIFO) is violated.
2. Which of the following activities require real-time processing:
   a. Displaying the letters typed at the keyboard on the monitor screen.
   b. Printing a sequence of mailing labels.
   c. Maintaining the checking and savings account balances of a bank's customers.
3. Which of the following activities can be handled conveniently in a batch processing environment:
   a. Printing mailing labels.
   b. Executing a program that predicts the state of next year's economy.
   c. Executing a video game.
4. Define time-sharing.
5. Explain how multitasking operating systems can obtain higher throughput than systems that insist on performing each task completely before starting the next.
6. What is an open network?

3-4 Operating System Architecture

A productive approach to understanding a complicated system is to analyze the system in terms of its parts and to understand how each of these parts is used as an abstract tool by the rest of the system. In this section we apply such a modular analysis to our study of operating systems.

Our approach is to assume that a user sitting at a workstation has just requested that a program (which is stored in mass storage) be executed. With this as our starting point, we will follow the activities of a simplified yet representative operating system as it obeys the request. We further assume that the system is an interactive multitasking one.

Operating System Components

The first unit we introduce is the *command processor* since this part of the operating system handles the dialogue with the user. The command processor "watches" the keyboards, mice, and other input devices attached to the machine and interprets the commands entered, as mentioned earlier in this chapter. Thus, this unit gives the system much of its personality by establishing the communication format to which any user of the system must conform.

Once the command processor determines that the command it received is valid and discovers that it is a request for the execution of a program, it resorts to the assistance of the *scheduler.* As the name suggests, the scheduler arranges for the execution of the program. In a batch processing environment, this would involve placing the program in the job queue according to its priority. In an interactive multitasking environment, the scheduler's job is to place the requested program within the collection of other activities currently sharing time.

Each of the activities sharing time within such a system is called a *process.* The term *process* is a technical term that refers to the execution of a program. Note that a single program can be associated with several processes. For example, in a time-sharing system two requests to sort different lists of data produce two separate processes, both of which may involve the execution of the same program; but each of these processes is a separate activity progressing at its own rate. In our example, the process being scheduled is the execution of the requested program. Other processes that might already be scheduled involve the execution of tasks previously requested by the user, execution of requests from other users of the system, and the execution of tasks required by the operating system itself. (The command processor and the scheduler are themselves implemented as processes that share the CPU with the other activities.)

Before the requested program is scheduled for execution, the scheduler must seek the services of two other units within the operating system. One is the *file manager,* the unit that maintains the records pertaining to the information stored in mass storage. This unit is required by the scheduler for accessing the requested program.

The file manager is also in charge of protecting files in mass storage against unauthorized access. In particular, if the file manager discovers that the user should not be allowed to execute the requested program, it reports to the scheduler, which in turn reports the problem back to the command processor instead of scheduling the program for execution. (In this case, the command processor would properly chastise the user for making an unauthorized request.)

The file manager needs space in main memory in which to place our program when it is retrieved from mass storage. To obtain this space, it requires the services of the *memory manager,* another unit within the operating system. The memory manager has the task of coordinating the use of the machine's main memory. It is this unit that keeps records of which areas of memory are currently being used and handles the allocation and deallocation of memory space to the other activities in the system.

Assuming all goes well with the file manager, the scheduler must also be assisted by the *resource allocator,* which coordinates the assignment of peripheral devices within the computer system. If the process being scheduled requires a resource not currently available, the resource allocator reports the situation to the scheduler. Otherwise, the required resources are allocated to the new process and the process, which in our case is the execution of the selected program, is scheduled.

The final step of executing the program is handled by the operating system unit called the *dispatcher.* This unit, in a time-sharing system, coordinates the switching of the machine's attention among the various processes scheduled for execution. We discuss the function of the dispatcher in more detail in the next section. For now we merely note that the dispatcher oversees the actual execution of the requested process (along with the other processes scheduled for execution) and reports back to the scheduler when the process is completed. At that time, the scheduler informs the resource allocator that the resources used by the process are no longer needed and reports the completion of the process to the command processor, which in turn may notify the user.

Our choice of approaching the structure of an operating system from the viewpoint of a machine user was not completely arbitrary. Such a point of view is also used to produce the onion-skin diagram of an operating system's architecture, as shown in Figure 3-4 on the following page. The purpose behind the diagram is to reflect the levels of abstraction within the system. We envision the computer users on the outside (of the onion). From there, all that is visible is the outer layer consisting of the command processor. The command processor in turn communicates with the scheduler, represented by the next inner layer of the onion. Within this layer are the file manager and resource allocator, and within that layer is the memory manager. Finally, deep inside the system is the dispatcher overseeing the execution of processes.

Utility Software

Today's operating systems contain (or are accompanied by) a variety of additional programs and partial programs called *utility software* (or *application software*). Utility software normally associated with an operating system includes a collection of programs for manipulating files. Within this collection one commonly finds programs for copying, deleting, merging, and sorting files.

Another important piece of utility software is an *editor,* which provides an interactive way of creating and modifying files by means of a keyboard, mouse, and monitor. Historically, an editor was designed as a programming tool and provided a

Figure 3-4 An onion-skin diagram of an operating system

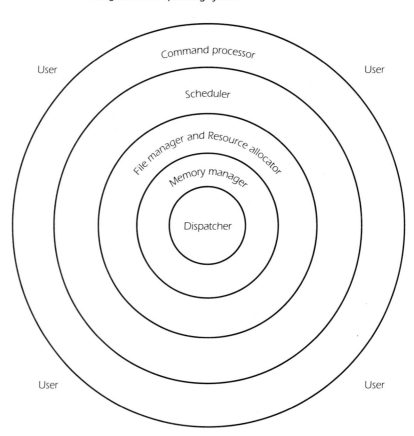

convenient means by which programs, in an appropriately coded form, could be typed at the keyboard, saved by the operating system, and later retrieved for modification. These early editors were developed with only rudimentary editing features such as the ability to delete unwanted lines or to insert new lines. Perhaps the most powerful feature of these early editors was their ability to search a document for the occurrence of a designated character pattern and possibly change those occurrences to another pattern. Today, editors have evolved into word processors that provide powerful features, including automatic page formatting, spelling checking, and grammar analysis.

In many applications, easy access to utility software is one of the more important features of an operating system, and many interactive systems are designed with this in mind. One result of this emphasis is the concept of viewing utility programs as building blocks from which larger programs (or more accurately program sequences) can be constructed. For example, in addition to providing separate utility programs to perform such tasks as searching documents for certain syntactic forms (such as underscored or boldfaced words), sorting lists, and printing files, an operating system can provide a means by which utilities can be strung together to produce the appearance of one large program that prints an index for a document by locating the underscored words, sorting these words, and then printing them along with their corresponding page numbers. The technique of stringing together activities so that the output of one becomes the input of the next is often called piping (not to be confused with the term *pipelining* introduced in Chapter 2, which refers to the technique of fetching instructions in advance). The string of activities is called a pipe; each activity in the string is called a filter.

The utility routines just discussed are stand-alone programs in the sense that they are ready to execute with no additional programming required by the user. Another class of utility software consists of partial routines for inclusion in user-written programs. An example of such software is the collection of routines for performing frequently needed calculations, including routines for statistical analysis, graphics applications, and economic forecasting. Such routines are commonly provided in a file called a **library** and are inserted into (or more accurately linked to) a user program by another stand-alone utility program called the linker. We discuss this process in more detail in Chapter 5.

Questions/Exercises

1. List the components of an interactive time-sharing operating system. Summarize the role of each component with a short phrase.
2. Draw an onion-skin diagram of the mail-order business described in Section 3-2.
3. From an editor's point of view, why is it convenient to have the computer's program divided into cells of byte sizes?
4. What is the difference between user-written programs and utility programs provided by the operating system?

3-5 Rudiments of Time-Sharing

In Section 3-4, we indicated that the illusion of several activities occurring at the same time within a single machine is created by the dispatcher through the technique of time-sharing, but we avoided a discussion of how this was actually accomplished. In this section, we investigate the rudiments of this technique. First, however, we need to understand the hardware **interrupt** feature.

Interrupt Handling

If you are interrupted while performing a task, you normally stop what you are doing, record in some manner where you are, take care of the interrupting entity, and later return to the original task. Interrupts in computers provide for a similar activity to occur in relation to the execution of a program. When an interrupt signal occurs within the computer system, it causes the CPU to stop the current process, save its position in that process, and then start another process. Let us take a closer look at the last two steps in this procedure.

First note that when you are interrupted while reading a book, your place in the book consists not only of the current page number but also of the information (some of which may be incomplete) that you have gained to that point. Your ability to continue reading at a later time depends on your ability to remember both the page number at which to start and the accumulated information. Similarly, the CPU's position in a process consists not only of the value in the program counter but also of the information in the other registers and memory cells being used by the process. This collection of information, including the value in the program counter, is called the *process's state.*

To save the CPU's position in the current process therefore involves saving the entire process's state. This is typically done by copying the contents of the registers into a collection of cells in memory. In this way, the complete state will be preserved in main memory so that the CPU can perform another process and later return to the original one by reloading the state from memory.

The last step in the interrupt procedure—to start another process—is implemented by changing the contents of the program counter to contain the location of the desired instructions and starting the fetch phase of the machine's cycle. The location of these instructions is predetermined and is called the interrupt entry point because it is the point at which the CPU enters the software system after an interrupt has occurred. The instructions stored at this location are collectively called the *interrupt routine* because they constitute the routine executed by the CPU immediately after being interrupted.

In summary, upon an interrupt signal being generated, the CPU completes its current machine cycle, saves the contents of its registers in memory, and starts executing the instructions located at the interrupt entry point.

Allocating Time Slices

Now that we have discussed the handling of interrupts, let us see how the dispatcher in an operating system can execute several processes at the same time. Suppose two processes are scheduled for execution, and their associated programs are stored in different locations in main memory. To start one of the processes, the dispatcher merely executes a jump to the appropriate location in memory. However, before doing this, it starts a timer circuit that will generate an interrupt signal after a certain time has lapsed.

The first process therefore is interrupted after a period of time, called a *time slice,* and the interrupt routine is started. Here the interrupt routine—a part of the dispatcher—again sets the timer and jumps to the beginning of the second process's program. Upon the completion of the next time slice, the second process is interrupted and control is again given to the interrupt routine within the dispatcher. Now the dispatcher, knowing where the first process's state was stored in memory, is able to reload the registers as they were when the first process was interrupted and continue that process. Thus, aided by interrupt circuitry, the dispatcher can coordinate the alternating execution of several processes (Figure 3-5).

The technique of alternating the CPU's attention between different processes is called time-sharing. On large machines it is not uncommon to find 50 or more processes sharing the time of a single CPU. Since the length of a time slice is in the range of 10 milliseconds to 100 milliseconds, the appearance of all these processes running at the same time is produced even though only one is actually executing at any instant. For example, if interactive processes are communicating with people through different terminals, then each person has the illusion of having his or her own machine. Thus, the operating system has created numerous virtual machines (one for each terminal), while in reality only one machine exists.

It is reasonable that each virtual machine created by a time-sharing system is slower than the real machine, and when many processes are sharing time, this slowness can become quite noticeable. Several techniques are available for controlling this machine sluggishness. One approach is to assign priorities to the processes in the sharing pool so that important processes execute quickly at the expense of less important ones. This might be done by either giving the high-priority processes longer time slices or giving them preferred treatment when selecting the process to receive the next time slice.

Questions/Exercises

1. We mentioned in the text that each process in a time-sharing system runs slower than it does in a nonsharing environment. What about several processes as a group? More precisely, does it take less total time to complete two processes by

Figure 3-5 Time-sharing between process A and process B

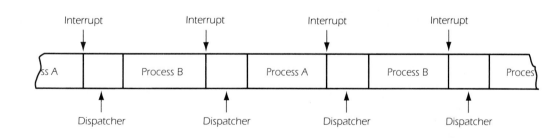

allowing them to share time or by executing the first completely and then running the second?

2. In a time-sharing system, how can high-priority processes be allowed to run faster than others?

3. Summarize the activities of a machine when handling an interrupt.

4. What are the major activities involved in restarting a process for the next time slice?

5. If time slices in a time-sharing system are 50 milliseconds, how many processes can share one second? (Disregard the time required by the dispatcher.)

3-6 Resource Allocation

In this section, we investigate the subtleties involved in the task of resource allocation.

Coordinating the Use of Resources

We begin by noting that the resources of a machine can be placed in one of two categories: those that are shareable and those that are not. Disk units go into the first category, because data for different processes can be stored on different tracks of the same disk without interference. Tape units are in the second category because, due to their sequential nature, two processes trying to use the same tape independently for data storage greatly interfere with one another. Printers also fall into the second category because the sharing of a printer results in rather confusing output.

The major role of the resource allocator is the prevention of such clashes over nonshareable resources. The first step in this direction is to establish the resource allocator as the central clearinghouse for all requests for resources. (In reality, some resources are controlled by other units in the system. For example, the dispatcher allocates time slices.) Closely associated with this step is the need to design the system in a way that enforces the policies of the resource allocator. After all, little is gained if, once in execution, a process is allowed to do as it pleases. To accomplish these goals, processes in multitasking environments are not allowed to communicate directly with the peripheral devices of the machine. Rather, all such communication is done through the operating system at the request of the processes. This places the operating system in a position whereby it can assure that once a process has been allocated a nonshareable resource, other processes are denied the use of that resource until the first process has finished.

The next step in the control of resources is to establish a reliable allocation procedure for the resource allocator. As a solution to this problem, one might first suggest a technique based on the concept of a flag. (A flag refers to a bit in memory that can be in one of two states: set or clear.) Our proposed solution is to establish a flag for each of the nonshareable resources. When we begin, all flags are clear. If a process requests the use of a nonshareable resource, the resource allocator checks the corresponding flag. If the flag is still clear, no other process is using the resource; the resource allocator grants the request and also changes the flag to its set state. If another process later requests the use of the same resource, the flag is found in its set state (indicating the resource is already in use) and the resource allocator denies the request of the second process. Finally, when a process finishes with a nonshareable resource, the resource allocator clears the corresponding flag, indicating the resource's availability.

Semaphores

Although this solution looks good at first glance, it has a serious problem. The task of testing and possibly setting the flag requires several machine steps. It is therefore possible for the task to be interrupted after a clear flag has been detected but before the flag has been set. In turn, the following scenario could take place.

Suppose a printer is currently available and a process requests use of it. The corresponding flag is checked and found to be clear, indicating that the printer is available. However, at this point, the process is interrupted and another process begins its time slice. It too requests the use of the printer. Again, the flag is checked and found still clear because the previous process was interrupted before the resource allocator had time to set the flag. Consequently, the resource allocator allows the second process to begin using the printer. Later, the original process resumes execution where it left off, which is immediately after the resource allocator found the flag to be clear. Thus, the resource allocator continues by granting the original process access to the printer. Two processes are now using the same nonshareable printer.

The problem here is that the task of testing and possibly setting the flag must be completed without interruption. One solution is to use the interrupt disable and interrupt enable instructions provided in most machine languages. When executed, the interrupt disable instruction causes the CPU to delay recognition of normal interrupt signals until an interrupt enable instruction is executed. Interrupt signals occurring in the interim must wait. Therefore, if the resource allocator starts the flag-testing routine with an interrupt disable instruction and ends it with an interrupt enable instruction, no other activity can interrupt the routine once it starts.

Another approach that leads to a solution to our flag maintenance problem is to use the test-and-set instruction that is available in many machine languages. This instruction directs the CPU to retrieve the value of a flag, note the value received, and then set the flag all within a single machine instruction. The advantage here is that since the CPU always completes an instruction before recognizing an interrupt, the task of testing and setting the flag cannot be interrupted when it is implemented as a single instruction.

A properly implemented flag, as just described, is called a *semaphore,* in reference to the railroad signals used to control access to sections of track. In fact, semaphores are used in software systems in much the same way as they are in railway systems. Corresponding to the section of track that can contain only one train at a time is a sequence of instructions that can be executed by only one process at a time. Such a sequence of instructions is called a critical region. A process must find the semaphore clear and set it before entering the critical region; then it must clear the semaphore once the critical region is completed.

Deadlock

Let us look at another problem that might arise when allocating resources. Suppose two processes are sharing time. One requests the use of the printer and receives it, while the other requests the use of the tape drive and receives it. Later, the first process needs the tape drive in addition to the printer but is denied its use because the other process is using it. The first process must therefore wait for the second one to finish with the tape drive. However, while the first process is waiting, the second process reaches a point where it needs the use of the printer. The operating system also denies this request since the printer is assigned to the first process; thus, each process ends up waiting for the other to finish. Such a condition is called *deadlock* and, just as in other settings (Figure 3-6), can severely degrade a system's performance if not properly handled.

Figure 3-6 A deadlock resulting from competition for nonshareable railroad intersections

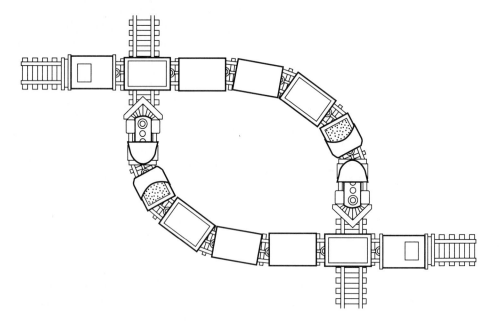

Analysis of deadlock has revealed that it cannot occur unless all three of the following conditions are satisfied:

1. There is competition for nonshareable resources.
2. The resources are requested on a partial basis; that is, having received some resources, a process will return later to request more.
3. Once a resource has been allocated, it cannot forcibly be retrieved.

The point of isolating these conditions is that deadlock in a system can be prevented by removing any one of them, and in fact techniques attacking each are used in systems today. For example, requiring each process to request all its required resources at one time removes the second condition, or allowing the operating system to take back resources removes the third condition. Perhaps the more imaginative techniques involve the removal of the first condition. Let us take a look at how this might be done.

One approach is not to remove the competition directly by controlling the requests but to remove it indirectly by converting nonshareable resources into shareable ones. For example, suppose the nonshareable resource in question is a printer and a variety of processes require its use. Each time a process requests the use of a printer, the operating system grants the request. However, instead of sending the data to an actual printer, the operating system sets aside storage area on a disk to hold the data until a printer becomes available. Thus, each process, thinking it has the use of a printer, executes in its normal way. In this manner the operating system has made the nonshareable resource appear shareable by creating the illusion of many virtual printers that can be used simultaneously. This technique of holding data for output at a later but more convenient time is called *spooling* and is quite popular on systems of all sizes.

Questions/Exercises

1. Suppose process A and process B are sharing time on the same machine, and each needs the same nonshareable resource for short periods of time. (For example, each process may be printing a series of independent, short reports.) Thus, each process may repeatedly acquire the resource, release it, and later request it again. What is a drawback to controlling access to the resource in the following manner:

    > Begin by assigning a flag the value 0. If process A requests the resource and the flag is 0, grant the request. Otherwise, make process A wait. If process B requests the resource and the flag is 1, grant the request. Otherwise, make process B wait. Each time process A finishes with the resource, change the flag to 1. Each time process B finishes with the resource, change the flag to 0.

2. Suppose a two-lane road converges to one lane to go through a tunnel. To coordinate the use of the tunnel, the following signal system has been installed:

A car entering either end of the tunnel causes red lights above the tunnel entrances to be turned on. As the car exits the tunnel, the lights are turned off. If an approaching car finds a red light on, it waits until the light is turned off before entering the tunnel. What is the flaw in this system?

3. Suppose the following solutions have been proposed for removing the deadlock that occurs on a single-lane bridge when two cars meet. Identify which condition for deadlock given in the text is removed by each solution.

   a. Do not let a car onto the bridge until the bridge is empty.

   b. If cars meet, make one of them back up.

   c. Add a second lane to the bridge.

4. Suppose we represent each process in a time-sharing system with a dot and draw an arrow from one dot to another if the process represented by the first dot is waiting for a resource being used by the second. Mathematicians call the resulting picture a directed graph. What property of the directed graph is equivalent to deadlock in the system?

3-7 Getting It Started

We began this chapter by asking how we get a computer to do something for us, and we answered by saying that the operating system, which is already running, is designed to respond to our requests. That leaves the question open as to how the operating system gets started. To understand this procedure, we first take a closer look at main memory technology.

Memory Technology

Memory techniques used in computers can be divided into two broad categories: volatile and nonvolatile. Volatile means that the memory circuit does not retain the stored information when it is turned off. Any information in it is lost each time power is disconnected, and when power is restored, the memory either is blank or contains miscellaneous garbage. An example of such memory is the capacitor technology discussed in Chapter 1: The tiny capacitors used for computer memory lose their charge in a few milliseconds if not recharged by what is known as the memory refresh circuit.

Nonvolatile techniques retain the stored information after power loss. An example of this technology is found in the use of magnetic media, which are popular in mass storage systems. For use in main memory systems, magnetic material can be formed into tiny donut-shaped rings called *cores,* each capable of representing one bit. Such technology was quite popular in the past, but its size, cost, and energy requirements have caused it to lose favor.

In an effort to construct memories that do not change when their power sources are removed, some technologies are used that might be considered extreme in the sense that the memory contents cannot be changed, even by the computer itself. Since the machine cannot write information into it, such memory is often referred to as *read-only memory (ROM)*. Once information is placed in ROM by a special process analogous to blowing tiny fuses on a chip, it remains there whether the machine is on or off. Common uses of ROM include storage of customized software used by the operating system to control the particular hardware in a machine as well as the bootstrap, which we explain below.

The Bootstrap

A CPU is constructed so that each time it is turned on it initializes its program counter to a predetermined address before starting its first machine cycle; therefore, it interprets the contents of the memory cells beginning at this predetermined location as the program that is to be executed. This area of the machine's memory consists of ROM. In home appliances such as microwave ovens, this ROM constitutes a majority of the machine's memory. The elementary operating system that monitors the keyboard on the front of the oven and correspondingly controls the (rather specialized) peripheral devices is stored here. Each time the oven is plugged into a power socket, the controlling computer automatically begins performing its supervisory tasks.

When greater flexibility is required, it is not practical to construct the majority of main memory in the form of ROM. In fact, most of the memory in today's general-purpose computers is volatile. The ROM in these machines is relatively small and contains a short program called the *bootstrap*. (Its role in loading the operating system is analogous to that of the small tab on a boot, which is necessary when putting on a boot but is of little use afterward.) This program is not the operating system but rather a program that reads a predetermined area of mass storage (normally on disk) into a volatile area of memory, assumes the data read is the beginning of the operating system, and executes a jump to the beginning of this memory area. In this manner, when the machine is turned on, the operating system, which is permanently held in mass storage, is automatically loaded into memory and then executed (Figure 3-7, on the following page). In keeping with the bootstrap terminology, this process is known as *bootstrapping* or sometimes simply booting.

Questions/Exercises

1. Suppose a computer's memory was constructed using a nonvolatile technology. Why should a section of ROM still be provided for the bootstrap?
2. What analogy can be drawn between the bootstrap routine in a computer and the starter in a car?
3. Summarize the bootstrapping process found in a general-purpose computer.

Figure 3-7 The bootstrap process

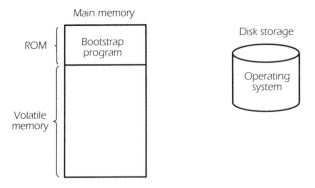

(Step 1) Machine starts by executing the bootstrap program already in memory. Operating system is stored in mass storage.

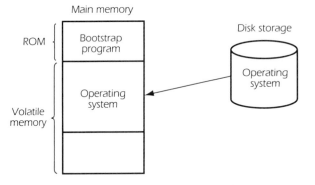

(Step 2) Bootstrap program directs the transfer of the operating system into main memory and then transfers control to it.

3-8 A Closer Look at Networks

The pattern in which the machines in a network are connected is known as the network's topology. Figure 3-8 represents some of the popular topologies including the ring, in which the machines are connected in a circular fashion; the bus, in which the machines are all connected to a common communication line; and the irregular network, in which the machines are connected in what appears to be a haphazard manner. The irregular topology is common in wide area networks, whereas the ring and bus topologies are usually found in local environments where network control is more likely to fall under a single authority.

For a computer network to operate correctly, a system of rules, called protocols, must be established and followed throughout the system. These protocols govern the

Figure 3-8

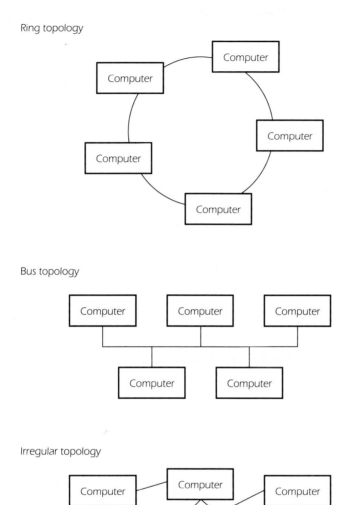

Ring topology

Bus topology

Irregular topology

communication between the machines in the network in much the same way that society uses protocols to govern interactions among people. (A common protocol in our society is to answer the telephone by saying, "Hello.") The use of these protocols streamlines communication; diverting from them causes delays and misunderstandings. (What would happen if you answered the telephone by merely picking up the receiver and listening?)

Protocols for Special Topologies

Some protocols are sometimes related to the topology of the network. In the case of a ring topology, protocols coordinate the transmission of messages around the ring. One example is the token system implemented by IBM. In this protocol, each machine transmits messages only to its right and receives messages only from its left, as shown in Figure 3-9. A message from one machine to another must therefore be forwarded counterclockwise around the ring until it reaches its destination. To coordinate the introduction of new messages to the ring, a unique bit pattern, called a token, is passed around the ring. Normally, each machine merely relays the token from left to right in the same manner in which it relays messages. If, however, the machine receiving the token has messages of its own to introduce to the network, it transmits one message before relaying the token. Likewise, when the next machine receives the token behind the new message, it can either forward the token immediately or introduce its own new message in front of the token. In this manner, each machine in the network has equal opportunity to introduce a message of its own as the token circles around the ring.

Another protocol is often associated with the bus topology. Here each message transmitted by any machine is broadcast to all the machines on the common communication line (Figure 3-10). In turn, each machine monitors all the messages but responds only to those addressed to it. In this environment, a machine in the network must wait until it detects that there are no messages on the line before transmitting a message of its own. At that time, the machine can begin transmitting but must continue to monitor the line because another machine may have also detected the absence of activity on the line and started transmitting. In that case, the

Figure 3-9 Communication over a ring topology

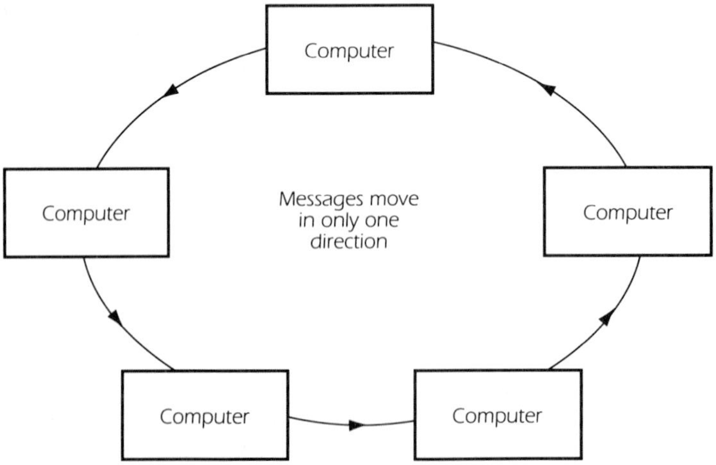

information on the line is a blend of the two messages. Once they detect this conflict, both machines must stop transmitting and pause for a brief, random period of time before trying to transmit again. Usually both machines do not pause for the same amount of time. Thus, one machine may begin transmitting before the other and hence gain priority. If, however, the pause periods happen to coincide, the machines clash again and are forced to pause once more. Moreover, a third machine might start transmitting while the two machines are waiting, in which case both machines would be forced to wait until the line is clear once again.

Irregular topologies present their own unique protocol demands. For instance, such networks usually offer several paths that a message can take from one machine to another. It is therefore the task of the network software to determine the route for each message and to coordinate the propagation of the message along the chosen path.

One technique for this is packet switching in which each message is first divided into small segments called packets, and then each packet, along with the address of that packet's destination, is sent out into the network to find its way to the destination. As the machines throughout the network receive packets, they consider each packet's destination and forward that packet to another machine based on the machine's knowledge of the network. Thus, the packets from a single message may follow different paths to their destination and may arrive at the destination out of sequence. It is the task of the destination machine to rebuild the message from the packets.

The Open System Interconnection Reference Model

As mentioned earlier, the International Standards Organization is addressing the task of developing protocol standards that can be adopted by all manufacturers so that their network products will be compatible. A major result of this effort is the Open System Interconnection (OSI) reference model. This is essentially a report that identifies and classifies the tasks required for communication over a network. To

Figure 3-10 Communication over a bus topology

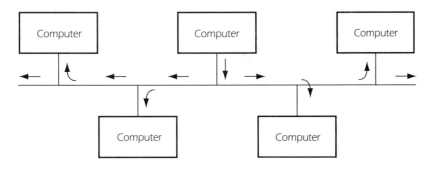

understand this classification scheme, let us first look at an analogy: Suppose your company wants to send replacement parts to a customer in a distant city.

Your task is to collect the parts and to package them according to the specifications of a shipping company. You then deliver the package to the shipping company of your choice and pay the appropriate fee. At this point, your job is complete; responsibility for the parts has been passed to the shipper.

Of course, the shipper does not view its task as transporting replacement parts. Instead, its task is to transport a package of a certain weight and certain dimensions to a designated location by a designated time. Although you may have chosen the less expensive surface rate, the shipper may decide that it is more cost effective to send your package by air. Hence, your package, along with others, may be placed in a container conforming to airline requirements. Having conformed to the specifications of the airline, the shipper transfers the responsibility for the parts to the airline.

At this point, the airline has the task of transporting a large container from one airport to another. Depending on its particular cargo load, it may choose to place that container on a direct flight, send it through an intermediate stop, or perhaps subcontract the transportation of the container to another airline.

In any case, the airline ultimately delivers the container to the shipping company in the destination city. The shipping company unpacks the container and delivers your package to your customer according to the address you provided.

In summary, the transporting of the parts is carried out by a three-level hierarchy (Figure 3-11): the user level (consisting of you and your customer), the shipping company, and the airline. Each level performs its task, using the lower levels as abstract

Figure 3-11 Our package-shipping example

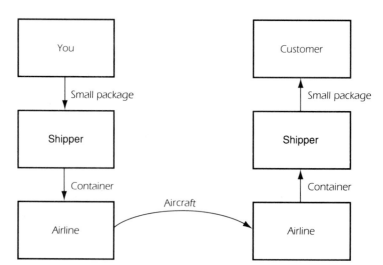

tools. Such is the case with the OSI reference model, except that it is a seven-level hierarchy rather than three, and each level consists of a collection of software routines rather than people and businesses.

Figure 3-12 summarizes the seven-level hierarchy of the OSI reference model, each level of which is called a layer. The division of labor into a hierarchy of layers is the heart of the OSI reference model and has two important consequences, which are common objectives in any hierarchical design. First, it breaks the overall task into manageable subtasks, each with its specific goals. In turn, the solution of each subtask can be used as an abstract tool in the solution of other subtasks.

Second, the hierarchy establishes well-defined boundaries between the subtasks at which standard interfaces can be implemented. By conforming to these standard interfaces, different solutions for the same subtask can be substituted for one another without disrupting the rest of the system.

Our goal is not to become experts in the particular activities of each layer in the OSI reference model. Rather, it is to appreciate the role the hierarchy plays in implementing a modular structure through which the benefits of abstraction can be reaped. With this as our goal, let us follow the transmission of a message through the seven layers of the model.

We will concentrate on the activities at the sending end of the communication with the understanding that the corresponding layers at the receiving end tend to undo the tasks performed at the sending end. (Each level of the hierarchy in our package example had a representative at both ends of the communication, with the representatives at corresponding levels tending to undo the task performed at the

Figure 3-12 The seven layers of the OSI reference model

Application layer	Handles the communication with the application software.
Presentation layer	Handles issues of data format such as encrypting data for security, or perhaps applying data compression to increase efficiency.
Session layer	Handles the task of establishing and maintaining communication between the two machines communicating over the network.
Transport layer	Packages messages into data units appropriate for the network being used and attaches the address of each message's final destination to each of the data units.
Network layer	Handles the routing of the data units through the network via intermediate machines.
Data link layer	Handles error detection, correction, and the retransmission of hopelessly garbled data.
Physical layer	Handles the actual communication of bit patterns in terms of voltage levels, radio frequencies, or optical signals as required by the particular communication method being used.

opposite end. You sent the parts, your customer received them; the shipper's representative at your end packaged the container and delivered it to the airline, the shipper's representative at your customer's end received the container from the airline and unpacked it.)

Let us assume that a user on the west coast of the United States needs to transfer a file to a machine on the east coast (Figure 3-13). The application layer on the west coast would handle the task of retrieving the file from mass storage (with the assistance of the local operating system) and pass it to the presentation layer. If the file is classified, the presentation layer may encrypt it before passing it on to the session layer. The presentation layer may also apply a data compression algorithm to the file to reduce its length before passing the file on to the session layer.

The session layer has the task of establishing a connection with the machine on the east coast and confirming that the machine at the other end of the connection is, in fact, the correct one based on some authentication technique. It is also the task of the session layer to reestablish contact if the connection is broken and to release the connection when the required communication is finished.

The transport layer packages the file appropriately for the particular network being used. This may involve breaking the file into uniformly sized packets or relaying the file as a single unit. In any case, the transport layer attaches the file's final

Figure 3-13 The OSI reference model at work

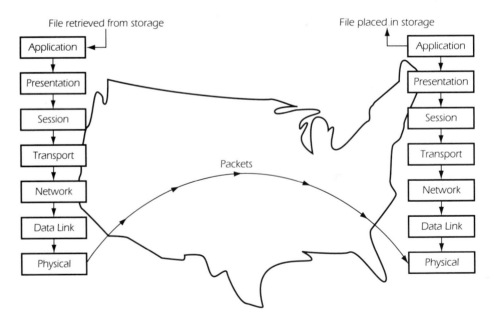

destination address to each unit as it passes the file down the hierarchy to the network layer.

The network layer, knowing the actual configuration of the network, is charged with coordinating the activities particular to the network structure being used. For example, in a token-ring network, the network layer is in charge of relaying the token and inserting new messages behind it. In our example, the network layer is in charge of routing the file through the network. Thus, to each data unit received from the transport layer, the network layer attaches the address of the next intermediate machine along the path to the final destination and then hands each data unit to the data link layer. It is the task of the network layer at each intermediate destination to send each data unit on to the next machine along the path.

The data link layer is in charge of seeing that the data units are communicated accurately. It may do this by applying some form of error detection and correction, such as recoding the data units using an error-correcting code. It then passes the resulting bit patterns to the physical layer for transmission. The physical layer converts these bit patterns into the proper electrical or optical signals and transmits them over the communication line.

Ultimately, the data units are received at the final destination on the east coast and are reassembled into the original file as they work their way up the OSI hierarchy, with each layer essentially reversing the process performed by its counterpart on the west coast. Then, the east coast's application layer places the file in mass storage.

Issues of Security

Although the file-transfer process just discussed consists of many steps, it requires little more time than transferring the file from one place to another within a single machine. Indeed, a person using a machine on a wide area network with the appropriate privileges can obtain real-time access to data anywhere on the system. In fact, in many cases (such as worldwide reservation or credit reference systems), remote data from several locations may be accessed via a network in a manner that gives the appearance of the data being stored on the local machine. In these cases, we say that the remote access is transparent to the user.

Of course, with this ease of communication between machines comes the disadvantage of unauthorized access. In general, the only way a machine has of distinguishing between authorized and unauthorized requests for access to data is by means of passwords. If the correct password is given, the machine grants the requests that follow. However, passwords can be obtained by trickery. One brute force method is to program one machine to repeatedly call another over a network, trying different passwords until the proper combination is achieved. In an effort to thwart such methods, many operating systems are designed to report any avalanche of incorrect passwords.

A more sophisticated defense is to create the illusion of success (called a trapdoor) when false passwords are given and to proceed to give misinformation to the intruder. This has the advantage of holding the interest of the intruder so the communication is maintained until its origin can be traced.

Unfortunately, no protection system is totally effective, and this leads to a multitude of questions regarding the wisdom of placing sensitive information on a networked machine and the liability for the release of inadequately protected information.

Another problem coupled with networks is vandalism, exemplified by the spread of viruses, which are self-replicating programs often designed to destroy files or perform some other malicious act when a predetermined condition is met. Such programs are also spread via floppy disks. Once an infected disk (a disk containing the virus program) is inserted into a machine, the virus can take up residence within that machine, infect other disks used on that machine, and wait for the predetermined condition to trigger its vandalism.

A worm is another type of program used in network vandalism. This program can multiply as it spreads through a network, thus increasing the network's overhead and decreasing the network's efficiency.

As the popularity of networks increases, the potential for damage from unauthorized access to information and vandalism also grows. In turn, the ethical and legal questions associated with these issues promise to lead to extensive debate in the near future.

Questions/Exercises

1. In a ring network, what are some disadvantages to restricting the transfer of messages to a single direction?

2. Suppose the machines in the network of Figure 3-9 are named A, B, C, D, and E (starting from top center and moving clockwise) and that the privilege to transmit a new message is controlled by a token moving counterclockwise. Moreover, suppose A has three messages to place on the network, C has two, D has one, and E has two. If the token is currently between A and B, in what order will the machines transmit their messages?

3. Design a method by which a ring network using a token can recover from the loss of the token due to a malfunction.

4. Identify some standards used at the interfaces between the levels in our shipping example. Explain how the use of these standards allows one shipping company to be substituted for another without altering your approach to sending the parts to your customer.

5. Would it be acceptable for a software developer to counter the problem of software piracy by designing software products that place a virus in those machines that execute an unauthorized copy of the software?

Chapter 3 Review Problems

(Asterisked problems are associated with optional sections.)

1. In each of the following cases, identify which item is hardware and which is software:
   a. newspapers, news
   b. music, player pianos
   c. recipe, cake

2. Explain the distinction between real and virtual characteristics.

3. Identify four virtual characteristics that may be created by an operating system.

4. Explain how operating systems can be used to make different machines appear to have the same characteristics.

5. List four activities of a typical operating system.

6. Summarize the distinction between batch processing and interactive processing.

7. What is the difference between interactive processing and real-time processing?

8. What is a multitasking operating system?

9. Explain how abstraction simplifies the task of solving a problem.

10. Identify three software utilities that normally accompany an operating system.

11. Identify three abstract tools provided by a typical operating system.

12. Identify two ways of classifying computer networks.

*13. Identify four components of an operating system other than the command processor, and summarize the activities of each.

*14. Draw an onion-skin diagram of a restaurant.

*15. Suppose a time-sharing operating system is allotting time slices of 50 milliseconds. If it normally takes 8 milliseconds to position a disk's read/write head over the desired track and another 17 milliseconds for the desired data to rotate around to the read/write head, how much of a program's time slice can be spent waiting for a read operation from a disk to take place? If the machine is capable of executing one instruction each microsecond, how many instructions can be executed during this waiting period? (This is why a time-sharing system normally allows another process to run while the first process is waiting for the services of a peripheral device.)

*16. What activities must the operating system perform when a process requests a logical record from a physical record that
   a. has not yet been read from mass storage?
   b. is already held in main memory because of a previous read request?
   In which of these cases is the process's time slice (in a time-sharing system) most likely terminated? Why?

*17. A process is said to be I/O-bound if it requires a lot of I/O operations, whereas a process that consists of mostly computations within the CPU/ memory system is said to be compute-bound. If both a compute-bound process and an I/O-bound process are waiting for a time slice, which should be given priority? Why?

*18. Would greater throughput be achieved by a system running two processes in a time-sharing environment if both processes were I/O-bound (refer to problem 17) or if one was I/O-bound and the other was compute-bound? Why?

*19. Identify the components of a process's state.

*20. Identify a situation in a time-sharing system in which a process does not consume the entire time-slice allocated to it.

*21. Explain an important use for the test-and-set instruction found in many machine languages. Why is it important for the entire test-and-set process to be implemented as a single instruction?

*22. List in chronological order the major events that take place when a program is interrupted.

*23. A banker with only $100,000 loans $50,000 to each of two customers. Later, both customers return with the story that before they can repay their loans they must each borrow another $10,000 to complete the business deals in which their previous loans are involved. The banker resolves this deadlock by borrowing the additional funds from another source and passing on this loan (with an increase in the interest rate) to the two customers. Which of the three conditions for deadlock has the banker removed?

*24. Students who want to enroll in Model Railroading II at the local university are required to obtain

permission from the instructor and pay a laboratory fee. The two requirements are fulfilled
independently in either order and at different
locations on campus. Enrollment is limited to 20
students; this limit is maintained by both the
instructor, who will grant permission to only 20
students, and the financial office, which will allow
only 20 students to pay the laboratory fee.
Suppose that this registration system has resulted
in 19 students having successfully registered for
the course, but with the final space being claimed
by two students—one who has only obtained
permission from the instructor and another who
has only paid the fee. Which requirement for
deadlock is removed by each of the following
solutions to the problem:

a. Both students are allowed in the course.
b. The class size is reduced to 19, so neither of
    the two students is allowed to register for the
    course.
c. The competing students are both denied
    entry to the class and a third student is given
    the 20th space.
d. It is decided that the only requirement for
    entry into the course is the payment of the
    fee. Thus, the student who has paid the fee
    gets into the course, and entry is denied to the
    other student.

*25. Explain how deadlock can occur as two pawns
approach each other in a chess game. What
nonshareable resources are involved? How is
such deadlock normally broken?

*26. Suppose each nonshareable resource in a com-
puter system is classified as a level 1, level 2, or
level 3 resource. Moreover, suppose each process
in the system is required to request the resources
it needs according to this classification. That is, it
must request all the required level 1 resources at
once before requesting any level 2 resources.
Once it receives the level 1 resources, it can
request all the required level 2 resources, and so
on. Can deadlock occur in such a system? Why or
why not?

*27. Processes in a time-sharing system are normally
considered as being in one of three states:
executing (the process enjoying the current time
slice), ready (the processes waiting for a time
slice), and not ready (the processes that couldn't
make use of a time slice because they are waiting
for the assignment of some required resource,

input from a terminal, or perhaps data to arrive
from a mass storage device). In each of the
following cases, identify the classification to
which the described program will be moved:

a. The executing process at the normal end of a
    time slice.
b. The process at the head of the ready queue at
    the end of a time slice.
c. The executing process that has just requested
    data from mass storage.
d. A process in the not ready state that has just
    been allotted the resource for which it has
    been waiting.

*28. Each of two robot arms is programmed to lift
assemblies from a conveyor belt, test them for
tolerances, and place them in one of two bins
depending on the results of the test. The assemblies arrive one at a time with a sufficient interval
between them. To keep both arms from trying to
grab the same assembly, the computers controlling the arms share a common memory cell. If an
arm is available as an assembly approaches, its
controlling computer reads the value of the
common cell. If the value is nonzero, the arm lets
the assembly pass. Otherwise, the controlling
computer places a nonzero value in the memory
cell, directs the arm to pick up the assembly, and
places the value 0 back into the memory cell.
What sequence of events could lead to a tug-of-
war between the two arms?

*29. Suppose each computer in a ring network is
programmed to transmit simultaneously in both
directions those messages that originate at that
station and are addressed to all the other stations
belonging to the network. Moreover, suppose
this is done by first acquiring access to the
communication path to the machine's left, retaining this access until access to the path to the right
is acquired, and then transmitting the message.
Identify the deadlock that occurs if all the
machines in the network tried to originate such a
message at the same time.

*30. Identify the use of a queue in the process of
spooling output to a printer.

*31. The pavement in the middle of an intersection
can be considered as a nonshareable resource for
which cars approaching the intersection compete. A traffic light rather than an operating
system is used to control the allocation of the
resource. If the light is able to sense the amount

of traffic arriving from each direction and is programmed to give the green light to the heavier traffic, the lighter traffic might suffer from what is called starvation. What is meant by starvation? What could happen in a multiuser computer system where routines are assigned priorities and competition for resources is always resolved strictly by priority?

*32. What problem can occur in a time-sharing system if the dispatcher always assigns time slices according to a priority system in which the priority of each task sharing time remains fixed? (Hint: What is the priority of the routine that just completed its time slice in comparison to the routines that are waiting, and consequently which routine gets the next time slice?)

*33. What is the similarity between deadlock and starvation? (Refer to problem 31.) What is the difference between deadlock and starvation?

*34. What problem arises as the length of the time slices in a time-sharing system are made smaller and smaller? What about as they become longer and longer?

*35. List five resources whose use a multitasking operating system might have to coordinate.

*36. In what way is deadlock avoided in the simple operating system described in Section 3-4?

*37. List the major steps in a general bootstrap process in chronological order.

*38. What is packet switching?

*39. What is the OSI reference model?

*40. Identify two goals of the OSI reference model.

*41. In a network based on the bus topology, the bus is a nonshareable resource for which the machines must compete in order to transmit messages. How is deadlock controlled in this context?

*42. Suppose the machines in Figure 3-9 are called A, B, C, D, and E (starting at the top center and moving clockwise) and that the privilege to transmit a new message is controlled by a single token. If machine D has a message to transmit, and the token is currently between machines B and C, which machines will have an opportunity to transmit before machine D?

*43. Suppose the privilege to transmit a new message in the network in Figure 3-9 is controlled by a single token and that each message, once transmitted, is terminated when it returns to its origin. What is the maximum number of messages that can be active on the network at any time?

Problems for the Programmer

1. What utility routines do you use to prepare and execute a program in your programming language?

2. What utility routines can you request from within a program in your programming language?

3. If you are using an interactive time-sharing system, how can you find out how many users are using the system with you? Does system response become sluggish as this number increases? Why might you expect it to?

4. Write a program that passes an imaginary token back and forth among four potential owners named A, B, C, and D under the restriction that the token can have only one owner at any given time. In particular, a request to give the token to a letter is implemented by typing that letter at the keyboard. If the token is available, your program should respond with the message "Token is now assigned to X" where X is the letter that was typed.

On the other hand, your program should respond with the message "Token is not available" if the token is not available (if it is currently owned by another letter). Typing the letter currently owning the token should cause the token to be released and the program to respond with the message "Token is now available." What similarities and dissimilarities does your program have with a resource allocator controlling access to a nonshareable resource?

5. Expand your program in programming problem 4 to control two tokens called X and Y that might be requested by any of the potential owners. Design your program to avoid deadlock.

6. Write an elementary operating system simulator consisting of a command processor, a file manager, and a scheduler. That is, write a program that accepts commands of the form:

EXECUTE name
DELETE name
CREATE name
LIST

(where "name" implies a character string identifying a fictitious file to be maintained by the system) from the keyboard and responds correctly. More precisely, the command LIST should cause the command processor to ask the file manager to list the names of the files currently being held in the simulated system, and the commands CREATE and DELETE should result in the file manager being requested to insert or remove (respectively) the indicated file. The EXECUTE command should cause the command processor to request the scheduler to schedule the identified program for execution. In this case, of course, the scheduler should check with the file manager to see that the requested program is in fact available. As a way of simulating the scheduling of a program for execution, design the scheduler so that it prints a message such as "PROGRAM X SCHEDULED FOR EXECUTION" at your terminal.

Additional Reading

Comer, D. *Operating System Design: The XINU Approach*. Englewood Cliffs, N.J.: Prentice-Hall, 1984.

Comer, D. *Operating System Design: Internetworking with XINU*. Englewood Cliffs, N.J.: Prentice-Hall, 1987.

Comer, D. *Internetworking with TCP/IP*, 2nd ed. Englewood Cliffs, N.J.: Prentice-Hall, 1991.

Dietel, H. M. *An Introduction to Operating Systems*, 3rd ed. Reading, Mass.: Addison-Wesley, 1994.

Forester, T. and Morrison, P. *Computer Ethics: Cautionary Tales and Ethical Dilemmas*. Cambridge, Mass.: MIT Press, 1990.

Raynal, M. *Distributed Algorithms and Protocols*. New York: John Wiley and Sons, 1988.

Stallings, W. *Local Networks,* 3rd ed. New York: Macmillan, 1990.

Stallings, W. *Operating Systems*. New York: Macmillan, 1992.

Tanenbaum, A. S. *Computer Networks,* 2nd ed. Englewood Cliffs, N.J.: Prentice-Hall, 1989.

Tanenbaum, A. S. *Modern Operating Systems*. Englewood Cliffs, N.J.: Prentice-Hall, 1992.

Walrand, J. *Communication Networks: A First Course*. Boston, Mass.: Aksen Associates, 1991.

CHAPTER FOUR

ALGORITHMS

We have seen that, before a computer can perform a task, it must be given an algorithm telling it precisely what to do, and consequently, the study of algorithms is the cornerstone of computer science. In this chapter, we introduce many of the fundamental concepts of this study, including the issues of algorithm discovery and representation as well as the major control concepts of iterative and recursive structures. In so doing we also present a few well-known algorithms for searching and sorting.

4-1 Definition

In the introductory chapter, we informally introduced the concept of an algorithm. We should now look more closely at the meaning of this term. Our situation is analogous to the need for more precise definitions of terminology in other fields, such as the terms *work* in physics and *real property* in law.

Technically speaking, computer science defines the term **algorithm** as a finite sequence of unambiguous, executable steps that ultimately terminate if followed. You may think that the latter part of this definition (requiring a finite sequence of steps to terminate) is redundant. However, the fact that a list of directions contains only a finite number of steps does not necessarily mean that the described task will ever be completed if followed. For example, the single instruction that reads "Do this step again" results in an endless process, whereas "If you have done this step four times, then stop; otherwise, do it again" terminates. In summary, the latter part of the definition of an algorithm means that an algorithm must be both definable in a finite number of instructions and executable in a finite amount of time.

The use of the term *unambiguous* in the definition of an algorithm means that at each step the action to be performed next must be uniquely determined by the instruction and the data available at that time. Observe that this does not mean that the instruction alone must be enough to determine the desired action. Merely knowing that a person is about to execute the "if" instruction from the previous paragraph is not enough information to determine what that person's action is going to be. We must also know how many times the person has already executed the instruction.

The requirement that each step in an algorithm be executable rules out the possibility of an algorithm containing steps whose execution is impossible. For instance, the sequence of steps

1. Make a list of all the positive integers.
2. Arrange this list in descending order (from largest to smallest).
3. Extract the first integer from the resulting list.
4. Stop.

is not an algorithm because the execution of some of its steps is impossible. One cannot make a list of all the positive integers as requested by step 1, and the positive integers cannot be arranged in descending order as requested by step 2. Computer scientists use the term *effective* to capture this concept of being executable. That is, they speak of an algorithm being effective, whereas we might say that an algorithm must be doable.

The technical definition of an algorithm given above originated in the study of computability, a subject we consider in Chapter 11. The underlying goal of this subject is to determine what problems have solutions that can be obtained by a computational process and thus can be solved by algorithmic machines. Inherent in the concept of computing the solution of a problem is the ability to recognize when the solution has been obtained and thus terminate the computational process. In this sense, then, one is interested in only those computational processes that ultimately stop. This is the source of the termination requirement in our formal definition of an algorithm.

On the other hand, numerous applications in data processing require a nonterminating computational process. For example, the monitoring of a patient's vital signs is a process that should continue performing its task indefinitely. Another example is a computer operating system that continues serving the needs of the machine's users in a cyclical fashion. Applications such as these and the lack of a definitive source of terminology within the computing community have resulted in the informal, and technically incorrect, use of the term *algorithm* in reference to processes that may not terminate. Thus, one must be aware of these variations and not jump to the assumption of termination without first considering the context of the discussion. In this text, however, those processes referred to as algorithms terminate.

Questions/Exercises

1. Give some examples of algorithms with which you are familiar. Are they really algorithms in the precise sense?
2. Why would a natural language such as English not be suited for the communication of algorithms?
3. Why is the following instruction sequence not an algorithm in the precise sense? Modify it so that it is an algorithm.

   Step 1. Take a coin out of your pocket and put it on the table.

   Step 2. Return to step 1.

4-2 Algorithm Representation

We begin by noting that an algorithm itself is purely conceptual. Thus, to communicate an algorithm (perhaps to another person or to a computer), we must find a way to represent the algorithm. The issues involved in algorithm representation constitute the subject of this section.

Syntax and Semantics

Paramount to the subject of algorithm representation is the distinction between syntax and semantics. The term *syntax* refers to the representation, whereas *semantics* refers to the concept represented. The syntactic structure *air* is merely a collection of three letters, but the object represented (the semantics) is a gaseous substance surrounding the entire world.

A major goal in algorithm representation is to ensure that the syntax accurately reflects the intended semantics. Examples abound in language in which such associations are not well defined. For instance, does the statement, "Visiting grandchildren can be nerve-racking" mean that the grandchildren can be nerve-racking when they visit or that going to see them can be nerve-racking?

Another concern is that the syntax should reflect the underlying semantics in an accessible manner. Let us explain by an example. Consider the algorithm for folding a bird from a square piece of paper as represented in Figure 4-1. Our first observation is that the representation of an algorithm can take on a variety of syntactic forms—even a sequence of pictures. Moreover, the form chosen can significantly affect the accessibility of the algorithm being represented. For instance, although you may argue that the representation in Figure 4-1 is not ideal, most would agree that the pictorial form is much more accessible than any representation we might develop if we chose to express the algorithm in a narrative form using ordinary English sentences and paragraphs.

The search for syntactic structures for representing algorithms in an unambiguous, accessible manner is a continuing effort in computer science.

Primitives

Let us reconsider Figure 4-1, which although superior to a narrative representation still has some communication deficiencies. One results from the fact that two-dimensional line drawings often fail to capture the reality of three-dimensional space, and thus the drawings are at times ambiguous. Another is that in some cases the difference between two consecutive drawings is too great to communicate the steps involved in bridging the gap.

These problems are actually special cases of general algorithm representation issues, one being the need for an unambiguous syntax, the other being the need for a well-established level of detail at which the algorithm should be expressed. Computer science attacks both of these issues through the use of primitives. A *primitive* consists of a well-defined semantic structure together with an unambiguous syntax for representing it. Using this approach, the aforementioned problems in algorithm representation are overcome by first establishing a rich enough collection of primitives so that any algorithm can be expressed as a combination of them and

Figure 4-1 Folding a bird from a square piece of paper

then expressing all algorithms in these terms. Such a collection of primitives along with the rules by which they can be combined to represent more complex structures constitutes a *programming language.*

As an example, we could go a long way toward producing a better representation of the bird-folding algorithm by first establishing the general origami primi-

Figure 4-2 Origami primitives

Syntax	**Semantics**

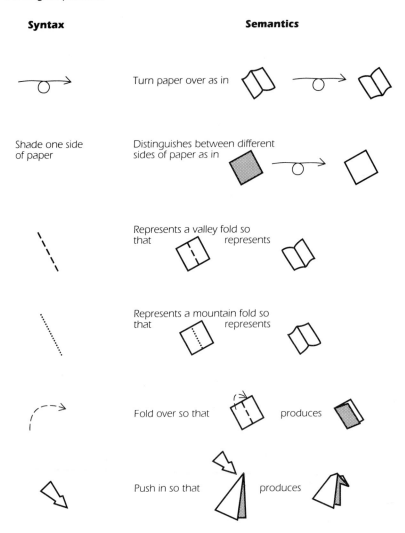

tives shown in Figure 4-2. Then, we could describe the algorithm for folding the bird using these primitives as building blocks. A portion of the result is shown in Figure 4-3, where we have concentrated on the process of forming the bird's head.

To obtain a collection of primitives to use in representing algorithms for computer execution, we could turn to the individual instructions that the machine is designed to execute. After all, if an algorithm is expressed at this level of detail, we will certainly have a program suitable for machine execution. However, expressing algorithms at this level is extremely tedious, and hence, one normally uses a collection

Figure 4-3 Forming the bird's head

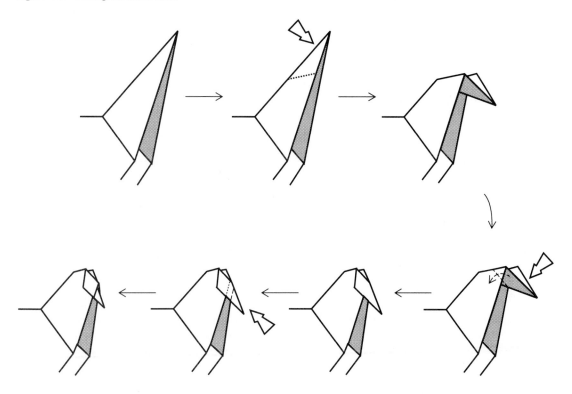

of "higher-level" primitives, each of which can be constructed by combining the primitives provided in the machine's language. The result is a programming language in which algorithms can be expressed in a conceptually higher form than in the actual machine language. Such languages are called high-level programming languages and are discussed in the next chapter.

Pseudocode

For now, we forego the introduction of a formal high-level programming language in favor of a less formal, more intuitive notational system known as *pseudocode.* In general, a pseudocode is a notational system in which ideas can be expressed informally during the algorithm development process.

One way to obtain a pseudocode is simply to loosen the rules of the formal language in which the final version of the algorithm is to be expressed. This is a common approach in those settings in which the target programming language is known in advance. There the pseudocode used during the early stages of program development consists of syntax-semantic structures similar to, but less formal than, those used in the target programming language.

Our goal, however, is to consider the issues of algorithm development and representation without confining our discussion to a particular programming language. Thus, our approach to pseudocode is to develop a consistent, concise notation for representing recurring semantic structures. In turn, these structures will become the primitives in which we attempt to express future ideas.

For example, the need to select one of two possible activities depending on the truth or falsity of some condition is a common algorithmic structure. Examples include:

> If the gross domestic product has increased, buy common stock;
> otherwise, sell common stock.

Buy common stock if the gross domestic product has increased and sell it otherwise.

> Buy or sell common stock depending on whether the gross domestic product has increased or decreased, respectively.

Each of these statements could be rewritten to conform to the structure

if *(condition)* **then** *(activity)*
else *(activity)*

where we have used the key words **if, then,** and **else** to announce the different substructures within the main structure and parentheses to delimit the boundaries of these substructures. By adopting this syntactic structure for our pseudocode, we acquire a uniform way in which to express this common semantic structure. This, then, is exactly what we do. In fact, we also adopt the shorter syntax

if *(condition)* **then** *(activity)*

for those cases not involving an **else** activity. Thus, whereas the statement

> Depending on whether or not the year is a leap year,
> divide the total by 366 or 365, respectively.

may possess a more creative literary style, we will consistently opt for the straightforward

if (year is leap year)
then (divide total by 366)
else (divide total by 365)

and

> Should it be the case that sales have decreased, lower the price by 5%.

will be reduced to

if (sales have decreased) **then** (lower the price by 5%)

Another common algorithmic structure involves the need to continue executing a statement or sequence of statements as long as some condition remains true. Informal examples include

As long as there are tickets to sell, continue selling tickets.

and

While there are tickets to sell, keep selling tickets.

For all such cases, we adopt the uniform pattern

while *(condition)* **do** *(activity)*

for our pseudocode. In short, such a statement means to check the *condition* and, if it is true, perform the *activity* and return to check the *condition* again. If the *condition* is ever found to be false, move on to the next instruction following the **while** structure. Thus, both of the preceding statements are reduced to

while *(tickets remain to be sold)* **do** *(sell a ticket)*

Modular Design

Up to this point, we have been discussing the role of syntax-semantic relationships in reference to the goal of producing unambiguous programs. However, the removal of ambiguity is not the only concern in algorithm representation. Equally important is that the final program be easy to understand and modify. This, in fact, is the reason we will use indentation in our pseudocode. The statement

if *(item is taxable)*
  then [**if** *(price > limit)*
    then *(pay x)*
    else *(pay y)*]
  else *(pay z)*

is easier to comprehend than the otherwise equivalent

if *(item is taxable)* **then** [**if** *(price > limit)* **then** *(pay x)*
  else *(pay y)*] **else** *(pay z)*

(Note that we have also introduced the use of brackets to alleviate the confusion of nested parentheses.)

We see, then, that the organization of an algorithm's representation is as important to clarity as the design and selection of primitives. One technique for obtaining a well-organized representation is to construct it in a modular fashion. That is, we divide the task performed by the algorithm into small units (or modules) and represent each of these modules separately. Then, these modules can be used as abstract tools to construct other modules that tackle larger portions of the overall task. The result is a representation that is organized in varying levels of detail. At the highest level, we find the steps of the algorithm stated in terms of large units whose functions are closely related to the overall task at hand. As we shift our attention to lower levels in the hierarchy, we find each individual task defined in more detail and in terminology more closely associated with the primitives in which all tasks are ultimately defined. Thus, anyone approaching such a representation is able to grasp its composition with relative ease and to evaluate it (or part of it) at the degree of detail desired.

If we apply the concept of modular design to our presentation of the bird-folding algorithm, the result might appear as in Figure 4-4. There we have described the algorithm in terms of major subtasks such as folding the base, forming the leg structure, and shaping the body. Each of these activities can then be presented in more detail in another drawing where the additional precision does not contribute to the clutter of detail from the other steps. In particular, the process of forming the head could be described as already shown in Figure 4-3.

With these examples in mind, we should extend our pseudocode to allow for the modular representation of algorithms. For this we first allow a module to be given a name by beginning that module with a statement of the form

procedure *name*

where *name* is the name to be given the module consisting of the instructions that follow this statement. Then, we allow that module to be used elsewhere merely by requesting its services. As an example, if two modules were given the names ProcessLoan and RejectApplication, then they could be used to simplify an otherwise complex **if-then-else** structure by writing

Figure 4-4 Folding a bird using modules

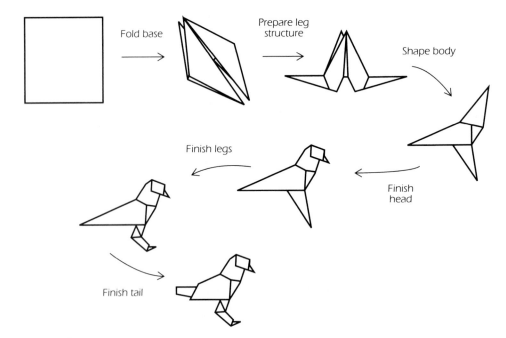

> **if** (. . .) **then** (Execute the module ProcessLoan)
> **else** (Execute the module RejectApplication)

which would result in the execution of the procedure ProcessLoan if the tested condition were true or in the execution of RejectApplication if the condition were false.

Modules should be designed to be as generic as possible. A module for sorting lists of names should be designed to sort any list—not a particular one. Thus, the module should be written in such a way that the list to be sorted is not specified in the module itself. Instead, the list should be referred to by a generic name within the module's representation.

In our pseudocode, we will adopt the convention of listing these generic names in parentheses on the same line on which we identify the module's name. In particular, a module named Sort, which is designed to sort any list of names, would begin with the statement

> **procedure** Sort (List)

Later in the representation where a reference to the list being sorted is required, the generic name List would be used. In turn, when the services of Sort are required in another module, we will identify which list is to be substituted for List in the procedure Sort. Thus, we write something such as

> Apply the procedure Sort to the organization's membership list

and

> Apply the procedure Sort to the wedding guest list

depending on our needs.

As a final example, suppose we want to apply the module EvenOdd as represented in Figure 4-5 to the values 4 and 7. Then the statement

> Apply EvenOdd to the values 4 and 7

results in the message

> Only the first value is even.

Figure 4-5 A module expressed in our pseudocode

> **procedure** EvenOdd (FirstValue, SecondValue)
>   **If** (FirstValue and SecondValue are even)
>   **then** (Print "Both values are even.")
>   **If** (FirstValue is even and SecondValue is odd)
>   **then** (Print "Only the first value is even.")
>   **If** (FirstValue is odd and SecondValue is even)
>   **then** (Print "Only the second value is even.")
>   **If** (FirstValue and SecondValue are odd)
>   **then** (Print "Both values are odd.")

whereas the statement

Apply EvenOdd to the values 7 and 4

results in the message

Only the second value is even.

Keep in mind that the purpose of our pseudocode is to provide a means of jotting down rough outlines of algorithms—not the writing of finished, formal programs. Thus, we will feel free to insert informal phrases that request activities whose details are not rigorously specified. (How these details are resolved is not so much a feature of the algorithm being expressed as it is a property of the language in which the formal program is ultimately written.) If, however, we find a particular idea recurring in our outlines, we will adopt a consistent syntax for representing it and thus extend our pseudocode.

Questions/Exercises

1. A primitive in one context may turn out to be a composite of primitives in another. For instance, our **while** statement is a primitive in our pseudocode, yet it is implemented as a composite of machine-language instructions. Give two other examples of this phenomenon in a noncomputer setting.

2. In what sense is the construction of modules the construction of primitives?

3. The Euclidean algorithm finds the greatest common divisor of two positive integers X and Y by the following process:

   As long as the value of neither X nor Y is zero, continue dividing the larger of the values by the smaller and assigning X and Y the values of the divisor and remainder, respectively. (The final value of X is the greatest common divisor.) Express this algorithm in our pseudocode.

4. Describe a collection of primitives that are used in a subject other than computer programming.

4-3 Algorithm Discovery

The development of a program consists of two activities—discovering the underlying algorithm and representing that algorithm as a program. Up to this point, we have been concerned with the issues of algorithm representation without considering the question of how algorithms are found in the first place. Yet algorithm discovery is usually the more challenging step in the software development process. After all, to discover an algorithm is to find a method of solving that problem whose solution the algorithm is to compute. Thus, to understand how algorithms are discovered is to understand the problem-solving process.

The Theory of Problem Solving

The techniques of problem solving and the need to learn more about them are not unique to computer science, but rather they are topics pertinent to almost any field. On the other hand, the close association between the process of algorithm discovery and that of general problem solving has caused computer scientists to join with those of other disciplines in the search for better problem-solving techniques. Ultimately, one would like to reduce the process of problem solving to an algorithm in itself, but this has been shown to be impossible. (This is a result of the material in Chapter 11, where we show that there are problems that do not have algorithmic solutions.) Thus, the ability to solve problems remains more of an artistic skill to be developed than a precise science to be learned.

As evidence of the illusive, artistic nature of problem solving, the loosely defined problem-solving phases presented by the mathematician G. Polya in the late 1940s remain the major principles on which attempts to teach problem-solving skills are based today. (Actually, Polya's work was preceded by the research of H. von Helmholtz [late 1800s], J. Dewey [1930s], and others who studied the problem-solving process in general settings. Polya is usually quoted by computer scientists because his work dealt with problem solving in the context of mathematics—a close cousin of computer science.) Polya's problem-solving phases are

Phase 1. Understand the problem.

Phase 2. Devise a plan for solving the problem.

Phase 3. Carry out the plan.

Phase 4. Evaluate the solution for accuracy and for its potential as a tool for solving other problems.

Translated into the context of program development, these phases become

Phase 1. Understand the problem.

Phase 2. Get an idea as to how an algorithmic procedure might solve the problem.

Phase 3. Formulate the algorithm and represent it as a program.

Phase 4. Evaluate the program for accuracy and for its potential as a tool for solving other problems.

Having presented Polya's list, we should emphasize that these phases are not steps to be followed when trying to solve a problem but rather phases that will be completed sometime during the solution process. The key word here is *followed*. You do not solve problems by following. Rather, to solve a problem, you must take the initiative and lead. If you approach the task of solving a problem in the frame of mind depicted by "Now I've finished phase 1, it's time to move on to phase 2," you are not likely to be successful. However, if you become involved with the problem and ultimately solve it, you most likely can look back at what you did and realize that Polya's four phases had been completed.

Another important observation is that Polya's four phases are not necessarily completed in sequence. Contrary to the claim made by many authors, successful problem solvers often start formulating strategies for solving a problem (phase 2) before the problem itself is entirely understood (phase 1). Then, if these strategies fail (during phases 3 or 4), the potential problem solver gains a deeper understanding of the intricacies of the problem and, based on this deeper understanding, can return to form other and hopefully more successful strategies.

Keep in mind that we are discussing how problems are solved—not how we would like them to be solved. Ideally, we would like to eliminate the waste inherent in the trial-and-error process just described. In the case of developing large software systems, discovering a misunderstanding as late as phase 4 can represent a tremendous loss in resources. Avoiding such catastrophes is a major goal of software engineers (Chapter 6), who have traditionally insisted on a thorough understanding of a problem before proceeding with a solution. One could argue, however, that a true understanding of a problem is not obtained until a solution has been found. The mere fact that a problem is unsolved implies a lack of understanding. Thus, to insist on a complete understanding of the problem before proposing any solutions is somewhat idealistic.

As an example, consider the following problem:

> Person A is charged with the task of determining the ages of person B's three children. B tells A that the product of the children's ages is 36. After considering this clue, A replies that another clue is required, so B tells A the sum of the children's ages. Again, A replies that another clue is needed, so B tells A that the oldest child plays the piano. After hearing this clue, A tells B the ages of the three children. How old are the three children?

At first glance the last clue seems to be totally unrelated to the problem. However, it is this clue that allows A to finally determine the ages of the children. How can this be? Let us proceed by formulating a plan of attack and following this plan, even though we still have many questions about the problem. Our plan will be to trace the steps described by the problem statement while keeping track of the information available to person A as the story progresses.

The first clue given A is that the product of the children's ages is 36. This means that the triple representing the three ages is one of those listed in Figure 4-6(a). The next clue is the sum of the desired triple. We are not told what this sum is, but we are told that this information is not enough for A to isolate the correct triple; therefore, the desired triple must be one whose sum appears at least twice in the table of Figure 4-6(b). But the only triples appearing in Figure 4-6(b) with identical sums are (1,6,6) and (2,2,9), both of which produce the sum 13. This is the information

Figure 4-6

(1,1,36)	(1,6,6)
(1,2,18)	(2,2,9)
(1,3,12)	(2,3,6)
(1,4,9)	(3,3,4)

(a) Triples whose product is 36

$1 + 1 + 36 = 38$	$1 + 6 + 6 = 13$
$1 + 2 + 18 = 21$	$2 + 2 + 9 = 13$
$1 + 3 + 12 = 16$	$2 + 3 + 6 = 11$
$1 + 4 + 9 = 14$	$3 + 3 + 4 = 10$

(b) Sums of triples from part **a**

available to A at the time the last clue is given. It is at this point that we finally understand the significance of the last clue. It has nothing to do with playing the piano; rather it is the fact that there is an oldest child. This rules out the triple (1,6,6) and thus allows us to conclude that the children's ages are 2, 2, and 9.

In this case, then, it is not until we attempt to implement our plan for solving the problem (phase 3) that we gain a complete understanding of the problem (phase 1). Had we insisted on completing phase 1 before proceeding, we would probably never have found the children's ages. Such irregularities in the problem-solving process are fundamental to the difficulties in developing systematic approaches to problem solving.

Another irregularity is the mysterious inspiration that may come to a potential problem solver who, having worked on a problem without apparent success, may at a later time suddenly see the solution while doing another task. This phenomenon was identified by Helmholtz as early as 1896 and was discussed by the mathematician Henri Poincaré in a lecture before the Psychological Society in Paris. There Poincaré described his experiences of realizing the solution to a problem he had worked on after he had set it aside and begun other projects. The phenomenon is as though a subconscious part of the mind continues working and, if successful, immediately forces the solution into the conscious mind. Today, the period between consciously working on a problem and the sudden inspiration is known as an incubation period, and its understanding remains a goal of current research.

Getting a Foot in the Door

We have been discussing problem solving from a somewhat philosophical point of view while avoiding a direct confrontation with the question of how we should go about trying to solve a problem. There are, of course, numerous problem-solving approaches, each of which can be successful in certain but not all settings. We will identify some of these shortly. For now, we note that there seems to be a common thread running through these techniques, which simply stated is "get your foot in the door." As an example, let us consider the following simple problem:

Before A, B, C, and D ran a race they made the following predictions:

A predicted that B would win.
B predicted that D would be last.
C predicted that A would be third.
D predicted that A's prediction would be correct.

Only one of these predictions was true, and this was the prediction made by the winner. In what order did A, B, C, and D finish the race?

After reading the problem and analyzing the data, it should not take long to realize that since the predictions of A and D were equivalent and only one prediction was true, the predictions of both A and D must be false. Thus, neither A nor D were winners. At this point we have our foot in the door, and obtaining the complete solution to our problem is merely a matter of extending our knowledge from here. If A's prediction was false, then B did not win either. The only remaining choice for the winner is C. Thus, C won the race and C's prediction was true. Consequently, we know that A came in third. That means that the finishing order was either CBAD or CDAB. But, the former is ruled out since B's prediction must be false. Therefore, the finishing order was CDAB.

Of course, being told to get our foot in the door is not the same as being told how to do it. Obtaining this toehold, as well as realizing how to expand this initial thrust into a complete solution to the problem, requires creative input from the would-be problem solver. There are, however, several general approaches that have been proposed by Polya and others for how one might go about getting a foot in the door. One of these is to try working the problem backward. For instance, if the problem is to find a way of producing a particular output from a given input, one might start with that output and attempt to back up to the given input. This approach is typical of someone trying to discover the bird-folding algorithm in the previous section. They tend to unfold a completed bird in an attempt to see how it is constructed.

Another general problem-solving approach is to look for a related problem that is either easier to solve or has been solved before and then try to apply its solution to the current problem. This technique is of particular value in the context of program development. Often the major difficulty in program development is not that of solving a particular instance of a problem but rather of finding a general algorithm that can be used to solve all instances of the problem. More precisely, if we were faced with the task of developing a program for sorting lists of names, our task would not be to sort a particular list but to find a general algorithm that could be used to sort any list of names. Thus, although the instructions

Interchange the names David and Alice.
Move the name Carol to the position between Alice and David.
Move the name Bob to the position between Alice and Carol.

correctly sort the list David, Alice, Carol, and Bob, they do not constitute the general-purpose algorithm we desire. What we need is an algorithm that can sort this list as well as other lists we may encounter. This is not to say that our solution for sorting a particular list is totally worthless in our search for a general-purpose algorithm. We might, for instance, get our foot in the door by considering such special cases in an attempt to find general principles that can in turn be used to develop the desired general-purpose algorithm. In this case, then, our solution is obtained by the technique of solving a collection of related problems.

Still another approach to getting a foot in the door is to apply *stepwise refinement,* which is essentially the technique of not trying to conquer an entire task (in all its gory detail) at once. Rather, stepwise refinement proposes that one first view the problem at hand in terms of several subproblems. The idea is that by breaking the original problem into subproblems, one is able to approach the overall solution in terms of steps, each of which is easier to solve than the entire original problem. In turn, stepwise refinement proposes that these steps be decomposed into smaller steps and these smaller steps be broken into still smaller ones until the entire problem has been reduced to a collection of easily solved subproblems.

In this light, stepwise refinement is a top-down methodology in that it progresses from the general to the specific. In contrast, bottom-up methodologies progress from the specific to the general. Although contrasting in theory, the two approaches actually complement each other in practice. For instance, the decomposition of a problem proposed by the top-down methodology of stepwise refinement is often guided by the problem solver's intuition, which is working in a bottom-up mode.

Solutions produced by stepwise refinement possess a natural modular structure, and herein lies a major reason for the popularity of stepwise refinement in algorithm design. Indeed, if an algorithm has a natural modular structure, then it is easily adapted to a modular representation, which we have seen is conducive to the development of a manageable program. Furthermore, the subproblems produced by stepwise refinement are compatible with the concept of team programming, in which several people are assigned the task of developing a software product as a team. After all, once the task of the software has been broken into subproblems (or potential modules), the personnel on the team can work independently on these subtasks without getting in each other's way.

These advantages of stepwise refinement in the context of software development have produced many followers of the technique. However, with all its good points, stepwise refinement is not the final word in algorithm discovery. Rather, it is essentially an organizational tool whose problem-solving attributes are consequences of this organization. Stepwise refinement is a natural methodology to use when organizing a nationwide political campaign, writing a term paper, or planning a sales convention. Similarly, most software development projects in the data processing community have a large organizational component. The task is not so much that of discovering a startling new algorithm as it is a problem of organizing the tasks to be performed into a coherent package. Thus, stepwise refinement has correctly become a major design methodology in data processing and is a technique in which potential programmers and systems analysts should be trained. But stepwise refinement remains only one of many design methodologies of interest to computer scientists, and thus one should not be misled into believing that all algorithm discoveries can be achieved by means of stepwise refinement.

In the last analysis, then, algorithm discovery remains a challenging art that must be developed over a period of time rather than taught as an isolated subject consisting of well-defined methodologies. Indeed, to train a potential problem solver to follow certain methodologies is to squash those creative skills that should instead be nurtured.

Questions/Exercises

1. a. Among all the lists of positive integers whose sum is 2001, find the list whose product is the largest.
   b. Use the insight gained from solving part a to obtain an algorithm for solving the same problem for values other than 2001.
2. a. Suppose we are given a checkerboard consisting of 2^n rows and 2^n columns of squares, for some positive integer n, and a box of L-shaped tiles, each of which can cover exactly three squares on the board. If any single square is cut out of the board, can we cover the remaining board with tiles such that tiles do not overlap or hang off the edge of the board?
   b. Explain how your solution to part a can be used to show that $2^{2n} - 1$ is divisible by 3 for all positive integers n.
   c. How are parts a and b related to Polya's phases of problem solving?
3. Decode the following message. Then, explain how you got your foot in the door.

   Pdeo eo pda yknnayp wjosan.

4. Design an algorithm that a magician could follow to predict (correctly) the sum of all the top and bottom faces of four dice that have been tossed on a table, assuming that the magician can see only one of the dice. To what extent does the development of this algorithm consist of following predetermined problem-solving steps? To what extent does it consist of creativity and insight? How did you get your foot in the door?

4-4 Iterative Structures

Our goal now is to study some of the repetitive structures used in describing algorithmic processes. In this section we discuss *iterative structures* in which a collection of instructions is repeated in a looping manner, and in the next section we introduce the technique of recursion. Moreover, as examples, we introduce some popular algorithms for searching and sorting—the sequential and binary searches and the insertion and quick sorts—since they involve applications of the repetitive structures being considered. We begin, then, by introducing the sequential search algorithm.

The Sequential Search Algorithm

Consider the problem of searching a list for the occurrence of a particular target value. We want to develop an algorithm that determines whether or not that value is in the list. If the value is in the list, we consider the search a success; otherwise, we consider it a failure. We assume that the list is sorted according to some rule for ordering its entries. For example, if the list is a list of names, we assume the names appear in alphabetical order, or if the list is a list of numbers, we assume its entries appear in order of increasing magnitude.

To get our foot in the door, we imagine how we might search a guest list of perhaps 20 entries for a particular name. In this setting, we might scan the list from its beginning, comparing each entry with the target name. If we find the target name, the search terminates as a success. However, if we reach the end of the list or reach a name greater than (alphabetically) the target name, our search terminates as a failure. (Remember, the list is arranged in alphabetical order, so reaching a name greater than the target name indicates that the target does not appear in the list.) In summary, our rough idea is to continue searching down the list as long as there are more names to be investigated and the target name is less than the name currently being considered.

In our pseudocode, this process can be represented as

> Select the first entry in the list as the test entry.
> **while** (target value > test entry and
> there remain entries to be considered)
> **do** (Select the next entry in the list as the test entry)

Upon terminating the **while** structure, either the test entry is no less than the target name or it is the last name in the list. In either case, we can detect a successful search by comparing the test entry to the target value. If these are equal, the search has been successful. Thus, we add the statement

> **if** (target value = test entry)
> **then** (Declare the search a success.)
> **else** (Declare the search a failure.)

to the end of the pseudocode routine presented above.

Finally, we observe that the first statement in our search routine is based on the assumption that the list in question contains at least one entry. We might reason that this is a safe guess, but just to be sure we can position our routine as the **else** option of the statement

> **if** (List empty)
> > **then** (Declare search a failure.)
> > **else** (. . .)

which produces the module shown in Figure 4-7. Note that this module can be used to perform searches in other modules by statements such as

> Apply the procedure Search to the passenger list to look for the name Darrel Baker.

to find out if Darrel Baker is a passenger and

> Apply the procedure Search to the list of ingredients using nutmeg as the target value.

to find out if nutmeg appears in the list of ingredients.

In summary, the algorithm represented by Figure 4-7 directs a sequential search that considers the entries in the order in which they occur in the list. For this reason, the algorithm is called the *sequential search algorithm.* Because of its simplicity, it is often used for short lists or in cases where other concerns dictate its use. However, in the case of long lists, sequential searches are not as efficient as other techniques (as we shall soon see).

Loop Control

The repetitive use of an instruction sequence is an important algorithmic concept. One method of implementing such repetition is the iterative structure known as the *loop,* in which a collection of instructions, called the body of the loop, is executed in a repetitive fashion under the direction of some control process. A typical example is found in the sequential search algorithm represented in Figure 4-7. Here we use a **while** statement to control the repetition of the single statement Select the next entry in List as the test entry. Indeed, the **while** statement

> **while** (condition) **do** (body)

Figure 4-7 The sequential search algorithm in pseudocode

> **procedure** Search (List, TargetValue)
> > **If** (List empty)
> > > **then**
> > > > (Declare search a failure.)
> > > **else**
> > > > [Select the first entry in List as the test entry;
> > > > **while** (TargetValue > test entry and
> > > > > there remain entries to be considered)
> > > > > **do** (Select the next entry in List as the test
> > > > > > entry.);
> > > > **If** (TargetValue = test entry)
> > > > > **then** (Declare search a success.)
> > > > > **else** (Declare search a failure.)]

exemplifies the concept of a loop structure in that its execution traces the cyclic pattern

> check the *condition*
> execute the *body*
> check the *condition*
> execute the *body*
>
> .
> .
> .

until the condition fails.

As a general rule the use of a loop structure produces a higher degree of flexibility than would be obtained merely by writing the body several times. For example, although the loop structure

> Execute the statement "Add a drop of sulfuric acid" three times.

is equivalent to the sequence

> Add a drop of sulfuric acid.
> Add a drop of sulfuric acid.
> Add a drop of sulfuric acid.

we cannot produce a similar sequence that is equivalent to the loop described by

> **while** (the pH level is greater than 4) **do**
> (add a drop of sulfuric acid)

because we do not know in advance how many drops of acid will be required.

Let us now take a closer look at the composition of loop control. You may be tempted to view this part of a loop structure as having minor importance. After all, it is typically the body of the loop that actually performs the task at hand (for example, adding drops of acid)—the control activities appear merely as the overhead involved because we chose to execute the body in a repetitive fashion. However, experience has shown that the control of a loop is the more error-prone part of the structure and therefore deserves our attention.

The control of a loop consists of the three activities initialize, modify, and test (Figure 4-8, on the following page), with the presence of each being required for successful loop control. The test activity has the obligation of causing the termination of the looping process by watching for a condition that indicates termination should take place. It is for the purpose of this test activity that we provide a condition within each **while** statement of our pseudocode. This is the condition under which the body of the loop should be executed. Thus, the termination condition is the negation of the condition stated in the **while** structure.

The other two activities in the loop control assure the termination condition will ultimately occur. The initialization step establishes a starting condition, and the modification step moves this condition toward the termination condition. For

Figure 4-8 Components of repetitive control

Initialize:	Establish an initial state that will be modified toward the termination condition
Modify:	Change the state in such a way that it moves toward the termination condition
Test:	Compare the current state to the termination condition and terminate the repetition if equal

instance, in Figure 4-7 initialization takes place in the statement preceding the **while** statement, where the current test entry is established as the first list entry. The modification step in this case is actually accomplished within the loop body, where our position of interest is moved toward the end of the list. Thus, having executed the initialization step, repeated application of the modification step results in the termination condition being reached. (If we never find the target value, we ultimately reach the end of the list.)

We should emphasize that the initialization and modification steps must lead to the appropriate termination condition. This characteristic is critical for proper loop control, and thus one should always double-check for its presence when designing a loop structure. Failure to make such an evaluation can lead to errors even in the simplest cases. A typical example is the use of a termination condition, such as testing a location for the value 6, initializing the location at 1, and then using the addition of 2 as the modification step. In this case, as the loop cycles, the location in question contains the values 1, 3, 5, 7, 9, and so on, but never the value 6. Thus, the loop never terminates.

There are two popular loop structures that differ merely in the order in which the loop control components are executed. The first is exemplified by our pseudocode statement

while (condition) **do** (activity)

whose semantics is represented in Figure 4-9. The test for termination is performed before the loop's body is executed.

In contrast, the structure in Figure 4-10 requests that the body of the loop be executed before the test for termination is performed. In this alternative structure, the loop's body is always performed at least once, whereas in the **while** structure the body is never executed if the termination condition is satisfied the first time it is tested.

We use the syntactic form

repeat (activity) **until** (condition)

Figure 4-9 The **while** loop structure

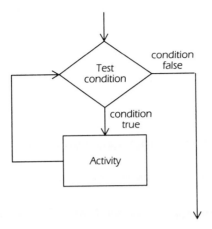

Figure 4-10 The **repeat** loop structure

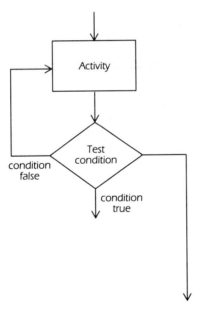

in our pseudocode to represent the structure shown in Figure 4-10. Thus, the statement

   repeat (take a coin from your pocket)
   until (there are no coins in your pocket)

assumes there is a coin in your pocket at the beginning, but

> **while** (there is a coin in your pocket)
> **do** (take a coin from your pocket)

does not.

The Insertion Sort Algorithm

As an additional example of the use of iterative structures, let us consider the problem of sorting a list of names into alphabetical order. But before proceeding, we should identify the constraints under which we will work. Simply stated, our goal is to sort the list "within itself." In other words, we want to sort the list by shuffling its entries as opposed to moving the list to another location. This rules out the technique of reconstructing the list in another location in such a way that the new version is sorted.

Our situation is analogous to the problem of sorting a list whose entries are recorded on separate index cards spread out on a crowded desk top. We have cleared off enough space for the cards but are not allowed to push additional materials back to make more room. This restriction is typical in computer applications, not because the work space within the machine is necessarily crowded like our desk top, but simply because we want to use the storage space available in an efficient manner.

Let us get a foot in the door by considering how we might sort the names on the desk top. Consider the list of names

> Fred
> Alice
> David
> Bill
> Carol

One approach to sorting this list is to note that the list consisting of only the top name, Fred, is sorted but a list consisting of the top two names, Fred and Alice, is not. Thus, we might pick up the card containing the name Alice, slide the name Fred down into the space where Alice was, and then place the name Alice in the hole at the top of the list, as represented by the first row in Figure 4-11. At this point our list would be

> Alice
> Fred
> David
> Bill
> Carol

Now the top two names form a sorted list, but the top three do not. Thus, we might pick up the third name, David, slide the name Fred down into the hole where David was, and then insert David in the hole left by Fred, as summarized in the second row of Figure 4-11. The top three entries in the list would now be sorted. Continuing in this fashion, we could obtain a list in which the top four entries are sorted by picking

Figure 4-11 Sorting the list Fred, Alice, David, Bill, and Carol

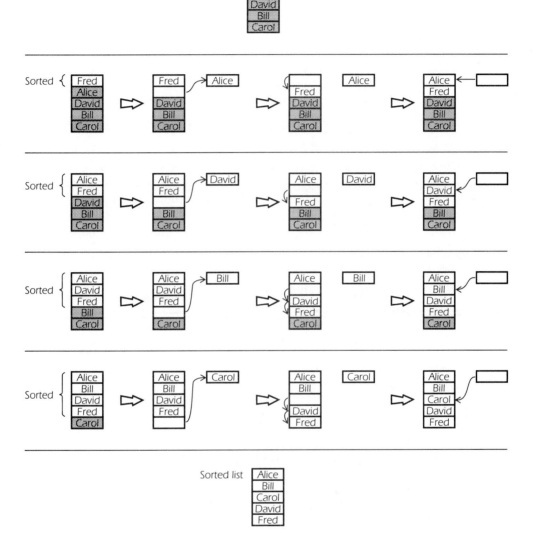

up the fourth name, Bill, sliding the names Fred and David down, and then inserting Bill in the hole (see the third row of Figure 4-11). Finally, we can complete the sorting process by picking up Carol, sliding Fred and David down, and then inserting Carol in the remaining hole (see the fourth row of Figure 4-11).

Having analyzed the process of sorting a particular list, our task now is to generalize this process to obtain an algorithm for sorting general lists. To this end, we observe that each row of Figure 4-11 represents the same general process: Pick up the first name in the unsorted portion of the list, slide the names greater than the extracted name down, and insert the extracted name back in the list where the hole appears. If we identify the extracted name as the pivot entry, this process can be expressed in our pseudocode as

```
Move the pivot entry to a temporary location leaving a hole in List;
while (there is a name above the hole and that name is greater than the pivot) do
        (move the name above the hole down into the hole leaving a hole above the name)
Move the pivot entry into the hole in List
```

Next, we observe that this process should be executed repeatedly, starting with the pivot being the second list entry and then advancing the pivot assignment one entry down the list before each additional execution until the last list entry has been positioned. This advancement of the pivot assignment is indicated in Figure 4-11 by means of shading. At any point in the figure, the portion of the list below the last pivot assignment is shaded. Each row in the figure begins by picking the top entry from the shaded portion to be the pivot and removing the shading from this position in the list. Thus, we can control the repetition of the preceding pseudocode routine with the statements

```
Shade the portion of List from the second entry through the last entry;
repeat
    (Remove the shading from the first name in the shaded portion of List and
        identify this name as the pivot entry

            .
            .
            .    )
    until (entire List is unshaded)
```

where the dots indicate the location where the previous routine should be placed.

Of course, our routine so far assumes that there are at least two entries in the list to be sorted, an assumption that should not be made in general. On the other hand, if the list in question has fewer than two entries, it must be sorted already. Thus, we can extend our routine to handle such cases merely by starting with the statement

```
if (there are two or more entries in List)
then (. . .)
```

Our complete pseudocode program is shown in Figure 4-12. In short, the program sorts a list by repeatedly removing an entry and inserting it into its proper place. It is because of this repeated insertion process that the underlying algorithm is called the *insertion sort*.

Note that the structure of Figure 4-12 is that of a loop within a loop, the outer loop being expressed by the **repeat** statement and the inner loop represented by the **while** statement. Each execution of the body of the outer loop results in the inner loop

Figure 4-12 *The insertion sort expressed in pseudocode*

```
procedure Sort (List)
If (there are two or more entries in List) then
    [shade the portion of List from the second entry
        through the last entry;
    repeat
        (Remove the shading from the first name in the shaded
            portion of List and identify this name as the
            pivot entry;
        Move the pivot entry to a temporary location leaving
            a hole in List;
        while (there is a name above the hole and that name
                is greater than the pivot) do
                (move the name above the hole down into the hole
                    leaving a hole above the name)
        Move the pivot entry into the hole in List)
    until (entire List is unshaded)]
```

being initialized and executed until its termination condition is obtained. Thus, a single execution of the outer loop's body will result in several executions of the inner loop's body.

The initialization component of the outer loop's control consists of shading the portion of the list from the second entry to the last. The modification component is handled by the statement

> Remove the shading from the first name in the shaded
> portion of List and identify this name as the
> pivot entry;

The termination condition occurs when the shaded portion of the list becomes empty, as indicated by the **until** clause.

The inner loop's control is initialized by removing the pivot entry from the list that creates a hole. The loop's modification step is accomplished by moving entries above the hole down, thus moving the hole up. The termination condition consists of the hole being immediately below a name that is not greater than the pivot or of the hole reaching the top of the list.

Questions/Exercises

1. Modify the sequential search program in Figure 4-7 to allow for lists that are not sorted.

2. Convert the pseudocode routine:

> assign Z the value 0;
> assign X the value 1;
> **while** (X < 6) **do**
>   (assign Z the value Z + X;
>   assign X the value X + 1)

to an equivalent routine using a repeat statement.

3. Suppose the insertion sort as presented in Figure 4-12 was applied to the list George, Cheryl, Alice, and Bob. Describe the organization of the list at the end of each execution of the body of the repeat structure.

4. Why would we not want to change the phrase "greater than" in the **while** statement in Figure 4-12 to "greater than or equal to"?

4-5 Recursive Structures

Recursive structures provide an alternative to the loop paradigm for repetitive structures. As an introduction to the technique, we consider the ***binary search*** algorithm that applies a divide-and-conquer methodology to the search process.

The Binary Search Algorithm

Let us again tackle the problem of searching a sorted list to see if it contains a particular entry, but this time we imagine that the list is a long tray of cards such as we might find in the reference section of a library. In this case, we probably would not approach the problem by interrogating the first card, then the second card, and so on. Rather, when faced with a search problem in this environment, we tend to begin by looking at a card in the area in which we believe the target entry will be found, or if we have no inclination as to where the target may be, we might pick an entry from the middle of the tray. If we are lucky, we pick the card we are looking for on our first try, in which case our search succeeds. If we are not so lucky, we must continue searching. But, knowing the value on the selected card and the order of the list, we can narrow the remaining search to a restricted portion of the list. If the target entry belongs in front of the chosen card, we narrow our search to the earlier portion of the list; otherwise, we search the latter portion.

In our pseudocode, this process could be represented as shown in Figure 4-13. Note that we have placed the word *middle* in quotation marks to indicate the possibility that a list with an even number of entries has no middle entry. In this case, the middle entry refers to the first entry in the second half of the list.

Our problem now is to decide how the search should continue if the entry chosen first is not the target one. In the routine in Figure 4-13, this is handled by a program module named Search. Thus, to complete our program we must provide a module named Search that describes how this secondary search is to be performed. Note that this module must be robust enough to handle a request to search an empty list. For instance, if the routine in Figure 4-13 is given a list containing only one entry that is not the target value, then the module is requested to search either the sublist above or below the single entry, both of which are empty.

We could use the sequential search developed in the previous section as the required module, but this is not the technique we probably would use when searching the card tray in a library. Rather, we probably would repeat the same process on the

Figure 4-13 The core of the binary search

```
Select the "middle" entry in List as the test entry;
Execute one of the following blocks of instructions
        depending on whether TargetValue is equal to, less
        than, or greater than the test entry.
    TargetValue = test entry:
        (Declare the search a success.)
    TargetValue < test entry:
        [Apply the module Search to see if TargetValue
                is in the portion of List preceding the test
                entry, and
        If (that search is successful)
            then (Declare this search a success.)
            else (Declare this search a failure.)]
    TargetValue > test entry:
        [Apply the module Search to see if TargetValue
                is in the portion of List following the test
                entry, and
        If (that search is successful)
            then (Declare this search a success.)
            else (Declare this search a failure.)]
```

restricted portion of the tray that we used for the whole tray. That is, we would select an entry toward the middle of that portion of the tray and use it to narrow our search further.

We can implement this in our pseudocode by first modifying the routine in Figure 4-13 to handle the case of an empty list and then giving the resulting program module the name Search to obtain the pseudocode program shown in Figure 4-14 (p. 160). Thus, if we were following the routine and came to the instruction "Apply the module Search . . . ," we would apply the same search technique to the smaller list that we were applying to the original one. If that search succeeded, we would return to declare our original search successful; if this secondary search failed, we would declare our original search a failure.

To clarify this process, let us apply the algorithm represented in Figure 4-14 to the list Alice, Bill, Carol, David, Evelyn, Fred, and George, with the target value being Bill. Our search begins by selecting David (the middle entry) as the test entry under consideration. Since the target value (Bill) must precede this test entry, we are instructed to apply the module named Search to the list of entries preceding David—that is, the list Alice, Bill, and Carol. Thus, we create a second copy of the search module and assign it to this secondary task.

For a while we have two copies of our search module being executed, as summarized in Figure 4-15 (p. 161). Progress in the original copy is temporarily suspended at the instruction

Apply the module Search to see if TargetValue is in the portion of List
preceding the test entry

Figure 4-14 The binary search algorithm in pseudocode

```
procedure Search (List, TargetValue)
    If (list empty)
        then
            (Declare the search a failure.)
        else
            [Select the "middle" entry in List as the test entry;
            Execute one of the following blocks of instructions
                depending on whether TargetValue is equal to, less
                than, or greater than the test entry.
            TargetValue = test entry;
                (Declare the search a success.)
            TargetValue < test entry;
                [Apply the module Search to see if TargetValue
                    is in the portion of List preceding the test
                    entry, and
                If (that search is successful)
                    then (Declare this search a success.)
                    else (Declare this search a failure.)]]
            TargetValue > test entry:
                [Apply the module Search to see if TargetValue
                    is in the portion of List following the test
                    entry, and
                If (that search is successful)
                    then (Declare this search a success.)
                    else (Declare this search a failure.)]]]
```

while we apply the second copy to the task of searching the list Alice, Bill, and Carol. When we complete this secondary search, we will discard the second copy of the module, report its findings to the original copy, and continue progress in the original. Thus, the second copy of the module executes as a subordinate to the original, performing the task requested by the original module and then disappearing.

The secondary search selects Bill as its test entry because that is the middle entry in the list Alice, Bill, and Carol. Since this is the same as the target value, it declares its search to be a success and terminates.

At this point, we have completed the secondary search as requested by the original copy of the module, so we are able to continue the execution of that original copy. Here we are told that if the secondary search was successful, we should declare the original search a success. Thus, our process correctly determines that Bill is a member of the list Alice, Bill, Carol, David, Evelyn, Fred, and George.

Let us now consider what happens if we ask our routine to search the list Alice, Carol, Evelyn, Fred, and George for the entry David. This time the original copy of the module selects Evelyn as its test entry and concludes that the target value must reside in the preceding portion of the list. It therefore requests another copy of the

Figure 4-15

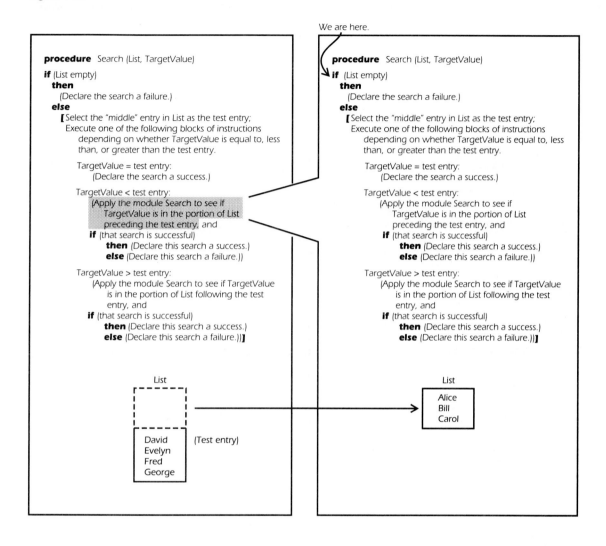

We are here.

module to search the list of entries appearing in front of Evelyn—that is, the two-entry list consisting of Alice and Carol. At this stage our situation is as represented in Figure 4-16 (p. 162).

The second copy of the module selects Carol as its current entry and concludes that the target value must lie in the latter portion of its list. Thus, it requests a third copy of the module to search the list of names following Carol in the list Alice and Carol. This sublist is empty, so the third copy of the module has the task of searching the empty list for the target value David. Our situation at this point is represented by

Figure 4-16

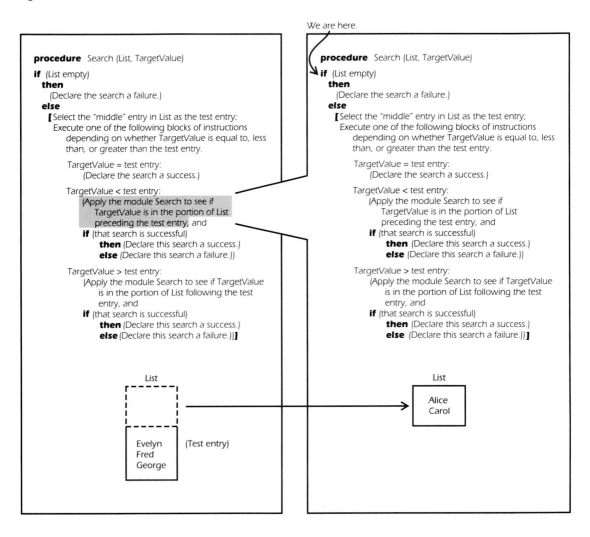

Figure 4-17. The original copy of the module has the task of searching the list Alice, Carol, Evelyn, Fred, and George, with the test entry being Evelyn; the second copy is searching the list Alice and Carol, with its test entry being Carol; and the third copy is about to begin searching the empty list.

Of course, the third copy of the module quickly declares its search to be a failure and terminates. The completion of the third copy's task allows the second copy to continue its task. It notes that the search it requested was unsuccessful, declares its

Figure 4-17

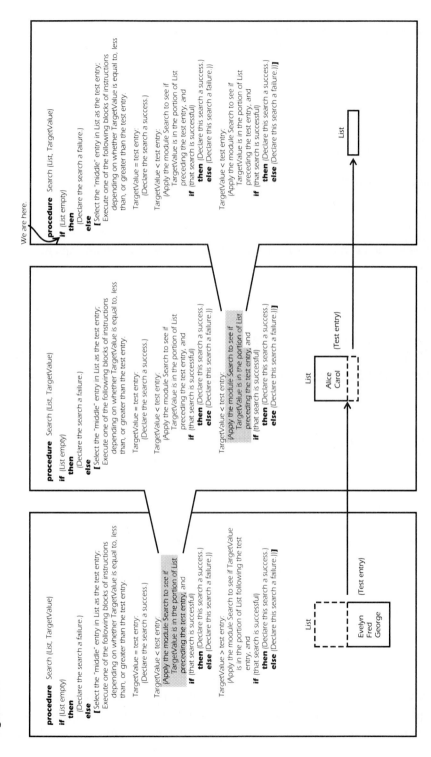

own task to be a failure, and terminates. This report is what the original copy of the module has been waiting for, so it can now proceed. Since the search it requested failed, it declares its own search to have failed and terminates. Thus, our routine has correctly concluded that David is not contained in the list Alice, Carol, Evelyn, Fred, and George.

In summary, if we were to look back at the previous examples, we could see that the process employed by the algorithm represented into Figure 4-14 is to repeatedly divide the list in question into two smaller pieces in such a way that the remaining search can be restricted to only one of these pieces. This divide-by-two approach is the reason why the algorithm is known as the binary search.

Recursive Control

The binary search algorithm is similar to the sequential search in that each algorithm requests the execution of a repetitive process. However, the implementation of this repetition is significantly different. Whereas the sequential search involves a circular form of repetition, the technique employed by the binary search is to have each stage of the repetition executed as a subtask of the previous stage. This technique is known as *recursion.*

As we have seen, the illusion created by the execution of a recursive algorithm is the existence of multiple copies of itself, called activations, that appear and disappear as the algorithm advances. Of those activations existing at any given time, only one is actively progressing. The others are effectively in limbo, with each waiting for another activation to terminate before it can continue.

Being a repetitive process, recursive systems are just as dependent on proper control as are loop structures. For example, just as in loop control, recursive systems are dependent on testing for a termination condition and on a design that assures this condition will be reached. In fact, proper recursive control involves the same three ingredients—initialization, modification, and test for termination—that are required in loop control.

In general, a recursive routine is designed to test for the termination condition (often called the base or degenerative case) before requesting further activations. If this condition is not met, the routine assigns an activation to the task of solving a revised problem that is closer to the termination condition than that assigned to the current activation. However, if the termination condition is met, a path is taken that avoids further recursive action, causing the current activation to terminate without creating additional activations. This means that one of the activations in limbo is allowed to continue execution, complete its task, and in turn allow yet another activation to continue. In this fashion, all the activations that are generated ultimately terminate, leaving the original task completed.

Let us see how the initialization and modification phases of repetitive control are implemented in our recursive binary search routine of Figure 4-14. In this case, the creation of additional activations is terminated once the target value is found or the task is reduced to that of searching an empty list. The process is initialized implicitly by being given an initial list and a target value. From this initial configuration, the routine modifies the task it is assigned to that of searching a smaller list. Since the original list is of finite length and each modification step reduces the length of the list in question, we are assured that the target value ultimately is found or the task is reduced to that of searching the empty list. Thus, we conclude that the repetitive process is guaranteed to cease.

Having seen both iterative and recursive control structures, you may wonder if the two are equivalent in power. That is, if an algorithm were designed using a loop structure, could another algorithm using only recursive techniques be designed that would solve the same problem and vice versa? Such questions are important in computer science because their answers tell us what features should be provided in a programming language in order to obtain the most powerful programming system possible. We return to these ideas in Chapter 11, where we consider some of the more theoretical aspects of computer science and its mathematical foundations. With this background, we then can prove the equivalence of iterative and recursive structures in Appendix E.

The Quick Sort Algorithm

For another application of recursion, we reconsider the problem of sorting a list of names. Once again, we work within the constraints of sorting the list within itself, as dictated by the crowded desk top analogy described in our introduction to the insertion sort in Section 4-4.

We approach our sorting task this time by selecting one name, which we call the pivot entry, finding this name's correct position, and placing the name in that position. To find the correct position for the pivot, we essentially divide the list into two smaller lists, the first consisting of the names that should precede the pivot in the final order and the second consisting of the names that should follow the pivot. Consequently, the correct location for the pivot entry is between these two sublists.

To start the process, we must select a list entry as the pivot. Not knowing anything about the list, we might as well pick the name currently at the top. Next, we must divide the list into the two sublists just described. For this purpose we place an arrow, which we call a pointer, at the first name in the list (which is the pivot entry) and another pointer at the last name. Our algorithm directs the movement of these pointers toward each other in such a way that the following assertion is always satisfied:

Assertion 1:
The names above the top pointer are less than (alphabetically) or equal to the pivot entry, while those below the bottom pointer are greater than the pivot.

This assertion states that the pointers identify two groups within the list. One group contains only entries that should precede the pivot entry (the names above the top pointer) in the final sorted list, while the other group contains only entries that should follow the pivot (the names below the bottom pointer).

To describe how the pointers are moved, we consider the problem of sorting the list:

Jane
Bob
Alice
Tom
Carol
Bill
George
Cheryl
Sue
John

We begin with the configuration:

→ Jane   (Pivot entry)
Bob
Alice
Tom
Carol
Bill
George
Cheryl
Sue
→ John

Next, we move the bottom pointer up the list, comparing the name pointed to with the pivot entry at each step. As long as this name is greater than the pivot entry, we keep moving the pointer. Ultimately we must reach a name less than or equal to the pivot entry, because the top name certainly fits this criterion. Once such a name has been reached, we stop moving the pointer. In our example, because this happens when the pointer reaches Cheryl, we stop moving the pointer at that position, producing the following configuration:

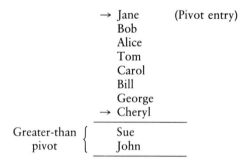

Now we begin moving the top pointer down the list, comparing the names pointed to with the pivot entry. This time, however, we keep moving the pointer as long as the name in the list is less than or equal to the pivot entry or until the two pointers coincide. As we will see, the latter condition indicates that the correct location for the pivot has been found. On the other hand, the former condition would present us with a dilemma, because any further movement of either pointer would destroy the validity of Assertion 1. This is demonstrated in our example, which at this stage appears as follows:

```
Less-than-      ⎧      Jane        (Pivot entry)
or-equal-to     ⎨      Bob
   pivot        ⎩      Alice
                    →  Tom
                       Carol
                       Bill
                       George
                    →  Cheryl
Greater-than    ⎰      Sue
   pivot        ⎱      John
```

Observe that this deadlock can be broken by interchanging the names designated by the pointers, after which we can again move the bottom pointer up (and then the top pointer down) without violating Assertion 1. This, then, is what we do. Immediately after the interchange, our example has the following configuration:

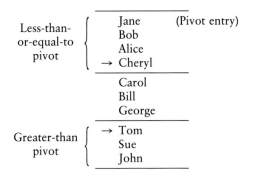

```
Less-than-      ⎧      Jane        (Pivot entry)
or-equal-to     ⎨      Bob
   pivot        ⎨      Alice
                ⎩   →  Cheryl
                       Carol
                       Bill
                       George
Greater-than    ⎰   →  Tom
   pivot        ⎱      Sue
                       John
```

By continuing the process of moving the pointers and then interchanging names to break the deadlock, the two pointers must at some point coincide. In our example, this meeting occurs after the bottom pointer has stopped at George and the top pointer has moved down to it, producing the situation that appears as follows:

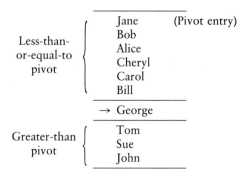

Once the pointers coincide, how does the identified entry compare to the pivot? To answer this question, we first justify the following assertion:

Assertion 2:
At the beginning of the sort process and after each interchange for breaking a deadlock, the top pointer points to a name less than or equal to the pivot.

This assertion is certainly true at the beginning of the sort, because at that time the top pointer points to the pivot entry itself. Furthermore, since each time a deadlock occurs the bottom pointer must point to a name less than or equal to the pivot entry, the interchange performed to break the deadlock results in the top pointer pointing to an entry that is less than or equal to the pivot. We conclude that Assertion 2 holds.

Based on Assertion 2, we claim

Assertion 3:
If the pointers coincide, the entry they identify is less than or equal to the pivot.

To justify this claim, we consider the two processes that can lead to the coincidence of the pointers. First, the bottom pointer can move up to the top pointer. In this case, Assertion 2 confirms that the top pointer must point to an entry less than or equal to the pivot before the bottom pointer can begin to move. Thus, if the bottom pointer reaches the top one, Assertion 3 is satisfied. The other process that can lead to common pointer positions is for the top pointer to move down to the bottom one. But in this case, the bottom pointer has previously stopped at an entry that is less than or equal to the pivot, so again, Assertion 3 is satisfied.

Combining Assertions 1 and 3, we conclude that once the pointers coincide, the entries in the list below the pointers are all greater than the pivot, and those entries at or above the common pointers are all less than or equal to the pivot. Indeed, in our example, we find the following configuration:

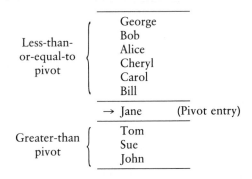

Less-than-
or-equal-to
pivot

    Jane   (Pivot entry)
    Bob
    Alice
    Cheryl
    Carol
    Bill
→ George

Greater-than
pivot

    Tom
    Sue
    John

We are now ready to position the pivot entry; it belongs between the two sublists we have formed. To place it there, we could remove the pivot from the list, repeatedly move names up one notch in the list until a hole is generated at the position of the common pointers, and then insert the pivot in this hole. This action would generate a tremendous amount of motion on our desk top as we pushed cards up to make room for the pivot. Therefore, we prefer to simply interchange the pivot with the entry identified by the common pointers. After all, this entry belongs in front of the pivot (by Assertion 3), and this interchange involves the movement of only two names instead of many. After this interchange, our example takes on the following appearance:

Less-than-
or-equal-to
pivot

    George
    Bob
    Alice
    Cheryl
    Carol
    Bill

→ Jane   (Pivot entry)

Greater-than
pivot

    Tom
    Sue
    John

What we have accomplished at this stage is the correct positioning of one name. Admittedly, this does not sound like much, but the fact is that we are almost done from the algorithm-development point of view. Indeed, if the portions of the list above and below the name just positioned were sorted, the entire list would now be sorted. Thus, the problem is reduced to sorting these two portions as though they were two separate lists.

Having started with the problem of sorting one list, we have arrived at the problem of sorting two lists. You might conclude that we are getting further from the

Figure 4-18 The quick sort algorithm in pseudocode

```
procedure Sort (List)
    If (List contains fewer than two entries)
        then (Declare List to be sorted.)
        else
            [Select the first entry in List as the pivot;
            Place pointers at the first and last entries of List;
            while (the pointers do not coincide) do
                (Move the bottom pointer up to the nearest
                    entry less than or equal to the pivot
                    but not beyond the top pointer;
                (Move the top pointer down to the nearest entry
                    greater than the pivot but not beyond the
                    bottom pointer;
                If (the pointers coincide)
                    then (Interchange the entries indicated by the
                        pointers.))
            Interchange the pivot with the entry indicated by the
                common pointers;
            Apply the module Sort to the portion of List above the pivot.
            Apply the module Sort to the portion of List below the pivot.]
```

solution rather than closer, but such a conclusion overlooks the fact that each of the two lists that must now be sorted is shorter than the original one. This observation leads to the conclusion that by applying this same algorithmic process to these shorter lists, we obtain even more but still shorter lists to sort. Successive applications of the process ultimately reduce the initial sort problem to the problem of sorting numerous lists, each of which contain no more than one name. (We use the phrase "no more than one" to allow for the occurrence of a list with no names in it. Such a case arises, for instance, if the pivot entry turns out to belong at the first of the list, resulting in the list of names above it being empty.) Since such lists are already sorted by default, we see that repeated applications of the process are, at some stage, no longer required; at that point, the original list is sorted.

Our completed solution, which is known as the **quick sort**[1] algorithm, is shown in Figure 4-18. We implement our solution as a module called Sort, which begins by testing the length of the list it is asked to sort. If that list has two or more entries, the module branches to the **else** portion of its **if-then-else** structure. There the module positions the pivot entry as we have described and then requests that the portions of the list above and below the pivot be sorted. These requests appear in the last two lines of the module as additional applications of the module Sort.

[1]The quick sort algorithm presented here differs slightly from the traditional version in the manner in which the pivot is handled. Interested readers are encouraged to consult the additional readings at the end of this chapter for other discussions of quick sort.

Let us apply the quick sort algorithm to the list

> Bob
> Elaine
> David
> Alice
> Cheryl

We check the length of the list, establish Bob as the pivot entry, position pointers at the top and bottom of the list, move the bottom pointer up to the name Alice, move the top pointer down to the name Elaine, and interchange Elaine and Alice. Our situation now is as follows:

> Bob,   (Pivot entry)
> → Alice
> David
> → Elaine
> Cheryl

Now we move the bottom pointer up to Alice but cannot move the top pointer down because the pointers already coincide. Thus, we interchange the names Bob and Alice. At this point our list appears as follows:

> Alice
> Bob   (Pivot entry)
> David
> Elaine
> Cheryl

We are now requested to sort the portion of the list above the pivot, which is the list containing the single name Alice. It is important to keep in mind that for a while we have two activations of our algorithm. One is temporarily suspended at the instruction

> *Apply the module Sort to the portion of List above the pivot.*

while the second is charged with the task of sorting the list Alice. Our situation is analogous to that represented in Figure 4-19 on the following page.

Actually, the second activation of the algorithm does not last long. It recognizes that the list it is charged with sorting has fewer than two entries and declares its task complete. Thus, we discard the second activation and return to continue in the first, where we find the instruction

> *Apply the module Sort to the portion of List below the pivot.*

which requests that we establish another activation of the sort algorithm and assign it the task of sorting the list David, Elaine, and Cheryl. This activation establishes David as its pivot entry, interchanges Elaine and Cheryl, and then interchanges David (the pivot) and Cheryl (the name identified by the common pointers). Thus, the list under consideration by this activation of the algorithm has the structure

Figure 4-19

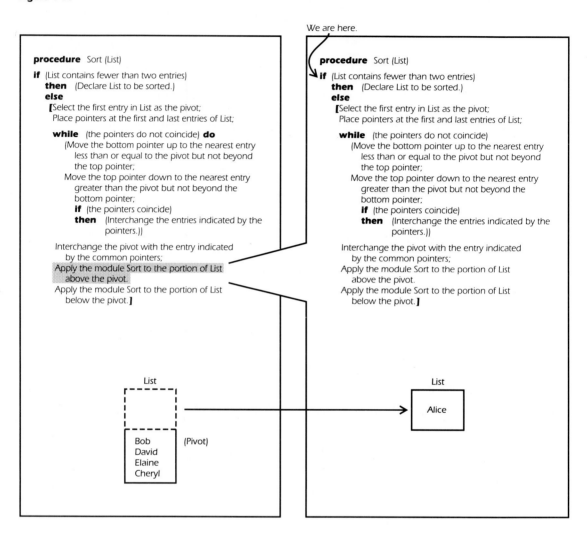

Cheryl
David   (Pivot entry)
Elaine

At this point the current activation reaches the instruction

Apply the module Sort to the portion of List above the pivot.

so it requests yet another activation to sort the list Cheryl. This results in a total of three activations currently underway. As the third of these activations begins, our situation is that of Figure 4-20. The original activation is waiting for the lower portion

Figure 4-20

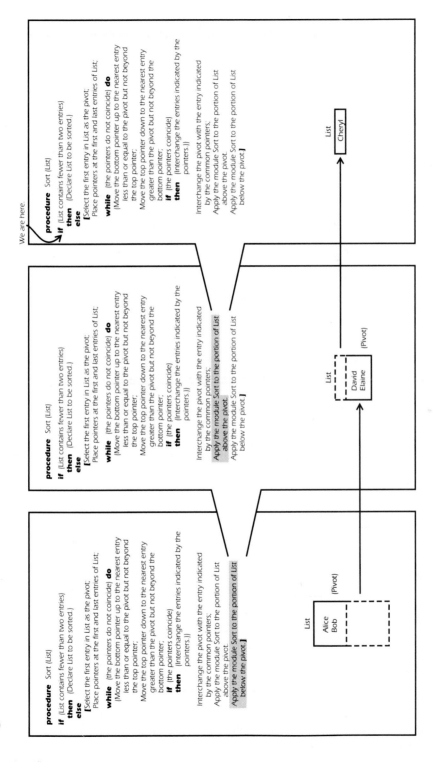

of its list to be sorted by the second activation. The second activation is waiting for the upper portion of its list to be sorted by the third activation. The third activation is about to begin its task.

Here again, the task of sorting a one-entry list does not take long. The third activation simply declares its list to be sorted and terminates. Thus, the second activation can proceed by requesting that the lower portion of its list be sorted. This, of course, creates a third activation charged with the task of sorting the list Elaine. This third activation does its job, terminates, and allows the second activation to continue once more.

At this stage, the second activation has completed its task. Thus, it terminates and allows the original activation to continue. The original activation had been suspended at its last instruction, which requested the lower portion of its list to be sorted. Since that request has now been fulfilled, the original activation is finished and terminates. Indeed, the entire list has now been sorted.

Questions/Exercises

1. What names are interrogated by the binary search (Figure 4-14) when searching for the name Joe in the list Alice, Bob, Carol, David, Evelyn, Fred, George, Henry, Irene, Joe, Karl, Larry, Mary, Nancy, and Oliver?
2. What is the maximum number of entries that must be interrogated when applying the binary search to a list of 200 entries? What about 100,000 entries?
3. If we apply the quick sort (Figure 4-18) to the list Carol, Alice, Bob, Larry, and John, what is the order of the names immediately after the first interchange of names? What about after executing the next-to-the-last instruction in the first activation of the program?
4. What happens if we apply the quick sort to a list that is already sorted? What if the list is in exactly reverse order?
5. What happens if we apply the quick sort to a list in which all the names are the same?

4-6 Efficiency and Correctness

Of the remaining topics we could discuss as a part of our formal introduction to algorithms, this section discusses two that should linger in your mind as you develop programs on your own. The first of these is efficiency, and the second is correctness.

Algorithm Efficiency

We discuss the issues of algorithm efficiency more thoroughly in Chapter 11 in the context of algorithm complexity. For now, however, we emphasize the importance of this topic by taking a few paragraphs to introduce the idea of comparative efficiency. Even though today's machines are capable of executing millions of instructions each second, efficiency remains a major concern in algorithm design. Often the choice between efficient and inefficient algorithms can make the difference between a practical solution to a problem and an impractical one.

Let us consider the problem of a university registrar who is faced with the task of retrieving and updating student records. Although the university has an actual enrollment of approximately 10,000 students during any one semester, its "current student file" contains the records of more than 30,000 students who are considered current students in the sense that they have registered for at least one course in the past few years but have not completed a degree. We envision these records as being stored in the registrar's computer in a list ordered by student identification numbers. Thus, to find a student's record, the registrar essentially searches a sorted list for a particular identification number.

We have presented two algorithms for searching such a list: the sequential search and the binary search. Our question now is whether the choice between these two algorithms makes any difference in the case of the registrar. We consider the sequential search first.

Given a student identification number, the sequential search algorithm starts at the beginning of the list and compares the entries it finds to the number desired. Not knowing anything about the source of the target value, we cannot conclude how far into the list this search must go. We can say, though, that after many searches we expect the average depth of the searches to be halfway through the list; some will be shorter, but others will be longer. We conclude that over a period of time, the sequential search will investigate roughly 15,000 records per search. Thus, if retrieving and checking a record for its identification number requires a millisecond (one thousandth of a second), each search will require an average of 15 seconds. Because an eight-hour workday contains 28,800 seconds, the sequential search allows the registrar to perform an average of no more than 2000 searches during a day. Thus, retrieving each of the 10,000 active student records represents more than a week's work. Moreover, this does not allow time for using or updating the information retrieved.

In contrast, the binary search proceeds by comparing the target value to the middle entry in the list. If this is not the desired entry, then at least the remaining search is restricted to only half of the original list. Thus, after interrogating the middle entry in the list of 30,000 student records, the binary search has at most 15,000 records still to consider. After the second inquiry, at most 7500 remain, and after the third retrieval, the list in question has dropped to no more than 3750 entries.

Continuing in this fashion, we find that if the target record is in the list, it will be found after retrieving at most 15 entries from the list of 30,000 records. Thus, if each of these retrievals can be performed in one millisecond, the process of searching for a particular record requires only 0.015 second. This means that the process of searching for each of the 10,000 active student records one at a time consumes at most 2.5 minutes—a substantial improvement over the sequential search algorithm.

The binary search seems preferable over the sequential one in our example. But, before we blindly accept this as a correct conclusion, we must admit that our example is somewhat simplistic. To use the binary search requires that the student records be stored in a manner that allows the middle entries of successively smaller sublists to be retrieved without undue hardship. In short, the ultimate efficiency of the algorithm is closely associated with the details of its implementation. Our example is rather typical in that a major concern regarding the algorithm's implementation is data organization. The relationship between algorithms and data organization is the underlying theme of Part Three of this text.

We conclude that the issue of efficiency is quite important. In fact, the search for efficient solutions to problems and for techniques of measuring efficiency is a major topic in the area of complexity theory. We discuss this topic in Chapter 11.

Software Verification

Recall that the fourth phase in Polya's analysis of problem solving (Section 4-3) is to evaluate the solution for accuracy and for its potential as a tool for solving other problems. The significance of the first part of this phrase is exemplified by the following example:

> A traveler with a gold chain of seven links must stay in an isolated hotel for seven nights. The rent each night consists of one link from the chain. What is the fewest

Figure 4-21 *Separating the chain using only three cuts*

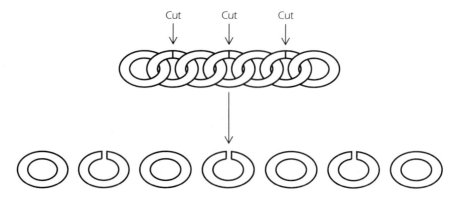

number of links that must be cut so that the traveler can pay the hotel one link of the chain each morning without paying for lodging in advance?

We first realize that not every link in the chain must be cut. For instance, if we cut the second link, we could free both the first and second links from the other five. Following this insight we are led to the solution of cutting only the second, fourth, and sixth links in the chain, a process that releases each link while cutting only three (Figure 4-21). Furthermore, any fewer cuts leaves two links connected, so we conclude that the correct answer to our problem is three.

However, upon reconsidering the problem, we might make the observation that when only the third link in the chain is cut, we obtain three pieces of chain of lengths one, two, and four (Figure 4-22). With these pieces we can proceed as follows:

On the first morning, give the hotel the single link.
On the second morning, retrieve the single link and give the hotel the two-link piece.
On the third morning, give the hotel the single link.

On the fourth morning, retrieve the three links held by the hotel and give the hotel the four-link piece.
On the fifth morning, give the hotel the single link.
On the sixth morning, retrieve the single link and give the hotel the double-link piece.
On the seventh morning, give the hotel the single link.

Consequently, our first answer, which we were sure was correct, is incorrect. How, then, can we be sure that our new solution is correct? We might argue as follows: Since a single link must be given to the hotel on the first morning, at least one link of the chain must be cut, and since our new solution requires only one cut, it must be optimal.

Translated into the programming environment, this example emphasizes the distinction between a program that is believed to be correct and a program that is correct. The two are not necessarily the same. The data processing community is rich

Figure 4-22 Solving the problem with only one cut

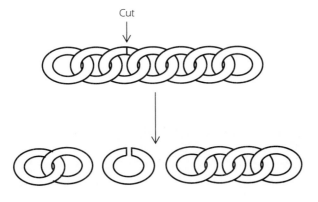

in horror stories involving software that although "known" to be correct still failed at a critical moment because of some unforeseen situation. Thus, verification of software is an important undertaking, and the search for efficient verification techniques constitutes an active field of research in computer science.

One current line of research in this area attempts to apply the techniques of formal logic to prove the correctness of a program. The underlying thesis is that by reducing the verification process to a formal procedure, one is protected from the inaccurate conclusions that may be associated with intuitive arguments, as was the case in the gold chain problem. Let us consider this approach to program verification in more detail.

Just as a formal mathematical proof is based on axioms (geometric proofs are often founded on the axioms of Euclidean geometry while other proofs may be based on the axioms of set theory), a formal proof of a program's correctness is based on the specifications under which the program was designed. To prove that a program correctly sorts lists of names, we are allowed to begin with the assumption that the program's input is a list of names, or if the program is designed to compute the average of one or more positive numbers, we can assume that the input does, in fact, consist of one or more positive numbers. In short, a proof of correctness begins with the assumption that certain conditions, called **preconditions,** are satisfied at the beginning of program execution.

The next step in a proof of correctness is to consider how the consequences of these preconditions propagate through the program. For this purpose, researchers have analyzed various program structures to determine how a statement, known to be true before the structure is executed, is affected by executing the structure. As a simple example, if a certain statement about the value of Y is known to hold prior to executing the instruction

assign X the value of Y

then that same statement can be made about X after the instruction has been executed. More precisely, if the value of Y is not 0 before the instruction is executed, then we can conclude that the value of X will not be 0 after the instruction is executed.

A slightly more involved example occurs in the case of an **if-then-else** structure such as

if (condition) then (instruction 1)
else (instruction 2)

Here, if some statement is known to hold before execution of the structure, then immediately before executing *instruction 1*, we know that both that statement and the condition tested are true, whereas if *instruction 2* is to be executed, we know the statement and the negation of the condition must hold.

Following rules such as these, a proof of correctness proceeds by identifying statements, called **assertions,** that can be established at various points in the program.

The result is a collection of assertions, each being a consequence of the program's preconditions and the sequence of instructions that lead to that point in the program at which the assertion is established. If the assertion so established at the end of the program corresponds to the desired output specifications, we can conclude that the program is correct.

For example, suppose we establish the assertion

All entries above the pivot are less than or equal to the pivot, and all entries below the pivot are greater than the pivot.

at the point in our quick sort algorithm (Figure 4-18) immediately after the pivot has been interchanged with the entry indicated by the common pointers. It then follows that once the remaining two instructions are executed, the entire list is sorted. Hence, the correctness of our program is verified.

As another example, consider the typical **repeat** loop structure represented in Figure 4-23. Suppose, as a consequence of the preconditions given at point A, we can establish that a particular assertion is true each time point B is reached during the repetitive process. (Such an assertion within a loop is known as a *loop invariant*.) Then, if the repetition ever terminates, execution moves to point C, where we can

Figure 4-23 The assertions associated with a typical repeat structure

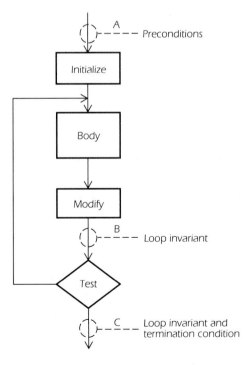

conclude that both the loop invariant and the termination condition hold. (The loop invariant still holds because the test for termination does not alter any values in the program, and the termination condition holds because otherwise the loop does not terminate.) If these combined statements imply the desired output, our proof of correctness can be completed merely by showing that the initialization and modification components of the loop ultimately lead to the termination condition.

You should compare this analysis to our example of the insertion sort shown in Figure 4-12. Indeed, the development of that program was based on the loop invariant

> Each time the loop body is completed the names in the unshaded portion of the list are sorted.

the termination condition

> The entire list is unshaded.

and the fact that by repeatedly unshading an additional name, the entire list ultimately is unshaded.

The fact that we informally identified the loop invariant in the process of developing the insertion sort program is not an uncommon phenomenon. It turns out that the assertions obtained when proving a program correct are often essentially the insights that led to the program in the first place. This, in turn, has caused many researchers to propose an assertion approach to program development. That is, they propose that the assertions for the various stages of a program be developed first and then the instructions that lead to these assertions be inserted. Note that this is quite similar to our development of the quick sort algorithm represented in Figure 4-18, where we used the assertion approach to record various relationships among the list entries during program development.

The ultimate goal among researchers working on the problem of program verification is to develop techniques by which the process of proving the correctness of programs can be automated. Unfortunately, mathematicians have shown that this goal, in its most general setting, cannot be achieved. Simply stated, there is no algorithm for determining whether or not programs are correct, and therefore it is impossible to program a machine to perform this task. On the other hand, programs have been written that perform a major part of the program verification task, and such programs will most likely form the foundation of tomorrow's program verification techniques.

Currently, however, the data processing community relies on other approaches to software verification, one of which is the use of redundancy. This is the technique of implementing two independent solutions to the same problem. If these solutions disagree, we know that at least one of them is wrong; if they agree, our confidence in correctness is reinforced.

Unfortunately, the use of redundancy proves to be inefficient in most applications. The result is that in most cases today, software is "verified" by applying it to test data—a process that is shaky at best. After all, verification by test data proves nothing more than that the program runs correctly for the test data. Any additional conclusions are merely projections based on statistical analysis. Thus, obtaining test data for use in program verification should be given the same careful consideration as obtaining a random sample in other statistical settings. It is this analogy that clarifies one of the major (yet often violated) rules of thumb in verification by test data: Test data should not be designed by a person involved in the software development. After all, a person so involved would tend to overlook the same possibilities when designing the test data that were overlooked when designing the software. Thus, the test data produced would be anything but a random sample, and consequently, errors in the software, just as our error in the gold chain problem, could go undetected.

Questions/Exercises

1. Below are a problem and a proposed answer. Is the proposed answer correct? Why or why not?

    Problem: Suppose a box contains three cards. One of three cards is painted black on both sides, one is painted red on both sides, and the third is painted red on one side and black on the other. One of the cards is drawn from the box, and you are allowed to see one side of it. What is the probability that the other side of the card is the same color as the side you see?

    Proposed answer: One-half. Suppose the side of the card you can see is red. (The argument would be symmetric with this one if the side were black.) Only two cards among the three have a red side. Thus, the card you see must be one of these two. One of these two cards is red on the other side, while the other is black. Thus, the card you can see is just as likely to be red on the other side as it is to be black.

2. The following program segment is an attempt to compute the quotient (forgetting any remainder) of two positive integers by counting the number of times the divisor can be subtracted from the dividend before what is left becomes less than the divisor. For instance, 7/3 should produce 2 because 3 can be subtracted from 7 twice. Is the program correct? Justify your answer.

    ```
    assign Count the value 0;
    assign Remainder the value of the dividend;
    repeat (assign Remainder the value of Remainder − divisor;
            assign Count the value of Count + 1)
    until (Remainder < the divisor)
    assign Quotient the value of Count
    ```

3. The following program segment is designed to compute the product of two nonnegative integers X and Y by accumulating the sum of X copies of Y—that is, 3 times 4 is computed by accumulating the sum of three 4s. Is the program correct? Justify your answer.

```
assign Product the value of Y;
assign Count the value 1;
while (Count < X) do
    (assign Product the value of Product + Y;
    assign Count the value of Count + 1)
```

4. Assuming the precondition that the value associated with N is a positive integer, establish a loop invariant that leads to the conclusion that if the following routine terminates, then Sum is assigned the value 0 + 1 + ... + N.

```
assign Sum the value 0;
assign I the value 0;
while (I < N) do
    (assign I the value I + 1;
    assign Sum the value Sum + I)
```

Give an argument to the effect that the routine does, in fact, terminate.

Chapter 4 Review Problems

1. Does the following program represent an algorithm in the strict sense? Why or why not?

    ```
    assign Count the value 0;
    while (Count not 5) do
        (assign Count the value of Count + 2)
    ```

2. In what sense do the following steps not constitute an algorithm?

    ```
    Draw a straight line segment between the points
        with rectangular coordinates (2,5) and (6,11).
    Draw a straight line segment between the points
        with rectangular coordinates (1,3) and (3,6).
    Draw a circle with radius two and center at the
        intersection of the previous line segments.
    ```

3. Rewrite the following program segment using a **repeat** structure rather than a **while** structure. Be sure the new version prints the same values as the original.

    ```
    assign Count the value 2;
    while (Count < 7) do
        (print the value assigned to Count and assign
        Count the value Count + 1)
    ```

4. Rewrite the following program segment using a **while** structure rather than a **repeat** structure. Be sure the new version prints the same values as the original.

    ```
    assign Count the value 1;
    repeat (print the value assigned to Count and
            assign Count the value Count + 1)
    until (Count = 5)
    ```

5. Design an algorithm that, when given an arrangement of the digits 0, 1, 2, 3, 4, 5, 6, 7, 8, 9, rearranges the digits so that the new arrangement represents the next larger value that can be represented by these digits (or reports that no such rearrangement exists if no rearrangement produces a larger value). Thus, 5647382901 would produce 5647382910.

6. What is the difference between a formal programming language and a pseudocode?

7. What is the difference between syntax and semantics?

8. a. Identify a benefit of modular design when designing an algorithm.
    b. Identify a benefit of modular design when reading an algorithm.

9. Design an algorithm that, given two strings of characters, tests whether the first string appears as a substring somewhere in the second.

10. Design an algorithm that a magician could follow to create the illusion of a rope being cut in half and then restored.

11. The algorithm represented below is designed to print the beginning of what is known as the Fibonacci sequence. Identify the body of the loop. Where is the initialization step for the loop control? The modification step? The test step? What list of numbers is produced?

assign Last the value 0;
assign Current the value 1;
while (Current < 100) **do**
    (print the value assigned to Current;
    assign Temp the value of Last;
    assign Last the value of Current; and
    assign Current the value of Last + Temp)

12. What sequence of numbers is printed by the algorithm represented below if it is started with input values 0 and 1?

    procedure MysteryWrite (Last, Current)
    if (Current < 100)
        then (print the value assigned to Current;
            assign Temp the value of Current +
            Last; and apply MysteryWrite to the
            values Current and Temp)

13. Modify the procedure MysteryWrite in the preceding problem so that the values are printed in reverse order.

14. What letters are interrogated by the binary search (Figure 4-14) if it is applied to the list A, B, C, D, E, F, G, H, I, J, K, L, M, N, O when searching for the value J? What about the value Z?

15. What name is interchanged with the pivot in the first activation of the quick sort (Figure 4-18) if it is applied to the list consisting of only Bill and Carol? What if the list is Carol and Bill?

16. On the average, how many times must two names be compared when searching a list of 6000 entries using the sequential search? What can be said about the binary search?

17. Identify the body of the following loop structure and count the number of times it will be executed. What happens if the test is changed to read "**while** (Count not 6)"?

    assign Count the value 1;
    while (Count not 7) **do**
        (print the value assigned to Count and
        assign Count the value Count + 3)

18. What problems do you expect to arise if the following program is implemented on a computer? (Hint: Remember the problem of round-off errors associated with floating-point arithmetic.)

    assign Count the value one-tenth;
    repeat (print the value assigned to Count and
            assign Count the value Count + one-
            tenth)
    until (Count equals 1)

19. Design a recursive version of the Euclidean algorithm (question 3 of Section 4-2).

20. Suppose we apply both Test1 and Test2 (defined below) to the input value 1. What is the difference in the printed output of the two routines?

    procedure Test1 (Count)
        assign Count the value of the input number;
        if (Count not 5)
            then (print the value assigned to Count
                and apply Test1 to the value
                Count + 1)

    procedure Test2 (Count)
        if (Count not 5)
            then (apply Test2 to the value Count + 1
                and print the value assigned to
                Count)

21. Identify the important constituents of the control mechanism in the routines of the previous problem. In particular, what condition causes the process to terminate? Where is the state of the process modified toward this termination condition? Where is the state of the control process initialized?

22. Write a program to generate the sequence of positive integers (in increasing order) whose only prime divisors are 2 and 3; that is, your program should produce the sequence 2, 3, 4, 6, 9, 12, 16, 18, 24, 27, ... Does your program represent an algorithm in the strict sense?

23. Redesign the quick sort algorithm using the last name in the list as the pivot entry.

24. Does the quick sort algorithm represented in Figure 4-18 still sort lists correctly if the last line is changed to read as follows:

Apply the module Sort to the portion of the list consisting of the pivot entry and all entries below the pivot.

Explain your answer.

25. Answer the following questions in terms of the list: Alice, Byron, Carol, Duane, Elaine, Floyd, Gene, Henry, Iris.
    a. Which search algorithm (sequential or binary) will find the name Gene quicker?
    b. Which search algorithm (sequential or binary) will find the name Alice quicker?
    c. Which search algorithm (sequential or binary) will detect the absence of the name Bruce quicker?

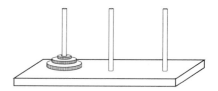

d. Which search algorithm (sequential or binary) will detect the absence of the name Sue quicker?

e. How many entries will be interrogated when searching for the name Elaine when using the sequential search? How many will be interrogated when using the binary search?

26. The factorial of 0 is defined to be 1. The factorial of a positive integer is defined to be the product of that integer times the factorial of the next smaller nonnegative integer. We use the notation $n!$ to express the factorial of the integer n. Thus, the factorial of 3 (written 3!) is $3 \times (2!) = 3 \times (2 \times (1!)) = 3 \times (2 \times (1 \times (0!))) = 3 \times (2 \times (1 \times (1))) = 6$. Design a recursive algorithm that computes the factorial of a given value.

27. What sequence of steps is executed if the quick sort algorithm (Figure 4-18) is applied to a list containing only one name?

28. a. Suppose you must sort a list of five names, and you have already designed an algorithm that sorts a list of four names. Design an algorithm to sort the list of five names by taking advantage of the previously designed algorithm.

b. Design a recursive algorithm to sort arbitrary lists of names based on the technique of part a.

29. The puzzle called the Towers of Hanoi consists of three pegs, one of which contains several rings stacked in order of descending diameter from bottom to top. The problem is to move the stack of rings to another peg. You are allowed to move only one ring at a time, and at no time is a ring to be placed on top of a smaller one. Observe that if the puzzle involved only one ring, it would be extremely easy. Moreover, when faced with the problem of moving several rings, if you could move all but the largest ring to another peg, the largest ring could then be placed on the third peg, and then the problem would be to move the remaining rings on top of it. Using this observation, develop a recursive algorithm for solving the Towers of Hanoi puzzle for an arbitrary number of rings.

30. Another approach to solving the Towers of Hanoi puzzle (problem 29) is to imagine the pegs arranged on a circular stand with a peg mounted at each of the positions of 4, 8, and 12 o'clock. The rings, which begin on one of the pegs, are numbered 1, 2, 3, and so on, starting with the smallest ring being 1. Odd-numbered rings, when on top of a stack, are allowed to move clockwise to the next peg; likewise, even-numbered rings are allowed to move counterclockwise (so long as that move does not place a ring on a smaller one). Under this restriction, always move the largest numbered ring that can be moved. Based on this observation, develop a nonrecursive algorithm for solving the Towers of Hanoi puzzle.

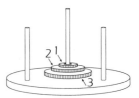

31. Analyze the loop in step 4 of this program for playing craps. Where is the loop initialized? In what sense is its state modified? Is termination guaranteed?

Step 1. Throw two dice and record their sum as "the original value."

Step 2. If the original value is 7 or 11 declare yourself the winner and stop.

Step 3. If the original value is 2, 3, or 12 declare yourself the loser and stop.

Step 4. Continue throwing the dice until their sum is either the original value or 7.

Step 5. If the new sum is 7, declare yourself the loser. Otherwise, declare yourself the winner.

32. Develop two algorithms, one based on a loop structure and the other on a recursive structure, to print the daily salary of a worker who each day is paid twice the previous day's salary (starting with one penny for the first day's work) for a 30-day period. What problems relating to number storage are you likely to encounter if you implement your solutions on an actual machine?

33. Design an algorithm to find the square root of a positive number by starting with the number itself as the first guess and repeatedly producing a new guess from the previous one by averaging the previous guess with the result of dividing the original number by the previous guess. Analyze the control of this repetitive process. In particular, what condition should terminate the repetition?

34. Design an algorithm that lists all possible rearrangements of the symbols in a string of five distinct characters.

35. Design an algorithm that, given a list of names, finds the longest name in the list. Determine what your solution does if there are several "longest" names in the list.

36. Design an algorithm that, given a list of five or more numbers, finds the five smallest and five largest numbers in the list without sorting the entire list.

37. Does the loop in the following routine terminate? Explain your answer. Explain what might happen if this routine is actually executed by a computer (refer to Section 1-6).

```
assign X the value 0;
assign Y the value ½;
while (X not equal 1) do
    (assign X the value of X + Y;
     assign Y the value of Y ÷ 2)
```

38. The following program segment is designed to compute the product of two nonnegative integers X and Y by accumulating the sum of X copies of Y; that is, 3 times 4 is computed by accumulating the sum of three 4s. Is the program segment correct? Explain your answer.

```
assign Product the value 0;
assign Count the value 0;
```

```
repeat (assign Product the value of Product +
        Y, and assign Count the value of
        Count + 1)
until (Count = X)
```

39. The following program segment is designed to report which of the positive integers X and Y is larger. Is the program segment correct? Explain your answer.

```
assign Difference the value of X − Y;
if (Difference is positive)
    then (print "X is bigger than Y")
    else (print "Y is bigger than X")
```

40. The following program segment is designed to find the largest entry in a nonempty list of integers. Is it correct? Explain your answer.

```
assign TestValue the value of the first list entry;
assign CurrentEntry the value of the first list
    entry;
while (CurrentEntry is not the last entry) do
    (if (Current Entry > TestValue)
        then (assign TestValue the value of
              CurrentEntry)
     assign CurrentEntry the value of the next list
        entry)
```

41. a. Identify the preconditions for the sequential search as represented in Figure 4-7. Establish a loop invariant for the **while** structure in that program that, when combined with the termination condition, implies that upon termination of the loop, the following **if** statement reports success or failure correctly.

    b. Give an argument showing that the **while** loop in Figure 4-7 does, in fact, terminate.

42. Based on the preconditions that X and Y are assigned nonnegative integers, identify a loop invariant for the following **while** structure that, when combined with the termination condition, implies that the value associated with Z upon loop termination must be X − Y.

```
assign Z the value of X;
assign J the value 0;
while (J < Y) do
    (assign Z the value of Z − 1;
     assign J the value of J + 1)
```

Problems for the Programmer

1. Implement the sequential search and insertion sort algorithms in a programming language you know.

2. Does your programming language support recursion? Design a short test program to check your answer. If it does, implement the quick sort algorithm.

3. Identify the statements in your programming language that are designed for loop control. In each case, identify what parts of the loop control are provided automatically and what parts you must still specify explicitly.

4. Implement your solutions to review problems 5, 6, 22, and 33.

5. If your programming language supports recursion, implement your solution to review problems 19, 26, 28, and 29.

6. Implement your solutions to review problem 32 so that the length of the pay period can be easily altered. For what length pay period are your answers computed correctly?

Additional Reading

Aho, A. V.; Hopcroft, J. E.; and Ullman, J. D. *Data Structures and Algorithms.* Reading, Mass.: Addison-Wesley, 1983.

Aho, A. V. and Ullman, J. D. *Foundations of Computer Science.* New York: Computer Science Press, 1992.

Cormen, T. H.; Leiserson, C. E.; and Rivest, R. L. *Introduction to Algorithms.* Cambridge, Mass.: MIT Press, 1990.

Dijkstra, E. W. *A Discipline of Programming.* Englewood Cliffs, N.J.: Prentice-Hall, 1976.

Gries, D. *The Science of Programming.* New York: Springer-Verlag, 1981.

Harbin, R. *Origami—The Art of Paper Folding.* London: Hodder Paperbacks, 1973.

Horowitz, E., and Sahni, S. *Fundamentals of Computer Algorithms.* Rockville, Md.: Computer Science Press, 1978.

Knuth, D. E. *The Art of Computer Programming,* Vol. 2 & 3, 2nd ed. Reading, Mass.: 1981.

Manber, U. *Introduction to Algorithms.* Menlo Park, Calif.: Addison-Wesley, 1989.

Polya, G. *How to Solve It.* Princeton, N.J.: Princeton University Press, 1973.

Roberts, E. S. *Thinking Recursively.* New York: John Wiley and Sons, 1986.

Sedgewick, R. *Algorithms,* 2nd ed. Reading, Mass.: Addison-Wesley, 1988.

Smith, J. D. *Design and Analysis of Algorithms.* Boston, Mass.: PWS-Kent, 1989.

Wirth, N. *Algorithms + Data Structures = Programs.* Englewood Cliffs, N.J.: Prentice-Hall, 1976.

CHAPTER FIVE

PROGRAMMING LANGUAGES

*Sections marked by an asterisk are optional in that they provide additional depth of coverage that is not required for an understanding of future chapters.

We have learned to appreciate the complexities involved in a software package such as an operating system and to understand the precision with which its algorithmic structure must be expressed. Moreover, this algorithmic structure must ultimately be described within the machine's memory as sequences of instructions coded as bit patterns according to the rules of the machine language. The process of designing software can be tedious enough without this additional error-prone task of expressing it in such obtuse form.

A system is needed by which the machine can be made to accept and understand algorithms in a form that is more compatible with humans. Such systems have been developed, with many allowing algorithms to be expressed in sentence form, much like the pseudocode used in Chapter 4. The success of these systems has led to an avalanche of programming languages. In this chapter, we take a look at some of the features of popular programming languages.

5-1 Historical Perspective

We begin by tracing the historical development of today's programming languages.

Early Generations

Before a computer can perform a task, it must be programmed to do so by placing an appropriate algorithm, expressed in machine language, in main memory. Originally this programming process was accomplished by the arduous method of requiring the programmer to express all algorithms in the machine's language. This approach added significantly to the already exacting task of an algorithm's design and more often than not led to errors that had to be located and corrected (a process known as debugging) before the job was finished.

The first step toward removing these complexities from the programming process was to do away with the tedious and error-prone use of numeric digits for representing the op-codes and operands found in a machine's language. To this end, it became popular to assign mnemonics to the various op-codes and to use them in place of hexadecimal representation during the design process. Thus, in place of the op-code for loading a register, a programmer might write LD, or to store the contents of a register, ST might be used. In the case of operands, rules were designed by which the programmer could assign names (often called identifiers) to locations in memory and use these names in place of the memory cell addresses in an instruction. A special case of this idea was the assignment of names such as R0, R1, R2, . . . to the registers in the CPU.

By choosing descriptive names for the memory cells and using mnemonics for representing op-codes, programmers could greatly increase the readability of a sequence of machine instructions. As an example, let us return to the machine-language routine at the end of Section 2-2 that added the contents of memory cells 6C and 6D and placed the result in location 6E. Recall that the instructions in hexadecimal notation appeared as follows:

```
156C
166D
5056
306E
C000
```

If we now assign the name PRICE to location 6C, TAX to 6D, and TOTAL to 6E, we can express the same routine as follows using the mnemonic technique:

```
LD R5,PRICE
LD R6,TAX
ADDI R0,R5 R6
ST R0,TOTAL
HLT
```

Most would agree that the second form, although still lacking, does a much better job of representing the purpose and meaning of the routine than does the first. (Note that the mnemonic ADDI is used to represent the add op-code to distinguish it from the op-code for adding floating-point numbers, which might be represented by ADDF.)

When these techniques were first introduced, programmers used such notation when originally designing a program on paper and later translated it into machine-usable form. It was not long, however, before this translation process was recognized as a straightforward procedure that could be performed by the machine itself. Consequently, the use of mnemonics was formalized into a programming language called an **assembly language,** and a program, called an **assembler,** was developed to translate other programs written in the assembly language into machine-compatible form. (The program was called an assembler because its task was to assemble machine instructions out of the op-codes and operands obtained by translating mnemonics and identifiers. The term *assembly language* followed this lead.)

Today, assemblers have become a common utility program in most computer systems. With such a system, a programmer can type a program in mnemonic form using the system's editor and then ask the operating system to use the assembler to translate the program and save the translated version as a file for later execution.

At the time assembly languages were first developed, they appeared as a giant step forward in the search for better programming environments. In fact, many considered them to represent a totally new generation of programming languages. Thus, assembly languages came to be known as second-generation languages, the first generation being the machine languages themselves.

Although second-generation languages had many advantages over their machine-language counterparts, they still fell far short of providing the ultimate programming environment. After all, the primitives used in an assembly language were essentially the same as those found in the corresponding machine language. The difference was simply in the syntax used to represent them.

A major consequence of this close association between assembly and machine languages is that any program written in an assembly language is inherently machine dependent. That is, the instructions within the program are expressed in terms of a particular machine's attributes. In turn, a program written in assembly language is not easily transported to another machine because it must be rewritten to conform to the new machine's register configuration and instruction set.

Another disadvantage of an assembly language is that a programmer, although not required to code instructions in bit pattern form, is still forced to think in terms of the small, incremental steps of the machine's language rather than being allowed to concentrate on the overall solution of the task at hand. The situation is analogous to designing a house in terms of concrete, boards, glass, nails, bricks, and so on. It is true that the actual construction of the house ultimately requires a description based on these elementary pieces, but the design process is easier if we think in terms of rooms, basements, windows, roofs, and so on.

In short, the elementary primitives in which a product must ultimately be expressed are not necessarily the primitives that should be used during the product's design. The design process is better suited to the use of high-level primitives, each representing a concept associated with a major feature of the product. Once the design is complete, these primitives can be translated to lower-level concepts relating to the details of implementation, just as a contractor ultimately translates a building's design into a bill of materials.

Following this philosophy, computer scientists began developing programming languages that were more conducive to software development than were the low-level assembly languages. The result was the emergence of a third generation of programming languages that differed from previous generations in that their primitives were both higher level and machine independent.

In general, the approach to third-generation programming languages was to identify a collection of high-level primitives (in essentially the same spirit as that in which we developed our pseudocode in Chapter 4) in which software could be developed. Each of these primitives was designed so that it could be implemented as a sequence of the low-level primitives available in machine languages. For example, the statement

assign Total the value Price plus Tax

expresses a high-level activity without reference to how a particular machine should perform the task, yet it can be implemented by the sequence of machine instructions discussed earlier. Thus, the structure

assign *identifier* **the value** *expression*

is a potential high-level primitive.

Once this collection of high-level primitives had been identified, a program, called a *translator,* was written that translated programs expressed in these high-level primitives into machine-language programs. All the translator needed to do was recognize the high-level primitives and convert them into their machine-level equivalents. Such a program was similar to the second-generation assemblers, except the third-generation translators often had to compile several machine instructions into short sequences to simulate the activity requested by a single high-level primitive. Thus, these programs came to be known as *compilers.*

Machine Independence and Beyond

With the development of third-generation languages, the goal of machine independence was largely achieved. Since the statements in a third-generation language did not refer to the attributes of any particular machine, they could be compiled as easily for one machine as for another. Thus, a program written in a third-generation language could theoretically be used on any machine simply by applying the appropriate compiler.

Reality, however, has not proven to be this simple. When a compiler is designed, certain restrictions imposed by the underlying machine are ultimately reflected as conditions on the language being translated. For example, the size of a machine's registers and memory cells places limits on the maximum size of integers that can be manipulated conveniently. Such conditions result in the fact that the "same" language tends to have different characteristics, or dialects, on different machines; consequently, it is often necessary to make at least minor modifications to a program to move it from one machine to another.

Compounding this problem of portability is the lack of agreement in some cases as to what constitutes the correct definition of a particular language. To aid in this regard, the American National Standards Institute (ANSI) and the International Standards Organization (ISO) have adopted and published standards for some of the popular languages. In other cases, informal standards have been developed because of the popularity of a certain dialect of a language and the desire of other compiler writers to produce compatible products.

In the overall history of programming languages, the fact that third-generation languages fell short of true machine independence is actually of little significance for two reasons. First, they were close enough to being machine-independent that software could be transported from one machine to another with relative ease, and therefore the demand for machine-independent languages was essentially satisfied. Second, the goal of machine independence turned out to be only a seed for more demanding goals. Thus, by the time machine independence was within reach, its significance had been diluted in comparison to the loftier ambitions of the time. Indeed, the realization that machines could respond to such high-level statements as

assign Total the value Price plus Tax

led computer scientists to dream of programming environments that would allow humans to communicate with machines in terms of abstract concepts rather than being forced to translate these concepts into machine-compatible data before processing and then to decode the machine's output afterward. Thus, instead of quenching a thirst, the third-generation languages whet an appetite for more advanced languages, each designed to transfer still more of the problem-solving burden onto the machine and away from the user.

More Recent Developments

Two problems arise if we try to continue with the history of programming languages from the generation point of view. One is that after the third generation we bump up against the edge of evolving terminology. The truth is that the lack of a central, definitive source of terminology has resulted in varying definitions of fourth- and fifth-generation languages.

As a general rule, however, the term *fourth-generation language* is used in reference to the numerous software packages that allow users to customize computer software to their applications without needing technical expertise. Programming in such languages normally involves selecting from choices presented on the monitor's screen in sentence or icon form. Such packages include spreadsheet systems that assist in maintaining tables of data in the form of traditional accounting records; database systems that assist in the maintenance and recall of information that might otherwise be stored in a traditional filing cabinet; graphics packages that assist in the development of graphs, charts, and other pictorial representations of information; and powerful word processors that allow documents to be merged, rearranged, and reformatted. Moreover, packages such as these are often bundled (as integrated software) to form one coherent system. With such a system, an economist can construct and modify economic models, analyze the effects various changes might have on the economy in general or a given business in particular, and present the results in a written document using graphs and charts as visual aids. Moreover, a small-business manager might customize the same package to develop a system for maintaining inventory and predicting the effects of stocking certain slow-moving items.

Such systems are considered to constitute another generation in programming languages because the programming environment they provide is noticeably closer to that of the application than the environments provided by third-generation languages. For example, instead of describing how information is represented within the machine, how a table of data can be represented on a computer screen, or how entries are actually updated within the machine, a programmer using fourth-generation software merely describes what data items are to appear on the spreadsheet and how they relate to each other. From then on, the software carries out the details of implementation. Thus, the user can customize and use a computerized spreadsheet without concentrating on (or even being aware of) the details associated with the technology being used.

The term *fifth-generation language* is being used more and more in reference to the concept of declarative programming, with an emphasis on the more specialized approach known as logic programming. We define these ideas more thoroughly later in this section. For now we merely note that the idea of declarative programming is to allow the computer user to solve a problem by concentrating on what the problem is rather than on how it is to be solved. At this point, such a goal probably seems outrageous to you. How can we hope to solve a problem without ultimately concentrating on how to solve it? The answer is that we do not solve the problem; rather, we let the computer system, with its underlying software, solve it. With this approach, then, our task is merely to declare what the problem is while the machine tackles the issues of its solution.

The concept of declarative programming brings us to the second problem encountered when trying to push the generation analysis of programming languages beyond the third generation. This problem is that the generation approach insists on classifying programming languages on a linear scale (Figure 5-1) according to the degree to which the user of the language must conform to the world of computer gibberish as well as the degree to which the task of solving a problem is placed on the machine as opposed to the user. In reality, the development of programming languages has not progressed in this manner but instead has branched as different approaches to the programming process (different paradigms) have surfaced and been

Figure 5-1 Generations of programming languages

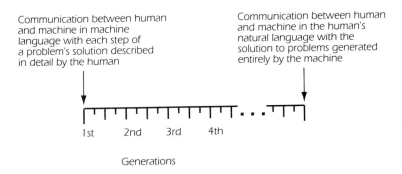

Communication between human and machine in machine language with each step of a problem's solution described in detail by the human

Communication between human and machine in the human's natural language with the solution to problems generated entirely by the machine

1st   2nd   3rd   4th

Generations

pursued. Thus, the historical development of programming languages is better represented by a multiple track diagram, in which the various paradigms are shown as new, emerging paths progressing independently of each other (Figure 5-2).

The *procedural paradigm,* also known as the *imperative paradigm,* represents the traditional approach to the programming process. Indeed, the procedural paradigm is the one on which a CPU's fetch-decode-execute cycle is based. As the name suggests, the procedural paradigm defines the programming process to be the development of procedures that when followed manipulate data to produce the desired result. Thus, the procedural paradigm tells us to approach a problem by trying to find a method for solving it.

In contrast, let us consider the *declarative paradigm.* As already mentioned, this paradigm emphasizes the question "What is the problem?" rather than "What procedure is required to solve the problem?" The trick here is to discover and implement a general problem-solving algorithm. Once this is done, problems can be solved merely by stating them in a form compatible with this algorithm and then applying the algorithm. In this context, the task of the programmer becomes that of developing a precise statement of the problem rather than of discovering an algorithm for solving the problem.

Of course, the major obstacle in developing a programming language based on the declarative paradigm is the discovery of the underlying problem-solving algorithm. For this reason early declarative languages tended to be special-purpose in nature, designed for use in particular applications. For example, the declarative approach has been used for many years in simulation languages with which computer technology is used to simulate a system (economic, physical, political, and so on) in order to test hypotheses. In these settings, the underlying algorithm is essentially the process of simulating the passage of time by repeatedly recomputing values of parameters (gross domestic product, trade deficit, and so on) based on the previously computed ones. Thus, to implement a declarative language for such simulations, all one must do is implement an algorithm that performs this repetitive procedure.

Figure 5-2 *The evolution of programming paradigms*

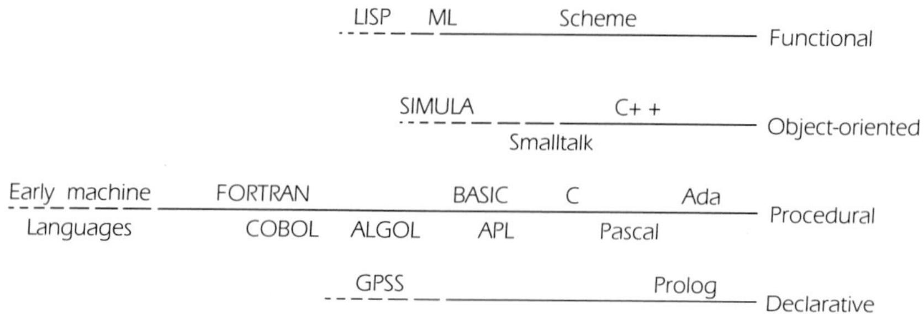

Following this, the only task required of a programmer using the language is to describe the relationships among the parameters to be simulated. Then the simulation algorithm merely simulates the passage of time using these relationships to perform its calculations.

More recently, the declarative paradigm has been given a tremendous boost by the discovery that the subject of formal logic within mathematics provides a simple problem-solving algorithm suitable for use in a general-purpose declarative programming system. The result has been increased attention to the declarative paradigm and the emergence of logic programming, a subject discussed in Section 5-6.

The *functional paradigm* views the process of program development as the construction of "black boxes," each of which accepts inputs (at the top) and produces outputs (at the bottom). Mathematicians refer to such "boxes" as functions, which is the reason this approach is called the functional paradigm. The primitives of a functional programming language consist of elementary functions (boxes) from which the programmer must construct the more elaborate functions required to solve the problem at hand. As an example, Figure 5-3 shows how a function for computing the

Figure 5-3 A function that computes the average of a list of numbers constructed from the simpler functions Add, Count, and Divide

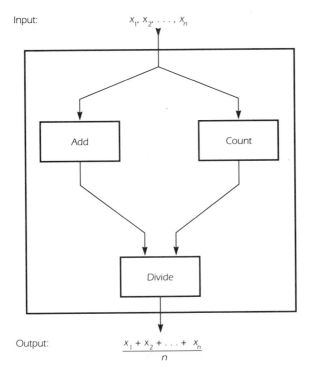

Input: $x_1, x_2, \ldots, x_n$

Add

Count

Divide

Output: $\dfrac{x_1 + x_2 + \ldots + x_n}{n}$

average of a list of numbers can be constructed from three simpler functions: One (Add) finds the sum of the entries in the list, another (Count) counts the number of entries in the list, and the third (Divide) determines the quotient of the preceding values. This construction can be represented in the syntax of LISP, a prominent functional programming language, by the expression

(Divide (Add Numbers) (Count Numbers))

whose nested structure reflects the fact that the function Divide operates on the results of Add and Count. As another example, an alphabetized list of the words in a document can be constructed by nesting three functions of the form DropPunc, which removes punctuation symbols from its input; DropDups, which removes duplicate words from its input; and Sort, which sorts its input, by the expression

(Sort (DropDups (DropPunc document)))

In short, the programming process under the functional paradigm is that of constructing functions as nested complexes of simpler functions.

An advantage of the functional programming paradigm over the procedural model is that it encourages a modular approach to program construction. Indeed, the fact that programs are viewed as functions that must be constructed from other functions forces one to think in modular terms. Thus, proponents of functional programming argue that their approach leads to well-organized programs more naturally than the procedural paradigm. Moreover, many claim that since the functional paradigm is based on building solutions from previously established pieces, new students of programming are able to develop solutions to complex problems more quickly than students who are taught the more traditional procedural techniques.

Another approach to program development is the *object-oriented paradigm,* which leads to the programming process called object-oriented programming (OOP). Using this approach, units of data are viewed as active "objects" rather than the passive units envisioned by the traditional procedural paradigm. To clarify this, consider a list of names. In the traditional procedural paradigm, this list is considered merely a collection of data. Any program accessing this list must contain the algorithms for performing the required manipulations. Thus, the list is passive in the sense that it is maintained by a controlling program rather than having the responsibility of maintaining itself. In the object-oriented approach, however, the list is considered an object consisting of the list together with a collection of routines for manipulating the list. These may include routines for entering a new entry in the list, detecting if the list is empty, and sorting the list. In turn, a program accessing this list does not need to contain algorithms for performing these tasks. Instead, it makes use of the routines provided in the object. In a sense, rather than sorting the list as in the procedural paradigm, the program asks the list to sort itself.

Many advantages of the object-oriented paradigm are consequences of the modular structure that emerges as a natural byproduct of the object-oriented philosophy. Indeed, each object is implemented as a separate, well-defined module whose characteristics are largely independent of the rest of the system. Thus, once an object representing a particular entity has been developed, that object can be reused any time that entity is required. In fact, a major feature of object-oriented programming languages is the ability to represent skeletal definitions of objects that can be used repeatedly to build multiple objects with the same properties or modified to build new objects with similar properties.

Object-oriented programming is rapidly gaining in popularity, and many believe it will dominate the programming scene in the future. Thus, the brevity of our introduction here does not represent the significance of the subject. We return to the object-oriented paradigm in our discussion of data structures in Chapter 7 and again in Chapter 9, where we consider the object-oriented approach to database design.

Clearly the development of programming languages is an ongoing process. New languages continue to evolve as we search for more convenient ways to communicate with machines. Thus, programming languages that represent the frontier of knowledge today are destined to be criticized as archaic tomorrow.

Questions/Exercises

1. In what sense is a program in a third-generation language machine independent? In what sense is it still machine dependent?
2. What is the difference between an assembler and a compiler?
3. We can summarize the procedural programming paradigm by saying that it places emphasis on describing a process that leads to the solution of the problem at hand. Give a similar summary of the declarative, functional, and object-oriented paradigms.
4. In what sense are the later-generation programming languages at a higher level than the earlier generations?

5-2 Language Implementation

The implementation of high-level programming languages is based on the process of converting programs in these languages into programs in machine language. In this section, we discuss the issues of this conversion process. Our motivation is twofold. First, an understanding of this process often helps in understanding the details of a particular programming language because these details are often traceable to concerns that arise during the conversion process. Second, our discussion of the translation of formal programming languages provides a preview to the issues involved in processing natural human languages such as English (an important topic of current research).

The Translation Process

The translation of a program consists of three activities: lexical analysis, parsing, and code generation (Figure 5-4). *Lexical analysis* is the process of recognizing which strings of symbols in the program to be translated (called the *source program*) actually represent a single, elementary object. For example, the string of three symbols 153 should not be interpreted as a 1 followed by a 5 followed by a 3 but should be recognized as representing a single numeric value. Likewise, the identifiers appearing in a program, although composed of several characters, should be interpreted collectively as a name, not as individual characters.

Note that humans perform lexical analysis with apparently little effort. When asked to read aloud, a person pronounces words rather than individual characters. On the other hand, if we expect a computer to perform this analysis, we must take care to describe what we want in an explicit, unambiguous manner. To this end, it is advantageous to design programming languages in a manner that simplifies the task of lexical analysis. Thus, most languages require that names referring to memory locations start with an alphabetic character rather than a digit. Such a restriction simplifies the task of distinguishing between a string representing a name and a string representing a numeric value.

The second activity in the translation process, *parsing,* is the process of analyzing the grammatical structure of a sentence and recognizing the role of its components. It is the technicalities of parsing that cause one to hesitate when reading the sentence

The man the horse that won the race threw was not hurt.

Likewise, it is the parsing process that distinguishes an **if-then-else** structure from a **while** structure and determines what statements belong to the **then** and **else** clauses.

To simplify the parsing task, the collection of statement structures found in a programming language is not as varied as in a natural language but normally is restricted to a few carefully chosen forms. After all, as the variety of statement structures allowed in a programming language increases, so does the complexity involved in distinguishing them from one another and identifying their various components.

Figure 5-4 The translation process

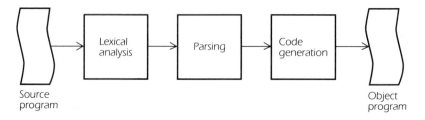

The final activity in translating a program, *code generation,* is the process of constructing sequences of machine-language instructions to simulate the statements recognized by the parser. It is this process, then, that produces the final product of the translation process—the *object program.*

Linking and Loading

The object program produced by the translation process, although expressed in machine language, is rarely in a form that can be executed directly by the machine. One reason is that most programming environments allow the modules of a program to be developed and translated as individual units at different times (which supports the modular construction of software). Thus, the object program produced from a single translation process is often only one of several pieces of a complete program, each piece of which requests services from the other modules in order to accomplish the task of the entire system. Even when a complete program is developed and translated as a single module, its object program is rarely prepared to stand alone at execution time because it most likely contains requests for services from utility software available through the operating system or from the operating system itself. Thus, an object program is actually a machine-language program containing several loose ends that must be connected to other object programs before an executable program is obtained.

The task of making these connections is performed by a utility program called a *linker.* Its job is to link several object modules (the result of previous and separate translations), operating system routines, and other utility software to produce a complete, executable program (sometimes called a load module) that is in turn stored as a file in the machine's mass storage system.

Finally, to execute a translated program, the load module must be placed in memory by a utility program called a *loader.* The significance of this step is most pronounced in the case of multitasking systems, in which the exact memory area available to the program is not known until it is time to execute the program (since it must share memory with other processes being executed) and varies from one execution to the next. In this setting, the task of the loader is to place the program in the memory area identified by the operating system and make any last-minute (last-microsecond) adjustments that might be needed once the exact memory location of the program is known. (A jump instruction in the program must jump to the correct address within the program.) It is the desire to minimize these last-minute adjustments by the loader that has encouraged the development of techniques by which explicit references to memory addresses within a program can be avoided, resulting in a program (called a relocatable module) that, without modification, executes correctly regardless of where it is placed in memory.

In summary, the complete task of preparing a high-level-language program for execution consists of the three-step sequence of translate, link, and load, as

Figure 5-5 The complete program preparation process

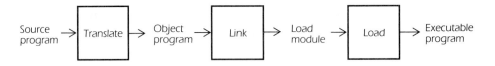

represented in Figure 5-5. Of course, once the translate and link steps have been completed, the program can be repeatedly loaded and executed without returning to the source version. If, however, a change must be made to the program, it is made to the source program, and then the modified source program is translated and linked to produce a new load module containing the change.

Translation Versus Interpretation

To alleviate the need for translation and linking after each program modification, an alternative to translation known as interpretation has been developed. In contrast to translation, interpretation uses a software package called an **interpreter** to scan the source program and perform the required activities. Thus, unlike a translator, which merely produces a machine-language copy of the program, an interpreter executes the program directly from its source-language form (Figure 5-6). Of course, we realize that because the machine executes only machine-language instructions, a certain translation process must be performed by the interpreter, but this step is hidden from the programmer; thus, the program appears to be executed without any required conversions.

Figure 5-6 Translation versus interpretation

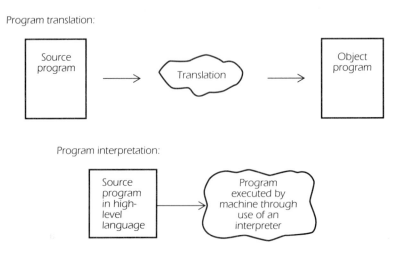

As you might imagine, the major advantage of using an interpreter is that once a program has been submitted to a machine in a high-level language form, it can be executed through a one-step process rather than the multiple translate/link/load/execute sequence required by translation.

The major disadvantage of an interpreter is that no permanent copy of the translation is produced and saved. Rather, the internal translation steps must be repeated each time the program is executed. The result is that a program being interpreted takes longer to execute than a similar program that is already translated. For this reason translation is often chosen for programs that are to be executed repeatedly, such as a payroll processor, or when real-time requirements demand timely execution. However, during program development and debugging or when programs are written on an experimental basis, executed only a few times, and then discarded, interpretation has proven extremely useful.

Questions/Exercises

1. Summarize the steps in the translation process.
2. a. What is the difference between a translator and an interpreter?
   b. Compare the process of making a change to a program that is translated to the process of making a similar change to a program that is interpreted.
3. In what sense is an object program not ready for execution?
4. What is a relocatable module, and how does its relocatable feature simplify the task of a loader?

5-3 Programming Language Design

Before considering detailed aspects of particular programming languages, we should discuss some of the general concerns of programming-language design. These concerns center around the choice and implementation of the primitives from which programs in the language must be constructed. Because each primitive consists of a semantic structure and its syntactic representation, our discussion is divided accordingly.

Semantic Concerns

The paradigm on which a language is based goes a long way toward establishing the semantic structures (ideas) that the language must be capable of expressing. If the paradigm is object-oriented, the language must allow the expression of objects; if the paradigm is procedural, the language will be called upon to express such control concepts as conditional branching, iteration, and recursion.

Of course, not all the concepts that must be expressible in the language need to be implemented as individual primitives. Instead, many concepts can be described in terms of other, less complex concepts, just as ideas that cannot be expressed in a single word of English can be expressed by combining well-established words to form sentences and paragraphs. This, combined with the fact that simple languages make for simple translators and interpreters, encourages the design of languages that are founded on small, well-chosen collections of basic semantic structures from which other, more complex structures can be constructed as needed.

Unfortunately, one cannot predict the applications for which a given programming language may ultimately be used, and one certainly would not want to discover at a later date that the use of the language is restricted because a critical semantic structure was not included in the language's design. One is therefore faced with conflicting goals. On the one hand, there is pressure to implement a large collection of primitives in hopes of covering all future needs; on the other hand, a cumbersome language is difficult to design, implement, learn, and use.

In Chapter 11 we learn that the theoretical foundations of computer science provide a solution to this problem. Only a few well-chosen primitives are required to ensure that a programming language has no hidden limitations. Indeed, most of the features in today's high-level languages are provided to increase a language's ease of use rather than its ultimate capabilities.

In addition to the choice of which semantic structures should be implemented as primitives, the design of a programming language requires that the chosen semantic structures be constructed in a manner that avoids ambiguities. The ambiguities occurring in natural languages are totally unacceptable in a programming environment. Anyone who has ever tried to match paint colors knows that the semantics of the statement "The kitchen wall is yellow" is ambiguous when it comes to the task of touching up the discolored area on the wall where an artifact has hung for 10 years. Moreover, some natural language statements have multiple meanings. The semantics of the statement "The better stock ran well ahead of the herd" varies depending on whether one is speaking of a financial market or stampeding cattle.

In the context of programming languages, the precise meaning of each primitive is relatively easy to control. It is when these primitives are combined to form more complex semantic structures that subtle ambiguities can arise. For instance, the semantics of addition and multiplication of integers are well established, yet when combined, as in $5 + 7 \times 2$, a potential ambiguity presents itself. Is the value represented 24 (the result of multiplying the sum $5 + 7$ by 2) or 19 (the result of adding 5 to the product 7×2)? This problem is often resolved by accepting the traditional precedence rules associated with numeric operations. In this case, given a numeric expression, all exponentiations are performed first, then multiplications and divisions, and finally additions and subtractions. Another option is to perform the operations as they are encountered from left to right or from right to left.

Other ambiguities arise when combining structures of the **if-then-else** and **if-then** variety. Each of these primitives has a well-defined meaning, yet when combined, as in the statement

if B1 **then if** B2 **then** X **else** Y

there is the potential for two different interpretations represented by

if B1 **then [if** B2 **then** X **]** **else** Y

and

if B1 **then [if** B2 **then** X **else** Y **]**

In the first case, action Y is executed if condition B1 is false, regardless of the condition B2. In the second case, Y is executed only if B1 is true and B2 is false. An example of how this problem might be resolved is to accept the rule that **else** clauses in a program are assigned to **if** statements by scanning the program from beginning to end while interpreting each **else** clause as the alternate activity associated with the nearest preceding **if** structure that has yet not been assigned an alternative. Thus,

if B1 **then if** B2 **then** X **else** Y

would be assigned the semantics represented by

if B1 **then [if** B2 **then** X **else** Y **]**

We see, then, that the definition of the semantics within a programming language encompasses more than the meaning of each individual primitive. It also includes the semantics of compound structures formed by combining primitives—a context that has the potential for producing numerous subtle distinctions, all of which must be carefully accounted for.

Syntactic Concerns

Let us now turn to the design issues involving syntax. These include the general structure and layout of a written program, notational conventions for representing the semantics of combined primitives, and the representation of the individual primitives themselves. The overall concern is that a program written in the language should be easily comprehensible to a human as well as to a translator or an interpreter.

We begin with the representation of individual primitives. Here, the symbols used to represent each primitive should reflect the semantics of the primitive in a clear, unambiguous manner. Indeed, examples of awkward syntax/semantic relationships occurring in programming languages are often the source of programming errors, especially for beginning programmers. For instance, consider the statement

Extra = Tax

which represents a common statement structure in the language FORTRAN. Without further explanation of the language, one is left with doubts as to the meaning of this statement. To the layperson, it appears to be a declarative statement indicating that the value referred to by Extra is the same as the value referred to by Tax. Even when it is explained that the statement is instructing the movement of data from one location to another, the syntax still is ambiguous about which direction the motion is to take place (from Extra to Tax or from Tax to Extra?).

In contrast, consider the equivalent statement from the language APL.[1] It appears as

$$\text{Extra} \leftarrow \text{Tax}$$

which most people would agree better represents the underlying semantics than its FORTRAN counterpart.

In addition to representing individual primitives, the syntax of a language should be designed to reflect the semantics of combined primitives. In particular, the syntax should reinforce the manner in which potential ambiguities in the semantics are resolved. As an example, consider the **if-then-else** and **if-then** structures in our pseudocode of Chapter 4. There we used parentheses to enclose the various components of the statements. One purpose of these symbols is to clarify the meaning of combined structures. For example, we could write

if B1 **then** (**if** B2 **then** X) **else** Y

when activity Y is to be executed if B1 is false and

if B1 **then** (**if** B2 **then** X **else** Y)

when Y is to be executed only if B1 is true and B2 false.

Similar uses of parentheses are common throughout many programming languages. For instance, parentheses are often used to clarify the interpretation of numerical expressions. The ambiguities inherent in the expression $5 + 7 \times 2$ are easily overcome by writing either $(5 + 7) \times 2$ or $5 + (7 \times 2)$, depending on the interpretation desired.

Another issue of syntax is the distinction between fixed-format and free-format design. The term *fixed format* means that the positioning of program statements on the written page must conform with certain rules. Early versions of FORTRAN required that instructions appear between the seventh and seventy-second columns on the printed page. Columns two through five were reserved for numeric labels that identify the various statements, and a nonblank symbol in column six indicated that the statement on that line was actually a continuation of the instruction on the

---

[1]We will not study the language APL in this text simply because we cannot do everything here. The language was developed by Kenneth Iverson in the early 1960s. You may want to investigate it on your own. By the way, APL stands for "a programming language."

previous line. Such restrictions allowed a translator to find the beginnings of the statements in a program as well as distinguish between the types of statements found. But this efficiency in parsing was at the expense of flexibility.

In contrast, newer programming languages tend to be based on a free-format design, in which the positioning of statements is not critical. The advantage is that programmers are free to organize the statements on the printed page in a way that enhances a program's readability. Thus, even though the use of parentheses is enough to avoid ambiguity in the statement

if B1 **then** (**if** B2 **then** X) **else** Y

the use of indentation to produce

if B1
   then (**if** B2 **then** X)
   else Y

increases the statement's readability.

Of course, with the advantages of a free-format design also come disadvantages. Because more than one statement can appear on a single line while other statements are spread over several lines, the syntax of a free-format language must include techniques for distinguishing the end of one instruction from the beginning of another. These include the use of punctuation such as semicolons and periods to separate statements; the use of key words such as **if, while,** and **repeat** to mark the beginning of certain structures; and parentheses and brackets for grouping components within statements.

Note that the use of key words for identifying certain components of a program often dictates that such words be used for that purpose only. If ADD were a key word representing the operation of addition, a programmer may experience difficulties if the data relating to an employee's address were referred to in a program as ADD. Thus, key words in a programming language are often also reserved words.

Finally, we note that the development of a parser for a particular programming language relies on a precise definition of the grammatical rules dictating how the symbols in the language can be combined to form programs. One technique for communicating these rules is to use *syntax diagrams.* These diagrams normally are provided as a set of charts, each describing a particular grammatical structure, perhaps in terms of other structures.

A syntax diagram describing the structure of the **if-then-else** statement in our pseudocode is shown in Figure 5-7 on the following page. Note that the **else** clause is shown to be optional, because by following the arrows through the diagram, one can either traverse the clause or bypass it. Note also that those terms that appear in an actual instance of the structure (such as the words **if** and **then**) are displayed within circles or ovals, whereas those terms representing components whose structures are not specified in this particular diagram (such as Boolean expression and statement) are

Figure 5-7 A syntax diagram of our if-then-else pseudocode statement

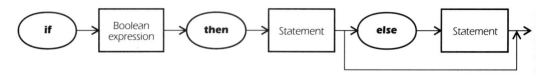

displayed within rectangles. In general, the structure of these latter components would be represented by additional diagrams that would collectively describe the entire pseudocode language.

As an example, Appendix D contains a set of syntax diagrams describing the Pascal programming language. First it describes a program as consisting of a program header followed by a declarative part that is followed by a procedural part and a period. Then additional diagrams are provided that describe these components in more detail. The second diagram, for example, shows that the structure program header begins with the word **program**. Thus, every Pascal program must begin with the word **program**.

Questions/Exercises

1. What ambiguities can arise when combining structures with the conjunctions *and* and *or*? How can parentheses be used to avoid these ambiguities?
2. Give three different values that might be obtained by evaluating the expression $2 \times 4 + 6/2$ and explain how each is obtained.
3. Based on the last diagram in Appendix D, which of the following strings are valid identifiers in the Pascal programming language?
   a. X7YZ   b. a8*2   c. 856   d. R33   e. XYZ
4. What properties of natural languages cause similar problems in both writing legal documents and expressing algorithms? How are these problems resolved in the legal profession? How are they resolved in a programming environment?
5. Give two different semantic meanings for the sentence:

    John ran after the parade.

5-4 Procedural Language Components

Let us now consider the class of third-generation procedural languages in more detail. Our examples are drawn from the languages Ada, C, FORTRAN, and Pascal. Our goal is not to learn how to program in any of these languages. Rather, our goal is to develop an understanding of the programming process dictated by the use of languages in this class.

Since these languages are based on the procedural paradigm, a program written in them consists of a description of the algorithmic process to be executed. However,

Figure 5-8 *The traditional organization of a source program*

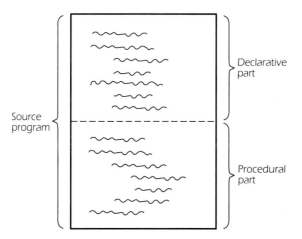

many of these languages also place a strong emphasis on the description of the data that the algorithm is to manipulate. Thus, a program in one of these languages tends to be divided into two parts: the declarative part, where pertinent facts about the data to be manipulated as well as other terminology particular to the program (subprogram names and descriptions) are described, and the procedural part, where the algorithmic process itself is described (Figure 5-8). We divide our discussion accordingly, beginning with the issues of the declarative portion of a program.

Data Description Statements

To use descriptive names for data within a program, it is necessary for the programmer to explain the names to the translator or interpreter. This explanation is usually done in the declarative part of a program using data description statements. Such statements provide a means of declaring the data names, often called identifiers, along with other associated information such as the data's type and structure (which we will explain shortly). With this information the translator or interpreter is able to set aside memory cells to hold the data, recall the addresses of these cells when the names are used later in the program, and construct the appropriate machine instructions to perform the data manipulation requested in the procedural part of the program.

Data Type

Data *type* refers to the interpretation given a bit pattern representing the data as well as the operations that can be performed on that data. Types with which we are familiar include integer, real, and character. The type *integer* refers to numeric data consisting of whole numbers, probably stored using two's complement notation. Operations that can be performed on integer data include the traditional arithmetic operations and comparison of relative size, such as determining whether the value of X is greater than value of Y. The type *real* refers to numeric data that may contain values other than whole numbers, probably stored in floating-point notation. Operations allowed on real data are similar to those performed on data of type integer. The type *character* consists of alphabetic, numeric, and punctuation symbols, probably stored in ASCII notation. Operations allowed on such data include relative comparison such as testing whether symbol X is before symbol Y in alphabetical order.

Another common type is **Boolean** (named in honor of the mathematician George Boole, 1815–1864), which refers to a data item that can have the value true or false. Examples occur as the result of comparisons such as Is Tax equal to Withholding? or as flags as in our proposed solution to the printer access problem of Section 3-6. Operations on data of type Boolean include assignment of a true or false value and inquiries as to whether the current value is true or false. Note that an item of type Boolean can be represented by a single bit.

Our example languages are rather similar in the manner in which they allow the association between identifiers and types to be declared in the declarative part of a program. For example, in the language C, the statements

```
float Length, Width;
int   Price, Tax, Total;
```

indicate that the identifiers Length and Width refer to memory locations containing floating-point representations while Price, Tax, and Total refer to integer values probably represented in two's complement notation. The same information in Pascal is expressed as

```
var
   Length, Width:  real;
   Price, Tax, Total: integer;
```

Knowing the type associated with each data item within a program is beneficial during the program translation process. For instance, imagine a compiler trying to translate the statement

```
MOVE Price PLUS Tax INTO Total
```

One of the first tasks the compiler might perform is to check that the operation requested (in this case, numeric addition) is appropriate for the data involved. Indeed, if Price is of type real and Tax of type character, then adding Price and Tax makes little sense and, in fact, should be reported as an error. If Price, Tax, and Total are all of type integer, then the translator knows to use the machine's integer addition instruction, whereas if they are of type real, the floating-point instruction is required.

Sometimes the action requested by a program may be meaningful even though the data types involved are not the same. For instance, the above instruction makes sense if Price and Tax are integer but Total is real. In this case, the compiler uses the integer addition instruction, but the sum must be recoded into floating-point format before being assigned to Total. Such implicit conversion between types is called **coercion.**

Coercion is frowned on by many language designers. They reason that the need for conversion usually indicates an error in the program's design and therefore should not be accommodated by the translator. The result is that most modern languages are **strongly typed,** which means that all activities requested by a program must involve data of agreeable types without coercion. In turn, compilers for these languages report all type conflicts as errors.

Data Structure

Another major concept associated with data is **structure,** which relates to the conceptual shape of the data. Perhaps the simplest example of this occurs when using a string of characters to represent an employee's name or a part identification number. It is not sufficient to know that the data item is of type character, but one must also know how many characters make up the item. If a translator must generate the machine instructions to move an employee's name from one location in memory to another, it must know how many memory cells to move. Thus, a FORTRAN program might contain the phrase

CHARACTER(LEN = 8) Name

indicating that Name is to refer to a string of eight characters. The same information would be expressed Ada as

Name: STRING(1..8);

Another common example of structured data is an **array.** The term *array* refers to a block of values such as a list (often called a vector), a two-dimensional table (a matrix), or tables of higher dimensions (these do not have special names). Elements of an array normally are identified within a program through the use of indices. That is, the third entry in a vector named Sales is referenced by the expression Sales (3), and the entry from the second row and fifth column of a matrix named Scores is identified by Scores(2,5). (A minor exception is found in the C language, in which row and column numbers start at 0 rather than 1. Hence, in C, the entry in the second row and fifth column is identified by Scores [1][4].) Note that it is customary to list the row number before the column number.

To describe an array in the declarative part of a program, most languages use a syntax similar to that used for referring to the array later in the program's procedural

Figure 5-9 The 2-by-9 array named SCORES

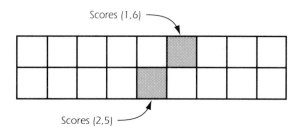

part. However, in the description statement, the values of the indices indicate the size of the array rather than a position in it. Thus, a matrix of integers containing two rows and nine columns (the shape of a baseball scoreboard, as shown in Figure 5-9) named Scores is described in FORTRAN by the statement

INTEGER Scores(2,9)

and in C by

int Scores [2][9];

The same structure is described in Pascal by

var
Scores: array [1..2,1..9] of integer;

Up to this point we have looked at examples of ***homogeneous arrays,*** meaning that all the entries of a given array are the same type. It is often convenient to deal with ***heterogeneous arrays,*** which are arrays in which different elements can be different types. For example, we might consider a block of employee data as a vector whose first entry is Name (type character), second entry is Age (type integer), and third entry is Rating (type real) (Figure 5-10). In Pascal, such a structure is described by

var
Employee: **record**
        Name: packed array [1..20] of char;
        Age: integer;
        Rating: real
    end

The rectangular shape associated with arrays actually exists only in the programmer's mind, not in the machine, and is therefore a virtual structure. In reality, the data contained in the array may be scattered over a wide area of the machine's memory. This is why we refer to structure as being the conceptual shape of data. It is the responsibility of the translator or interpreter to set aside, based on the data descriptions we have been discussing, a suitable block of memory for holding the data

Figure 5-10 *A heterogeneous array named* Employee

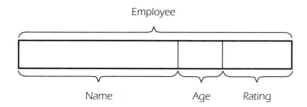

and later be able to locate the correct item within this block when an expression in the program such as Scores [1,4] is reached. In a sense, then, the translator or interpreter simulates the conceptual structure.

User-Defined Types

The expression of an algorithm is often more convenient if types other than those provided as primitives in the programming language are available. For this reason, most modern programming languages allow programmers to define additional types, using the primitive types and structures as building blocks. These additional types are known as *user-defined types.*

As an example, suppose we develop a program involving numerous identifiers, each consisting of the same heterogeneous structure as the Employee example earlier in this section. We could declare the structure of each identifier using a separate statement in which we explicitly repeat the common information. A more succinct approach, however, is to define an additional type, perhaps called EmployeeType, that incorporates the common structure of each identifier. Then we can declare each identifier to be of that type. This is accomplished in Pascal by first defining the type EmployeeType with the statement

```
type
    EmployeeType = record
                Name:    packed array[1 . . 20] of integer;
                Age:     integer;
                Rating:  real
            end
```

and then declaring the variables DistManager, Sales1, and Sales2 to be of type EmployeeType using the statement

```
var
    DistManager, Sales1, Sales2: EmployeeType;
```

In addition to being more succinct than describing the structure of each identifier separately, this latter approach clarifies the fact that all the identifiers have a common structure. Hence, the program we obtain would be more accessible than had we described the structure of each identifier separately.

Variables Versus Constants

Thus far we have related descriptive names to data by associating the name with the memory cell (or cells) that holds the data. With this arrangement, the value associated with a name can be varied as the program executes by changing the bit pattern of the related memory location. The data associated in this manner with the name is said to be variable, and the name is called a variable name or sometimes simply a *variable.* (Note that this terminology does not mean that the name varies but that the value associated with the name can vary.) This terminology is the origin of the key word **var** in the Pascal statements in the preceding paragraphs.

In contrast, it is often helpful to assign a descriptive name to a value that does not change later in a program. For instance, in a program for controlling air traffic around an airport, the airport's altitude above sea level might be used in many computations. If we associate the name AirportAlt with this value, say 645 feet, then this descriptive name can be used when expressing computations instead of the less descriptive value 645. (To anyone reading the program, the name AiportAlt conveys the purpose of a computation in which it appears more readily than the appearance of the actual value 645.) Note that the value associated with AiportAlt does not change during program execution. That is, the value associated with the name is constant rather than variable, and thus such a name is referred to as a symbolic constant or simply a *constant.* Many programming languages allow the programmer to specify such constants. For example, AirportAlt can be associated with the constant value 645 in Pascal by

const AirportAlt = 645;

The technique of naming constants is also helpful if the program ever needs to be changed. For example, if our air traffic control program is installed at another airport, the altitude of the airport must be changed inside the program. If we used the value 645 in all the computations requiring this information, we must find and change each of these values within the program. The problem is further complicated if the value 645 also occurs in reference to a quantity other than the airport's altitude. How do we know which occurrences of 645 to change and which to leave alone? On the other hand, if we define the name AirportAlt to refer to the constant 645, as in the preceding statement, and use this descriptive name in the program, changing the program for another airport at the altitude 267 feet simply requires changing the preceding statement to

const AirportAlt = 267;

This simple modification causes all occurrences of AirportAlt in the associated program to refer to the value 267 rather than 645.

Assignment Statements

When we discussed machine languages, we separated the instructions for moving data into a different group from those that performed arithmetic or logic operations. However, in high-level languages, these steps are often combined into a single syntactic structure called an *assignment statement.* For example, although the FORTRAN statement

Extra = Tax

that we discussed earlier is only a data-movement statement, the same syntactic structure is used to represent instructions for performing computations. This is done by replacing the right-hand side of the movement statement with an expression describing the operation to be performed and using the left-hand side to indicate the location in which the result is to be stored. Thus, to add Price and Tax giving Total in C and FORTRAN, one would write

Total = Price + Tax

Likewise, in Ada and Pascal the preceding assignment statements would be written as

Extra : = Tax

and

Total : = Price + Tax

respectively.

In general, any algebraic expression can be used in place of the expression Price + Tax in our examples, with the arithmetic operations of addition, subtraction, multiplication, division, and exponentiation typically represented by the symbols +, −, *, /, and **, respectively, although care should be taken to observe the order in which these operations might be performed. For instance, the expression 2 * 4 + 6 / 2 could be associated with different values depending on the semantic rules of the language (Section 5-3).

Again you should be cautioned not to consider computers as predominately number crunchers (that is, machines that perform numeric computations). Many computations other than the arithmetic operations are expressible in high-level languages. One important group consists of those operations performed on strings of characters. Examples include finding occurrences of one string in another, concatenating two strings to form a single long one, or replacing a part of a string with another. For instance, if First and Last are names of character strings, the FORTRAN statement

Both = First//Last

causes the name Both to be associated with the long string formed by concatenating the contents of First and Last.

Many languages use the symbol + to represent the concatenation operation. In this case, the symbol + has different meanings depending on the type of its operands: If its operands are numeric, it represents addition; if its operands are strings of characters, it represents concatenation. Such multiple use of a symbol is called **overloading.**

We will introduce other string operations later in our discussion of string-processing functions.

Statement-Level Control Statements

Control statements control or alter the execution sequence of the program. Of all the programming statements, those from this group have probably received the most attention and generated the most controversy. The major villain is the simplest control statement of all, the GOTO statement. It provides a means of directing the execution sequence to another location that has been labeled for this purpose by a name or number. It is therefore nothing more than a direct application of the machine-level jump instruction. The problem with such a feature in a high-level programming language is it allows programmers to write rat's nests like

```
        GOTO 40
20      Total = Price + 10
        GOTO 70
40      IF Price < 50 GOTO 60
        GOTO 20
60      Total = Price + 5
70      STOP
```

when a two-statement program like this does the job:

```
IF Price < 50 THEN Total = Price + 5
              ELSE Total = Price + 10
STOP
```

To avoid such complexities, modern languages are designed with more elaborate control statements, such as **if-then-else,** that allow a certain branching pattern to be expressed within a single syntactic structure. The choice of which control structures to incorporate into a language is a significant design decision. The object is to provide a language that not only allows algorithms to be expressed in a readable form but also assists the programmer in obtaining such readability. This is done by restricting the use of those features that have historically led to sloppy programming while encouraging the use of better-designed features. The result is the often misunderstood practice known as **structured programming,** which encompasses an organized design methodology combined with the appropriate use of the language's control statements. The idea is to produce a program that can be readily comprehended and can be easily shown to meet its specifications.

The more common branching structures as they appear in the Pascal language together with their corresponding flowchart representations are listed in Figure 5-11.

Figure 5-11 Fundamental Pascal control structures

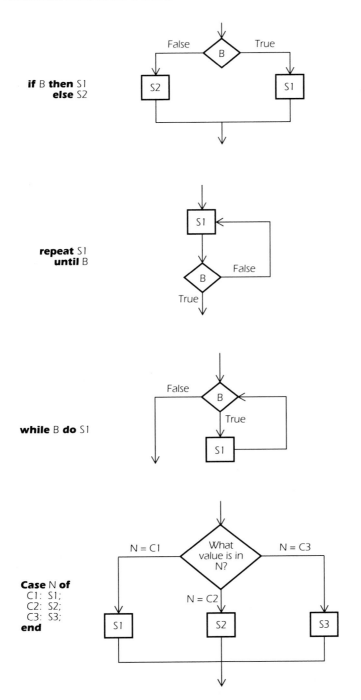

if B **then** S1
    else S2

repeat S1
    until B

while B **do** S1

Case N **of**
  C1: S1;
  C2: S2;
  C3: S3;
end

In each case, the notation S1, S2, and so on, represents arbitrary instructions, and B represents the occurrence of a phrase such as "I < 5" or "Name = 'Smith' " that produces a Boolean result. In the **case** statement, N represents the name of a data item, and C1, C2, C3 represent the possible values of that item.

Statements expressing the control structures in Figure 5-11 are found with varying degree in numerous programming languages, especially the newer ones. One control structure, however, that appeared in the early procedural languages has maintained its popularity through the years. This is a form of the loop structure discussed in Chapter 4. Here the repetition of the loop's body is controlled by maintaining an auxiliary data element that is automatically modified each time the loop is traversed in addition to being tested for a programmer-defined termination condition. An example of this structure as it appears in each of our example languages is shown in Figure 5-12. In each case, we use the name K for the auxiliary data element and request that the body of the loop (represented by dots) be executed five times.

Unit-Level Control Statements

We now consider statements that control the execution of entire subprograms.

Subprograms

A subprogram (also known as a procedure or subroutine) is nothing more than a collection of instructions forming a program unit written independently of the main program yet associated with it through a transfer/return process (Figure 5-13). Control is passed to the subprogram at the time its services are required, and then control is returned to the main program after the subprogram has finished.

Figure 5-12 Traditional loop control structures

```
        Ada:   for K in 1 . .5 loop
                   .
                   .
                   .
               end loop;
          C:   for (K = 1; K<6; ++K)
               {. . .}
     FORTRAN:   DO K = 1,5
                   .
                   .
                   .
               END DO
       Pascal:   for K: = 1 to 5 do
                   begin
                   .
                   .
                   .
                   end
```

The syntax used to represent the request of a subprogram varies among the different languages. FORTRAN uses the key word CALL. In contrast, C, Pascal, and Ada identify the required subprogram by its name alone. Thus, if we write subprograms called GetNames (to get a list of names from a person at a keyboard), SortNames (to sort a list of names), and WriteNames (to write a list of names at a monitor), we can combine them to form a larger program to get a list and write it in sorted order in FORTRAN with the statement sequence

        CALL GetNames
        CALL SortNames
        CALL WriteNames

or in C, Pascal, and Ada with

        GetNames;
        SortNames;
        WriteNames;

The technique used to describe a subprogram itself varies from language to language. In fact, many systems allow such program units to be written in languages other than that of the main program. In such cases, the subprograms are translated individually, and then their object versions are linked to the object version of the main program, forming a load module containing the entire program package.

Parameters

In most procedural programming languages, a subprogram is implemented as though it were a completely separate entity with its own data and algorithm so that an item of data in either the main program or the subprogram is not

Figure 5-13 The flow of control involving a subprogram

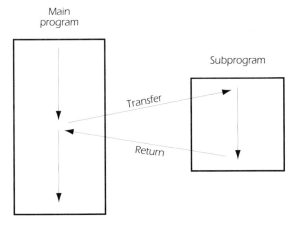

automatically accessible from within the other. (In fact, data names within the sub-program can be identical to those in the main program without implying any relationship among the data, just as members of different households may have the same name even though no relationship exists between them.) With this arrangement, any transfer of data between the two program parts must be specified explicitly by the programmer. This is usually done by listing the items called *parameters* (or sometimes arguments) to be transferred in the same syntactic structure used to request the subprogram's execution (usually by means of a parenthetical statement).

In its most general form, the transfer of data through parameters takes place in two directions. When execution of the subprogram is requested, the parameters are effectively transferred to the subprogram, the subprogram is executed, the (possibly modified) parameters are transferred back to the main program, and the main program continues. In other cases, the transfer can take place in only one direction: either to the subprogram before it is executed or to the main program after the subprogram's execution. Languages that provide more than one of these transfer techniques also provide a means by which the programmer can specify which option is desired.

Perhaps the most straightforward example among our example languages is found in Ada. Here the key words **in, out,** and **in out** are used to indicate the direction in which data is transferred. For example, consider a subprogram named Larger, defined with three parameters named I, J, and K in such a way that, when called, the subprogram compares the numbers assigned to I and J and places the larger one in location K. Such a subprogram can be written in Ada as

```
procedure Larger(I,J: In INTEGER; K: out INTEGER) is
begin
  if I < J then K := J
           else K := I
end Larger;
```

Here the parameters I and J are designated as **in** parameters, while the parameter K is designated as an **out** parameter. These designations describe the direction in which information is to be transferred in relation to the subprogram. That is, information is to be transferred into the parameters I and J but out of the parameter K.

Once our subprogram has been defined, it can be used from within a main program to place the larger of the two numbers associated with locations Num1 and Num2 in location L by inserting the statement

Larger(Num1, Num2, L);

in the program where this action is desired. When this statement is executed, the following sequence of events is performed (see Figure 5-14):

Figure 5-14 An example of parameter passing

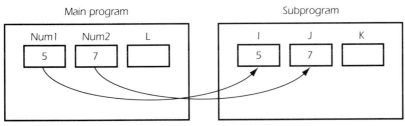

(a) Num1 and Num2 are effectively
transferred to I and J.

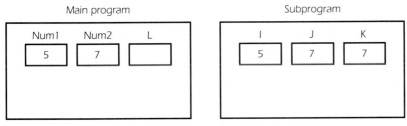

(b) Subprogram places the larger value
in location K.

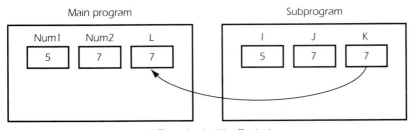

(c) The value in K is effectively
returned to the main program.

1. The values associated with Num1 and Num2 in the main program are effectively copied[1] into the locations I and J, respectively, in the subprogram.
2. The subprogram is executed, leaving the larger value in location K.
3. The value in K (in the subprogram) is copied into the location L in the main program.
4. Execution of the main program continues with the statement following the statement that invoked the subprogram.

From this sequence of events, we see that the names used for the parameters within the subprogram can be thought of as merely standing in for the actual data values that are supplied when the subprogram is requested. As a result, you often hear them called *formal parameters,* whereas the data values supplied from the main program are referred to as *actual parameters.*

A significant benefit of this substitution system is that the same subprogram can be asked to perform its task on different sets of data at different points in the main program. In particular, our Larger subprogram can be used at one point to find the larger of the two values Num1 and Num2 with the statement

Larger(Num1, Num2, L);

and later to find the larger of the values X and Y with the statement

Larger(X, Y, L);

Functions

A useful variation from the strict parameter list form of communication between a main program and a subprogram is found in the concept of a *function.* A function is a subprogram in which input values are transferred through a parameter list. However, information is returned from a function to the main program in the form of the "value of the function." That is, the value returned by a function is associated with the name of the function in a manner similar to the association between a value and a variable name. The difference is that the value associated with a function name is computed (according to the function's definition) each time it is required, whereas when a variable's value is required, it is merely retrieved from memory.

Students of trigonometry are familiar with the functions sine and cosine. These functions are often referenced by expressions such as sin(x) and cos(x), in which the

[1]We use the words *effectively copied* to reflect the fact that different programming languages transfer parameters in different ways. In some cases, the data is actually copied from its location in the main program into memory cells associated with the subprogram. This technique is inefficient when the amount of data associated with the parameters being passed is large. A more efficient method is to transfer only the address of the memory cells that contain the required data. This gives the subprogram access to the data without the overhead of producing a duplicate copy. In the latter case, the information in the memory cells is said to be passed to the subprogram by reference. If, however, the information is actually copied, it is said to be passed by value.

input parameter is designated by x and the result of executing the function is represented by the expression itself. Thus,

$$sin(x) + cos(x)$$

expresses the sum of the results from computing sin(x) and cos(x).

Likewise, if we implement our Ada subprogram Larger as a function called Max, we can store the larger of Num1 and Num2 in L using the statement

$$L := Max(Num1, Num2);$$

More precisely, the meaning of this statement is that the larger of the values Num1 and Num2 is returned as the value associated with Max, and this value is then assigned to L.

A major advantage of a function over a subprogram is that, with a function, the value being returned is immediately available for further computation. For example, if Min is a function that returns the smaller of its two parameters, the statement

$$Z := Max(Num1, Num2) - Min(Num3, Num4);$$

assigns to the variable Z the largest difference that can be obtained by subtracting either Num3 or Num4 from one of Num1 or Num2. To accomplish this same task using similar subprograms requires a sequence of statements, such as

```
Larger(Num1, Num2, L);
Smaller(Num3, Num4, S);
Z := L - S;
```

String-Processing Functions

One method of extending the operations available in a programming language is to design a collection of functions that perform the operations desired and then to place this collection in a library file from which the functions can be linked to programs that require their services. A common example of this is the implementation of operations for manipulating strings of characters.

One of the most common string-processing functions computes the length of (the number of symbols in) a string. In C, this function is known as strlen (short for string length), whereas some dialects of Pascal call the function Length. Thus, if Name is the identifier of a string having the value *William*, then

$$strlen(Name)$$

and

$$Length(Name)$$

each return the value 7, whereas if the value of Name is *Shakespeare*, the result is 11.

Another common string operation is concatenation. We have already seen that this operation appears in FORTRAN as // and in some dialects of Pascal by overloading the symbol +. In C, however, it is implemented as a library function known as strcat.

Finding the location of one string within another is also a common operation with strings. In some dialects of Pascal this operation is implemented as a function named Pos (short for Position), and in C it appears as a function known as strstr (short for string substring). In particular, if LongString represents the string *touched* and SubString represents *ouch*, then

Pos(SubString, LongString)

returns the value 2, because *ouch* begins at the second position in *touched*. Similarly, in C,

strstr(LongString, SubString)

returns the location (in the form of a memory address) of the starting position of *ouch* in the string *touched*.

Implicit Subprogram Activation

Until now, our discussion of the control of program units has centered around explicit control techniques. That is, when using these techniques, we must explicitly request the execution of the desired program unit. In contrast, numerous implicit techniques exist by which program units can be activated. One example is the interrupt routine discussed earlier in terms of time-sharing operating systems, where we saw that the execution of the dispatcher is initiated by the expiration of a program's time slice rather than by an explicit request by the program. In fact, the program whose time slice has terminated would probably prefer to keep running and not call the dispatcher. Thus, we have an example of a program unit being activated by the occurrence of an event rather than by an explicit request.

Another instance of this phenomenon is found in software such as spelling checkers, calendars, and notebook systems for personal computers. These programs are designed to lie dormant in the machine's memory until a particular event occurs. At that time, the currently active program is interrupted and the dormant program becomes active. The program relinquishing control does not explicitly request the activation of the dormant program. In fact, the producers of the relinquishing program have no way of knowing what dormant software will be available on the machines of their various customers.

Ada has numerous features for implementing such implicit control of software units. With these, programs can be developed as individual units, each of which essentially waits in the background until the occurrence of the particular event that activates it. Since this might happen in the case of several units at the same time, programs of this nature are excellent candidates for parallel processing environments and promise to be quite popular in the coming years.

I/O Statements

We learned earlier that operating systems contain prewritten routines for controlling the peripheral devices attached to a machine. From the high-level language point of view, these routines are nothing more than subprograms that can be invoked by the program being written simply by requesting their execution when needed. For this, the programmer merely needs to know the correct subprogram names and any special syntax rules associated with them. For example, to receive a value from the keyboard and place it in a location named Value, a Pascal programmer writes

readln (Value)

and to write the value on a monitor:

writeln (Value)

is used (**readln** indicates "read line" and **writeln** indicates "write line").

As with string manipulations, I/O activities sometimes are not considered part of a programming language itself but are viewed as additions to the language. In these cases, subroutines for performing these activities normally are provided in a library from which the required routines can be accessed as desired.

Most implementations of C, for example, contain a library with functions called scanf and printf for performing data input and output, respectively. These routines use parameters for communicating both the data to be transferred and the organization of that data in its printed form. The result is known as formatted input and output. For example, a C programmer writes

printf("%d %d \n", Value1, Value2);

to cause the values of the variables Value1, and Value2 to be printed in decimal notation on a single line. The string in quotation marks indicates the data's format. Each %d indicates a position that is to be filled by a value in decimal notation. The values are supplied by the remaining parameters. The pattern \n indicates that a new line should be started after these values have been printed. Assuming the values of Age1 and Age2 are 16 and 25, respectively, the statement

printf("The ages are %d and %d \n", Age1, Age2);

causes the message

The ages are 16 and 25.

to appear on the monitor.

Internal Documentation

Experience has shown that no matter how well the syntax of a language is designed or how well the language's features are used, additional information is either helpful or mandatory when trying to understand a program that someone else has written.

For this reason, languages are designed to allow additional comments to be inserted within a program for documentation purposes. This is done by providing a syntactic structure that informs the translator or interpreter to ignore certain parts of the written program. Any remarks placed in this ignored portion are available to a human reading the program but not to the translator or interpreter.

Two popular syntax structures are used for inserting comments. One is to enclose the comment within special characters. For example, the beginning of a comment in Pascal is indicated by the symbol {, and the end of the comment is marked by the symbol }. C uses the notation /* and */. The other technique is to mark the beginning of the comment with a special character and end the comment by starting a new line. Using this technique, Ada starts comments with a double hyphen (--) and FORTRAN with the symbol !.

A few words are in order about what constitutes a meaningful comment. Beginning programmers, when told to use comments for internal documentation, tend to follow a program statement such as:

Total := Price + Tax;

with a comment such as "Calculate Total by adding Price and Tax." Such redundancy adds length rather than clarity to the program. Remember that the purpose of internal documentation is to explain the program, not to repeat it. A more appropriate comment associated with the preceding statement might be to explain why the total is being calculated if that is not obvious. For example, the comment "Total is used later to compute GrandTotal and not needed after that" is more helpful than the previous one.

Program Examples

We close this section by showing how the insertion sort algorithm can be implemented in Ada, C, FORTRAN, and Pascal. In each case, you will observe that the list to be sorted is defined as an array. The procedural part of each program consists of three smaller routines. The first gets the names to be sorted from the keyboard, the second is the sort routine itself, and the third writes the names in alphabetical order on the monitor screen.

To appreciate the benefits of high-level languages, you should compare the example programs in this section to Appendix C, which presents the insertion sort algorithm expressed in assembly language.

Ada Example

The language Ada, named after Augusta Ada Byron (1815–1851), who was an assistant of Charles Babbage and the daughter of poet Lord Byron, is the newest of the languages presented here, with its design being established as recently as 1979.

It was developed at the initiative of the U.S. Department of Defense in an attempt to obtain a single, general-purpose language for all its software development needs. A major emphasis during Ada's design was to incorporate features for programming real-time computer systems used as a part of larger machines, such as missile guidance systems, environment control systems within buildings, and control systems in automobiles and small home appliances. Ada thus contains features for expressing activities in parallel processing environments as well as convenient techniques for handling special cases (called exceptions) that might arise in the application environment.

The insertion sort routine expressed in Ada is shown in Figure 5-15. Although not a feature in the actual language, our example adopts the convention of writing Ada's reserved words in boldface to enhance readability.

Figure 5-15 The insertion sort in Ada

```
--Insertion sort in Ada
with TEXT __ IO;
use TEXT __ IO;
procedure MAIN is
      subtype NAME __TYPE is STRING (1 .. 8);
      LIST __ LENGTH: constant := 10;
      NAMES: array (1 . . LIST __ LENGTH) of NAME __TYPE;
      PIVOT: NAME __TYPE;
      HOLE: INTEGER;
begin
-- First, get the names from the terminal.
      for K in 1 . . LIST __ LENGTH loop
         GET(NAMES(K));
      end loop;
-- Sort the list (HOLE contains the location of the
--             hole in the list from the time the
--             pivot is removed until it is
--             reinserted.)
      for N in 2 . . LIST __ LENGTH loop
         PIVOT := NAMES(N);
         HOLE := N;
         for M in reverse 1 .. N − 1 loop
           If NAMES(M) > PIVOT
              then NAMES(M + 1) := NAMES(M);
              else exit;
           end if;
             HOLE := M;
         end loop;
         NAMES(HOLE) := PIVOT;
      end loop;

-- Now, print the sorted list.
      for K in 1 . . LIST __ LENGTH loop
         NEW __ LINE;
         PUT(NAMES(K));
      end loop;
end MAIN;
```

C Example

The language C was developed and implemented by Dennis Ritchie at Bell Laboratories in the early 1970s. Although originally designed as a language for developing operating systems and compilers, C has obtained popularity throughout the programming community and is enjoying the benefits of standardization through the efforts of the American National Standards Institute.

C was originally envisioned as merely a step up from machine language. Consequently, its syntax is terse compared to other high-level languages that use complete English words to express some primitives that are represented by special symbols in C. This terseness is one of the reasons for C's popularity, because it allows for efficient representations of complex algorithms. (Often a concise representation is more readable than a lengthy one.)

C has also given rise to various extensions, the most prominent being C++ (pronounced "see plus plus"), which incorporates those features required for object-oriented programming.

Figure 5-16 shows the insertion sort implemented in C.

Figure 5-16 The insertion sort in C

```
/* the insertion sort in C */

#include <stdio.h>
#include <string.h>

main ( )
{
  char names [10][9],pivot[9];
  int i,j;

/*get the names */
  for (i = 0;i < 10; ++i)
    scanf("%s",names[i]);

/*sort the list */
  for (i = 1;i < 10; ++i)
    {
    strcpy(pivot,names[i]);
    j = i - 1;
    while ((j > = 0) && (strcmp(pivot,names[j]) < 0))
      (strcpy(names[j + 1],names[j]); --j;};
    strcpy(names[j + 1], pivot);
    }

/* print the sorted list */
  for (i = 0;i < 10; ++i)
    printf("%s \n",names[i]);
}
```

FORTRAN Example

FORTRAN is an acronym for FORmula TRANslator. This language was one of the first high-level languages developed (announced in 1957) and the first to gain wide acceptance within the computing community. Over the years, its official description has undergone numerous extensions, so you may hear computer scientists mention FORTRAN IV or FORTRAN 77. The latest in the series is FORTRAN 90, which extended FORTRAN 77 to include such features as recursion and user-defined data types. Although criticized by many, FORTRAN continues to be a popular language within the scientific community. In particular, many numerical analysis and statistical packages are, and will probably continue to be, written in FORTRAN. The insertion sort routine implemented in FORTRAN is shown in Figure 5-17.

Pascal Example

Pascal is named after the French mathematician and inventor Blaise Pascal (1623–1662). Announced by Niklaus Wirth in 1971, it incorporates many of the later design features such as an emphasis on data type in addition to structure, a free-format syntax, and numerous control structures. Today, Pascal is used extensively in computer science education because its design reinforces an organized approach to program development.

Figure 5-17 The insertion sort in FORTRAN

```
!       Insertion sort in FORTRAN
        INTEGER J,K
        CHARACTER(LEN=8)  Pivot
        CHARACTER(LEN=8)  DIMENSION(10)  Names
!       First, get the names.
        READ(UNIT=5, FMT=100)  (Names(K), K=1,10)
100     FORMAT(A8)
!          Now, sort the list.
OuterLoop: DO J=2,10
        Pivot = Names(J)
  InnerLoop: DO K=J-1,1,-1
        IF (Names(K) .GT. Pivot) THEN
            Names(K+1) = Names(K)
        ELSE
            EXIT InnerLoop
        ENDIF
        END DO InnerLoop
        Names(K+1) = Pivot
        END DO OuterLoop
!       Now, print the sorted list.
        WRITE(UNIT=6,FMT=400) (Names(K),K=1,10)
400     FORMAT ('',A8)
        END
```

Figure 5-18 The insertion sort in PASCAL

```
      {Insertion sort in Pascal}
program InsertSort(Input, Output);
Const
      Blanks = '            ';
      ListLength = 10;
type
      NameType = packed array [1 .. 8] of char;
var
      Names:array [1 . . ListLength] of NameType;
      Pivot: NameType;
      LocationFound: Boolean;
      J,M,N: Integer;
{GetName is a procedure for reading an entire name.}
procedure GetName(var Name: NameType);
var J: Integer;
begin J : = 1;
      repeat read(Name[J]); J := j + 1; until (J>8) or eoln;
      readln
end;
begin
{First, get the names from the terminal.}
      for J:= 1 to ListLength do
            begin Names[J]:= Blanks; GetName(Names[J]) end;
{Sort the list.}
      N := 2;
      repeat
            Pivot : = Names[N];
            M := N − 1;
            LocationFound := false;
            while (not LocationFound) do
                  if Names[M] > Pivot
                        then begin Names[M + 1] := Names[M];
                                    M := M − 1;
                                    if M = 0 then LocationFound := true
                              end
                        else LocationFound := true;
            Names[M + 1] := Pivot;
            N := N + 1
      until N > ListLength;
{Now print the sorted list.}
      for J := 1 to ListLength do writeln (Names[J])
end.
```

The insertion sort routine implemented in Pascal is shown in Figure 5-18. As with Ada, we have adopted the convention of writing the reserved words in boldface to increase our program's readability.

Questions/Exercises

1. What syntax would you expect to use in a third-generation programming language to refer to the entry in the third row and fifth column of a 10-by-6 matrix named XYZ?

2. What is the result of assigning 26.1 to a variable of each of the following types:
   a. integer   b. real   c. character
3. What structure is associated with the following data examples:
   a. The individual daily sales of five employees for a one-week period.
   b. The data from part a for 52 weeks.
   c. The attendance for each of six football games.
   d. The block of information pertaining to an item in a store's stock, such as name, quantity, stock number, supplier, or cost.
4. What is the difference between a constant and a variable?
5. When moving data as a result of an assignment statement from a location of type integer to a location of type real, what action must take place in addition to the transfer of data?
6. In each of the sample programs in this section, identify the point where the declarative part ends and the procedural part begins.
7. In each of the sample programs in this section, identify the statements that would be ignored by a translator or an interpreter. Why are these statements included if they do not affect the program's performance?

5-5 Parallel Computing

A growing area of research in the field of programming languages involves the development of languages for expressing algorithms consisting of different pieces implemented as individual processes that execute simultaneously. In reality, these processes might actually execute at the same time on different processors (in a multiprocessor environment) or perhaps only appear to execute simultaneously (in a time-sharing environment).

An example might be a program for weather forecasting based on a two-level model of the atmosphere. One process might be given the task of projecting conditions in the upper atmosphere (such as the path and strength of the jet stream), while another process would be charged with projecting the conditions in the lower atmosphere. Of course, these two tasks would not be totally independent, so it would be necessary for the two processes to communicate with one another. To fulfill this need, the system could be designed so that each process would begin by independently projecting the current conditions one hour into the future; once these projections had been made, the processes would share their predictions before making their independent predictions for the next one-hour period. In this manner, the two processes would produce a 24-hour forecast by coordinating their efforts over 24 steps.

To write programs for such parallel computing applications, language features are needed that allow programmers to express the activities involved in coordinating the actions of the various processes in the system. In some cases, these features have been incorporated as primitives in a language; in others, they are implemented as extensions to an existing language.

Ada is an example of the former approach. Indeed, as we noted in the previous section, a major goal in the design of Ada was to produce a language that could be used for expressing programs for use in parallel processing environments.

A popular example of the language extension approach is based on the collection of features known as Linda. Linda is not a programming language but rather a collection of primitives that, when added to an existing language, produces an extended language with parallel computing capabilities. Using Linda, researchers have created and experimented with parallel extensions of such languages as C, FORTRAN, LISP, Pascal, and Prolog.

The central concept of Linda is that of a shared storage area called the tuple space, in which each process in the system can deposit and retrieve data bundles called tuples. A process can deposit a tuple in the tuple space at any time. It can also attempt to remove a tuple from the tuple space at any time, but an attempt to remove a nonexistent tuple results in the process being forced to wait until a tuple with the desired properties is deposited by another process.

A tuple is a collection of one or more data items with an associated order. We often represent a tuple by listing its data items within parentheses. Thus, the tuple containing the values 5, 3.2, and "Fred" is written

$$(5, 3.2, \text{"Fred"})$$

which is not the same as the tuple

$$(3.2, \text{"Fred"}, 5)$$

because the order is different.

Linda provides the primitives named out and in for expressing the basic operations of depositing and retrieving tuples to and from the tuple space. The primitive in is used to retrieve tuples from the tuple space; out is used to deposit tuples. (The terms *in* and *out* express the action from the context of the process, not the tuple space. Thus, the primitive out is used to transfer a tuple out of the process into the tuple space, whereas in is used to transfer a tuple into the process from the tuple space.) For example, the statement

$$\text{out } (5, 17)$$

is used by a process to deposit the tuple (5, 17) into the tuple space, and the statement

$$\text{in } (5, 17)$$

is used to retrieve such a tuple.

Variables preceded by a question mark can be used to save components of the tuple being retrieved. In particular, if Value is a variable of type integer, then the statement

in ("final cost", ?Value)

can be used to retrieve any tuple whose first component is the character string "final cost" and whose second component is an integer. The integer value occurring in the chosen tuple is then assigned to the variable Value. If no such tuple exists in the tuple space, the process is forced to wait until such a tuple is deposited. When such a deposit is finally made, the tuple is removed from the tuple space, the assignment is made to Value, and the process is allowed to continue.

We should note that the operations in and out must be implemented as atomic routines; that is, each must be executed as an indivisible unit in the sense of a critical region. Indeed, if a process begins an in operation and finds a tuple of the desired type, it must be allowed to retrieve that tuple before another process is allowed to find the same tuple. Remember, in a multiprocessing environment, many processes can be rummaging through the tuple space at the same time.

Figure 5-19 shows how the processes in our weather forecasting example can be expressed if we extend our pseudocode to include the Linda primitives. Here the two processes are represented by the procedures LowLevel and HighLevel If LowLevel completes its forecast for the next one-hour period first, it deposits the tuple ("low-level done") in the tuple space and tries to retrieve the tuple ("high-level done"). But that tuple is not present, so the LowLevel process is forced to wait. When the HighLevel process completes its forecast for the first one-hour period, it deposits the tuple that the LowLevel process is waiting for and then retrieves the tuple deposited by the LowLevel process. At that time, both processes continue their tasks by beginning their forecasts for the next one-hour period.

We close by identifying the other primitives found in most Linda implementations. These include rd (short for read), which is the same as in except that the tuple is not removed from the tuple space. A major use of rd is to allow several processes to detect the presence of the same tuple in the tuple space. The primitives inp and rdp are similar to in and rd; the difference is that these primitives do not require the

Figure 5-19 A pseudocode representation of our weather-forecasting program

```
procedure LowLevel                      procedure HighLevel
assign Count the value 1;               assign Count the value 1;
while (Count ≤ 24) do                   while (Count ≤ 24) do
    (Prepare the low-level forecast          (Prepare the high-level forecast
        for the next one-hour period;            for the next one-hour period;
    out ("low-level done");                  out ("high-level done");
    in ("high-level done");                  in ("low-level done");
    Assign Count the value Count + 1)        Assign Count the value Count + 1)
```

process to wait if the desired tuple is not present in the tuple space. Finally, the primitive eval is used to start the execution of processes that are executed in parallel. For example, the statements

$$\text{eval (LowLevel)}$$
$$\text{eval (HighLevel)}$$

can be used to start our weather forecasting processes.

Questions/Exercises

1. If ValueA and ValueB are variables declared to be of type integer, which of the following tuples can be retrieved by the statement

$$\text{in (?ValueA, ?ValueB)}$$

  a. (5.3, 6)   b. (6, 7, 8)   c. (5, 12)   d. (3)
2. Explain how a critical region can be implemented using the Linda primitives in and out.
3. Suppose the tuple space contains only the tuple (5, 7), and Value is a variable of type integer. What would be the result of each of the following commands?
  a. in (4, 2)   b. out (8, 3.4)
  c. rd (?Value, 7)   d. in (?Value, 7)

5-6 Declarative Programming

Earlier we claimed that formal logic provides a general problem-solving algorithm around which a declarative programming system can be constructed. In this section, we investigate this claim by first introducing the rudiments of the algorithm and then taking a brief look at a declarative programming language based on it.

Logical Deduction

Suppose we already know that either John is at school or John is sick. If we are then told that John is not sick, we can conclude that John is at school. This is an example of a deductive-reasoning principle called **resolution.** To better understand this principle, let us first agree to represent statements by single letters and the negation of a statement by preceding the letter representing the statement with the symbol $\neg$. For instance, we might represent the statement "John is at school" by P, the statement "John is sick" by Q, and the statement "John is not sick" by $\neg$Q. Then the reasoning described above can be summarized as

$$\left. \begin{array}{c} P \text{ or } Q \\ \neg Q \end{array} \right\} \text{ imply } P$$

In a more general form, the resolution principle says that if P, Q, and R are statements, then the statements

P or Q

and

R or ¬Q

collectively imply the statement

P or R

as represented in Figure 5-20. In this case, we say that the two original statements resolve to produce the third statement, which is called the **resolvent.** (You may want to stop here while you convince yourself that the resolvent is, in fact, a logical consequence of the parent statements.)

Note that resolution can be applied only to pairs of statements that appear in clause form—that is, statements whose elementary components are connected by the word *or*. Thus,

P or Q or R

is in clause form, whereas

if P then Q

is not. The fact that this potential problem poses no serious concern is a consequence of a theorem in mathematical logic to the effect that any statement expressed in the first-order predicate logic (a system for representing statements with extensive expressive power) can be expressed in clause form. We will not prove this important theorem here, but for future reference, observe that the statement

if P then Q

is equivalent to the clause form statement

Q or ¬P

Logicians have shown that by means of resolution we can confirm the inconsistency of any collection of contradictory clause form statements. More precisely, a collection of clauses is contradictory if and only if repeated applications

Figure 5-20 Resolving the statements (P or Q) and (R or ¬Q) to produce (P or R)

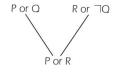

Figure 5-21 *Resolving the statements (P or Q), (R or ⌐Q), ⌐R, and ⌐P*

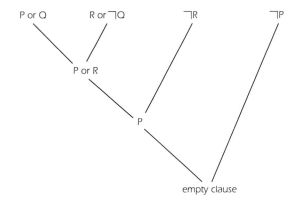

of resolution can ultimately lead to an empty clause (the result of applying resolution to two clauses of the form P and ⌐P). For example, Figure 5-21 indicates how this can arise in the case of the initial clauses

P or Q   R or ⌐Q   ⌐R   ⌐P

To appreciate the significance of this, suppose a collection of consistent statements implies some other statement P and we want to demonstrate this implication. Implying the statement P is the same as contradicting the statement ⌐P. Thus, to demonstrate that the original collection of statements implies P, all we need to do is express the original statements as well as the statement ⌐P in clause form, and then apply resolution until an empty clause occurs. Upon obtaining an empty clause, we can conclude that statement ⌐P is inconsistent with the original statements, and thus the original statements must imply P.

One final point remains before we are ready to apply resolution in an actual programming environment. Suppose we have the two statements

if Mary is at X then Mary's lamb is at X

and

Mary is at home

where X is intended to represent any location. In clause form, the two statements become

(Mary's lamb is at X) or ⌐(Mary is at X)

and

(Mary is at home)

which at first glance do not have components that can be resolved. On the other hand, the components (Mary is at home) and ⌐(Mary is at X) are quite close to being opposites of each other. The problem is to recognize that X, being a statement about locations in general, is a statement about home in particular. Thus, a special case of the first statement is

(Mary's lamb is at home) or ¬(Mary is at home)

which can be resolved with the statement

(Mary is at home)

to produce the statement

(Mary's lamb is at home)

The process of assigning values to variables (such as assigning the value *home* to X) so that resolution can be performed is called unification. It is this process that allows general statements to be applied to specific applications in a deduction system.

Prolog

The language Prolog (short for PROgramming in LOGic) is a declarative programming language whose underlying problem-solving algorithm is based on repeated resolution. A program in Prolog consists of a collection of initial statements upon which the underlying algorithm bases its deductive reasoning. The components from which these statements are constructed are called predicates. A predicate consists of a predicate identifier followed by a parenthetical statement listing the predicate's arguments. A single predicate represents a fact about its arguments, and its identifier is usually chosen to reflect this underlying semantics. Thus, if we want to express the fact that Bill is Mary's parent, we can use the predicate form

parent(bill, mary).

(Note that the arguments in this predicate start with lowercase letters, even though they represent proper nouns. This is because Prolog distinguishes between constants and variables by insisting that constants begin with lowercase letters and variables begin with uppercase letters.)

Statements in a Prolog program are either facts or rules (each of which must be terminated by a period). A fact consists of a single predicate. For example, the facts that Bob is taller than Carol and Carol is taller than Sue can be represented by the Prolog statements

taller(bob, carol).

and

taller(carol, sue).

A Prolog rule is an if-then statement. (Prolog accepts the responsibility of converting if-then statements into clause form.) An if-then statement in Prolog (such as "if X then Y") is represented with the consequence first (as in "Y if X"). The symbol

:- is used in place of the word *if*. Thus, the rule "Z is taller than X if Z is taller than Y and Y is taller than X" can be expressed as

$$taller(Z,X) :- taller(Z,Y), taller(Y,X).$$

The comma separating taller(Z,Y) and taller(Y,X) represents the conjunction *and*.

Keep in mind that the Prolog system does not know the meaning of the predicates in a program; it simply manipulates the statements in a totally symbolic manner according to the resolution inference rule. Thus, it is up to the programmer to describe all the pertinent features of a predicate in terms of facts and rules. In this light, Prolog facts tend to be used to identify specific instances of a predicate, whereas rules are used to describe general principles. This is the approach followed by the preceding statements regarding the predicate taller. The two facts describe particular instances of "tallerness" while the rule describes a general property. Note that the fact that Bob is taller than Sue, though not explicitly stated, is a consequence of the two facts combined with the rule.

Most Prolog implementations are designed to be used interactively. In this context, the task of a programmer is to develop the collection of facts and rules that constitute the set of initial statements to be used in the deductive system. Once this collection of statements is established, conjectures (called *goals* in Prolog terminology) can be proposed to the system by typing them at a computer's keyboard. When such a goal is presented to a Prolog system, the system applies resolution to try to confirm that the goal is a consequence of the initial statements. Based on our collection of statements describing the relationship taller, each of the goals

> taller(bob, carol).
> taller(carol, sue).
> taller(bob, sue).

could be so confirmed because each is a logical consequence of the initial statements. (The first two are identical to facts appearing in the initial statements, whereas the third requires a certain degree of deduction by the system.)

More interesting examples are obtained if we provide goals whose arguments are variables rather than constants. In these cases, Prolog tries to derive the goal from the initial statements while keeping track of the unifications required to do so. Then, if the goal is obtained, Prolog reports these unifications. For example, consider the goal

> taller(W, sue).

In response to this, Prolog reports

> taller(carol, sue).

Indeed, this is a consequence of the initial statements and agrees with the goal via unification. Furthermore, if we asked Prolog to tell us more, it finds and reports the consequence taller(bob, sue).

In contrast, we can ask Prolog to find people shorter than Carol by proposing the goal

taller(carol, W).

In fact, if we started with the goal

taller(V, W).

Prolog ultimately reports all the height relationships that can be derived from the initial statements. Thus, a single Prolog program can be used to confirm that a particular person is taller than another given person, to find those who are taller than a given person, to find those who are shorter than a given person, or to find all height relationships. This versatility is one of the features that has captured the imagination of computer scientists.

Let us now consider the Prolog program in Figure 5-22 for sorting a list of numbers. Although it uses some features that we have not discussed, such as square bracket notation for representing lists, we can still grasp the main structure of the program—an understanding that provides insight into the power of declarative programming. Let us look at the purpose of the program's statements.

The first statement

sort(L,S) :- permutation(L,S), ordered(S).

represents the rule that a list S is the sorted version of the list L, if S is a permutation of L and S is ordered. However, the Prolog system does not know the meaning of the predicates permutation and ordered, so the remaining statements are provided to define these predicates. The next two statements represent the fact that the empty list is a permutation of itself and the rule that a nonempty list is a permutation of another list if the two contain the same entries.

Figure 5-22 A Prolog program for sorting a list of numbers

```
sort (L,S) :- permutation(L,S), ordered(S).

permutation([ ],[ ]).
permutation[Q,[X|T]] :- append(A,[X|B],Q),
                        append(A,B,P),
                        permutation(P,T).

ordered ([ ]).
ordered ([_|[ ] ]).
ordered ([A|[B|T]]) :- A < B, ordered ([B|T]).

append([ ],Z,Z).
append([X|L],M,[X|N]) :- append(L,M,N).
```

The next three statements define the predicate ordered. The first states that the empty list is ordered; the next states that a list with only one entry is ordered; and the third is the rule stating that a list with at least two entries is ordered if its first entry is less than its second and the entries after the first are in order.

Finally, the statements regarding the predicate append describe the condition of one list being the result of appending two other lists. (This concept was required in the definition of permutation.)

To use our sort program to sort the list 8, 2, 4, 3, we enter the goal

sort([8,2,4,3],X).

to which the Prolog system responds

sort([8,2,4,3],[2,3,4,8]).

Note that our sort program says nothing about how the sort process is to be done. Rather, the program concentrates on expressing what a sorted list is. Thus, the process of developing the program is one of describing the problem to be solved, not of describing a sequence of events that solve the problem. This is the distinction between the declarative and procedural paradigms.

Questions/Exercises

1. Which of the statements R, S, T, U, and V are logical consequences of the collection of statements (¬R or T or S), (¬S or V), (¬V or R), (U or ¬S), (T or ¬U), and (S or V)?

2. Is the following collection of statements consistent? Explain your answer.

P or Q or R
¬R or Q
R or ¬P
¬Q

3. Suppose a Prolog program consisted of the statements

smaller(carol, john).
smaller(bill, sue).
smaller(sue, carol).
smaller(X,Z) :- smaller(X,Y), smaller(Y,Z).

List the results that can be produced from each of the following goals:

a.   smaller(sue, V).
b.   smaller(U, carol).
c.   smaller(U,V).

Chapter 5 Review Problems

(Asterisked problems are associated with optional sections.)

1. a. Using our pseudocode, design a program for simulating the interaction between the fox and rabbit populations in a certain region over a ten-year period. Make the following assumptions:

   1. The initial fox population is $F_0 = 18,000$ and the initial rabbit population is $R_0 = 98,000$.

   2. If the fox and rabbit populations at the end of one month are F_i and R_i, respectively, then the populations at the end of the next month are given by

   $$F_{i + 1} = F_i + (.038 \times R_i F_i - .218 \times F_i)/12$$

   and

   $$R_{i + 1} = R_i + (.934 \times R_i - .041 \times R_i \times F_i)/12$$

   b. Circle the portions of your program that are specific to this particular simulation problem. Then modify your program so that these portions can be easily altered.

   In what sense does your modified program constitute a general-purpose simulation system?

2. Suppose the function f expects two numeric values as its parameters and returns the smaller of the two values as its output value. If w, x, y, and z represent numeric values, what is the result returned by f(f(w,x),f(y,z))?

3. Suppose f is a function that returns the result of reversing the string of symbols given as its input, and g is a function that returns the concatenation of the two strings given as its input. If x is the string *abcd*, what is returned by g(f(x),x)?

4. Show how a function whose input consists of three lists of words and whose output is an alphabetized list of all the words common to all of the input lists can be constructed from a function that alphabetizes a list and another function that finds the words common to two lists.

5. Suppose your checking account is represented as an object in an object-oriented program for maintaining your financial records. What data is stored inside this object? What messages can that object receive and how does it respond to each? What are other objects that might be used in the program?

6. Translate the high-level statement

   Assign Halfway the value of Length + Width

   into the machine language of Appendix B, assuming that Length, Width, and Halfway are all represented in floating-point notation.

7. Translate the high-level statement

   IF X EQUALS 0 THEN MOVE Y PLUS W INTO Z
   ELSE MOVE Y PLUS X INTO Z

   into the machine language of Appendix B, assuming that W, X, Y, and Z are all represented as binary values occupying 1 byte of memory each.

8. Why was it necessary to identify the type of data associated with the variables in problem 7 in order to translate the statements? Why do many high-level programming languages require the programmer to identify the type of each variable at the beginning of a program?

9. Common data types include integer, real, and character. Describe a likely technique for representing data of each of these types inside a machine.

10. Summarize the distinction between a machine language and an assembly language.

11. Design an assembly language for the machine described in Appendix B.

12. Draw a syntax diagram representing the structure of the **while** statement in the pseudocode of Chapter 4.

13. Which of the following contain errors in syntax, and which contain errors in semantics?
    a. All humans have feathers.
    b. Bumble bees finish carrots.
    c. Finish carrots bees bumble.
    d. Over twelve asparagus.

14. Identify two semantic interpretations for each of the following:
    a. Stampeding horses can be dangerous.
    b. William saw a painting in a museum that he liked.

c. The circus had a man on an elephant with an artificial leg.

d. If taxes rise, then if inflation rises, then hold stock, otherwise sell stock.

15. Draw a picture of the array described by each of the following Pascal statements:

a. **var**
   xxx: **array** [1..4,1..2] **of** integer;

b. **var**
   yyy: **array** [3..6,1..3] **of** integer;

c. **var**
   zzz: **array** [1..3,1..4,1..3] **of** integer;

16. What ambiguities can be introduced in a program if a function with two parameters of type integer are given the same name as a two-dimensional array? What subtle technique is used in Pascal to avoid this problem?

17. What is the difference between a homogeneous array and a heterogeneous array?

18. John Programmer argues that the ability to declare constants within a program is not necessary because variables can be used instead. For example, our example of AirportAlt in Section 5-4 can be handled by declaring AirportAlt to be a variable and then assigning it the required variable at the beginning of the program. Why is this not as good as using a constant?

19. Summarize the distinction between the declarative and procedural parts of a program written in a procedural programming language.

20. Summarize the distinction between the **repeat** and **while** loop structures.

21. Summarize the following rat's-nest routine with a single **if-then-else** statement:

   if X > 5 **goto** 80
   X = X + 1
   goto 90
   80 X = X + 2
   90 **stop**

22. Summarize the following nested **if-then-else** structure with a single **case** statement:

   if X = 4
      then X = X + 1
      else if X = 5
         then X = X + 2
         else if X = 6
            then X = X + 3

23. Using the case statement structure to handle the opponent's possibilities, design an algorithm to play tic-tac-toe (naughts and crosses). Your algorithm should take the first move by placing an X in the upper-left-hand corner. (Use symmetry to reduce the number of options.)

24. If your tic-tac-toe algorithm in problem 23 is changed to always select the middle square for its first move, how can the use of symmetry reduce the rest of the algorithm to one large **if-then-else** structure?

25. In what way is the "for . . ." loop structure in Pascal less flexible than its "repeat . . ." and "while . . ." counterparts?

26. The following Ada program sequence is designed to make use of the subprogram Larger discussed in this chapter. What values are assigned to the variables A, B, and C at the end of the routine?

   A := 5;
   B := 6;
   C := 7;
   Larger(A, B, C);
   Larger(C, B, A)

27. The following is the first statement of a subprogram written in the programming language Ada. Would the parameter password be passed by reference or value?

   procedure CheckPassword (password: **in**
      PASSTYPE; reply: **out** INTEGER) **is**

28. Why would a large array probably not be passed to a subroutine by value?

29. Using the subprogram Larger from the text, describe a sequence of instructions that accomplishes the same objective as the single statement

   $Z = Max(I,J) + Max(A,B)$

   where Max is the function introduced in the text.

30. Explain the difference between explicit subprogram activation and implicit subprogram activation.

31. Summarize the distinction between a traditional subprogram and a function.

32. If Long represents the string *detached* and Short represents the string *ache*, what will be the result of executing the Pascal expression Pos(Short, Long)?

33. Identify some manipulations of symbol strings that may appear as primitive operations in programming languages.

34. Suppose a Pascal-like program contained the following three lines, where SubProg is the name of a subprogram:

    x := 5;
    SubProg(x, y, z);
    w := x;

    What can be said about the value assigned to the variable w in the last statement if parameters are passed by value that cannot be concluded if parameters are passed by reference?

35. What ambiguity exists in the statement

    Assign X the value of 3 + 2 ∗ 5

36. Suppose a small company has five employees and is planning to increase the number to six. The following are excerpts from two equivalent programs used by the company that must be altered to reflect the change in the number of employees. Both programs are written in a Pascal-like language. Indicate what changes must be made to each program. What complications arise in the case of program 1 that are avoided by the use of constants in program 2?

    Program 1
    ─────────
            .
            .
            .
    DailySalary := TotalSal/5;
    AvgSalary := TotalSal/5;
    DailySales := TotalSales/5;
    AvgSales := TotalSales/5;
            .
            .
            .

    Program 2
    ─────────
            .
            .
      const
        NumEmpl = 5;
        DaysWk = 5;
            .
            .

    DailySalary := TotalSal/DaysWk;
    AvgSalary := TotalSal/NumEmpl;
    DailySales := TotalSales/DaysWk;
    AvgSales := TotalSales/NumEmpl;
            .
            .
            .

*37. Using the Linda primitives in and out as a way of extending the pseudocode in Chapter 4, describe two parallel processes A and B such that A generates widgets that B then checks for defects before it declares them finished.

*38. Using the Linda primitives in and out as a way of extending the pseudocode in Chapter 4, describe two parallel processes A and B such that each generates widgets that are inspected by the other for defects before receiving final approval.

*39. Give an example in which the Linda primitive rd is used rather than the primitive in.

*40. Give an example in which the Linda primitive inp is used rather than the primitive in.

*41. Draw a diagram (similar to Figure 5-21) representing the resolutions needed to show that the collection of statements (Q or ¬R), (T or R), ¬P, (P or ¬T), and (P or ¬Q) are inconsistent.

*42. Is the collection of statements ¬R, (T or R), (P or ¬Q), (Q or ¬T), and (R or ¬P) consistent? Explain your answer.

*43. What conclusions can Prolog find if faced with the goal

    bigger(X, lassie).

    and the initial statements

        bigger(rex, lassie).
        bigger(fido, rex).
        bigger(spot, rex).
        bigger(X,Z) :- bigger(X,Y), bigger (Y,Z).

*44. What conclusions can Prolog find if faced with the goal

    eq(X,Y).

    and the initial statements

        grteq(a,b).
        grteq(b,c).
        grteq(c,a).
        grteq(U,W) :- grteq(U,V), grteq(V,W).
        eq(X,Y) :- grteq(X,Y), grteq(Y,X).

Problems for the Programmer

1. Pick a third-generation programming language and identify any reserved words in it. If there are reserved words, identify statements in the programming language that would become ambiguous if these words were not reserved.

2. What features are present in your third-generation programming language that allow a translator to isolate the various statements in a program?

3. What data types and structures are available in your programming language? What syntax is provided for declaring these characteristics? Are any of these characteristics declared implicitly?

4. Implement your own version of the Pascal function Pos in the programming language of your choice. (If your programming language already has these functions, ignore them for the purpose of this exercise.)

5. Write a program that searches for the value 5 within a two-dimensional array of integers. What control structures does the programming language you are using provide for stopping the search process once this value is found?

6. Suppose that a savings and loan association determines the maximum amount it can loan to an individual for a home mortgage using the following system: The individual's job and the home being purchased are each rated on a scale from 1 to 10. If the job rating is 1, no loan is given. If the job rating is greater than 1 but less than 7, the loan limit is determined by the formula

((job rating)/10)(annual salary)(2)((home rating)/10)

If the job rating is 7 or more, the mortgage limit is determined by

((job rating)/10)(annual salary)(3)((home rating)/10)

Write a program that computes the loan limit based on a customer's ratings and annual salary.

7. A palindrome is a character string that appears the same when read backward as when read forward, such as madam or noon. Write a program that accepts a character string and reports whether or not it is a palindrome.

8. Design a set of mnemonics for the machine language in Appendix B, and write an assembler to translate the programs expressed with these mnemonics into hexadecimal form.

9. Implement your solutions to review problem 1.

Additional Reading

Aho, A. V.; Sethi, R.; and Ullman, J. D. *Compilers: Principles, Techniques, and Tools.* Reading, Mass.: Addison-Wesley, 1986.

Andrews, G. R. *Concurrent Programming: Principles and Practice.* Redwood City, Calif.: Benjamin/Cummings, 1991.

Booch, G. *Software Engineering with Ada.* Menlo Park, Calif.: Benjamin/Cummings, 1983.

Carriero, N. and Gelernter, D. *How to Write Parallel Programs: A First Course.* Cambridge, Mass.: MIT Press, 1990.

Clocksin, W. F., and Mellish, C. S. *Programming in Prolog,* 3rd ed. New York: Springer-Verlag, 1987.

Cox, B. J. *Object-Oriented Programming: An Evolutionary Approach.* Reading, Mass.: Addison-Wesley, 1986.

Davis, R. E. *Truth, Deduction, and Computation.* Rockville, Md.: Computer Science Press, 1989.

Delahaye, J.-P. *Formal Methods in Artificial Intelligence.* New York: John Wiley and Sons, 1987.

Kernighan, B. W., and Ritchie, D. M. *The C Programming Language,* 2nd ed. Englewood Cliffs, N.J.: Prentice-Hall, 1988.

Maier, D., and Warren, D. S. *Computing with Logic.* Redwood City, Calif.: Benjamin/Cummings, 1988.

Pohl, I. *C + + for C Programmers.* Redwood City, Calif.: Benjamin/Cummings, 1989.

Pratt, T. W. *Programming Languages,* 2nd ed. Englewood Cliffs, N.J.: Prentice-Hall, 1984.

Rogers, J. B. *A Prolog Primer.* Reading, Mass.: Addison-Wesley, 1986.

Sebesta, R. W. *Concepts of Programming Languages,* 2nd ed. Redwood City, Calif.: Benjamin/Cummings, 1993.

Sethi, R. *Programming Languages.* Reading, Mass.: Addison-Wesley, 1989.

Wilensky, R. *Common LISPcraft.* New York: Norton, 1986.

CHAPTER SIX

SOFTWARE ENGINEERING

We began our study of software by discussing operating systems that create the environment in which interaction between humans and machines is conducted. We then turned our attention to the study of algorithms and the programming process. In this chapter, we consider topics relating to the overall process of software development and maintenance. Many of the techniques applied here are similar to those applied by engineers in the development of automobiles, bridges, and television sets. In fact, the topic is called software engineering.

Our discussion concerns large software systems, the complete comprehension of which exceeds the short-term memory capabilities of the human mind. Examples might include business inventory systems, university registration systems, or automated systems for maintaining customer records of stock brokerage firms. The problems faced when developing such systems are more than enlarged versions of those problems faced when writing small programs. For instance, the development of such systems requires the efforts of more than one person over an extended period of time during which the requirements of the proposed system may be altered and the personnel assigned to the project may change, due to promotions, job transfers, and so on. Consequently, the subject of software engineering includes topics, such as personnel and project management, that are more readily associated with business management than computer science. You should be aware of this close association between software engineering and the business world, but we avoid these side tracks here. Instead, we focus on those topics generally considered to lie within the established bounds of computer science.

6-1   The Software Engineering Discipline

Beginning computer science students are somewhat disadvantaged when approaching the study of software engineering. They have never participated in the development of large software systems and therefore cannot fully comprehend the problems involved. Their experiences most likely encompass programming projects that can be completed in a few days. Moreover, they have probably not been required to live with and maintain the programs they have written.

It might be helpful therefore to begin our study of software engineering by selecting any large complex device you want (an automobile, a multistory office building, or perhaps a cathedral) and imagine being asked to design it and then to supervise its construction. How can you estimate the cost in time, money, and other resources to complete the project? How can you divide the project into manageable pieces? How can you assure that the pieces produced are compatible? How can those working on the various pieces communicate? How can you measure progress? How can you cope with the wide range of detail (the selection of the door knobs, the design of the gargoyles, the availability of blue glass for the stained glass windows, the strength of the pillars, the design of the duct work for the heating system)? Questions of the same scope must be answered during the development of a large software system.

Since engineering is a well-established field, you might think that there is a wealth of previously developed engineering techniques that can be applied toward answering such questions. This reasoning, however, overlooks the many distinctions between the properties of software and those of other fields of engineering.

One of these distinctions deals with the role of tolerances. Traditional areas of engineering deal with the development of products that are acceptable as long as they perform their task within certain bounds. A washing machine that cycles through its wash-rinse-spin cycle within a 2% tolerance of the desired time is acceptable. Software, in contrast, performs either correctly or incorrectly. An accounting system that is accurate only to within a 2% tolerance is not acceptable.

Another distinction relates to the lack of quantitative systems, called metrics, for measuring the properties of software. What metric, for example, can be used for measuring the quality of software? The quality of a mechanical device is often measured in terms of the mean time between failures, which is a measurement of how well the device endures wear and tear. Software, in contrast, does not wear out, so this method of measuring quality does not carry over into software engineering.

The inability to measure software properties in a quantitative manner is one of the major reasons that software engineering has not yet found a rigorous footing in the same sense as mechanical and electrical engineering. Whereas these subjects are founded on the established science of physics, software engineering is still searching for its roots.

Thus, research in software engineering is currently progressing on two levels: Some researchers work toward developing techniques for immediate application, while others search for underlying principles and theories on which more stable techniques can someday be constructed. Being based on a subjective foundation, many methodologies developed on the first level, which were preached as fact in the past, have been replaced by other approaches that may themselves fade with time. Meanwhile, progress on the other level continues to be evasive.

The need for progress on both levels is enormous. Our society has become addicted to computer systems and their associated software. Our economy, health care, government, law enforcement, transportation, and defense depend on large software systems. Yet there continue to be major problems with the reliability of these systems. Software errors have caused such disasters and near disasters as the rising moon being interpreted as a nuclear attack, the loss of $5 million by the Bank of New York in only one day, the loss of the Mariner 18 space probe, radiation overdoses that have killed and paralyzed, and the simultaneous disruption of telephone communications over large regions.

While science continues to search for methods of developing better-quality software, professional organizations have contributed their efforts indirectly by promoting high standards of ethics and professional conduct among their membership. The Association of Computing Machinery (ACM) has adopted a code of professional conduct, while the Data Processing Management Association (DPMA) and the Institute of Electrical and Electronics Engineers (IEEE) have each adopted their own codes of ethics. Such codes enhance the professionalism of software developers and counter nonchalant attitudes toward each individual's responsibilities.

In this chapter, we introduce some of the results of software engineering research, including some of the basic principles of software engineering (the software life cycle, modularity, coupling, and cohesion) as well as some of the development tools and techniques that are used today.

Questions/Exercises

1. Why is the number of lines in a program not a good measure of the complexity of the program?
2. What technique can be used for determining how many errors are in a piece of software?
3. Suggest a metric for measuring software quality. What weaknesses does your metric have?

6-2   The Software Life Cycle

The most fundamental concept in software engineering is the software life cycle.

The Cycle as a Whole

The software life cycle is shown in Figure 6-1. This figure represents the fact that once software is developed, it enters a cycle of being used and modified that continues for the rest of the software's life. Such a pattern is common for many manufactured products as well. The difference is that, in the case of other products, the modification phase is more accurately called a repair or maintenance phase because other products tend to move from being used to being modified as their parts become worn.

Software, on the other hand, does not wear out. Instead, a piece of software moves into the modification phase because errors that were not discovered earlier in the development phase force changes to be made, because changes in the program's application occur that require corresponding changes in the software, or because changes made during a previous modification are found to induce problems elsewhere in the software. For example, changes in tax laws often require modifications to payroll programs that calculate witholding taxes, and all too often these changes have adverse effects in other areas of the program that may not be discovered until some time later.

Figure 6-1 The software life cycle

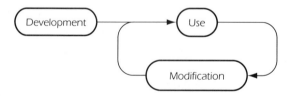

Regardless of the reason for a piece of software entering the modification phase, this process requires that a person (often not the original author) study the program and its documentation until the program, or at least the pertinent part of the program, is understood. Otherwise, any modification could introduce more problems than it solves. Acquiring this understanding can be a difficult task even when the software is well designed and documented. In fact, it is often within this phase that a piece of software is finally discarded under the pretense (too often true) that it is easier to develop a new system from scratch than to modify the existing package successfully.

In our discussion of data description statements in Chapter 5, we saw how the name *AirportAlt* might be used in lieu of the nondescriptive value 645 in a program and reasoned that if a change became necessary, it would be easier to change the value associated with the name instead of finding and changing numerous occurrences of the value 645. The point is that a little effort during the development phase can make a tremendous difference in the modification phase. In turn, most of the research in software engineering is directed toward the activities in the development stage and their effects on later modifications.

The Traditional Development Phase

Let us, then, take a closer look at the stages within the development phase of the software life cycle (Figure 6-2). These consist of analysis, design, implementation, and testing, as described below.

1. *Analysis.* It is in this early stage of software development that the needs of an organization are recognized as a potential computer application and the decision is made that an automated system should be developed. It is here that software engineering is most closely aligned with the field of business administration. Indeed, these early decisions are more involved with the operation of the organization than with the study of algorithms.

    Once the decision is made to develop an automated system, the true analysis phase begins. The major goal of this process is to identify the needs of the user of the proposed system. For example, if the system is to be an inventory maintenance system for the purchasing department, then the needs and

Figure 6-2 The development phase of the software life cycle

expectations of the purchasing department must be identified. One popular way of doing this is to analyze the system currently in use (which may be a manual system or perhaps an outdated automated one) and to identify its inputs, outputs, the changes that should be incorporated in the new system, and those features that should be maintained. The premise is that the first step toward learning what the new system should do is to understand what the old system does and how it does it.

One of the formal results of the analysis phase is a set of requirements that the new system must satisfy. These requirements are stated in terms of the application rather than in the technical terminology of the data processing community. One requirement might be that access to data must be restricted to authorized personnel. Another might be that the data must reflect the current state of the inventory as of the end of the last business day or that the arrangement of the data as displayed on the computer screen must adhere to the format of the paper forms currently in use.

After the system requirements are identified, they are converted into more technical system specifications. For example, the requirement that data be restricted to authorized personnel might become the specification that the system will not respond until an approved five-digit password has been typed at the keyboard or that data will be displayed in coded form unless preprocessed by a routine known only to authorized personnel.

2. *Design.* It is in the design phase that the technical details of the proposed system are developed. It is here that the system is broken into manageable units called modules, with each module constituting a small part of the overall system.

It is by means of this modular decomposition that the implementation of large systems becomes a possibility. Without such a breakdown, the technical details required in the implementation of a large system would exceed a human's comprehensive powers. With a modular design, however, only the details pertaining to the module under consideration need be mastered. This same modular design is also conducive to future maintenance because it allows changes to be made on a modular basis. (If a change is to be made to the way each employee's health benefits are calculated, then only modules dealing with health benefits need be considered.)

We see, then, that a good modular structure is important to the implementation as well as later modification of the system. This is why we concentrate on this structure in the next few sections.

3. *Implementation.* This phase involves the actual writing of programs, creation of data files, and development of databases. With a good modular design this implementation process can be accomplished by several people working independently on different modules.

4. *Testing.* This phase is closely associated with the previous one, because each module of the system is normally tested as it is implemented. Indeed, each

module in a well-designed system can be tested independently of the other modules by using simplified versions of the other modules, called stubs, to simulate the interaction between the target module and the rest of the system. Of course, this individual testing gives way to overall system testing as the various modules are completed and combined.

Unfortunately, the testing and debugging of a system is extremely difficult to perform successfully. Research has shown that large software systems contain three to five errors for every 100 program statements, even after significant testing. Many of these errors may go undetected for the life of the system, while others may cause major malfunctions, such as train doors opening while the train is between stations and false alerts from automated national defense systems. The elimination of such errors is one of the goals of software engineering. The fact that they are still prevalent means that a lot of research remains to be done.

Early approaches to software engineering were based on a strict adherence to the analysis, design, implementation, and testing sequence of software development. The feeling was that too much was at risk during the development of a large software system to allow for trial-and-error techniques. Thus, software engineers insisted that the entire analysis of the system be completed before beginning the design and, likewise, that the design be completed before beginning implementation. The result was a development process now referred to as the waterfall model, an analogy to the fact that the development process was allowed to flow in only one direction.

More Recent Trends

You will notice a similarity between the four problem-solving phases identified by Polya (Section 4-3) and the analysis, design, implementation, and testing phases of software development. After all, to develop a large software system is to solve a problem. On the other hand, the traditional waterfall approach to software development is in stark contrast to the "free-wheeling," trial-and-error process that is often vital to creative problem solving. Whereas the waterfall approach seeks to establish a highly structured environment in which development progresses in a sequential fashion, creative problem solving seeks a nonstructured environment in which one can drop previous plans of attack to pursue sparks of intuition without explaining why.

In recent years, software engineering techniques have begun to reflect this underlying contradiction. A major force behind this shift in philosophy has been the development of *computer-aided software engineering* (abbreviated as *CASE*) tools. These tools include software systems that assist in the development of dataflow diagrams, entity-relationship diagrams, and data dictionaries (all of which we discuss later), which are used to model the projected system. Some CASE systems even include code generators that, when given specifications for a part of a system, produce high-level language programs that implement that part of the system. The use of these automated tools significantly reduces the effort required in the analysis, design, and implementation phases of software development so that it is much easier to back up and change previous decisions if they are found to be wrong. The result has been a relaxation of the strict waterfall approach to software engineering.

One of the more prominent consequences of this newer approach to software development has been the use of prototyping, a technique that is also supported by many CASE tools. *Prototyping* refers to the construction of simplified versions or parts of the proposed system that can be analyzed before further development is done. Items that are readily conducive to prototyping include screen and document formats, database and file structures, and system protocols. Moreover, prototyping techniques are now being applied to construct simplified working versions of entire software systems.

The result of prototyping is that software development ceases to be a sequential process in which one phase is completed before the next begins. Instead, it becomes an iterative process in which analysis, design, and prototyping are repeated until the correct design is obtained. In many cases, the prototypes that are constructed during this iterative process are discarded in favor of a fresh implementation of the final design. This approach is known as throwaway prototyping. In contrast is the process of evolutionary prototyping in which the prototype is continually refined until it, itself, becomes the final system.

Questions/Exercises

1. What is the difference between system requirements and system specifications?
2. Summarize each of the four stages (analysis, design, implementation, and testing) within the development phase of the software life cycle.
3. Summarize the distinction between the traditional waterfall model of software development and the newer prototyping paradigm.

6-3 Modularity

One of the key statements in Section 6-2 was that to modify software one must understand the program or at least the pertinent parts of the program. Such an understanding is often difficult enough to obtain in the case of small programs and would be close to impossible when dealing with large software systems if it were not for the concept of *modularity*. This refers to the practice of dividing the software into manageable units, with each unit designed to perform only a part of the overall task.

We have already encountered the concept of modularity in this chapter as well as in Chapters 4 and 5. There we observed that by isolating the details of certain activities within subprograms, we could obtain a main program that more readily expresses its purpose and methods than would be available if we insisted on including complete descriptions of the activities in a single program unit.

An Example

Let us now consider a particular example of modularity as represented by the structure chart in Figure 6-3. A *structure chart* is a pictorial representation of a modular structure in which each module is represented by a rectangle and dependencies between modules are represented by arrows connecting them. In our example, the module ProcessPayroll is dependent on the module ComputeTax; that is, module ProcessPayroll uses module ComputeTax (most likely in the context of calling it as a subprogram) to accomplish its goal.

The structure chart in Figure 6-3 represents a simple payroll system for a small business. The division of labor among the modules is as follows:

ProcessPayroll is the controlling module charged with the task of computing the appropriate pay for each employee.

ComputeEarnings queries the work record of a particular employee and determines that employee's total earnings for the current pay period.

ComputePretaxWithholding determines the amount a given employee should contribute to the company's retirement program.

ComputeTax determines how much should be withheld from an employee's pay for state and federal taxes. It uses the modules ComputeFederalTaxes and Compute-StateTaxes to accomplish its task.

Figure 6-3 A structure chart of a simple payroll system

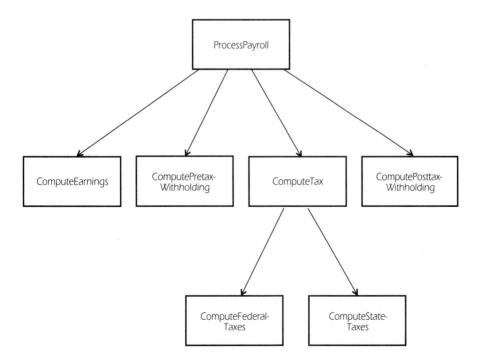

ComputePosttaxWithholding determines how much additional money should be withheld from an employee's income to cover company charges such as child care, parking, and cafeteria bills.

Coupling

We have introduced modularity as a way of obtaining manageable software. The idea is that a future modification will likely apply to only a few of the modules so that one's attention can be restricted to that portion of the system during the modification process. This, of course, depends on the assumption that changes in one module will not unknowingly affect other modules in the system. Consequently, one's goal when designing a modular system should be to maximize independence between modules.

Working against this objective is the fact that some connection between modules is necessary for them to form a coherent system. This connection is referred to as *coupling.* The goal of maximizing independence therefore corresponds to minimizing coupling.

Intermodule coupling actually occurs in several forms. One is *control coupling,* which occurs when one module passes control to another, as in the transfer/return relationship associated with subprograms. Another is *data coupling,* which refers to the sharing of data between modules.

The structure chart in Figure 6-3 already represents the control coupling in our simple payroll system. Data coupling is traditionally represented in a structure chart with additional arrows, as represented in Figure 6-4. This chart indicates the data items that are passed to a module when its services are first requested and those data items that are passed back to the original module when the requested task is completed. In particular, when *ProcessPayroll* requests action from *ComputePretaxWithholding*, it passes the pertinent *EmployeeID* and *TotalEarnings* to *ComputePretaxWithholding*; and upon completing its task, *ComputePretaxWithholding* reports its conclusions to *ProcessPayroll* through the data item *Withholding*.

This intermodule data coupling is normally implemented by means of subprogram parameter lists, as introduced in Chapter 5. Indeed, the use of subprograms is the most popular technique for implementing modular systems, and the use of parameters provides a natural method for implementing any data coupling between a module and its subordinates. Such a coupling technique is explicit in that its existence is readily recognizable in the high-level language version of the program.

A different, and potentially dangerous, form of data coupling between modules is the implicit coupling obtained by the use of global data. Global data refers to data elements that are automatically available to the modules throughout a system as opposed to local data elements that are accessible only within a particular module unless explicitly passed to another. Most high-level languages provide methods for implementing both global and local data.

In our payroll example, implicit data coupling may occur through the use of a global employee database to which each module may refer without being granted

Figure 6-4 A structure chart showing data coupling

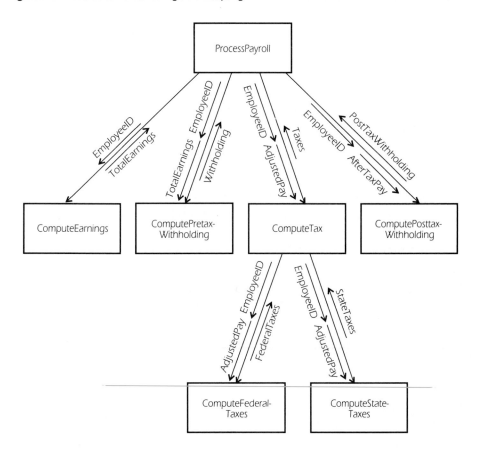

explicit permission. More precisely, ComputeEarnings may interrogate this database to find the total number of hours worked by an employee, while ComputePretaxWithholding might consult the same database to confirm that the employee in question participates in the company's retirement program.

The potential problem here is that one module may alter information used by other modules in a manner that is not anticipated by the rest of the system. This is especially likely after the system has been modified over a period of time. The result is that an apparently straightforward change to the system can have unforeseen and possibly disastrous side effects.

Side Effects

In a programming environment, the term **side effect** refers to an action performed by a program that is not readily represented by the program's syntax. Consider, for example, a module called CheckPassword whose task is to determine the privileges associated with different passwords. (Some users of the system may have passwords that allow the user to change data, while others may have passwords that allow only data retrieval.) If the privilege information were implemented as local data and passed through the parameter list, a request for services from the module CheckPassword might appear as

CheckPassword(Password, Privilege)

In contrast, if Privilege were implemented as a global data element, then a request for CheckPassword might appear as

CheckPassword(Password)

which does not explicitly reflect the fact that Privilege is involved. Indeed, in this case the action of CheckPassword has been demoted to a side effect.

Being inherently transparent, side effects constitute a major source of programming errors, and because implicit data coupling is one of the major sources of side effects, its use is sometimes scorned by software engineers. On the other hand, the proper use of global data can often simplify a program's presentation and hence increase its reliability. This, then, is an example of when the use of comment statements in the source program can be helpful. In particular, good programming style encourages the use of comments to identify any global data used by a module.

Cohesion

Just as important as minimizing the coupling between modules is maximizing the internal binding within each module. The term **cohesion** has been adopted for referring to this internal binding, or the degree of relatedness of a module's internal parts. Intuitively, one would expect a module that projects future income from real estate investments to be more cohesive than a module that projects income from a variety of investments.

To appreciate the importance of cohesion, we must look beyond the initial development of the system and consider the entire software life cycle. If it becomes necessary to make changes in a module, the existence of a variety of activities within it can easily confuse what would otherwise be a simple process. Thus, in addition to seeking low intermodule coupling, software designers strive for high intramodule cohesion.

A weak form of cohesion is known as **logical cohesion.** This is the cohesion within a module induced by the fact that its internal elements perform activities logically similar in nature. For example, consider a module that performs all of a system's communication with the outside world. The "glue" that holds such a module together is that all the activities within the module deal with communication. However, the subjects of the communication can vary greatly. Some may deal with obtaining data, while others deal with reporting errors.

A stronger form of cohesion is known as *functional cohesion,* which means that all the parts of the module are geared toward the performance of a single activity. What constitutes a single activity depends on the tools available. The module ProcessPayroll in Figure 6-3 are not functionally cohesive if the details of computing taxes and determining retirement contributes are included. However, by isolating these activities in other modules and using them as abstract tools, each step in the ProcessPayroll module can be focused on performing a single task (processing payroll) among all the other activities involved in the company's operation.

Questions/Exercises

1. Do modular systems always have a hierarchical-like structure?
2. How does a novel differ from an encyclopedia in terms of the degree of coupling between its units such as chapters, sections, or entries? What about cohesion?
3. A hand of bridge is divided into two phases: the bidding and the actual playing of the cards. Analyze the coupling between these phases by identifying the information that is passed from the first phase to the second explicitly. What is passed implicitly?
4. Is the goal of maximizing cohesion compatible with minimizing coupling? That is, as cohesion increases, does coupling naturally tend to decrease?
5. Identify the cohesive property that binds the various parts together in each of the following settings. Also identify how the natural divisions in each setting are related to cohesion:
   a. a club
   b. a department store
   c. a university registration system
   d. a newspaper

6-4   Development Tools and Techniques

In this section, we consider how modular designs are obtained. The development of design techniques is a major topic within software engineering, and its study has resulted in the development of design strategies general enough to be applied uniformly over a wide range of applications. In fact, the concepts discussed in this section are applicable whether the system being designed is to be automated or not.

Top-Down Design

Perhaps the most common concept associated with system design is that of top-down design methodology, which we met in Chapter 4 as stepwise refinement. The point of this concept is that one's first step when performing a task, such as a system design or the programming of a module, should be to produce a short, undetailed summary of the solution rather than a final detailed version of the solution. This summary often takes the form of little more than a restatement of the problem itself.

The next step is to refine the solution produced in the preceding step. Here one considers the solution in slightly more detail and divides the preceding summarized activity into its major units. The important point is that each of these units, although being more detailed, encompasses only a part of the overall task. The original problem thus gets divided into several smaller and simpler problems whose solutions collectively provide a solution to the original problem. This refinement process continues successively until problems with manageable solutions are obtained.

The result of top-down design is a hierarchical system of refinements that often can be translated directly into a modular structure. That is, the smallest units in the hierarchy become modules that perform simple tasks, while the superior units become modules that perform more complex tasks using the lower modules as abstract tools.

Bottom-Up Design

In contrast to the top-down design methodology is the bottom-up approach, in which one starts the design of a system by identifying individual tasks within the system; one then considers how solutions to these tasks can be used as abstract tools in the solution to more complex problems.

For many years, this approach has been considered inferior to the top-down design paradigm. Today, however, the bottom-up design methodology is gaining support. One reason for this shift in opinion is that the top-down methodology tends to seek a solution with a hierarchical structure. Indeed, the process of dividing tasks into subtasks naturally leads to a design consisting of a dominant module that uses submodules, each of which relies on subsubmodules, and so on. On the other hand, the best design for some systems is not of a hierarchical nature. A design consisting of two modules interacting as equals (Figure 6-5a) may be a better solution than a design consisting of a superior module that relies on subordinates to perform its task (Figure 6-5b). For example, a multinational economic model might be implemented as several modules, one for each nation, that communicate directly with each other to simulate the interaction between nations.

Another reason for the increased interest in bottom-up design rests in the emphasis on constructing abstract tools that can be used as building blocks in a variety of applications. Much of the momentum for this approach stems from the popularity of object-oriented programming, in which programs are often constructed from stand-alone objects, each having the ability to interact with other objects directly rather than through a supervising module. In turn, these objects are also available as ready-made units for use in other designs. In this atmosphere, then, the design of a new system conforms more closely to the process of building complex solutions from pieces than to the process of refining global approaches into subtasks.

Figure 6-5 Contrasting modular designs

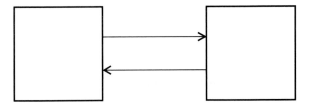

(a) Modules interacting as equals

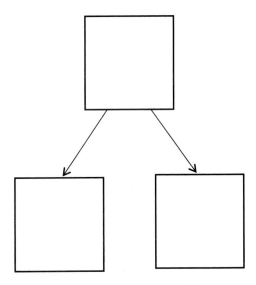

(b) Modules under control of a supervising module

Dataflow Diagrams

Software engineering has produced a variety of design techniques and notational systems to aid in the system design process, many of which are applicable in either top-down or bottom-up paradigms. One of these emphasizes the data, or information, that will flow through the proposed system as opposed to the procedures, or algorithms, that will be executed. The idea behind this approach is that by following the data paths through the proposed system, we discover where data units merge, split, or are otherwise altered. Because computational activity is needed at these locations in the system, such activities, or groupings of activities, should form the modules of the system. Consequently, concentrating on flow of data helps us discover a modular structure for a system instead of forcing us to break it into pieces according to intuition.

A *dataflow diagram* is a pictorial representation of the data paths in a system. The various symbols in such a diagram have specific meanings: Arrows represent data paths, rectangles represent data sources and sinks, circles (bubbles) represent locations of data manipulation, and heavy straight lines represent data storage. In each case the symbol is labeled with the name of the object represented either within it or alongside it.

A dataflow diagram for our simple payroll system is shown in Figure 6-6. Note that the dataflow diagram, in which emphasis is placed on the data, more readily reflects the role of the underlying employee database than the structure chart in Figure 6-4.

Entity-Relationship Diagrams

Another tool used in the analysis and design of software systems is the *entity-relationship diagram,* which is a pictorial representation of the items of information (entities) manipulated by the system and the relationships between these pieces of information. As an example, let us consider part of an entity-relationship diagram for a software system for maintaining information about professors, students, and classes at a university.

We first identify the data entities manipulated by the system. These include the entity professor, which we think of as representing a single professor at the university; the entity student, which represents a single student; and the entity class, which represents a section of a given course. With each occurrence of the professor entity is associated a name, address, employee identification number, salary, and so on; with each occurrence of the student entity is associated a name, address, student identification number, grade point average, and so on; and with each occurrence of the class entity is associated a course identification (History 101), semester and year, classroom, time of day, and so on.

Having identified the entities in our system, we now consider the relationships among the entities. We first note that each professor teaches classes and each student attends classes. We therefore identify the relationship between the entities professor and class as the relationship teaches and that between the entities student and class as the relationship attends. (Note that entities are referred to by nouns, whereas relationships are referenced by verbs.)

Figure 6-6 A dataflow diagram of a simple payroll system

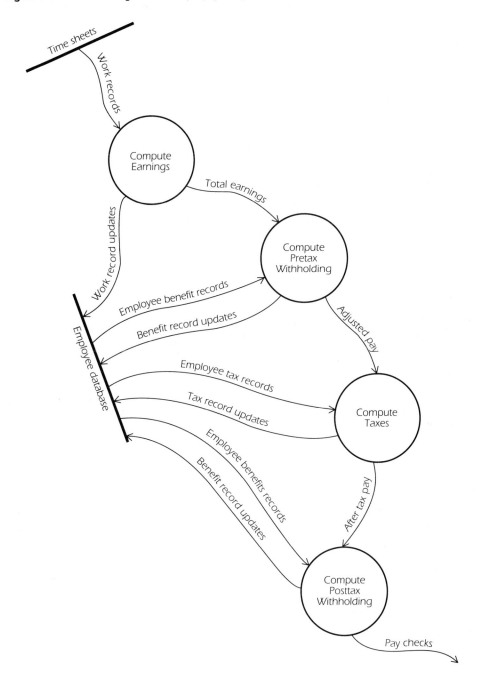

Figure 6-7 An entity-relationship diagram

To represent these entities and relationships, we use the entity-relationship diagram in Figure 6-7. Here each entity is represented by a rectangle and each relationship is represented by a diamond. The diagram clearly shows that professors are related to classes by means of the relationship *teaches* and students are related to classes by means of the relationship *attends*.

There is, however, a different structure associated with the two relationships in our example. The relationship between *professor* and *class* is a one-to-many relationship in that each professor teaches several classes but each class is taught by only one professor. In contrast, the relationship between *student* and *class* is a many-to-many relationship because each student attends several classes and each class is attended by several students. This additional information is represented in Figure 6-7 by the presence of pointers on the lines connecting relationships to entities. In particular, a single pointer toward an entity indicates that only one occurrence of that entity is involved in each occurrence of the relationship, whereas a double pointer indicates that more than one occurrence of the entity may be involved.[1] Thus, the pointer toward the entity *professor* in Figure 6-7 indicates that only one professor teaches a class, while the double pointer toward the entity *class* in the *teaches* relationship indicates that each professor may teach more than one class.

Although different, entity-relationship diagrams are quite compatible with dataflow diagrams. Indeed, the two are often used in conjunction with each other. Dataflow diagrams are helpful when trying to understand the flow of data, whereas entity-relationship diagrams are used when studying the structure of the data itself.

Data Dictionaries

Still another tool in the development of a software system is the ***data dictionary***—a central depository of information about the data items appearing throughout the system. This information includes the identifier used to reference each item, what constitutes valid entries in each item (Will the item always be numeric or perhaps always alphabetic? What will be the range of values that might be assigned to this item?); where the item is stored (Will the item be stored in a file or a database and, if so, which one?); and where the item is referenced in the software (Which modules will refer to the item?).

---

[1]No universal standard exists for representing multiplicity within an entity-relationship diagram. The single/double pointer system used here may not agree with other material you will read.

There are several goals associated with the development of a data dictionary. One is to enhance communication between the potential user of the system and the analyst who is charged with the task of converting the user's needs into requirements and specifications. It would be discouraging to find, after the system has been implemented, that part numbers are not really numeric or that the size of the inventory exceeds the maximum allowed by the system. The process of constructing a data dictionary helps avoid such misunderstandings.

Another goal associated with the data dictionary is to establish uniformity throughout the system. It is usually by means of constructing the dictionary that redundancies and contradictions surface. For example, the item referred to as PartNumber in the inventory records may be the same as the PartId in the sales records. Moreover, the personnel department may use the item Name to refer to an employee while inventory records may contain the item Name in reference to a part.

Questions/Exercises

1. Draw a dataflow diagram depicting the flow of information between an instructor, a student, and a textbook. Include the fact that quizzes are given.
2. Suppose that a certain receptionist receives requests for appointments. The response to a request is either a schedule for a future appointment or an immediate appointment. Draw a dataflow diagram representing this part of the receptionist's job.
3. Give a short definition of a dataflow diagram, an entity-relationship diagram, and a data dictionary.
4. Draw an entity-relationship diagram representing airline companies, flights flown by each company, and the passengers on the various flights.

6-5 Documentation

A software system is of little use unless people can learn to use it and maintain it. Hence, documentation is an important part of a software package, and in turn its development is an important topic in software engineering.

Documentation of a software package is normally produced for two purposes. One is to explain the features of the software and describe how to use them. This is known as user documentation because it is designed to be read by the user of the software. Hence, user documentation tends to be nontechnical.

Today, user documentation is recognized as an important marketing tool. Good user documentation (combined with a well-designed user interface) makes a software package accessible and thus increases its sales. Recognizing this, many software developers hire technical writers to produce this part of their product, or they provide preliminary versions of their products to independent manual writers so that how-to books are available in book stores when the software itself is released to the public.

User documentation traditionally takes the form of a manual that presents an introduction to the most commonly used features of the software (often in the form of a tutorial), a section explaining how to install the software, and a reference section describing the details of each feature of the software.

This manual is often available in book form, but in many cases it is provided as a file that is stored on the same medium as the software. This allows a user of the software to review portions of the manual at the computer monitor while using the software. In this case, the information may be broken into small units, sometimes called help packages, that are presented as a part of the software system itself. That is, the ability to request access to one of the help packages is an option built into the software system. In some systems, help packages may appear on the monitor screen automatically if the user dallies too long between commands.

The other purpose for documentation is to describe the software itself so that the system can be maintained later in its life cycle. Documentation of this type is known as system documentation and is inherently more technical than user documentation. In the past, system documentation consisted of the final source programs and some sketchy explanations that were written after the software was developed—an approach with which most beginning programmers can identify. However, such haphazard documentation is simply not acceptable for today's large software systems.

Today, system documentation begins with the development of the original system specifications and continues throughout the software's life cycle. Ultimately, it consists of all the documents that were prepared during the software's development, including the specifications by which the system was verified, the dataflow and entity-relationship diagrams from which the software was designed, the data dictionary, and the structure charts representing the modular structure of the system.

Of major importance is the source version of all the programs in the system. It is important that these programs be presented in a readable format, which is why software engineers support the use of well-designed, high-level programming languages, the use of comment statements for annotating a program, and a modular design that allows each module to be presented as a coherent unit.

The fact that the development of system documentation is an ongoing process leads to a conflict between the goals of software engineering and human nature. It is highly unlikely that the initial specifications, dataflow diagrams, entity-relationship diagrams, or structure charts will remain unchanged as the system development progresses. It is more likely that changes will be made as the people involved in the project recognize problems that were not foreseen. (This phenomenon is the driving force behind the development of prototyping techniques.) At issue in this case is the temptation to make ongoing changes in the system's design without going back to update the earlier design documents. The result is a strong possibility that these documents will be incorrect and hence their use in the final documentation misleading.

Herein lies another argument in favor of CASE tools. They make the tasks of redrawing diagrams and updating dictionaries much easier than they were with the older manual methods. Moreover, combining this advantage with the newer prototyping methodologies, which accept the idea of analysis and design being iterative processes involving implementation, brings the task of document alteration into the realm of accepted practice rather than that of discouraged exception. In turn, updates are more likely to be made in this environment, and the final documentation is more likely to be accurate.

We close by emphasizing that the example of updating documents is only one of many instances in which software engineering must encompass both the cold, hard facts of a science and the realistic understanding of human nature. Others include the inevitable personality conflicts, jealousies, and ego clashes that arise when people work together. Thus, as we have mentioned before, the subject of software engineering covers much more than those subjects directly associated with computer science.

Questions/Exercises

1. In what forms can software be documented?
2. At what phase (or phases) in the software life cycle is documentation prepared?
3. Which is more important, a program or its documentation?

Chapter 6 Review Problems

1. Give an example of how efforts in the development of software can pay dividends later in software maintenance.

2. What is evolutionary prototyping?

3. Summarize how the use of CASE tools has changed the software development process.

4. Explain how the lack of metrics for measuring certain software properties affects software engineering discipline.

5. How does software engineering differ from other, more traditional fields of engineering.

6. a. Identify a disadvantage of the traditional waterfall model for software development.
   b. Identify an advantage of the traditional waterfall model for software development.

7. What is the difference between explicit and implicit data coupling? Give an example of each.

8. What is the difference between coupling and cohesion? Which should be minimized and which should be maximized? Why?

9. Which of the following statements is an argument for coupling, and which is an argument for cohesion:
   a. For a student to learn, the subject should be presented in well-organized units with specific goals.
   b. A student doesn't really understand a subject until the subject's overall scope and relationship with other subjects has been grasped.

10. In the text, we mentioned control coupling but did not pursue it. Contrast the coupling between two program units obtained by a simple GOTO statement with the coupling obtained by a subprogram call.

11. Answer the following questions in relation to the accompanying structure chart:
    a. To which module does module Y return control?
    b. To which module does module Z return control?
    c. Are modules W and X linked via control coupling?
    d. Are modules W and X linked via data coupling?
    e. What data is shared by both module W and module Y?
    f. In what way are modules Y and X related?

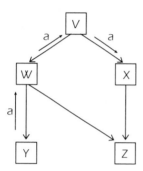

12. In relation to the structure chart in problem 11, what stubs are necessary to test module V? What characteristics might these stubs have?

13. Answer the following questions in relation to the accompanying structure chart:
    a. What is different between the way modules A and B use data items x and y?
    b. If one of the modules was in charge of obtaining data item z from a user at a remote terminal, which module would that apparently be?

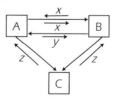

14. Here are sketches of subprograms A, B, C, D, E, and F expressed in an Ada-like syntax. Draw a structure chart representing the control and data coupling indicated by these sketches. Within which module is a person's address apparently determined? What about a person's age? The skills required for a job?

procedure A(Name: **in** String; Addr: **out** String);
.
.
end;
procedure B(Job: **in** String);
.
.
F(Job, Skills);
.
.
end;
procedure C(Name: **in** String);
.
.
D(Name, Age);
.
.
A(Name, Addr):
.
.
end;
procedure D(Name: **in** String; Age: **out** int);
.
.
end;
procedure E(EmplID: **in** String);
.
.
C(Name);
.
.
B(Job);
.
.
end;
procedure F(Job: **in** String; Skills: **out** SkillType);
.
.
end;

15. Here are sketches of subprograms A, B, and C expressed in an Ada-like syntax. Draw a structure

chart representing the control and data coupling among them.

procedure A(x: **in** integer; y: **in out** integer);

  .

  .

end;

procedure B(z: **out** integer);

  .

  .

end;

procedure C;

  .

  .

B(z);

A(x, y);

  .

  .

end;

16. Design a modular structure for an on-line inventory/customer records system for a mail-order business and represent it with a structure chart. What modules in your system must be modified because of changes in sales tax laws? What if the length of the postal system's ZIP code changes?

17. Suppose you are about to change the type associated with the variable Total in a FORTRAN program containing the statement:

    CALL GetTax (Rate, Price, Tax, Total)

What warning does this statement give you about additional changes you should make?

18. Suppose the function Handicap were designed to compute and return the handicap of the golfer identified in the parameter list, but in so doing suppose it also adds one to the value of a global variable called Par. If the value of Par is initially 4 and Bill's handicap is 2, how will the result of the computation

    Par + Handicap(Bill)

vary depending on the order in which the values needed in the computation are obtained?

19. Give a definition for the term *side effect*.

20. What potentially disastrous side effects are lurking in a software system whose modules use global rather than local variables?

21. What side effects does the order of execution have in performing the calculation 4 / 2 + 6?

22. A major role of the personnel department of a medium-size manufacturing business is the filling of vacancies as they occur on the shop floor. Draw a dataflow diagram depicting the flow of data through the portion of a personnel department charged with this responsibility.

23. Draw a dataflow diagram depicting the registration process at a university.

24. Contrast the information represented in dataflow diagrams with that given in structure charts.

25. What is the difference between a one-to-many relationship and a many-to-many relationship?

26. Draw an entity-relationship diagram representing the relationships between the cooks, waitresses, customers, and cashiers in a restaurant.

27. Draw an entity-relationship diagram representing the relationships between magazines, publishers of magazines, and subscribers to magazines.

28. In each of the following cases, identify whether the activity relates to a structure chart, a dataflow diagram, an entity-relationship diagram, or a data dictionary.
    a. Identifying the data pertinent to the system to be developed.
    b. Identifying the relationship between the various items of data appearing in the system.
    c. Identifying the characteristics of each item of data in the system.
    d. Identifying which items of data are shared among the various parts of the system.

29. Summarize the distinction between top-down and bottom-up design strategies.

30. What is the difference between user documentation and system documentation?

31. Suppose that 100 errors were intentionally placed in a large software system before the system was subjected to final testing. Moreover, suppose that a total of 200 errors were discovered and corrected during this final testing, of which 50 errors were from the group intentionally placed in the system. If the remaining 50 known errors are then corrected, how many unknown errors would you estimate are still in the system?

32. Why would it not be desirable for the same person who wrote a program to also design the test data?

Problems for the Programmer

1. Does the programming language you are using provide for both global and local data elements? Using a function similar to the handicap function of review problem 18, write a test program to find out if your programming language evaluates expressions from right to left or left to right.

2. Extend your simple operating system of programming problem 6 in Chapter 3 to include a resource allocator and a dispatcher. Assume that the system has access to four nonshareable resources. Modify the file manager so that it randomly associates a collection of these resources to each file when it is CREATEd to simulate that program's resource requirement list. Then to execute a program, the resource allocator must approve that program's resource request. After a suitable amount of time, the dispatcher in your system should report to the scheduler that the program has completed. Design your system so that more than one program can be under the control of the dispatcher at the same time.

3. Draw a structure chart for a software system that simulates the machine described in Appendix B.

4. What features are provided by the programming language you use for implementing data coupling between modules? How can data be implicitly passed between modules? How can data be explicitly passed between modules?

5. What features are provided by the programming language you use to encourage well-designed programs?

Additional Reading

Arthur, L. J. *Rapid Evolutionary Development*. New York: John Wiley, 1992.

Connell, J. L., and Shafer, L. *Structured Rapid Prototyping: An Evolutionary Approach to Software Development*. Englewood Cliffs, N.J.: Prentice-Hall, 1989.

Conte, S. D.; Dunsmore, H. E.; and Shen, V. Y. *Software Engineering Metrics and Models*. Redwood City, Calif.: Benjamin/Cummings, 1986.

Forester, T. and Morrison, P. *Computer Ethics: Cautionary Tales and Ethical Dilemmas in Computing*. Cambridge, Mass.: MIT Press, 1990.

Pressman, R. S. *Software Engineering: A Practitioner's Approach,* 3rd ed. New York: McGraw-Hill, 1992.

Schach, S. R. *Software Engineering*. Boston, Mass.: Aksen Associates, 1993.

Sommerville, I. *Software Engineering,* 4th ed. Reading, Mass.: Addison-Wesley, 1992.

Yourdon, E. *Structured Walkthroughs*. Englewood Cliffs, N.J.: Prentice-Hall, 1979.

Yourdon, E. *Modern Structured Analysis*. Englewood Cliffs, N.J.: Prentice-Hall, 1989.

PART THREE

DATA ORGANIZATION

We have seen that the information stored inside a machine is represented in a coded form and stored either in memory cells or in some mass storage system. However, the information in this form is rarely conducive to use in an application. Rather, the application normally suggests that we imagine the data as being organized in a manner different from the actual storage structure in the machine. For example, data representing the weekly sales of a company's sales force might be envisioned in tabular form, with a separate column for each day of the week and a separate row for each member of the sales force; the names and positions of a company's employees might be pictured in the form of an organization chart; or a company may want its inventory records organized by part number for one application and by cost for another.

Part Three introduces the study of how a machine can be programmed to present its internal data to a user as though it were stored in these conceptual and more useful forms and how this goal affects the way the data items are actually stored within the machine. In Chapter 7, we concentrate on data stored in a machine's main memory; in Chapter 8, we consider data stored in mass storage; and in Chapter 9, we introduce the topic of database systems.

CHAPTER SEVEN

DATA STRUCTURES

*Sections marked by an asterisk are optional in that they represent additional depth of coverage that is not required for an understanding of future chapters. (Section 7-7 is a minor exception. It is required background for Section 9-5.)

We have used the terms *virtual* and *conceptual* several times in reference to properties that, although appearing to belong to hardware, are actually simulated through a combination of hardware and software. For example, we saw that a single machine can appear to be many machines through the use of a time-sharing system or that a machine can appear to understand the words in a high-level programming language by means of an interpreter. This chapter is concerned with another conceptual feature, the structure (or organization) of data.

Recall that any information stored in a machine's memory must be organized to fit into a row of memory cells, even though this data may be more useful as a rectangular table of values. In this case, our problem is to simulate the rectangular shape using the tools provided by the machine. The goal is to allow the user of the data to think of the data as having this simulated shape without being concerned with the data's actual organization within the machine.

7-1 Arrays

We begin our study of data structures by considering the organizations known as arrays encountered earlier in our discussion of high-level programming languages. There we saw that many high-level languages allow a programmer to express an algorithm as though the data being manipulated were stored in a rectangular arrangement; the programmer might refer to the fifth element in a one-dimensional array or the element in the third row and sixth column of a two-dimensional array. Since the array is actually stored in the memory cells of the machine, it becomes the job of either the translator or the interpreter to convert such references into the terminology of memory cells and addresses.

One-Dimensional Arrays

Suppose an algorithm for manipulating a series of 24 hourly temperature readings is expressed in a high-level language. The programmer would probably find it convenient to think of these readings arranged as a one-dimensional array, that is, a list called Readings whose various entries are referenced in terms of their position in the list. This position is often called an index. The first reading might be referenced by Readings[1], the second by Readings[2], and so on.

The conversion from the conceptual one-dimensional array organization to the actual arrangement within the machine can be rather straightforward. The data can be stored in a sequence of 24 memory cells in the same order envisioned by the programmer. Knowing the address of the first cell in this sequence, an interpreter or translator can then easily convert terms such as Readings[4], into the proper memory terminology. In this case, to find the actual address, one merely subtracts one from the position of the desired entry and then adds the result to the address of the first

Figure 7-1 The array of Readings stored in memory starting at address 13

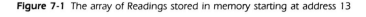
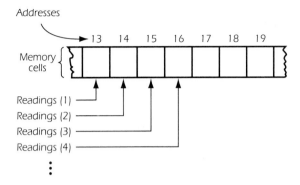

cell in the sequence. (If the first cell in the sequence is at address 13, the reading referenced by Readings[4] is located at location $13 + (4 - 1) = 16$, as shown in Figure 7-1.)

Multidimensional Arrays

The conversion is not quite so simple with multidimensional arrays. Consider, for example, a record of the sales made by a company's sales force during a one-week period. We can think of such data arranged in tabular form, with the names of the sales personnel listed down the left side and the days of the week listed across the top. Hence we can think of the data being arranged in rows and columns; the values across each row indicate the sales made by a particular employee, while the values down a column represent all the sales made during a particular day. Extracting information from the table therefore involves finding the value common to both a given row and a given column.

A machine's memory is arranged not in a rectangular fashion but rather as a row of memory cells; thus, the rectangular structure required by the sales table must be simulated. To do this, we first recognize that the size of the array does not vary as updates are made. We can therefore calculate the amount of storage area needed and reserve a block of contiguous memory cells of that size. Next, we store the data in the cells row by row. That is, starting at the first cell of the reserved block, we copy the values from the first row of the table into consecutive memory locations; following this we copy the next row, then the next, and so on (Figure 7-2, on the following page). Such a storage system is said to use ***row major order*** in contrast to ***column major order,*** in which the array is stored column by column.

With the data stored, the problem now becomes locating particular entries as they are requested. Recall that because the user will be thinking in terms of rows and columns, a request will be in the form of wanting, for example, the value of the entry in the third row and fourth column (that is, the sales made by the third employee on

Figure 7-2 A two-dimensional array with four rows and five columns stored in row major order

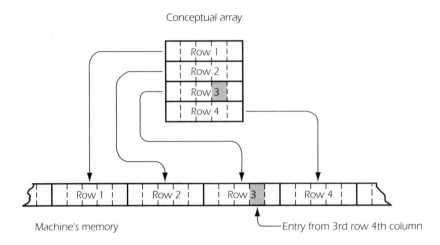

Thursday). To find this entry, we first envision ourselves as being at the first location in the reserved block of the machine's memory. The cells following this location contain the data in the first row of the array followed by the second, then the third, and so on. To get to the data in the third row, we must move beyond both the first and second rows. Since each row contains five entries (one for each day from Monday through Friday), we must move beyond a total of ten entries to reach the first entry of the third row. From the beginning of the third row, we must move beyond another three entries to reach the entry in the fourth column of the array. Altogether, to reach the entry in the third row and fourth column, we must move beyond 13 entries from the beginning of the block.

The preceding calculation is a special case of a general process that can be used for finding entries in a two-dimensional array when it is stored in row major order. In particular, if we let C represent the number of columns in the array (which is the number of entries in each row), to find the entry in the Ith row and Jth column, we must move beyond.

$$(C \times (I - 1)) + (J - 1)$$

entries from the beginning of the array. (This expression is sometimes called the address polynomial.) That is, we must move beyond $I - 1$ rows, each of which contains C entries, to reach the Ith row and then $J - 1$ more entries to reach the Jth entry in this row. In our prior example, C was equal to 5, I to 3, and J to 4: $(5 \times (3 - 1)) + (4 - 1)$ equals 13.

With this information, software routines can be written to convert requests in terms of rows and columns into locations within the block of memory containing the array. A translator, for example, uses this technique to convert a reference such as Sales[2,4] into an actual memory address. Thus, a programmer can enjoy the luxury of thinking of the data in tabular form (the conceptual structure) even though it is actually stored in a single row (the actual structure) within the machine.

Questions/Exercises

1. Show how the array $\begin{smallmatrix} 5 & 3 & 7 \\ 4 & 2 & 8 \\ 1 & 9 & 6 \end{smallmatrix}$ appears in memory when stored in row major order.

2. Give a formula for finding the entry in the Ith row and Jth column of a two-dimensional array if it is stored in column major order rather than row major order.

3. If a two-dimensional array of 8 rows and 11 columns are stored in row major order beginning at memory address 25, what is the address of the entry in the third row sixth column if each entry occupies two memory cells?

4. In the C programming language, indices of arrays start at 0. Thus the entry in the first row, fourth column of an array named Array is referenced by Array[0][3]. In this case, what address polynomial is used by the translator to convert references of the from Array[I][J] into memory addresses?

7-2 Lists

An important property of arrays is that their size and shape are constant, so simulating them in a machine's memory is essentially a process of converting the conceptual location of an element into the actual location. In contrast are dynamic structures, which vary in size and shape. For instance, an organization's membership list grows as new members join and shrinks as old members leave. In such cases, we find that in addition to locating elements in the structure, we must accommodate variations in the structure itself.

Pointers

A prominent concept in the maintenance of dynamic structures is that of a pointer, so let us introduce this idea before proceeding. Recall that the various storage locations in a machine's memory are identified by numeric addresses. If we know the address of a piece of data, we can find that data with little difficulty. Being merely numeric values, these addresses themselves are easily stored in a machine's memory. Thus, having stored an item of data in one cell of memory we can store the address of that data in another memory cell. Later, if we want to retrieve the data item and we have access to the cell containing its address, we can find the data by referring to its address.

In a sense, then, a memory cell containing the address of a data item can be thought of as pointing to that data item. Such cells are called **pointers.** (Note that we have already encountered the idea of a pointer in our discussion of a machine's fetch-decode-execute cycle, in which a program counter is used to hold the address of the next instruction to be executed. In fact, another but somewhat outdated term for program counter is **instruction pointer.**)

Many programming languages today allow for the declaration, allocation, and manipulation of pointers, just as they allow for such operations for integers or character strings. Using such a language, a programmer can design elaborate networks of data items within a machine's memory. For example, suppose a library has its holdings represented in a machine's memory in alphabetical order by title. Although convenient in many applications, this arrangement makes it difficult to find all the books by a particular author, because the books are scattered throughout the list. To solve this problem we can reserve an additional memory cell of type pointer within the block of cells representing each book. In each of these pointer cells, we can place the address of another block representing a book by the same author so that each collection of books with common authorship is linked in a loop (Figure 7-3). Thus, once we find one book by a given author, we can find all the others by following the pointers from one book to another.

Let us now return to our discussion of dynamic data structures by considering two methods of maintaining a list of names within a machine's memory. The first of these methods (dense list) is similar to array storage systems and does not use pointers; the other method (linked list) takes advantage of pointer techniques to overcome some of the disadvantages encountered with a dense list.

Dense Lists

One technique for storing a list of names in a machine's memory is to store the entire list in a single block of consecutive memory cells. Assuming that each name is no longer than eight letters, we can divide this large block of cells into a collection of subblocks, each containing eight cells. Into each subblock, we can store a name by recording its ASCII code using one cell per letter (Figure 7-4, on p. 276). If the name alone does not fill all the cells in the subblock allocated to it, we can merely fill the remaining cells with the ASCII code for a space. Using this system requires a block of 80 consecutive memory cells to store a list of ten names.

Such an organization is referred to as a **dense list** and appears to be straightforward and convenient. It is really nothing more than a one-dimensional array in which each element consists of eight memory cells. However, problems can arise when we try to modify a list stored in this way. Suppose we need to delete a name. If this name is currently toward the beginning of the list and we need to keep the list in the same (possibly alphabetical) order, we must move all the names occurring later in the list forward in memory to fill the hole left by the deleted name.

Figure 7-3 Library holdings arranged by title but linked according to authorship

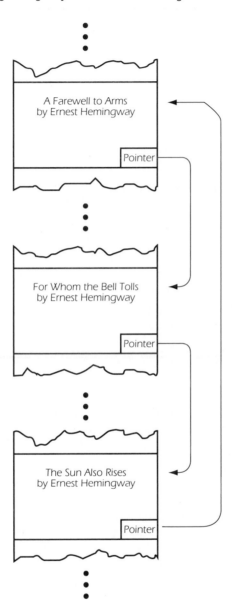

A more serious problem can occur if we need to add a name, because this requires not only moving names to create a hole for the new entry but also checking that there is room in memory to make this extension. In particular, if we originally reserve a block of 80 memory cells for our list of ten names, the addition of one name creates

Figure 7-4 Names stored in memory as a dense list

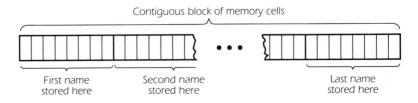

Contiguous block of memory cells

First name stored here

Second name stored here

Last name stored here

the need for a block of 88 cells. If we are lucky, eight unused cells are adjacent to the current block. However, if they are not, the addition of a single name forces us to move the entire list to a new area of memory that has room.

Linked Lists

Such problems can be avoided if we allow the individual names in the list to be stored in different areas of memory rather than together in one large, contiguous block. To do this, we store each name in a string of nine memory cells. The first eight of these cells are used to hold the name itself, and the last cell is used as a pointer to the next name in the list. In this form, the list can be scattered among several small nine-cell blocks linked together by pointers. Because of this linkage system, such an organization is called a *linked list.*

To keep track of where the first entry of a linked list is located, we set aside a memory cell in which we save the address of the first entry. This cell points to the beginning of the list and is normally called the ***head pointer.*** To read the list, we start at the location indicated by this head pointer and find the first name along with the pointer to the next entry. Following this pointer, we can find the second entry and so forth throughout the list. In this manner, we can traverse the entire list by hopping from one name to the next. (Searching a linked list for a particular entry is similar to a treasure hunt. The head pointer provides the first clue that directs us to another location. If we do not find the treasure there, we follow the next clue and so on.)

At this point, we have considered the problem of moving from one member of the list to the next but have ignored the problem of detecting the end of the list. This problem is solved by using a ***NIL pointer,*** a special bit pattern appearing in the pointer cell of the last entry that indicates that no further entries appear in the list. For example, if we agree never to start an entry at address 0, the value zero never appears as a legitimate pointer value, and we can use it as the NIL pointer in the list storage. Thus, we place the value zero in the pointer cell of the last entry in the list. Later, when the list is traversed, this special value can be interpreted as marking the end of the list rather than as being the address of yet another entry.

The final linked list storage organization is represented by the diagram in Figure 7-5. We depict the scattered blocks of memory used for the list by individual

Figure 7-5 The structure of a linked list

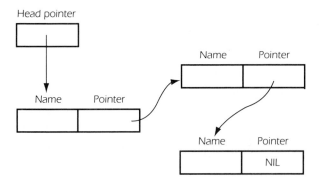

rectangles. Each rectangle is labeled to indicate its composition. Note that the information stored in each pointer is represented by an arrow that leads from the pointer itself to the pointer's addressee.

Let us return now to the problems of deleting and inserting entries in the list to see how the use of pointers alleviates the movement of names encountered when storing the list in a single contiguous block. First we note that a name can be deleted by changing a single pointer. This is done by changing the pointer that formerly pointed to the name being deleted so that it points to the name following the deleted entry (Figure 7-6). From then on, when the list is traversed, the deleted name is passed by because it no longer is part of the chain.

Inserting a new name is only a little more involved. We first find an unused block of nine memory cells, store the new name in the first eight cells, and fill the ninth cell with the address of the name in the list that should follow the new name. Finally, we change the pointer associated with the name that should precede the new name so that

Figure 7-6 Deleting an entry from a linked list

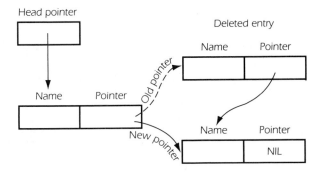

it points to the new name (Figure 7-7). Observe that after this is done, the new entry is found in the proper place anytime the list is traversed.

In reality, the deletion or insertion of an entry in a linked list is not quite as simple as our description implies, because we might want to keep track of those blocks of cells that have been removed from the list. Indeed, the information in these blocks is no longer important, so these blocks of cells can be reused at a later date to hold new entries in the list. One technique for keeping track of blocks available for reuse is to maintain a record of pointers to reusable blocks or perhaps maintain another linked list consisting of these blocks. Thus, as a block is removed from the main list, it is added to the list of available storage blocks, and as new entries are needed, blocks to contain them can be removed from the list of available blocks and inserted in the list. The process of collecting reusable memory space is called garbage collection.

Supporting the Conceptual List

Regardless of whether one chooses to implement a list as a dense structure or as a linked one, the user of the list should not have to consider the technicalities of the implementation each time a list access is required. Rather, the user should be able to forget about these details and merely use the list as though the storage system is actually organized in the same way as the conceptual structure (just as a programmer is allowed to refer to a particular element in an array without being concerned with the technicalities of how the array is actually stored).

For example, consider the task of developing a software package for maintaining the class enrollments for a university registrar. The person developing this package might approach the problem by establishing a separate list structure for each class, with each list containing an alphabetically ordered list of the students in that class.

Figure 7-7 Inserting an entry into a linked list

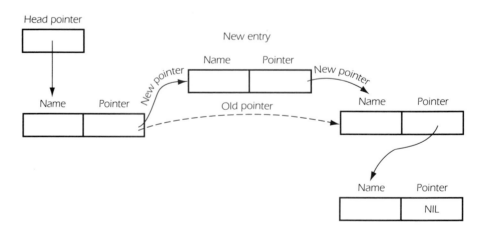

Figure 7-8 A subprogram for printing a linked list

```
procedure PrintList (List)
    Assign CurrentPointer the value in the head pointer of List.
    while (CurrentPointer is not NIL) do
        (Print the name in the entry pointed to by CurrentPointer;
        Observe the value in the pointer cell of the List entry
            pointed to by CurrentPointer, and reassign CurrentPointer
            to be that value.)
```

Once this is done, the programmer's attention should be allowed to shift to the more general concerns of the problem and not be repeatedly distracted by the details of how data might be moved within a dense list or what shifting of pointers is required in a linked list.

What we need is a collection of subprograms for performing the activities, such as inserting a new entry, deleting an old entry, searching for an entry, or printing the list, that otherwise require an understanding of the underlying list structure. These routines, together with the actual storage cells being used, fill the needs of the remaining software package while hiding the technicalities of how the list is actually implemented. For example, to place J. W. Brown in the course Physics 208, the programmer can write a statement such as

insert ("Brown, J. W.", "Physics 208")

and rely on the subprograms to carry out the details of the insertion.

As an example of such a routine, a subprogram named PrintList for printing a linked list of names is shown in Figure 7-8. Recall that the first entry of the list is pointed to by a pointer called the head pointer, and each entry in the list consists of two pieces: a name and a pointer. Once this subprogram has been developed, it can be used by a programmer to print the list without concern for how the list is actually stored. For example, to obtain a printed class list for Economics 301, the programmer need only write

PrintList ("Economics 301")

Questions/Exercises

1. If you know the address of the beginning of the first entry in a dense list, how can you find the address of the fifth entry? What about the case of a linked list?
2. What condition indicates that a linked list is empty?
3. Modify the subprogram in Figure 7-8 so it stops printing once a particular name has been printed.
4. Design an algorithm for finding a particular entry in a linked list and then deleting it.

7-3 Stacks

One of the properties of a list that makes a linked structure more inviting than a dense one is the need to insert and delete entries inside the list. Recall that it was such operations that had the potential of forcing the massive movement of names to fill or create holes in the case of a dense list. If we restrict such operations to the ends of the structure, we find that the use of a dense structure becomes a more convenient system. An example of this phenomenon is a *stack*, which is a list where all insertions and deletions are performed at the same end of the structure. The end at which these operations occur is called the *top* of the stack. The other end is sometimes called the stack's base.

To reflect the fact that access to a stack is restricted to the topmost entry, we use special terminology when referring to the insertion and deletion operations. The process of inserting an object on the stack is called a *push* operation, and the process of deleting an object is called a *pop* operation. Thus, we speak of pushing an entry onto a stack and popping an entry off a stack.

We are quite familiar with stack structures in everyday life. For example, consider a stack of books on a table. Such an organization yields itself to the particular insertion and deletion operations of placing books on top of the stack (a push operation) and lifting books off the top (a pop operation). Disaster can result, however, from an attempt to remove or insert a book in the middle of a tall stack. Indeed, the structure of a stack dictates that the last object inserted must be the first one removed. This observation results in a stack often being referred to as a *last-in-first-out (LIFO)* structure.

Stack Applications

Before considering how a stack can actually be implemented in a computer's memory, let us take a moment to see where such structures might be useful. A common example is found within an interpreter for a high-level programming language where a stack is used to manage the execution of subprograms. Recall that when the execution of a subprogram is requested, the machine must transfer its attention to the subprogram; yet later, when the subprogram is completed, it must return to the original location before continuing (Figure 7-9). Thus, when the initial transfer is made, there must be a mechanism for remembering the location to which execution ultimately returns.

The situation is further complicated by the fact that the subprogram may itself request the execution of another subprogram, which may request still another, and so on. Consequently, the return locations being remembered begin to pile up. Later, as each of these subprograms is completed, execution must be returned to the proper place within the program unit that called the completed subprogram. Thus, a system is needed to save the return locations and later retrieve them in the proper order.

Figure 7-9 Nested subprogram terminating in the opposite order to that in which they were requested

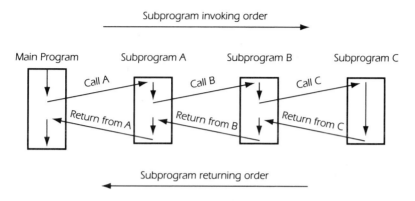

A stack is an ideal structure for such a system. As each subprogram is called, the interpreter merely pushes a pointer to the pertinent return location on the top of a stack, and as each subprogram is completed, the interpreter extracts the top entry from the stack with the assurance of obtaining a pointer to the proper return location. Indeed, the return locations are required in exactly the opposite order from which the subprogram calls were made. (The last subprogram called is the first one finished.)

This example is representative of stack applications in general because it demonstrates the relationship between stacks and the process of backtracking. The concept of a stack is inherent in any process that entails backing out of a system in the opposite order from which it was entered.

Stack Implementation

We turn now to the problem of implementing a stack structure in a computer's memory. It is customary to reserve a block of contiguous memory cells large enough to accommodate the stack as it grows and shrinks. (Determining the size of this block can often be a critical design problem. If too much room is allocated, the result is a waste of memory space, whereas if too little room is reserved, the stack ultimately exceeds the allotted storage space.) Having reserved a block of memory, we select one end to serve as the stack's base. This is where we place the first entry that is pushed on the stack, with each additional entry being placed next to its predecessor as the stack grows toward the other end of the reserved block.

One additional tool is needed in our system: a way of keeping track of the top of the stack. After all, as entries are pushed and popped, the stack top moves back and forth within the reserved block of memory cells. We must therefore maintain a record of the location of the top entry. For this purpose we set aside another memory cell in which we store the address of the cell currently residing at the top of the stack. This

Figure 7-10 A stack in memory

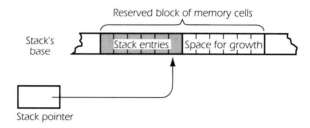

additional cell is known as the *stack pointer.* The complete system, as illustrated in Figure 7-10, works as follows: To push a new entry on the stack, we first adjust the stack pointer to point to the vacancy just beyond the top of the stack and then place the new entry at this location. To pop an entry from the stack, we read the data pointed to by the stack pointer and then adjust the pointer to point to the next entry down on the stack.

When a stack is organized in this manner, there is little difference between the conceptual structure and the actual structure of the data in memory. Suppose, however, that we cannot estimate the maximum size to which a particular stack may grow, so we cannot reserve a fixed block of memory and be assured that the stack will always fit. A solution is to implement the stack as a linked structure similar to that discussed in Section 7-2. This avoids the limitations of restricting the stack to a fixed-size block since it allows the entries in the stack to be stuffed into small pieces of available space anywhere in memory. (The expense, however, is a higher overhead.) In such a situation the conceptual stack structure will be quite different from the actual arrangement of the data in memory.

To complete the implementation of a stack, one must develop subprograms to perform the push and pop operations as well as a subprogram to test whether or not the stack is empty. These three routines would allow the stack to be used by a programmer without demanding that the programmer pay attention to the internal implementation of the stack itself.

A Particular Stack Application

As a closing example, we return to the list-printing problem considered at the end of Section 7-2. Suppose that now we want the names in the linked list printed in the opposite order. The problem is that the only way we can access the names is by following the linked structure; thus, the first name accessed must be the last one printed. We need a way of holding each name retrieved until all the following names have been retrieved and printed. Our solution is to traverse the list from its beginning to its end while pushing the names we find onto a stack (Figure 7-11). After reaching the end of the list, we print the names as we pop them off the stack. The subprogram for this process is presented in Figure 7-12, on p. 284

Figure 7-11 Using a stack to print a linked list in reverse order

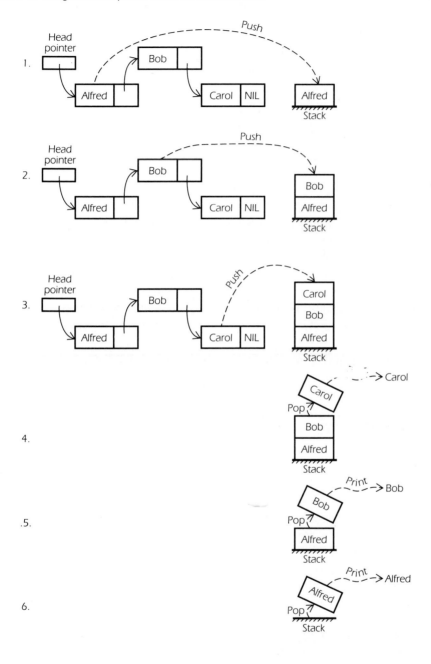

Figure 7-12 A subprogram (using an auxiliary stack) for printing a linked list in reverse order

> **procedure** ReversePrint (List)
>   Assign CurrentPointer the value in the head pointer of List.
>   **while** (CurrentPointer is not NIL) **do**
>   (Push the name pointed to by CurrentPointer onto the stack;
>   Observe the value in the pointer cell of the List entry
>   pointed to by CurrentPointer, and reassign CurrentPointer
>   to be that value.)
>   **while** (the stack is not empty) **do**
>   (Pop a name off the stack and print it.)

Questions/Exercises

1. List some additional occurrences of stacks in everyday life.
2. Suppose a main program calls subprogram A, which in turn calls subprogram B, and after B is completed, subprogram A calls subprogram C. Follow this scenario maintaining the stack of return locations.
3. Based on the technique of this section for implementing a stack in a contiguous block of cells, what condition indicates that the stack is empty?
4. Design an algorithm for popping an entry off a stack that is implemented with a stack pointer. Your algorithm should print an error message if the stack is empty.
5. Describe how a stack can be implemented in a high-level language in terms of a one-dimensional array.

7-4 Queues

A queue is another form of a restricted access list. In contrast to a stack in which both insertions and deletions are performed at the same end, a queue restricts all insertions to one end while all deletions are made at the other. We have already met and discussed this structure in relation to waiting lines in Chapter 3, where we recognized it as being a first-in-first-out (FIFO) storage system. Actually, the concept of a queue is inherent in any system in which objects are served in the same order in which they arrive.

The ends of a queue get their names from this waiting-line relationship. More precisely, the end at which entries are removed is called the **head** (or sometimes the front) of the queue just as we say that the next person to be served in a cafeteria is at the head (or front) of the line. Similarly, the end of the queue at which new entries are added is called the **tail** (or rear).

As we have mentioned before, terminology tends to evolve over time. Our definition of a queue as a strictly FIFO structure is traditional, but you will also hear the term *queue* used to refer to any structure in which each entry is removed from the head, regardless of when it entered the structure. This more relaxed definition includes structures in which new entries may be inserted in front of previous entries to maintain alphabetical order or to give certain entries higher priority than others. It also allows a stack to be classified as a particular type of queue.

Queue Implementation

Let us consider how we can implement a queue in a computer's memory. We can do this within a block of contiguous cells in a way similar to our storage of a stack. We need to perform operations at both ends of the structure, so it makes sense to set aside two memory cells to use as pointers instead of just one, as we did for a stack. Thus, we establish one pointer, called the **head pointer,** that always points to the head of the queue, and another pointer, called the **tail pointer,** that keeps track of the tail. We begin with an empty queue by setting both these pointers to the same location (Figure 7-13). Each time an entry is inserted, we place it in the location pointed to by the tail pointer and then adjust the pointer to point toward the next unused location. In this manner, we see that the tail pointer is always pointing to the first vacancy at the tail of the queue. To remove an entry, we extract the object occupying the location pointed to by the head pointer and then adjust this pointer to point toward the entry that followed the removed one.

Figure 7-13 A queue implemented with head and tail pointers

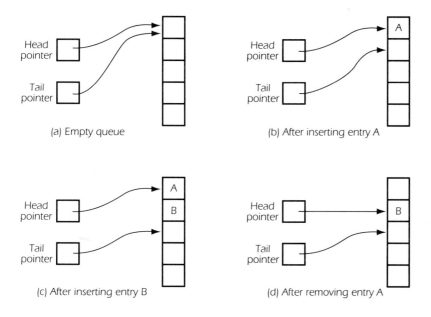

(a) Empty queue

(b) After inserting entry A

(c) After inserting entry B

(d) After removing entry A

Figure 7-14 A queue "crawling" through memory, shown here containing entries A, B, and C and later containing C, D, E, and F

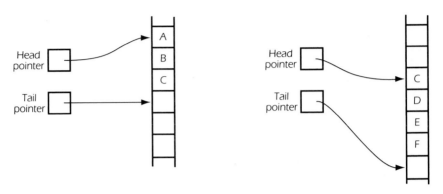

A problem remains with the storage system as described thus far. If left unchecked, the queue crawls slowly through memory like a glacier, destroying any other data in its path (Figure 7-14). This movement is the result of the rather egocentric policy of inserting each new entry by merely placing it next to the previous one and repositioning the tail pointer accordingly. If we add enough entries, the tail of the queue ultimately extends all the way to the end of the machine's memory.

This greed for memory is not the result of the queue's size but is a side effect of the queue's access procedure. (A small yet active queue can easily require more of a machine's memory resources than a large, inactive one.) One solution to this memory space problem is to move the entries in a queue forward as the leading ones are removed, in the same manner as people waiting to buy theater tickets step forward each time a person has been served. However, it was such mass movement of data that drove us to the concept of linked structures in the discussion of lists. What we want is a way of confining the queue to one area of memory without being forced to perform major rearrangements of data.

A common solution to this dilemma is to set aside a block of memory for the queue, start the queue at one end of the block, and let the queue migrate toward the other end of the block. When the tail of the queue reaches the end of the block, we merely start inserting additional entries back at the original end of the block, which by this time is vacant. Likewise, when the last entry in the block finally becomes the head of the queue and is removed, we adjust the head pointer back to the beginning of the block where other entries are by this time waiting. In this manner, the queue chases itself around within the block rather than wandering off through memory.

Such a technique results in an implementation that is called a *circular queue* because the effect is that of forming a loop out of the block of memory cells allotted to the queue (Figure 7-15). As far as the queue is concerned, the last cell in the block is adjacent to the first cell.

Figure 7-15 (a) A circular queue containing the letters F through O as actually stored in memory, and (b) in its conceptual form in which the last cell in the block is "adjacent" to the first cell

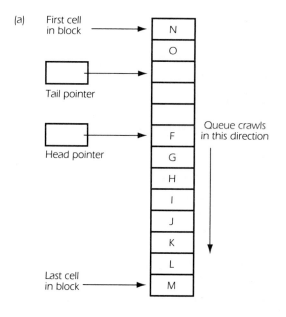

(a)

First cell in block

Tail pointer

Head pointer

Queue crawls in this direction

Last cell in block

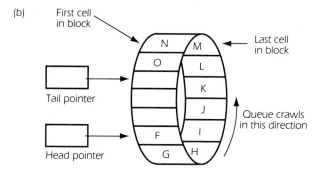

(b)

First cell in block

Last cell in block

Tail pointer

Head pointer

Queue crawls in this direction

Once again, we should recognize the difference between the conceptual structure envisioned by the user of a queue and the actual cyclic structure implemented in the machine's memory. As in the case of the previous structures, these differences are bridged by software. That is, along with the collection of memory cells used for data storage, the queue implementation includes a collection of subprograms that interpret the stored data according to the rules of a queue. These subprograms consist of routines to insert and remove entries from the queue as well as routines to detect whether the queue is empty or full. Then, by means of these routines, a programmer can request that entries be inserted or removed by executing prewritten software

Figure 7-16 A subprogram (using an auxiliary queue) for printing separate listings of undergraduates and graduates

```
procedure PrintSeparateListings (List)
    Assign CurrentPointer the value in the head pointer of List.
    while (CurrentPointer is not NIL) do
        [If (CurrentPointer points to the name of an undergraduate)
            then (Print the name.)
            else (Insert the name in the queue called Graduates.)
        Observe the value in the pointer cell of the List entry
            pointed to by CurrentPointer, and reassign CurrentPointer
            to be that value.]
    while (the queue called Graduates is not empty) do
        (Remove an entry from the queue and print it.)
```

routines that perform these operations without reflecting the details of the actual storage system in memory.

A Particular Queue Application

In closing, we return to the idea of manipulating a linked list of names, but this time we assume the list represents a combined alphabetized listing of both undergraduate and graduate students at a university. Moreover, we assume that with each name in the list is an additional item of data indicating whether the student is an undergraduate or a graduate student. Our task is to produce an alphabetized listing of the undergraduate students followed by an alphabetized listing of the graduate students.

One technique would be to traverse the linked list twice, producing the undergraduate list the first time and the graduate list the second. However, such a procedure is very inefficient because the second pass through the list repeats the same separation process already done during the first pass.

A more efficient system temporarily stores the names of the graduate students found during the first pass (while the undergraduate names are being printed) and then produces the graduate list from the auxiliary storage instead of searching through the linked list a second time. Note that once we are ready to produce the list of graduate students, we want to retrieve the names from the auxiliary storage system in the same order in which they were inserted so that the final listing is in alphabetical order. Thus, this auxiliary system is organized as a queue. An algorithm for solving the printing problem takes the form shown in Figure 7-16.

Questions/Exercises

1. Using paper and pencil, keep a record of the circular queue structure described in this section during the following scenario (assume the block reserved for the queue can contain four entries):

Insert entry A.
Insert entry B.

Insert entry C.
Remove an entry.
Remove an entry.
Insert entry D.
Insert entry E.
Remove an entry.
Insert entry F.
Remove an entry.

2. When a queue is implemented in a circular fashion as described in this section, what is the relationship between the head and tail pointers when the queue is empty? What about when the queue is full? How can one detect whether a queue is full or empty?

3. Design an algorithm for inserting an entry in a circular queue.

7-5 Trees

The last data structure that we will consider is the *tree,* which is the structure reflected by an organizational chart of a typical company (Figure 7-17). Here, the president is represented at the top, with lines branching down to the vice-presidents, who are followed by regional managers, and so on. To this intuitive definition of a tree structure we impose one additional constraint, which (in terms of an organizational chart) is that no individual in the company reports to two different people. That is, different branches of the organization do not merge at a lower level.

Terminology

In the terminology of tree structures, each position in the tree is called a *node.* The single node at the top is called the *root node* (since if we turned the drawing upside down, this node would represent the base or root of the tree). The nodes at the other

Figure 7-17 An example of an organizational chart

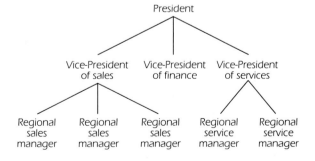

extreme are called **terminal nodes** (or **leaf nodes**). A line connecting two nodes is called an **arc**.

If we position ourselves at any node in a tree, we find that this node together with those nodes below it again have the structure of a tree. This, in fact, is a major advantage of such an organizational structure, because it divides a company into different suborganizations, each of which has the same type of structure. (A regional manager is effectively the president of that region.) We call these smaller structures **subtrees.**

Additional terminology has its origins in the concept of each node giving birth to those nodes immediately below it. We often speak of a node's ancestors or descendants. We refer to its immediate descendants as its **children** and its immediate superior as its **parent.** Moreover, we speak of nodes with the same parent as being **twins** or **siblings.**

Finally, we often refer to the **depth** of a tree, which is nothing more than the number of nodes in the longest path from the root to a leaf. In other words, the depth of a tree is the number of horizontal layers within it.

We encounter tree structures repeatedly in subsequent chapters, so rather than elaborate on applications now, we simply mention the uses that are discussed later. In Section 7-6 as well as in our discussion of index organization in Chapter 8, we find that information that must be searched quickly for data retrieval is often organized as a tree; and in Chapter 10, we see how games can be analyzed in terms of trees.

Tree Implementation

In our discussion of the storage of a tree structure in a machine's memory, we restrict our attention to **binary trees**—trees in which each node has at most two children. Such trees normally are stored in memory using a linked structure similar to that of linked lists. However, rather than each entry consisting of two components (the data followed by a next-entry pointer), each entry (or node) of the binary tree contains three components: the data, a pointer to the node's first child, and a pointer to the node's second child. Although there is no left or right inside a machine, it is helpful to refer to the first pointer as the **left child pointer** and the other pointer as the **right child pointer** in reference to the way we would draw the tree on paper. Thus, each node of the tree is represented by a short, contiguous block of memory cells with the format shown in Figure 7-18.

Figure 7-18 The structure of a node in a binary tree

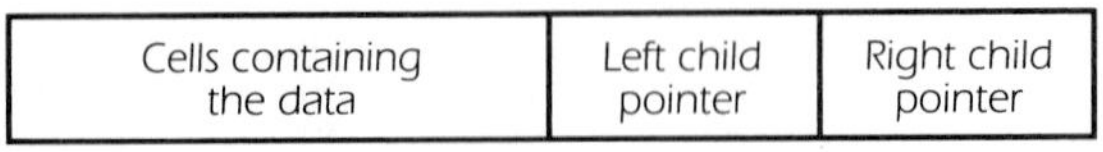

Cells containing the data	Left child pointer	Right child pointer

Storing the tree in memory involves finding available blocks of memory cells to hold the nodes and linking these nodes according to the desired tree structure. That is, each pointer must be set to point to the left or right child of the pertinent node or assigned the NIL value if there are no more nodes in that direction of the tree. Thus, a terminal node is characterized by having both of its pointers assigned NIL. Finally we set aside a special memory location where we store the address of the root node. We call this the *root pointer.*

An example of this linked storage system is presented in Figure 7-19, where a conceptual binary tree structure is exhibited along with a representation of how that tree might actually appear in a computer's memory. With this system we can always find the root node by means of the root pointer and then trace any path down the tree by following the appropriate pointers from node to node.

An alternative to a linked storage system for binary trees is the technique of setting aside a contiguous block of memory cells, storing the root node in the first of these cells (for simplicity, we assume that each node of the tree requires only one memory cell), storing the left child of the root in the second cell, storing the right child of the root in the third cell, and in general storing the left and right children of the node found in cell n in the cells $2n$ and $2n + 1$, respectively. Cells within the block that represent locations not used by the current tree structure are marked with a unique bit pattern that indicates the absence of data. Following this technique, the

Figure 7-19 The conceptual and actual organization of a binary tree using a linked storage system

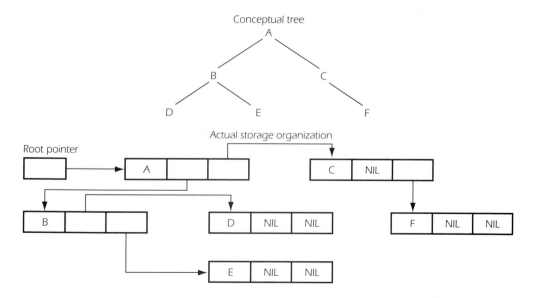

Figure 7-20 *The tree of Figure 7-19 stored without pointers*

1	2	3	4	5	6	7
A	B	C	D	E		F

conceptual tree shown in Figure 7-19 is stored as shown in Figure 7-20. Note that the system is essentially that of storing the nodes across successively lower levels of the tree as segments, one after the other. That is, the first entry in the block is the root node, followed by the root's children, followed by the root's grandchildren, and so on.

In contrast to the linked structure described earlier, this alternate storage system provides a convenient method for finding the parent or sibling of any node. (Of course, this can be done in the linked structure at the expense of additional pointers.) Indeed, the location of a node's parent can be found by dividing the node's position in the block by 2 while discarding any remainder (the parent of the node in position 7 would be the node in position 3), and a node's sibling can be found by adding 1 to the location of a node in an even-numbered position or subtracting 1 from the location of a node in an odd-numbered position (the sibling of the node in position 4 is the node in position 5, while the sibling of the node in position 3 is the node in position 2). Moreover, this storage system makes efficient use of space in the case of binary trees that are approximately balanced (in the sense that both subtrees tend to have the same depth) and full (in the sense that they do not have long, thin branches). For trees without these characteristics, though, the system can become quite inefficient, as shown in Figure 7-21.

We see then that, as in the case of the other structures we have studied, there are a variety of systems for storing binary trees, each with its advantages and disadvantages, and once again we find it advantageous to shield the user of the tree from the technicalities of the implementation chosen. Consequently, one normally identifies the activities that will be performed on a tree by the external software and then writes subprograms to accomplish these activities while hiding the technicalities of the actual storage system. These subprograms together with the storage area then form a package that allow a programmer to use the tree without being distracted by the details of the implementation.

A Binary Tree Package

To demonstrate such a package, let us return to the problem of storing a list of names in alphabetical order. We assume that the operations to be performed on this list are the following:

Figure 7-21 A sparse, unbalanced tree shown in its conceptual form and as it would be stored without pointers

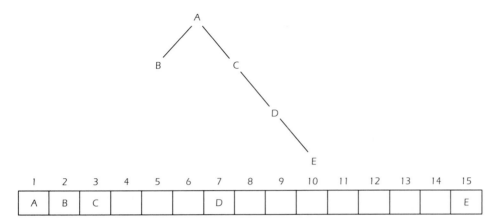

search for the presence of an entry,
print the list in alphabetical order, and
insert a new entry

Our goal is to develop a storage system along with a collection of subprograms to perform these operations.

We begin by considering options regarding the subprogram for searching the list. If the list were stored according to the linked list model in Section 7-2, we would be forced to search the list in a sequential fashion, a process that, as we discussed in Chapter 4, could be very inefficient if the list should become long. Thus, we can try to find an implementation that allows us to use the binary search algorithm (Chapter 4) for our search subprogram. To apply this algorithm, our storage system must allow us to find the middle entry of successively smaller portions of the list. Such an operation is possible when using a dense list, since we can compute the address of the middle entry in much the same manner as we can compute the locations of entries in an array. But using a dense list introduces problems when making insertions, as observed in Section 7-2.

Our problem can be solved by implementing the list as a binary tree rather than using one of the traditional list systems. We make the middle list entry the root node, the middle of the remaining first half of the list the root's left child, and the middle of the remaining second half the root's right child. The middle entries of each remaining fourth of the list become the children of the root's children and so forth. For example, under this process, the tree in Figure 7-22 can represent the list of letters

Figure 7-22 The letters A through M arranged in an ordered tree

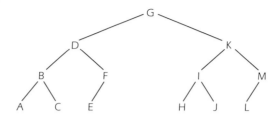

A, B, C, D, E, F, G, H, I, J, K, L, and M. (We consider the larger of the middle two entries as the middle when the part of the list in question contains an even number of entries.)

To search the list stored in this manner, we compare the target value to the root node. If the two are equal, our search has succeeded. If they are not equal, we move to the left or right child of the root, depending on whether the target is less than or greater than the root, respectively. There we find the middle of the portion of the list necessary to continue the search. This process of comparing and moving to a child continues until we find the target (meaning that our search was successful) or we reach the bottom of the tree without finding the target (meaning that our search was a failure). Figure 7-23 shows how this search process can be implemented in the case of a linked tree structure. (Annotative comments are bracketed by asterisks.)

Figure 7-23 The binary search applied to a linked binary tree

```
**   The variable CurrentPointer is used to hold a pointer   **
**   to the current position in the tree. The node at        **
**   this location is called the current node.               **

procedure BinarySearch (Tree, TargetValue)
    Assign CurrentPointer the value in the root pointer of Tree.
    Assign Found the value "false."
    while (Found is "false" and CurrentPointer is not NIL) do
        [Select the applicable case from those listed below and
        perform the associated activity:
            TargetValue = current node:

                (Assign Found the value "true.")

            TargetValue < current node:

                (Assign CurrentPointer the value in the current
                node's left child pointer.)

            TargetValue > current node:

                (Assign CurrentPointer the value in the current
                node's right child pointer.)]
    If (Found = "false") then (Declare the search a failure.)
                        else (Declare the search a success.)
```

Having altered the natural sequential order of our stored list for the sake of search efficiency, you may think that the process of printing the list in alphabetical order would now be difficult. This hypothesis, however, proves to be false. To print the list in alphabetical order, we merely need to print the left subtree in alphabetical order, print the root node, and then print the right subtree in alphabetical order (Figure 7-24). After all, the left subtree contains those elements that are less than the root node, while the right subtree contains the elements larger than the root. Thus, a sketch of our print routine looks like this:

if (tree not empty)
then (print the left subtree in alphabetical order,
    print the root node,
    print the right subtree in alphabetical order)

You may argue that this outline achieves little toward our goal of developing a complete print subprogram, because it involves the tasks of printing the left subtree and the right subtree in alphabetical order, both of which are essentially the same as our original task. The only difference in the task of printing the entire tree and that of printing the left or right subtree is in the size of the trees involved. Thus, solving the problem of printing a tree involves the smaller task of printing subtrees. This suggests a recursive system in which our subprogram is applied to smaller and smaller trees.

Following this lead, we can expand our outline into a complete pseudocode subprogram for printing our tree in alphabetical order as shown in Figure 7-25, on the following page. We have assigned the routine the name PrintTree and then requested the services of PrintTree for printing the left and right subtrees. You should confirm for yourself that the termination condition of the recursive process (reaching

Figure 7-24 Printing a search tree in alphabetical order

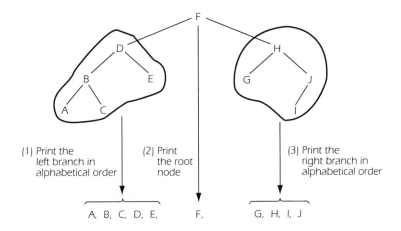

Figure 7-25 A subprogram for printing a linked tree in alphabetical order

```
procedure PrintTree (Tree)
    If (Tree is not empty)
        then (Apply the procedure PrintTree to the tree that
                appears as the left branch in Tree;
              Print the root node of Tree;
              Apply the procedure PrintTree to the tree that
                appears as the right branch in Tree.)
```

an empty subtree) is guaranteed to be reached, because each activation of the routine operates on a smaller tree than the one causing the activation.

The task of inserting a new entry in the tree is also easier than it may at first appear. You may guess that certain insertions would require cutting the tree open to allow room for the new entry, but actually the new node can always be attached to the bottom of the tree as a leaf, regardless of the value involved. To find the proper place for this new leaf, we move down the tree along the path that we would follow if we were searching for the value to be inserted. Then, when we reach the bottom of the tree, we have found the proper location for the new node. Indeed, we have found the location to which a search for the new data would lead.

A program segment expressing this process in the case of a linked tree structure is shown in Figure 7-26. It first searches the tree for the value being inserted and then places the new node at the proper location. Note that a slightly special case occurs if the tree is empty in the first place. This case is detected by testing for the condition of CurrentPointer still being the same as the root pointer after the search process has been completed. Moreover, if the data being inserted is actually found in the tree during the search, no insertion is made.

We see, then, that a software package consisting of a linked ordered tree together with our subprograms for searching, printing, and inserting provides an excellent system for implementing the list required by our hypothetical application.

Questions/Exercises

1. Identify the root and leaf nodes in the following tree. Identify the subtrees below node 9. Identify the groups of siblings within the tree.

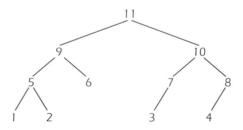

2. What condition indicates that a linked tree in a machine's memory is empty?

Figure 7-26 A subprogram for inserting an entry in a linked ordered tree

```
**   The variable CurrentPointer is used to hold a pointer    **
**   to the current position in the tree. The node at         **
**   this location is called the current node. Likewise,      **
**   PreviousPointer holds a pointer to the parent of the     **
**   current node, which is called the previous node.         **

procedure Insert (Tree, TargetValue)

**   First, find the correct location for the new node.       **

Assign CurrentPointer the value in the root pointer of Tree.
Assign Found the value "false."
while (Found is "false" and CurrentPointer is not NIL) do
     [Select the applicable case from those listed below and
     perform the associated activity:
          TargetValue = current node:

               (Assign Found the value "true.")

          TargetValue < current node:

               (Assign PreviousPointer the value of CurrentPointer;
               Assign CurrentPointer the value of the current
                    node's left child pointer.)

          TargetValue > current node:

               (Assign PreviousPointer the value of CurrentPointer;
               Assign CurrentPointer the value of the current
                    node's right child pointer.)]

**   Now, insert the new node as a child of the current node. **
**   A special case occurs if CurrentPointer is still the same **
**   as the root pointer, meaning that the original Tree was   **
**   empty.                                                    **

If (Found = "false")
     then [Create a new node containing TargetValue;
          If (CurrentPointer equals the root pointer)
               then (Establish the new node as the root node of Tree.)
               else (If (TargetValue < previous node)
                    then (Establish the new node as the left
                         child of the previous node.)
                    else (Establish the new node as the right child of
                         the previous node.))]
```

3. Draw a diagram representing how the tree

appears in memory when stored using the left and right child pointers, as described in this section. Then, draw another diagram showing how the tree would appear in contiguous storage using the alternate storage system described in this section.

4. Draw a binary tree structure you can use to store the list R, S, T, U, V, W, X, Y, and Z for future searching.

5. Indicate the path traversed by the binary search algorithm in Figure 7-23 when applied to the search tree in Figure 7-22 when searching for the entry J. What about the entry P?

6. Draw a diagram representing the status of activations of the recursive tree-printing algorithm in Figure 7-25 at the time node K is printed within the ordered tree in Figure 7-22.

7-6 Abstract Data Types

In Chapter 5, we introduced user-defined data types as a means of extending the types available in a language beyond those provided as primitives. We must now reconsider this idea, because traditional user-defined data types fall short of creating new data types in the full sense. Indeed, the data types provided as primitives in a language consist of two parts: a predetermined storage system (such as two's complement or floating-point notation) and a collection of predefined operations (such as addition and subtraction). Traditional user-defined types, however, merely allow programmers to define new storage systems. They do not provide a means of defining the set of operations that can be performed on the objects having the new type. (Recall that in Section 5-4, we used the user-defined type EmployeeType to clarify the fact that the identifiers DistManager, Sales1, and Sales2 represented structures of the same form, but our discussion did not identify the operations that are applied to these structures.)

An *abstract data type* is a more complete way of extending the types available in a language. It encompasses both the storage system and the associated operations. Usually, an abstract data type is implemented as a software unit consisting of a storage structure (or structures) and a collection of program segments defining the operations that can be performed on the structure.

Programming languages that support abstract data types normally provide a syntax for describing such a unit as well as a way of declaring variables of the new type. For example, we can define an abstract data type known as ListOfNames as a linked list structure along with the collection of routines insert, delete, search, and print, as discussed in Section 7-2. Then, we can define the variables MembershipList and InactiveList to be of that type, thus creating two lists, each of which is an ordered list of names. On each list, the operations insert, delete, search, and print are performed simply by requesting the services of the prewritten routines associated with the type.

Abstract Data Types as Templates

We must distinguish between an abstract data type and an object having that type (the latter is called an instance of the type). An abstract type is essentially a template (or a cookie cutter) that is used in constructing instances of the type. It describes the properties that all instances of that type will have but does not itself constitute an actual occurrence of that type. In the preceding example, the abstract data type ListOfNames was used to construct two instances of that type, one known as MembershipList and the other known as InactiveList.

Thus, an abstract data type is a convenient way to construct abstract tools consisting of customized data systems and the routines for manipulating these systems, especially when multiple copies of the tool are required. For instance, we can define an abstract data type called StackOfIntegers that encompasses a description of the data structures required to implement a stack together with the push and pop operations for manipulating these structures. Then, we can use this type as a template for establishing numerous stacks.

Figure 7-27 demonstrates this approach implemented in the Ada programming language. Loosely translated, this figure defines a program unit (a package, in Ada terminology) named StackPackage, which contains the description of a new type named StackOfIntegers, and identifies two procedures named push and pop. StackOfIntegers is described as an array (called StackEntries) of 25 integers together with an additional integer named StackPointer used to hold the position within the array of the stack's top (see question/exercise 5 in Section 7-3). The details of the procedures push and pop must be described in another program unit called a package body. It is there that the instructions for actually pushing and popping entries (as well as initializing the StackPointer) would be described.

Using this package as a template, actual stacks of integers (instances of the type StackOfIntegers) can be declared by statements, such as

StackOne: StackOfIntegers;

and

StackTwo: StackOfIntegers;

Figure 7-27 An abstract data type in Ada

```
package StackPackage is
  type StackOfIntegers is
    record
      StackEntries: array(1..25) of integer;
      StackPointer: integer;
    end record;
  procedure push(Value: in integer; Stack: in out StackOfIntegers);
  procedure pop(Value: out integer; Stack: in out StackOfIntegers);
end StackPackage;
```

that declare the variables StackOne and StackTwo to be of type StackOfIntegers. Later, the value 106 can be pushed onto StackOne using the statement

push(106, StackOne);

or the top entry from StackTwo can be retrieved in the variable OldValue using the statement

pop(OldValue, StackTwo);

Encapsulation

The idea of using a software package to represent an otherwise abstract object is a recurring theme in this chapter. So far, we have continually emphasized the role of subprograms for supporting conceptual interpretations of the underlying data. We have not, however, emphasized that it is important that all transactions between an instance of the given type and the instance's environment be performed by these routines. To do otherwise would be to open the doors to unforeseen complications.

The situation is analogous to a bank teller who also has a checking account with the bank. The system works well as long as the teller makes deposits and withdrawals through accepted procedures. But the stage is set for disaster if the teller decides to borrow lunch money from the teller drawer with the idea of replenishing the drawer later in the afternoon.

Likewise, it is often tempting to circumvent the established protocol of an abstract data type for the sake of shortsighted efficiency. For example, suppose a programmer needs to reference the third entry on a stack of type StackOfIntegers (Figure 7-27). The programmer, who knows how the stack is actually implemented, might be tempted to violate the stack's integrity by referencing the array StackEntry directly, rather than going through the formal process of popping the first two entries. Such a tactic usually leads to complications later in the software's life cycle and is considered to be one of the worst of evils by software engineers.

The problem is that future maintenance programmers, seeing that the object is described as a stack of integers, will not be aware of any nonstandard operations and could make changes that are not compatible with these anomalies. For instance, to extend the maximum size of the stack, the internal structure of the type StackOfIntegers can be changed from an array to a linked structure, which certainly is not compatible with the earlier modification.

To prevent such circumvention of abstract data types, newer programming languages, such as Ada, provide techniques by which a software package can be *encapsulated,* meaning that the package is constructed in such a manner that its internal structure can be accessed only by means of the approved package routines. If instances of the abstract data types occurring in a software system are encapsulated, the integrity of these data types is protected from poorly conceived modifications.

Figure 7-28 An abstract data type in Ada using encapsulation

```
package StackPackage is
   type StackOfIntegers is private;
   procedure push(Value: in integer; Stack: in out StackOfIntegers);
   procedure pop(Value: out integer; Stack: in out StackOfIntegers);
private
   Type StackOfIntegers is
      record
         StackEntries: array(1..25) of integer;
         StackPointer: integer;
      end record;
end StackPackage;
```

Figure 7-28 shows a modified version of the abstract data type StackOfIntegers, originally presented in Figure 7-27. The difference is that the new version takes advantage of Ada's encapsulation features. Note that we have moved the details of the stack's structure to the private part (the part following the key word **private**) of the package. Only the information in the public part (the part preceding the key word **private**) of the package is accessible outside the package. The information in the private part is local to the package. In our example, then, only the existence of a type called StackOfIntegers and the procedures push and pop are known outside the package; the fact that such a stack is implemented as an array called StackEntries is encapsulated within the package. In turn, statements such as

```
StackOne: StackOfIntegers;
StackTwo: StackOfIntegers;
push(106, StackOne);
```

and

```
pop(OldValue, StackTwo);
```

are still valid outside the package, but direct references to the array StackEntries or the integer StackPointer are not.

Of course, if an abstract data type is properly designed and implemented, a programmer will not need to violate the type's integrity nor even want to be aware of its internal details. Such is the essence of abstract tools.

In closing, we observe that the use of abstract data types along with encapsulation allows general-purpose programming languages to be customized to particular applications. A programmer charged with the task of developing a university registration system might start by defining an abstract type similar to a list in which the students enrolled in a course are stored, whereas a biologist studying the nervous system might develop and encapsulate a package whose internal data structures and routines simulate the pertinent characteristics of a single neuron. In either case, once these abstract types have been defined, the programmer can use them as building blocks as though they were primitives in the language. Thus, although each programmer started with the same language, the effect is that each has access to a language providing those primitives particular to the task at hand.

Questions/Exercises

1. In what way is a checking account at a bank encapsulated?
2. What is the difference between an abstract data type and an instance of that type?
3. What is the difference between a traditional program module and an instance of an abstract data type?
4. Describe two underlying structures that might be used to implement an object of type queue-of-integers.

7-7 Object-Oriented Programming

A list implemented in the traditional procedural paradigm can be represented as a simple data structure, such as a linked or dense list. The routines for manipulating this list (for example, inserting entries, deleting entries, and so on) appear in the procedural part of the program. When using an abstract data type, however, the routines for manipulating the list are bundled with the list structure to form a package (an abstract data type). Thus, the task of performing list manipulations shifts from the procedural part of the program to the package representing the list: Rather than manipulating the list itself, the procedural part of the program requests the package to do the manipulation by activating the proper routine within the package.

We see, then, that the concept of abstract data types involves converting passive data structures that are manipulated by the procedural part of a program into active units that manipulate themselves. This shift from passive to active units captures much of the philosophy of the object-oriented paradigm, which we introduced in Chapter 4.

In the object-oriented paradigm, such active units are called **objects.** The paradigm is to approach a problem by first identifying the objects involved and then implementing them as self-contained packages. At this point, the task of solving the problem is well underway. Indeed, since the objects are active rather than passive, all that remains is to activate the routines in the objects in the proper order.

The degree to which this activation of objects is performed by a separate control algorithm rather than by the objects themselves varies with different programming languages. Languages, such as Ada, that are essentially procedural languages onto which the ability to construct objects has been added tend to rely on a traditional procedural routine to initiate actions within objects as they are required. In contrast, the language Smalltalk[1] dictates that this controlling task be given to the objects

---

[1]The programming language Smalltalk, developed at the Xerox Palo Alto Research Center, was the pioneering language in the object-oriented philosophy. We will not study it in detail here.

themselves. As each object performs its internal activities, it sends messages to the other objects in the system. Thus, if a particular manipulation of an object should cause an action in another object, the original object notifies the other directly, rather than relying on the services of an overseeing algorithm.

As an example, consider the problem of constructing a worldwide model for economic forecasting. In the traditional procedural paradigm, each nation is represented as a collection of data structures containing that nation's gross domestic product, trade surplus/deficit, monetary exchange rate, and so on. The procedural part of the program contains a controlling algorithm that simulates the passage of time by repeatedly interrogating the various data items, deciding how the values found in each affect those of other nations, and making the changes it determines are appropriate (Figure 7-29). Thus, the data structures in the system are passive; all decisions and actions are performed by the controlling algorithm.

In contrast, consider solving this same problem using the object-oriented language Smalltalk. Each nation is represented by an object. Each object is an encapsulated package containing the appropriate data structures (for holding that nation's gross domestic product and so on) as well as a collection of subroutines, called methods, defining how that object (that nation) reacts to various stimuli (messages it receives or changes occurring within itself). For instance, an object may contain a method describing how that object reacts to receiving an offer of trade from another object. Similarly, it may contain a method that, when an increase in the object's trade deficit is detected, may increase tariffs on incoming goods or try to increase exports to other objects. The result is a collection of self-governing objects that solve the problem by communicating among themselves rather than being manipulated by a supervisory algorithm (Figure 7-30, on the following page).

The development of an object in an object-oriented program may not be a simple task, because the object may need to respond in complex ways to many different

Figure 7-29 The procedural approach to an economic model: A controlling algorithm makes decisions and manipulates values in the data structures representing nations

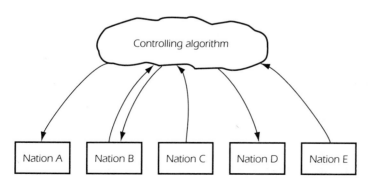

Figure 7-30 The object-oriented approach to an economic model: The objects (nations) communicate among themselves

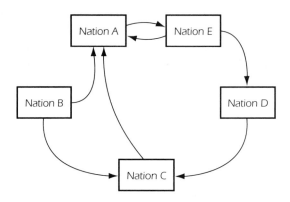

stimuli. Thus, most programming languages designed for object-oriented applications provide features to reduce the burden of object description.

One such feature is a template system with which the properties of an entire collection of similar objects can be described, together with a system for constructing actual instances of those objects. This, of course, is essentially a reincarnation of abstract data types. However, in an object-oriented programming environment, the equivalent of an abstract data type is called a *class*. A class, then, is a template from which objects are created. (The term *class* can also be used to refer to the collection of objects created from a single template, but we avoid such use here.)

In addition to a system for describing classes, object-oriented programming languages also provide for **inheritance,** which allows classes to be described in a hierarchical manner, with each class inheriting the properties of those higher in the hierarchy. Using inheritance, a biologist can develop a class describing objects that simulate the basic properties of a biological cell. Then the biologist can define additional classes to simulate different types of cells, such as muscle cells, bone cells, and neurons. Each of these more specialized classes can be described as a subclass of the original class and thus inherit the properties of a general cell but include additional features specific to the particular type of cell. (Inheritance also allows new features to override those of a previously defined class, so that the properties of a subclass may not be a true extension of those found in its parents.) Continuing in this fashion, the biologist can define additional subclasses to simulate particular types of neurons, such as those leading from the retina as distinguished from the motor neurons leading to muscles in the legs and arms. At each level of this hierarchy, the classes become more complex, but by applying inheritance, the effort already invested in defining simple classes need not be repeated when defining more specialized ones.

The existence of a variety of objects with similar yet different characteristics leads to a phenomenon reminiscent of overloading, which we met in Chapter 5. (Recall that overloading referred to the use of a single symbol, such as +, for representing different operations depending on the type of its operands.) Suppose that we develop an object-oriented graphics package. In this package, we define a variety of objects, each representing a shape (circle, rectangle, triangle, and so on). A particular image consists of a collection of these objects. Each object knows its size, location, and color as well as how to respond to messages telling it, for example, to move to a new location or to print itself. Hence, to draw the image, we merely send each object in the collection the message to print itself.

However, the routine used to perform this print operation varies depending on the shape of the object—printing a square is not the same process as printing circle. This customized interpretation of a message is known as *polymorphism;* the message is said to be polymorphic. Thus, in our biological example, it is polymorphism that allows cells of different types to respond differently to the same stimulus, or in our economic model, it allows capitalistic countries and socialistic countries to respond differently to the initiation of tariffs by one of the other countries in the system. In short, polymorphism determines the meaning of a command in terms of the entity that is asked to perform it, whereas overloading determines the meaning of a command in terms of the command's operands.

We close by considering Figure 7-31, which shows how our StackOfIntegers example might be implemented in the object-oriented language C++. (Statements following a double slash // are comments.) Although we have not discussed the details of C++, we can appreciate the overall structure of this simple example.

Our first observation is that StackOfIntegers is defined as a class, meaning that the code here merely defines the properties of a StackOfIntegers—actual instances are established later in the program when they are required. Each time an instance of

Figure 7-31 The class StackOfIntegers implemented in C++

```
const   int   MaxStack = 25;

class StackOfIntegers
{int StackPointer;                  //  Data structures are private.
int StackEntries [MaxStack];
public:                             //  Access to functions is public.
void StackOfIntegers( )            //  Initialization routine
   {StackPointer = 0;}
void push (int *Entry)             //  Response to push command
   {if (StackPointer < MaxStack)
       StackEntries[StackPointer + +] =  *Entry;}
void pop(int *Entry)               //  Response to pop command
   {if (StackPointer > 0)
       *Entry = StackEntries[StackPointer − −];}
}
```

StackOfIntegers is established the initialization routine (which sets that instance's StackPointer to 0) is executed. (An initialization routine is identified as a function whose name is the same as the class.) Only the portion of a class that is designated public can be referenced outside an instance of the class. Thus, the data maintained by each instance of StackOfIntegers is private, whereas the functions push and pop can be accessed from other parts of the program.

Questions/Exercises

1. Identify the objects that might be used in an object-oriented simulation of the pedestrian traffic in a shopping mall. What actions should each of these objects be able to perform?
2. In what sense are the objects in an object-oriented system functionally cohesive?
3. In what sense is a single object in an object-oriented system divided into submodules?

Chapter 7 Review Problems

(Asterisked problems are associated with optional sections.)

1. Draw pictures showing how the following array appears in a machine's memory when stored in row major order and in column major order:

A	B	C	D
E	F	G	H
I	J	K	L

2. Suppose an array with 6 rows and 8 columns is stored in row major order starting at address 20 (decimal). If each entry in the array requires only one memory cell, what is the address of the entry in the third row and fourth column? What if each entry requires two memory cells?

3. Work problem 2 assuming column major order rather than row major order.

4. Suppose the list of letters A, B, C, E, F, and G is stored in a contiguous block of memory cells. What activities are required to insert the letter D in the list if the alphabetical order is to be maintained?

5. The following table represents the contents of some cells in a computer's main memory along with the address of each cell represented. Note that some of the cells contain letters of the alphabet, and each such cell is followed by an empty cell. Place addresses in these empty cells so that each cell containing a letter together with the following cell form an entry in a linked list in which the letters appear in alphabetical order. (Use zero for the NIL pointer.) What address should the head pointer contain?

Address	Contents
11	C
12	
13	G
14	
15	E
16	
17	B
18	
19	U
20	
21	F
22	

6. The following table represents a portion of a linked list in a computer's main memory. Each entry in the list consists of two cells: The first contains a letter of the alphabet; the second contains a pointer to the next list entry. Alter the pointers so that the letter N is no longer in the list. Then replace the letter N with the letter G and

alter the pointers so that the new letter appears in the list in its proper place in alphabetical order.

Address	Contents
30	J
31	38
32	B
33	30
34	X
35	46
36	N
37	40
38	K
39	36
40	P
41	34

7. The following table represents a linked list using the same format as in the preceding problems. If the head pointer contains the value 44, what name is represented by the list? Change the pointers so that the list contains the name Jean.

Address	Contents
40	N
41	46
42	I
43	40
44	J
45	50
46	E
47	00
48	M
49	42
50	A
51	40

8. Which of the following routines correctly inserts New Entry immediately after the entry called Previous Entry in a linked list? What is wrong with the other routine?

Routine 1
    1. Copy the value in the pointer field of Previous Entry into the pointer field of New Entry.
    2. Change the value in the pointer field of Previous Entry to the address of New Entry.

Routine 2
    1. Change the value in the pointer field of Previous Entry to the address of New Entry.

    2. Copy the value in the pointer field of Previous Entry into the pointer field of New Entry.

9. Design an algorithm for concatenating two linked lists (that is, placing one before the other to form a single list).

10. Design an algorithm for combining two sorted dense lists into a single sorted dense list. What if the lists are linked?

11. Design an algorithm for reversing the order of a linked list.

12. In Figure 7-12 we presented an algorithm for printing a linked list in reverse order using a stack as an auxiliary storage structure. Design a recursive algorithm to perform this same task without making explicit use of a stack. In what form is a stack still involved in your recursive solution?

13. Sometimes a single linked list is provided with two different orders by following each entry with two pointers rather than one. Fill in the following table so that by following the first pointer after each letter one finds the name Carol, but by following the second pointer after each letter one finds the letters in alphabetical order. What values belong in the head pointer of each of the two lists represented?

Address	Contents
60	O
61	
62	
63	C
64	
65	
66	A
67	
68	
69	L
70	
71	
72	R
73	
74	

14. The following table represents a stack stored in a contiguous block of memory cells, as discussed in the text. If the base of the stack is at address 10 and the stack pointer contains the value 12, what value is retrieved by a pop

instruction? What value is then in the stack pointer?

Address	Contents
10	F
11	C
12	A
13	B
14	E

15. a. Draw a table showing the final contents of the memory cells if the instruction in problem 14 had been to push the letter D on the stack rather than to pop it. What would the value in the stack pointer be after the push instruction?

b. How would your answer to part a change if the base of the stack had been at address 14 rather than 10 (that is, if the cells used for the stack precede the stack rather than follow it)?

16. Design an algorithm to remove the bottom entry from a stack.

17. Design an algorithm to compare the contents of two stacks.

18. Suppose we want to create a stack of names that vary in length. Why is it advantageous to store the names in separate areas of memory and then build the stack out of pointers to these names rather than allowing the stack to contain the names themselves?

19. Does a queue crawl through memory in the direction of its head or its tail?

20. Suppose the entries in a queue require one memory cell each, the head pointer contains the value 11, and the tail pointer contains the value 17. What are the values of these pointers after one entry is inserted and two are removed?

21. a. Suppose a queue implemented in a circular fashion is in the state shown in the following diagram. Draw a diagram showing the structure after the letters G and R are inserted, three letters are removed, and the letters D and P are inserted.

b. What error occurs in part a if the letters G, R, D, and P are inserted before any letters are removed?

22. Describe how an array can be used to implement a queue in a high-level language.

23. The following table represents a tree stored in a machine's memory. Each node of the tree consists of three cells. The first cell contains the data (a letter), the second contains a pointer to the node's left child, and the third contains a pointer to the node's right child. A value of 0 represents a NIL pointer. If the value of the root pointer is 55, draw a picture of the tree represented.

Address	Contents
40	G
41	0
42	0
43	X
44	0
45	0
46	J
47	49
48	0
49	M
50	0
51	0
52	F
53	43
54	40
55	W
56	46
57	52

24. The following table represents the contents of a block of cells in a computer's main memory. Note that some of the cells contain letters of the alphabet, and each such cell is followed by two blank cells. Fill in the blank cells so that the memory block represents the tree following the table. Use the first cell following a letter as the pointer to that node's left child and the next cell as the pointer to the right child. Use 0 for NIL

pointers. What value should be in the root pointer?

Address	Contents
30	C
31	
32	
33	H
34	
35	
36	K
37	
38	
39	E
40	
41	
42	G
43	
44	
45	P
46	
47	

25. Design a nonrecursive algorithm to replace the recursive one represented in Figure 7-25. Use a stack to control any backtracking that may be necessary.

26. Apply the recursive tree-printing algorithm of Figure 7-25 to the tree represented in problem 23. Draw a diagram representing the nested activations of the algorithm (and the current position in each) at the time node X is printed.

27. While keeping the root node the same and without changing the physical location of the data elements, change the pointers in the tree of problem 23 so the tree-printing algorithm of Figure 7-25 prints the nodes alphabetically.

28. Draw a diagram showing how the following binary tree appears in memory when stored without pointers using the alternate storage system presented in this chapter.

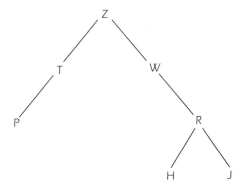

29. Describe a data structure suitable for representing a board configuration during a chess game.

30. Describe a data structure suitable for representing a Rubik's cube. What subprograms should be provided to support the conceptual image?

31. Modify the subprogram in Figure 7-25 to print the list in reverse order.

32. Describe a tree structure that can be used to store the genealogical history of a family. What operations are performed on the tree? If the tree is implemented as a linked structure, what pointers are associated with each node? Design subprograms to perform the operations you identified above, assuming that the tree is implemented as a linked structure with the pointers you just described.

33. Design an algorithm for finding and deleting a given value from a tree ordered in the fashion of Figure 7-22.

34. What is the difference between an abstract data type and an instance of that type?

35. Give a definition of *encapsulation*.

36. What is the difference between the public and private parts of an abstract data type?

37. Identify the data structures and procedures you can include in an abstract data type representing an address book.

38. Identify the data structures and procedures you can include in an abstract data type representing a spacecraft in a video game.

*39. Define each of the following:
    a. class
    b. object

c. inheritance

d. polymorphism

*40. Summarize the distinction between the object-oriented programming paradigm and the procedural programming paradigm.

*41. Identify some of the objects you would use to develop an object-oriented program for a checker-playing program. What data structures would be in each object? What actions would each of these objects perform?

Problems for the Programmer

1. Does your programming language provide statements for requesting and releasing pieces of memory as entries of a linked list are added and deleted? If so, what are they?

   What garbage-collection features must be provided in the underlying software to support these dynamic memory allocation requests?

2. How can you simulate a stack using the data types and structures available in your programming language? Write routines to perform the push and pop operations.

3. Extend your solution to the token problem of Chapter 3 (programming problem 4) to store the token requests made while the tokens are not available, and then grant those requests later as their turns come.

4. How can you simulate a tree structure using the data types and structures available in your programming language? Implement the tree-printing algorithms using this technique.

5. Implement your solutions to review problems 9, 10, 11, 16, and 17.

Additional Reading

Budd, T. *A Little Smalltalk.* Reading, Mass.: Addison-Wesley, 1987.

Cox, B. J. *Object-Oriented Programming: An Evolutionary Approach.* Reading, Mass.: Addison-Wesley, 1986.

Helman, P., and Veroff, R. *Intermediate Problem Solving and Data Structures,* 2nd ed. Redwood City, Calif.: Benjamin/Cummings, 1991.

Knuth, D. E. *The Art of Computer Programming,* Vol. 1, 2nd ed. Reading, Mass.: Addison-Wesley, 1973.

Kruse, R. L. *Data Structures and Program Design,* 3rd ed. Englewood Cliffs, N.J.: Prentice-Hall, 1994.

Ullman, J. D. *Structures and Algorithms.* Reading, Mass.: Addison-Wesley, 1983.

CHAPTER EIGHT

FILE STRUCTURES

In Chapter 7, we discussed various ways of organizing data. In terms of actual implementation, we focused on how those organizations might be simulated within a machine's main memory. In this chapter, we concentrate on data storage techniques used in mass storage. A major theme is the study of the relationship between the way in which the information is to be accessed and the way in which it should be stored.

Recall that a collection of data stored in mass storage is called a file, which in turn is subdivided into records. The subject of this chapter concerns how these records can be organized in mass storage to provide convenient access by the user. As in the case of data structures, we find that the organization ultimately presented to the user may not be the same as the actual storage system. Thus, as in Chapter 7, we find ourselves discussing and comparing both conceptual and real organizations.

8-1 Sequential Files

Suppose we want to maintain information about the employees in a business. The information consists of such items as name, address, employee identification number, Social Security number, pay scale, hours worked, date hired, and job title. We may want this employee information stored in mass storage rather than in main memory for several reasons. One is that there probably is not enough space in main memory. Another might be that the memory in our machine is volatile and the data would be lost if power were disconnected. Still another is that we want to keep a copy of our data in off-line storage (perhaps even at another location) for backup purposes.

For whatever reason, we assume that the information about the employees is to be recorded in mass storage with one logical record for each employee. Each record in turn consists of units, called *fields,* that contain the individual items of information about the employee.

Suppose our employee file is used for payroll processing, for which the entire file must be accessed each pay period. As each employee record is retrieved, that employee's pay is calculated and the appropriate check produced. Since all records are processed, it makes little difference which records are processed first. The most straightforward technique therefore is to consider the records as organized in a list and then to retrieve and process them one at a time from the beginning to the end. Such an organization is called a *sequential file.*

Rudiments of Sequential Files

This sequential organization may, of course, be only conceptual in nature. Depending on the physical characteristics of the storage device being used, we may choose to store the file in another form and present it to the user as a sequential system. If the storage device is a tape system, we normally remain faithful to the conceptual sequential order because of the sequential nature of the tape itself. However, if the device is a disk system, we might choose to disperse the records of the file over the disk to take advantage of unused portions (Figure 8-1). In this case, we link the records with a pointer system very similar to the linked list system in Chapter 7, except that here the pointers represent locations on the disk rather than in main memory.

Regardless of the storage system used, the end of a sequential file usually is indicated by an *EOF (end-of-file) mark.* In the linked structure, this mark might be similar to the NIL pointer in a linked list. Another approach is to store a special record, called a *sentinel,* as the last record of the file to mark the end. Of course, to avoid confusion, the fields in such a record must contain values that will never occur as data in the application. Still other implementations record the length of the file at its beginning and then use this information to detect the end of the file.

The user of a sequential file is allowed (or from another point of view, forced) to view the records in a simple sequential order. The only way to retrieve records is to start at the beginning of the file and extract them in the order provided.

Figure 8-1 A sequential file storage on a disk

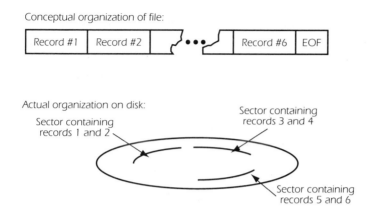

Conceptual organization of file:

| Record #1 | Record #2 | • • • | Record #6 | EOF |

Actual organization on disk:

Sector containing records 1 and 2

Sector containing records 3 and 4

Sector containing records 5 and 6

Although convenient for the processing of payroll checks, this sequential nature has some undesirable aspects. For example, suppose that before processing the payroll from the employee file, we must update the records to reflect the amount of time worked by each employee during the current pay period. To accomplish this, we note the time worked by a particular employee, search through the file to find the employee's record, and update the record. Next we select another employee's time sheet and search for the corresponding record.

This process is simplified if the order in which the time sheets are selected agreed with the order of the employee records in the file. This means that after updating an employee record, we need not return to the beginning of the file to initiate the search for the next record to be updated. Instead, we initiate the search from our current position in the file. For this reason sequential files are normally stored in alphabetical or numerical order according to the contents of a selected field, known as the **key field**. For example, we might choose to store the employee file in alphabetical order by last name or, since two employees may have the same last name, we may choose numerical order by Social Security number or employee identification number. If we then arrange the time sheets according to this same key field, updating the payroll file reduces to the process of merely updating the records one after the other as they appear in the sequential file.

Having seen the advantage of order, you probably will not be surprised to learn that a lot of sorting takes place in relation to processing sequential files. To update a sequential file, the new information (such as the collection of time sheets) is first recorded in the form of a sequential file known as a transaction file. Then, this transaction file is sorted to match the order of the file to be updated. Finally, the records in the original file are updated in the order in which they appear.

Programming Concerns

Now that we have discussed the rudiments of sequential files, we need to take a brief look at how such files (or more accurately, their records) are manipulated from the programmer's point of view. This we do in the context of programming in a high-level procedural language. These languages tend to express file manipulation through subroutines that are either defined as a part of the formal language itself or provided as language extensions supplied in an adjoining library. In either case, the parameters of these subroutines identify the target file and the area of main memory that is to receive or supply the data in the record being manipulated. For example, in Pascal, statements such as:

read (MailList, MailRecord)

and

write (MailList, MailRecord)

are used to retrieve and deposit information relative to a sequential file identified as MailList. Note that along with the file identifier within the parameter list, we find the name MailRecord (probably a heterogeneous array) that is used within the program to identify the block of data being transferred. Similar statements in FORTRAN are

READ (UNIT = 10,FMT = 150) Name, Address

and

WRITE (UNIT = 10,FMT = 150) Name, Address

The file referenced by these statements is indicated by the number 10 (which would have been assigned as the file identifier earlier in the program), the organization of the record itself is defined by the number 150 (which is a reference to another statement in the program where the record structure is described), and the individual fields in the record are identified as Name and Address.

Note that these statements include no explicit information as to the location in the file of the record being manipulated. Because the file is sequential, there is no choice to be made: The record being read is the one immediately following the current position in the file or the record being written is placed immediately following the current position.

In addition to subroutines for the manipulation of records in a sequential file, most high-level procedural language systems provide features that assist with the problem of detecting the EOF mark. This may appear as a special condition within the retrieve instruction itself or as a test to be performed independently of actual record retrieval.

In particular, FORTRAN uses the former system, allowing an extra parameter in the READ statement to indicate where control should be transferred if the record retrieved is, in fact, the EOF mark rather than a regular record. Thus, a statement to retrieve an employee record might have the following form:

READ (UNIT = 10,FMT = 150,END = 900) Name, Address

where the phrase END = 900 means that if the record obtained is the EOF mark, control should be transferred to the instruction labeled 900.

In contrast to this FORTRAN system of combining the EOF test with the retrieval statement, Pascal essentially uses a flag whose interrogation is independent of record retrieval. With this system, one can test for the EOF mark on the file identified as EmplData with the syntax eof(EmplData). The result is the value true if the EOF mark has been reached and false if not. Thus, a program sequence of the form

while (not eof(EmplData)) **do**
(read the next record and
process the appropriate check)

is used to process the payroll from the employee file. The result is that the read and process statements are repeated as long as there are employee records to be processed. However, once the last employee record is processed, execution goes on to the next part of the program. Such an application typifies the **while** loop structure.

The traditional merge algorithm provides an excellent medium in which to observe the need for EOF detection while at the same time presenting a classical example of sequential file processing. The setting is that new records have been collected that are to be inserted into an existing sequential file. This insertion is done in the context of producing a totally new copy of the sequential file with the updates inserted. The new records are stored in a file called the transaction file, the file to be updated is called the old master file, and the updated file is called the new master file (Figure 8-2). Both the transaction file and the old master file are assumed to be sorted according to a field referred to as the key field. We assume that all new records are indeed new; that is, no record in the transaction file can be found with an identical key field to that of a record in the old master file.

Figure 8-2 The traditional merging of two sequential files

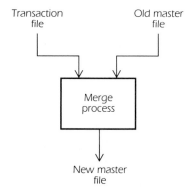

Observe that with these assumptions the problem becomes one of merging the two existing files, which we call the input files, into one large output file (the new master file). The algorithm accomplishes this by starting at the beginning of the two input files, accessing a record from each file, comparing the records, writing the smaller one into the new master file, and then reading another record from the appropriate input file before returning to compare again.

Within this basic framework we must also maintain a vigil for the end of either input file and, if this is found, respond accordingly. This leads to the algorithm represented in Figure 8-3.

Questions/Exercises

1. Follow the merge algorithm presented in Figure 8-3, assuming that the transaction file contains records with key field values equal to B and E while the old master file contains A, C, D, and F.

2. The merge algorithm is the heart of a popular sort algorithm called the merge sort. Can you discover this algorithm? (Hint: A file containing only one record is sorted.)

3. Identify the tape motions involved in inserting a new record into a sequential file stored on tape if the file is to remain on the same tape. (Assume all records are the same size. Why is this assumption important?)

Figure 8-3 The sequential file update (or merge) algorithm represented in pseudocode

```
Read a record (called the current transaction record)
     from the transaction file.
Read a record (called the current master record)
     from the old master file.
while (neither file has reached EOF) do
     [If (the key field of the current transaction record is)
          less than that of the current master record)
          then (write the current transaction record on the new
               master file and read the next record from the transaction file)
          else (write the current master record on the new
               master file and read the next record from the old
               master file)]
while (not EOF on old master file) do
     (write the current master record on the new master file
     and read the next record from the old master file)
     while no EOF on transaction file) do
          (write the current transaction record on the new master
          file and read the next record from the transaction file)
Write the sentinel on the new master file.
```

8-2 Text Files

By restricting the size of the logical records in a sequential file to a single byte, we obtain another file type known as a **text file.** (Some refer to these files as stream files, but others reserve the term *stream* to refer to a series of bytes that are passed from one process to another without necessarily being stored as a file in mass storage.) The name *text file* reflects the fact that files of this type are commonly used for storing documents consisting of text, with each logical record consisting of a single symbol or control code (such as a carriage return, line feed, or font indicator). When reading such a file, one receives the characters of the document in the sequential order in which they appear when the document is displayed on a monitor or a print out. Moreover, if the document is the source version of a program, this character-by-character order is appropriate as input to a translator.

An alternative to viewing a text file as a stream of individual bytes is to view the file as a sequence of lines separated by end-of-line markers. This conceptual image is a consequence of document storage applications and is promoted by the Pascal programming language.

For storage purposes a text file is broken into multiple-byte units that form physical records of a size compatible with the mass storage system being used. The manipulation of physical records is normally handled by the underlying software, so when either reading from or writing to a text file, the user has the image of a file consisting of a sequence of individual bytes or lines as desired.

In reality, when the first byte or line is requested from the file, the underlying software retrieves one or more entire physical records from the mass storage device and holds these records in a buffer in main memory. From this buffer, the request for a portion of the file as well as future requests are honored. As the underlying software passes the contents of the buffer to the user, additional physical records are retrieved into the buffer until the end of the file is reached.

As a user writes to a text file, the underlying software collects the individual bytes in a buffer until a complete physical record accumulates, or until the user indicates that the end of the file has been reached. It is then that a physical record is transferred to mass storage.

In some cases, the underlying software disguises the strict sequential nature of a text file. A word processor, for example, might store documents as text files but not limit the processing of the file strictly to its sequential form. Instead, a word processor normally reads several physical records into main memory and displays this text on the monitor as it would appear in the printed form of the document. Then the processor allows the user to move back and forth within this block of text while making changes. As the user moves farther down the text, more physical records are retrieved from mass storage and displayed on the screen, while the earlier updated portions of the document are redivided into physical records and placed back into mass storage. Thus, the word processor provides random access to that portion of the file that is currently held in main memory.

Most high-level procedural programming environments provide subroutines for manipulating text files. Once again these subroutines may be dictated as a part of the formal definition of the language or offered in libraries as extensions to the language.

Pascal is an example of the first case. It includes the routines read and write for accessing text files. In particular, if Symbol is declared as a variable of type character, then the statement

read(OldManuscript, Symbol);

retrieves one byte from the text file identified as OldManuscript and assigns that byte to the variable Symbol. Similarly, the statement

write(NewManuscript, Symbol);

places the byte currently assigned to Symbol at the current location in the file NewManuscript.

Commands for manipulating text files in a C language environment are provided as a language extension by means of prewritten subroutines within a library. These routines include getc and putc for retrieving and depositing bytes in a text file. Hence, in a C program the statements

getc(OldManuscript, Symbol);

and

putc(NewManuscript, Symbol);

would be used to accomplish the same goals as the preceding read and write Pascal statements.

To support the line-by-line image of a text file, Pascal provides routines called readln and writeln that manipulate text files by lines rather than individual characters. For example, the command

readln(OldManuscript);

advances the current position in the file OldManuscript to the beginning of the next line and

writeln(NewManuscript);

places an end-of-line marker at the current position in the file NewManuscript.

Questions/Exercises
1. In what sense is a text file a special case of a sequential file?
2. Identify two applications in which the use of text files is appropriate.

3. Suppose a word processor stores documents in a strict text file format. What problems might be encountered when the word processor is required to backtrack a long distance within a document that is being updated?

8-3   Indexed Files

Let us suppose now that in addition to processing payroll with the employee file, we want to use the file in an interactive query system. For instance, we may want to have a workstation available in the personnel office on which the records of employees can be displayed to answer questions regarding time in service, available skills, past promotions, and so on. In this atmosphere, records in the file are requested in an arbitrary order throughout the day.

This is a significant departure from the naturally sequential payroll application of Section 8-1. If we store the employee data as a sequential file and attempt to use it in this interactive application, we could easily find a lengthy delay between a request for a record and the displaying of that record. Indeed, to satisfy each request, the program handling the retrieval must apply a sequential search from the beginning of the file.

We have already discussed the disadvantages of such a process in relation to searching a list data structure. Compounding the problem in the present application is that the accessing of records from mass storage requires the additional time-consuming, mechanical motion associated with the storage device being used. The result is that sequential search techniques are even more sluggish when applied to mass storage than when applied to main memory.

What we need is a way of storing the employee file that reduces this search time. One approach is based on the same idea used in textbooks with an index that allows a topic to be located more directly than through a sequential search of the entire book. This index concept is easily applied to file storage, resulting in what is called an *indexed file.*

Index Fundamentals

An index for a file consists of a listing of the key field values occurring in the file along with the location in mass storage of the corresponding record. For example, in an employee file, we might build an index listing all the employee identification numbers. Finding the record for a particular employee in such a file requires searching for the pertinent employee number in the file's index and then retrieving the record stored in the indicated mass storage location.

Of course, this approach requires that we know the key field value (employee identification number) of the desired record. In some cases, it may be necessary for our file to be accessible by more than one key field, perhaps by either Social Security number or employee identification number. In such cases, a multiple index system is often the solution. In particular, in addition to constructing an index listing employee identification numbers, we might build a second index based on the key field being Social Security numbers (Figure 8-4). Then, regardless of whether one starts with an employee number or a Social Security number, the desired record can be accessed quickly by interrogating the appropriate index. (You often hear such a file referred to as an *inverted file,* with one key field designated as the *primary key* and the other as the *secondary key.*) The luxury of multiple indexes is not without its disadvantages, however. Indeed, as records are inserted and deleted, all indexes must be updated, so the existence of additional indexes can increase the time required to update the file.

Keep in mind that the index for a file is stored in mass storage along with the file itself. To access a record, we first retrieve the index into main memory, where we search through it for the desired entry before returning to mass storage for the record in question. Thus, the mere introduction of an index transfers the search process from the file in mass storage to the index, which can be searched in main memory. This transfer alone significantly increases the efficiency of searching the file. Indeed, it avoids numerous time-consuming retrievals of records from mass storage as each is considered in the search process. But, additional efficiency can be gained by proper index organization.

Index Organization

Consider now the question of index size. Since the index must be moved to main memory to be searched, it (or perhaps sections of it) must remain small enough to fit within a reasonable memory area. This requirement can produce problems if the

Figure 8-4 An inverted file

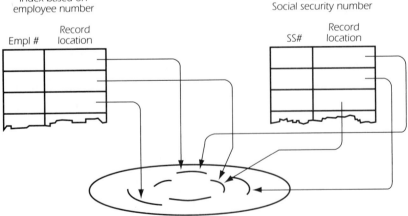

Records stored on disk

number of records in the file becomes large. One technique used to overcome such a growth problem is based on the idea of using the index to find an approximate, rather than the precise, location of the desired record. This can be accomplished by first organizing the file in a sorted sequential order and then chopping it into short, multirecord segments. Each segment (consisting of several records) is then represented in the index by a single entry, which is normally the last key field value in the segment. The result is a partial index containing only a few of the key field values appearing in the file.

The partial-index structure is summarized in Figure 8-5, in which we have indicated only the key field entry in each record and have assumed that these entries are single, alphabetic letters. The retrieval of a record from this system consists of finding the first entry in the index that is equal to or greater than the desired entry and then searching the corresponding sequential segment for the target record. For example, to find the record with key field entry E in the file in Figure 8-5, we follow the pointer associated with the index entry F and then search that segment to find the desired record.

A common implementation of the partial-index idea is based on the physical characteristics of disk storage systems where the size of the file segments is chosen so that each segment fits on a separate track of the disk being used. When retrieving a record, one uses the index to determine which track contains the target record, after

Figure 8-5 A file with a partial index

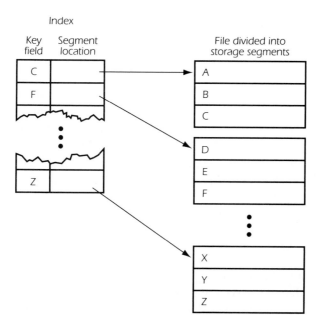

which that track can be searched as a short, sequential file. You might expect that since larger segments mean a smaller index, the segment size should be chosen to fill the tracks completely. This is true if no records will be added to the file in the future. However, if file growth is anticipated, only a fraction (called the *load factor*) of each track is initially filled. This leaves room to insert new records where they properly belong. Of course, even a very small load factor does not guarantee that a segment will not ultimately outgrow its track. Thus, in the case of dynamic files, provisions must be made either to split large segments into smaller ones or to store the overflow records on a separate part of the disk.

Another approach to the large-index problem is to divide the index into pieces using the concept of an index to the index. Thus, the overall index takes on a layered or tree structure. We might envision such a system as an extension of the partial-index idea. More precisely, if the sequential segments represented by the index entries were to become inefficiently large, we can construct a separate index for each of them. Thus, the original index no longer directs the search to a file segment but rather to the correct segment index, which then is used to find the location of the record in question (Figure 8-6).

Programming Concerns

Just as with sequential files, some high-level languages provide subroutines for manipulating records in an indexed file. By using these routines, programs can be written without the programmer being concerned with the actual structure of the index system being applied. As an example, in some dialects of FORTRAN, a record in an indexed version of the employee file can be retrieved with a statement of the form

READ (UNIT = 10,FMT = 150,REC = EmpIID,ERR = 950) Name, Address, . . .

which is similar to the sequential file statement presented in Section 8-1. We have simply deleted the END phrase (since an EOF mark has no meaning when retrieving a particular record from an indexed file) and inserted the phrases REC = EmpIID and ERR = 950. The first phrase indicates that the RECord being sought is one with its key field entry equal to the value currently assigned to the variable EmpIID; the second phrase states that if such a record is not found (an ERRor condition), execution of the program should be transferred to the statement labeled 950.

In a similar manner, the FORTRAN statement

WRITE (UNIT = 10,FMT = 150,REC = EmpIID) Name, Address, . . .

is used to store a record in the file. If a record already exists with a key field equal to the current value of EmpIID, the new record replaces the old one. However, if no record currently exists with that key field, a new record is inserted along with any updates needed in the index.

Figure 8-6 A hierarchical index

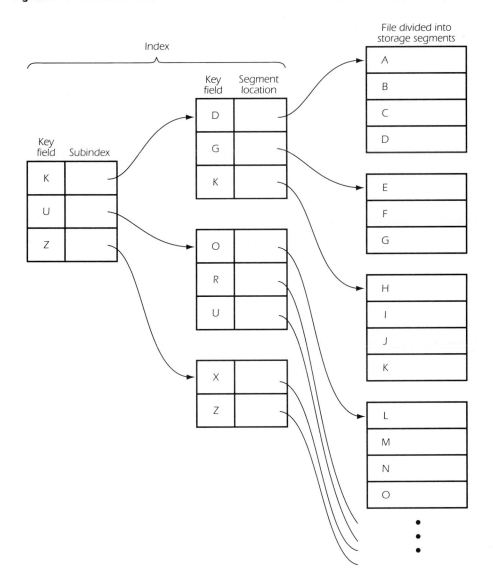

Questions/Exercises

1. Within a partial index, why is it advantageous to represent each segment of the file with its largest key field rather than its smallest? (Hint: Compare the algorithms needed to search the index in each case.)
2. The concepts of sequential and indexed files are often combined by supplying an index to an otherwise sequential file, producing what is called an indexed sequential file. What advantages does such an organization have?

3. Identify some pros and cons to organizing a file's index as a list rather than as a tree.

4. In the case of an inverted file, can both the primary and secondary indexes be organized as partial indexes using the technique presented in this section?

8-4   Hashed Files

At this point we have discussed examples of two general approaches to file organization. The first, known as sequential access, is represented by sequential and text files. It insists that the file be processed according to a particular serial order. The second is called direct access (sometimes called random access) and allows individual records to be retrieved without interrogating other records in the file. Indexed files provide an example of this paradigm.

Note that by properly traversing the index, an indexed file can also provide sequential access to the file. Hence, an index system is a way of obtaining both sequential and direct access to a file, a duality obtained at the expense of index maintenance.

Hashed files represent a file storage system that provides direct access only, without the overhead encountered with indexed maintenance. The idea behind a hashed file is to compute the location of a record in mass storage by applying some algorithm (the hash algorithm) to the value of the key field in question. The result is a system that (knowing the desired key field) can determine the location of a record quickly without the use of auxiliary tables that must be maintained.

A Particular Hashing Technique

Let us apply the hashing concept to our employee file. First, we divide the mass storage area allotted to the file into several sections called buckets. How many buckets we use is a design decision that we return to later. For now, let us assume that we have divided the storage region into 40 buckets. Next, assuming that records in the file will always be requested in terms of the employee identification number, we establish that field in each record as the key field.

Our first task is to convert any key field value into a numeric value. This step may seem meaningless to you since the key field is, in fact, the employee identification number. However, the actual value of this field may not be numeric. That is, identification "numbers" may take the form 25X3Z or J2-X35. On the other hand, recall that any information stored in the machine is represented in terms of a string of 0s and 1s. Thus, we can always interpret an item of data simply as a binary number whether or not that was the original intention when the information was coded.

Using this numeric interpretation, we can divide any key field value stored in memory by the number of buckets, which in our case is 40. Note that the result of this division process is an integer value, called the quotient, and another integer value known as the remainder. The important point is that this remainder is always in the range from 0 to 39. That is, if we consider only the remainder from the division, we always find one of the 40 possible values 0, 1, 2, 3, . . . 39. Thus, we can relate exactly one of the 40 buckets to each of these possible remainders (Figure 8-7).

With this system, we can convert any key field value into an integer (the remainder of the division) that identifies one of the buckets in mass storage, and we can use this system to determine the bucket in which to store the corresponding record. That is, we can consider each record individually, convert its key field value to an integer, apply our hash function to identify a bucket in mass storage, and then store the record in that bucket (as summarized in Figure 8-8, on the following page). Later, if we need to retrieve a record with a certain key field value, we can simply transform this value to a bucket number as before, retrieve the records in that bucket, and then search the retrieved records for the one in question.

Distribution Problems

Our simplified explanation has thus far overlooked a few complications inherent in a hashed file. At the root of these complications is the fact that once we have chosen the hash algorithm, we have no more control over the distribution of records in mass storage. For instance, if we use the divide-by-40 algorithm previously presented, and if the numeric interpretation of the key field values tends to be multiples of 40, a disproportionate number of the records are placed in the bucket assigned to the remainder zero. The result is that searching through that bucket approximates a

Figure 8-7 *The rudiments of a hashing system, in which each bucket holds those records that hash to that bucket number*

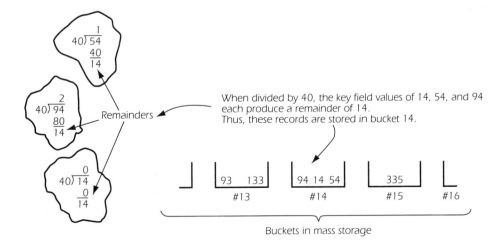

When divided by 40, the key field values of 14, 54, and 94 each produce a remainder of 14. Thus, these records are stored in bucket 14.

Buckets in mass storage

Figure 8-8 Hashing the key field value 25X3Z to one of 40 buckets

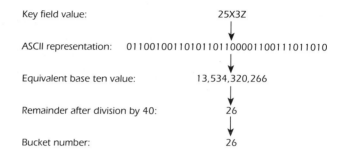

search through the entire file, resulting in little advantage over a sequential file structure. Moreover, unless the buckets are extremely large, some system must be provided for handling buckets that overflow.

It is therefore to our advantage to select a hash algorithm that evenly distributes the records among the buckets provided in mass storage. However, the selection process is complicated by the fact that we normally do not know in advance exactly what the key field values will be (because of employee turnover, the employee identification numbers used today will not be those used tomorrow). Thus, the choice of a hash algorithm must be based on a combination of one's artistic abilities, statistical analysis, and rules of thumb.

One such rule of thumb concerns our decision to divide mass storage into 40 buckets, which is generally not a good choice. To see why, recall that if a dividend and a divisor both have a common factor, this factor is present in the remainder. In turn, the remainders produced by the division process tend to be multiples of this common factor, while other values are ignored. We have already seen this effect when we conjectured the possibility of the key fields being multiples of 40 (which consistently produced remainders of zero). However, a similar problem exists if the key fields are multiples of 5. Since 40 is also a multiple of 5, the factor of 5 appears in the remainder of our division process, and the records in the file cluster in those buckets associated with the remainders 0, 5, 10, 15, 20, 25, 30, and 35.

Similar situations occur in the case of key field values that are multiples of 2, 4, 8, 10, and 20, because they are all also factors of 40. Of course, the observation of this fact suggests a partial solution. That is, the chance of clustering due to this phenomenon can be minimized by selecting the number of buckets to have as few factors as possible. Thus, one usually selects the number of buckets to be a prime number. For instance, the chance of clustering in the employee file example can be greatly reduced by dividing mass storage into 41 buckets rather than 40, because the only factors of 41 are 1 and 41.

Sometimes clustering can be reduced by selecting a hash algorithm based on principles other than division. One suggested technique (called the midsquare method) is to multiply the key field value by itself and select the middle digits from the product to represent the bucket number. Still another (called the extraction method) is to select the digits appearing in certain positions within the key field and construct the bucket number by combining these selected digits using some predetermined process. In any case, one often tests the performance of several hash algorithms on sample records before settling on a final choice.

Unfortunately, regardless of the hash algorithm we ultimately use, clustering of records will most likely occur as a file is modified over a period of time. We can gain an understanding of how quickly this might occur by considering what happens as we initially insert records into the modified 41-bucket employee file.

Assume that we have found a hash algorithm that arbitrarily distributes records among the buckets, that our file is empty, and that we are going to insert records one at a time. When we insert the first record, that record must go into an empty bucket. However, when we insert the next record, only 40 of the 41 buckets are empty. Thus, the probability that the second record will be placed in an empty bucket is only 40/41. Assuming that the second record is placed in an empty bucket, the third finds only 39 empty buckets, and the probability of its being placed in one of them is 39/41. Continuing this process, we find that if the first seven records are placed in empty buckets, the eighth record then has a 34/41 probability of being placed in one of the remaining empty buckets.

This analysis allows us to compute the probability of the first eight records being placed in empty buckets, because it is the product of the probabilities of each record being placed in an empty bucket, assuming that the preceding records were so placed. This probability is therefore

$$(41/41)(40/41)(39/41)(38/41) \ldots (34/41) = .482$$

The point is that the result is less than one-half. That is, it is more likely than not that at least two of the first eight records will hash to the same bucket, a phenomenon called a collision. Thus, clustering probably begins with only eight records stored among 41 buckets.

Handling Section Overflow

The high probability of collisions indicates that a hashed file should never be implemented under the assumption that clustering will not occur; thus, some plan must be established for handling the associated problems.

In particular, we must allow for the fact that certain buckets might fill up and that records that should go into these buckets must then be placed elsewhere. A typical technique for handling this is to reserve an additional area of mass storage to hold overflow records. Then, if a bucket fills up, records that normally are added to it are

Figure 8-9 Handling bucket overflow

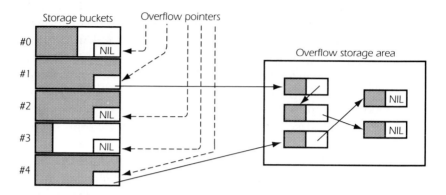

placed in the overflow area and linked to the appropriate bucket through an organization analogous to a linked list. With such a system, a hashed file stored in five buckets might have the structure shown in Figure 8-9, in which the storage area actually occupied by records is indicated by shading. (Note that buckets 1 and 4 have spilled into the overflow area, whereas one additional record in bucket 2 will cause bucket 2 to do the same.)

When trying to retrieve a record from such a file, one would first extract the proper bucket using the hash algorithm. If, however, the desired record was not found there, one would search the overflow records linked to that bucket. We conclude that if a lot of overflowing takes place, the efficiency of searching the file can drop significantly. Thus, the design of a hashed file requires a careful analysis involving the choice of the hash algorithm, the number and size of the buckets in mass storage, and the size and structure of the overflow area.

Programming Concerns

Few, if any, high-level procedural programming languages in use today offer direct implementations of hashed files. In part, this is due to the application-dependent issues (hash algorithm, number of buckets, size of buckets) involved in the design of these files. It is therefore the task of the programmer to develop the abstract tools required by a hashed file. This may be done in terms of the primitives in the language or perhaps by resorting to subroutines written in another language that provide more convenient tools.

Some languages provide primitives for manipulating a file structure known as a direct file.[1] Records in this type of file are referenced by relative record numbers; that

---

[1]Be careful not to confuse the terms *direct file* and *direct access*. The first refers to a particular way of obtaining the second. Direct files, indexed files, and hashed files all provide direct access.

is, the first record is referenced as record 1, the next as record 2, and so on. In these cases, constructing the abstract tools for a hashed file is rather straightforward. One merely implements a direct file in which each record represents a bucket in the abstract hashed file. Then the hash algorithm is designed to convert key field values into relative record numbers.

Once the abstract tools for implementing a hashed file have been constructed, actual use of a hashed file is similar to that of an indexed file. The statements for inserting a record or retrieving a record from the two types of files often contain the same information. In each case, one must identify the file itself, the key field value, the main memory location of the record to be recorded or the location in which the retrieved record should be placed, and perhaps what should be done in the case of an attempt to retrieve a nonexistent record.

In recent years hashing techniques have found applications outside the traditional mass storage arena. Today hashing is sometimes used to distribute data within an extremely large one-dimensional array in main memory. The components of such an array, which are designed with the capacity to hold several data entries, play the role of buckets, and a hash algorithm is used to identify the component in which each data entry belongs.

This expansion in the application of hashing techniques from mass storage systems into main memory systems is exemplary of the continuing evolution in data processing that is a problem for those who attempt to classify topics in the field. Indeed, hashing, which traditionally has been a topic of file structures, may soon be more accurately classified within the subject of data structures.

Questions/Exercises

1. Suppose an employee record system is implemented as a hashed file using 1000 buckets of mass storage with the Social Security number field as the key field. Observe that one possible hash algorithm is to select the first three digits from the Social Security number, because this would always result in a value between 0 and 999, inclusive. Why is this not a good choice?

2. Explain how a poorly chosen hash algorithm can result in a hashed file system becoming little more than a sequential file.

3. Suppose a hashed file is constructed using the division hash algorithm as presented in the text but with six mass storage buckets. For each of the following key field values, identify the bucket in which the record with that key field value is placed. What goes wrong and why?

   a. 24   c. 3   e. 15   g. 9   i. 27
   b. 30   d. 18   f. 21   h. 39   j. 0

4. How many people must be gathered together before the odds are that two members of the group will have birthdays on the same day of the year?

5.   How might the concepts of a hashed file blend with the physical characteristics of disk storage?

8-5   The Role of the Operating System

We have seen that associated with each file structure is a variety of details relating to the retrieval or insertion of records. However, we concluded our discussion of each structure by indicating that such details are often of no concern when accessing the file from within a high-level programming language environment, because these environments tend to provide prewritten subroutines for manipulating files. These subroutines, in turn, communicate with the operating system to perform their assigned tasks. Thus, much of the obligation for file manipulation ultimately falls on the operating system.

To fulfill this obligation, the operating system must have access to information about the file being manipulated. For example, it must know the structure of the file, which item within a record is the key field (if applicable), and whether the file is to be saved after the program using it is finished. Furthermore, some items of information must be remembered by the operating system between the retrieval of one record and the next. Depending on the type of file being manipulated, this may include the current position in the file, which physical record is currently in memory, and whether any abnormal conditions occurred during the previous access (for example, in an indexed file, was the requested record actually found?).

To manage this information, the operating system maintains a table, often called a *file descriptor* or file control block, for each file being processed. All the information relating to the processing of a single file is kept there in an organized manner and made available to the various routines in the operating system as needed. Thus, if a program involves the processing of three files, the operating system must construct three file descriptors to assist in the file management.

In a high-level programming language, the construction of a file descriptor normally is initiated by a prewritten subroutine named open. A typical statement in FORTRAN has a form similar to:

    OPEN(UNIT = 10, FILE = 'EmplFile', STATUS = OLD, ACCESS = SEQUENTIAL)

which requests the operating system to construct a file descriptor for the file named EmplFile. The parameters indicate that the file is referred to later in the program as unit number 10 (UNIT = 10), the name of the file is EmplFile (FILE = 'EmplFile'), the operating system should find this file already in mass storage (STATUS = OLD), and the structure of the file is sequential (ACCESS = SEQUENTIAL).

In Turbo Pascal (a popular dialect of Pascal provided by Borland International), file descriptors can be created by means of the predefined procedures called assign and reset. For example, the statements

assign(InText, 'RawManuscript');
reset(InText);

cause the operating system to construct a file descriptor for the file named RawManuscript and tell the translator that this file is referred to throughout the program by the name InText.

Note that both our Pascal and FORTRAN examples have shown that a file can be referenced later in a program by an identifier other than the file's proper name; future references to the file EmplFile in our FORTRAN example are in terms of the unit number 10, whereas in our Pascal example, the RawManuscript file is referred to as InText. This distinction between a file's external name and the term used to reference it within a program reflects the distinction between the syntax rules of operating systems and programming languages. A name used to identify a file in the context of an operating system may not be a syntactically valid identifier in the programming language being used. Thus, a means of name conversion is required. Once established, this distinction between internal and external file identification also provides flexibility in that a subroutine designed to manipulate a file in terms of its internal identifier can be used to process different files merely by assuring that each was given the proper internal identifier when it was opened.

Having been directed to construct a file descriptor, the operating system must also be told when it is no longer needed. After a file has been processed, many programming languages require the use of a subroutine named close. Basically this routine informs the operating system that the memory space used for the file descriptor can be used for something else; however, in some settings, the statement initiates more than this simple release of memory space. For instance, in the case of a text file that has been created by the program, the close routine causes the operating system to transfer the last physical record to mass storage. In any case, the syntax of the close statement is rarely anything more than a simple instruction, such as

CLOSE (UNIT = 10)

which, in FORTRAN, means the file identified as file number 10 can no longer be used in the program (or if it is used again, it must be reopened); the equivalent statement in Pascal is

close(InText);

Questions/Exercises

1. Identify the sequence of events followed by an operating system when retrieving a record from a partially indexed file.

2. What might be added to your answer to exercise 1 if the operating system is also controlling a time-sharing system?

3. Could a file that was originally built as a sequential file be opened as an indexed file?

Chapter 8 Review Problems

1. Suppose a sequential file is to be stored with a blocking factor of five. Explain how updating the file can be simplified if the file was originally stored with each physical record containing only three actual records and two blank records.

2. If the merge algorithm in Figure 8-3 is to be applied to two sequential files, does it matter which file plays the role of the master file and which plays the role of the transaction file?

3. List the steps that are executed in the merge algorithm in Figure 8-3 if the transaction file is empty at the start.

4. Modify the algorithm in Figure 8-3 to handle the case in which a transaction record has a key field value equal to a record already in the old master file. In this case, the transaction record should appear in the new master file and the old master record should be omitted.

5. Why must a high-level programming language statement for reading a record from an indexed file require more information than it does for reading a sequential file? What is this additional information?

6. Explain how a single file can be implemented on a disk so that it can be processed as a sequential file with either of two different sequential orderings.

7. Why is a company-assigned employee identification number a better choice for a key field than the last name of each employee?

8. In what sense is the advantage of an index lost if, to keep the index small, the segments used for a partial-index system are made extremely large?

9. Below is a table representing the contents of a partial index. Indicate which segment should be retrieved when searching for the record with each of the following key field values:
    a. 24X17   b. 12N67
    c. 32E75   d. 26X28

Key field	Segment number
13C08	1
23G19	2
26X28	3
36Z05	4

10. Based on the index in problem 9, what is the largest key field value in the file? What do you know about the smallest?

11. Give an advantage and a disadvantage of using a partial index rather than an index that contains all the key fields in a file.

12. What is the difference between a sequential file and an indexed sequential file?

13. What problems arise if all the indexes for an inverted file are partial indexes?

14. What file structure do you recommend for a file containing descriptions of a library's holdings, assuming that books must be referenced by author's name, book title, and subject? Support your recommendation.

15. If the only way to extract information from a hashed file is by actually hashing the key of each record, what information is required to obtain a complete listing of all the records?

16. If a hashed file is partitioned into 10 buckets, what is the probability of at least two of three arbitrary records hashing to the same section? (Assume the hash algorithm gives no bucket priority over the others.) How many records must be stored in the file until it is more likely for collisions to occur than not?

17. Solve the previous problem assuming that the file is partitioned into 100 buckets instead of 10.

18. If we are using the division technique discussed in this chapter as a hash algorithm and the file storage area is divided into 23 buckets, which section should we search to find the record whose key field value, when interpreted as a binary value, reduces to the integer 124?

19. If the division hash algorithm as presented in the text is being used, why is clustering more likely to occur when the file storage space is divided into 60 sections rather than 61?

20. Why is it advantageous to keep the list of overflow records (from a bucket in a hashed file) sorted according to key field values?

21. If we divided the storage area for a hashed file into 41 buckets that can each hold exactly one record, we expect at least one section to overflow after only eight records are stored. On the other hand, if we combine the same storage area into one section that can hold 41 records, we can always store 41 records before overflow occurs. What keeps us from deciding to implement hashed files using this latter configuration?

22. Suppose a record's key field value is XY. Using the division technique for hashing discussed in the text, convert this value into the section number that should contain the record in a hashed file consisting of 41 buckets. (Assume characters are stored using ASCII, 1 byte per character, with a zero in the most significant bit of each byte.)

23. Suppose a hashed file is to be constructed containing information about the residents of a local community in the United States. If the key field of this file is to consist of seven-digit telephone numbers, why would it not be a good idea to base the hashing algorithm on the first three digits in the key field?

24. A hashed file using the division hash algorithm discussed in the text is to be constructed with 50, 51, 52, or 53 buckets. Which of these choices is best? Why?

25. Suppose a hashed file was constructed using the division technique discussed in this chapter as the hash algorithm. Moreover, suppose that a record from bucket 3 is found to have a key field value that, when interpreted as a binary value, reduces to the integer 26. Into how many buckets was the mass storage area for this file divided?

26. Give an advantage that
    a. a sequential file has over an indexed file.
    b. a sequential file has over a hashed file.
    c. an indexed file has over a sequential file.
    d. an indexed file has over a hashed file.
    e. a hashed file has over a sequential file.
    f. a hashed file has over an indexed file.

27. In each of the following cases, indicate which file structure (sequential, indexed, or hashed) you recommend. Support your recommendations.
    a. a rough draft of a speech
    b. a file of a dentist's patient records
    c. a mailing list
    d. a file of 50,000 words and their definitions used for reference

28. What problems can arise when a large number of new records having similar key field values is inserted into an indexed file? How can these problems be reduced if the file is initially generated with a small load factor?

29. In what way is a sequential file similar to a linked list?

30. Identify two techniques that might be used for identifying the end of a text file.

31. Explain how a sequential file of employee records can be implemented using a programming language's primitives for manipulating text files?

32. How is a direct file similar to a one-dimensional array?

33. Define each of the following:
    a. text file
    b. indexed file
    c. hashed file
    d. direct file

34. Why would a programmer want to write a program using an internal identifier to refer to a file rather than the file's actual external name?

35. Identify three items of information that might be found in a file descriptor.

36. What is the purpose of opening a file? What is the purpose of closing a file?

37. How does the implementation of a sequential file differ if it is stored on tape rather than disk?

38. Suppose a sequential file contains 2000 records. If, over an extended period, various records are retrieved from the file, what do you expect to be the average number of records interrogated per retrieval? Explain your answer.

39. Suppose a file containing 50,000 words is used by a word processor to check for typographical errors in documents by checking each word in a document for its presence in the file. Why should this file not be stored as a text file?

40. Estimate the amount of space on an 80-megabyte disk drive that is required to store a term paper consisting of 40 double-spaced typed pages represented as a text file. How many such documents can the disk hold?

Problems for the Programmer

1. Assume the existence of a sequential file pertaining to airline flights with three fields: The first is the flight number (used as the key field), the second is the three-letter code of the origin airport, and the third is the three-letter code for the destination airport. Write a program that accepts an origin code and a destination code from the terminal, searches the file, and either prints the flight numbers of all flights between those airports or reports that there are no such flights, if such is the case.

2. Write a program based on the merge algorithm (Figure 8-3) that allows the addition of flights to the airline file of programming problem 1.

3. Using the record structure of programming problem 1, modify the merge algorithm (Figure 8-3) to allow both the addition of new flights and the modification of the information about existing flights.

4. Assume that the airline file described in programming problem 1 is indexed by the key field flight number. Write a program that accepts a flight number from the terminal and responds by printing the information about that flight or responds with a message that there is no such flight.

5. Extend the program written for programming problem 4 so that, once the correct flight is found, a search is made to print all other flight numbers of flights between the same airports as the requested flight.

6. Write a program to check the spelling of words. That is, your program should accept a word typed at the terminal, compare the word to its dictionary, and report whether or not the word was found. Do not search the dictionary sequentially, but use a hashing system to narrow the search to a section of the dictionary. (Use a dictionary of at least 100 words.)

7. Write a program to perform the hash algorithm discussed in Section 8-4. Using this program, experiment with the effects of dividing the available mass storage area into 40 versus 41 buckets.

Additional Reading

Bradley, J. *File and Data Base Techniques*. New York: Holt, Rinehart and Winston, 1982.

Folk, M. J. and Zoellick, B. *File Structures: A Conceptual Toolkit*, 2nd ed. Reading, Mass.: Addison-Wesley, 1992.

Hanson, O. *Design of Computer Data Files*. Rockville, Md.: Computer Science Press, 1982.

Miller, N. E. *File Structures Using Pascal*. Redwood City, Calif.: Benjamin/Cummings, 1987.

Miller, N. E., and Petersen, Charles G. *File Structures with Ada*. Redwood City, Calif.: Benjamin/Cummings, 1990.

Smith, P. D., and Barnes, G. M. *Files and Databases*. Reading, Mass.: Addison-Wesley, 1987.

Tremblay, J., and Sorenson, P. G. *An Introduction to Data Structures with Applications*. New York: McGraw-Hill, 1984.

CHAPTER NINE

DATABASE STRUCTURES

This final chapter regarding data organization represents a combination of data structures and file structures discussed previously. Indeed, a database is formed by combining techniques from both of these more traditional areas to obtain a single mass storage data system that can appear to have a multitude of organizations for serving a variety of applications. Such structures eliminate the duplication (providing separate data systems for each application even though these applications may require much of the same information) found in the more traditional file-oriented approach.

*Sections marked by an asterisk are optional in that they provide additional depth of coverage that is not required for an understanding of future chapters.

9-1   General Issues

The term *database* has evolved through its use in the popular press, in the business world, and among computer scientists. It is not surprising therefore to find varying definitions of the term, depending on whom you ask. Loosely speaking, any collection of data can be considered a database, although the term is usually reserved to mean a collection of data stored in mass storage that can take on a variety of appearances depending on the requirements at the time and can thus serve as the data source for a variety of applications.

We have already seen an elementary example of this phenomenon in our discussion of employee records in Chapter 8. There we envisioned times, such as during payroll processing, when we want the data to appear as a sequential file, while on other occasions, as in general employee information retrieval, a direct access configuration is more convenient. We discovered that an indexed system can provide this dual appearance, and some argue that such indexed files are simple databases. Others, citing the diversity achievable through large modern databases, say that this example is merely an amoeba in the evolution of databases. After all, databases in use today contain information encompassing the full spectrum of business activities and can provide access to selected portions of this data in a large number of formats.

To grasp a fuller meaning of the term *database,* we might look at the concept from the opposite direction. That is, we have just introduced a database as a data collection injected with the ability to emulate a variety of organizational forms depending on the needs of the application. From the other point of view, one often considers a database as the result of combining a variety of data collections (each of which was originally designed for a particular application) into a single integrated collection.

This consolidation approach to the database concept reflects the historical development of automated data storage and maintenance. As computing machinery found wider and wider uses in information management, each application tended to be implemented as a separate system with its own collection of data. Typically, the need to process payroll gave rise to a sequential file, and later the need for interactive data retrieval produced an entirely different system using a direct access file.

Although each of these systems represented an improvement over the corresponding manual techniques previously used, taken as a whole the collection of individual automated systems still constituted a limited and inefficient use of resources when compared to the possibilities of a combined database system. For example, different departments were not able to share the data they all needed, so much of the information required by an organization was duplicated in storage. The result was that when an employee moved, visits were required to numerous departments throughout the organization where address change cards were filed. Typographical errors, misplaced cards, and employee apathy could soon result in erroneous and conflicting data within the various data systems. Thus, after a move, an employee's newsletter might begin to arrive at the new address but with the wrong name, while the payroll records could continue to reflect the old address. In this atmosphere, database systems emerged as a means of consolidating the information stored and maintained by a particular organization (Figure 9-1). With such a system, both payroll and the mailing of newsletters could be processed from a single integrated data system.

Another advantage of a consolidated data system is the control achieved by an organization when the information it owns is placed in one common pot. As long as each department has complete control over its own data, those data tend to be used for the good of the department rather than for the good of the organization. In contrast, when a central database is implemented in a large organization, the control of information is normally concentrated in the administrative position known as the **database administrator (DBA)**, which may or may not be held by a single individual.

Figure 9-1 A file versus a database organization

File-oriented information system:

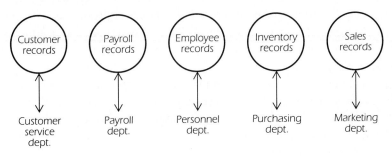

Database-oriented information system:

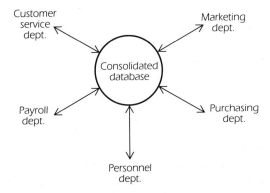

This central administrator (or administrative position) is cognizant of both the data available within the organization and the needs of the various departments. It is thus within this structure that decisions regarding data organization and access can be made with the entire organization in mind.

Along with the benefits of data consolidation come disadvantages. One significant concern is the control of access to sensitive data. For example, someone working on the organization's newsletter might need access to employee names and addresses but should not have access to payroll data; similarly, an employee processing payroll should not have access to the other financial records of the corporation. Thus, the ability to control access to the information in the database is often as important as the ability to share it.

To provide for this distinction of access privileges, database systems often rely on schemas and subschemas. A *schema* is a description of the entire database structure that is used by the database software to maintain the database. A *subschema* is a description of only that portion of the database pertinent to a particular user's needs. For example, consider a schema for a university database that indicates that each student record contains such items as the current address and phone number of that student in addition to that student's academic record. Moreover, it indicates that each student record is linked to the record of that student's faculty advisor. In turn, the record for each faculty member contains that person's address, employment history, and so on. Based on this schema, a pointer system is maintained that ultimately links the information about a student to the employment history of a faculty member.

To keep the university's registrars from using this linkage to obtain privileged information about the faculty, the registrar's access to the database must be restricted to a subschema whose description of the faculty records does not include employment history. Thus, under this subschema, a user can find out which faculty member is a particular student's advisor but cannot obtain access to additional information about that faculty member. In contrast, the subschema for the payroll department provides the employment history of each faculty member but does not include the linkage between students and advisors. Thus, the payroll department can modify a faculty member's salary but cannot find the students advised by that person.

There are other disadvantages connected to the evolution of database technology in addition to those directly associated with security. The size and scope of databases have increased rapidly. Today, extremely large collections of data can be assembled and interrogated with little effort over wide geographic areas, and with this increase in magnitude comes an increase in misinformation and misapplications of information. Incidents abound of injustices due to inaccurate credit reports, faulty criminal records, and discrimination resulting from unauthorized or unethical access to personal information.

In many cases, the underlying problem deals with the right to collect and hold information in the first place. What kind of information does an insurance company have a right to collect regarding its clients? Does a government have the right to maintain accounts of an individual citizen's voting record? Does a credit card company have the right to sell records of its customers' purchasing patterns to marketing firms? These questions represent some of the issues with which society must deal as a result of the influx of database technology.

Questions/Exercises

1. Identify two departments in a manufacturing plant that would have different uses for the same or similar inventory information.
2. Identify a variety of data collections found in a university environment that might be collected into one common database.
3. Describe how the subschema for the two departments in question 1 might differ.

9-2 The Layered Approach to Database Implementation

A person using a database is called the user, or at times the end user. You may imagine this person being an airline reservation clerk who interrogates the database from a terminal at an airport counter or perhaps an executive who retrieves information from the database at a workstation in an office. In either case, the user is most likely not trained in computer science and should not be required to consider the details of computer technology and techniques but rather should be allowed to concentrate on the problems of the application at hand. It is therefore the duty of the overall database system to present its information in terms of the application and not in computer gibberish.

To accomplish this goal in an organized manner, a database system is constructed from layers of abstraction (Figure 9-2). The image of the data given to the end user is produced by the application software, which is normally a system of programs, often written by the programming staff within the business itself, that communicates with the user in an interactive manner and in the application's terminology. It is in

Figure 9-2 The conceptual layers of a database

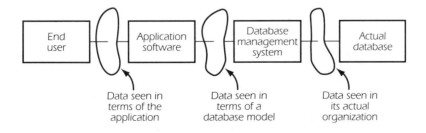

the design of this software that the overall system is given its personality. It may, for example, communicate with the user through such means as a question-and-answer dialogue or a fill-in-the-blanks scenario. Regardless of the user interface ultimately adopted, the application software communicates with the user to learn what information is required and later, having obtained the requested information, presents it to the user in a meaningful format.

Note that we did not say that the application software retrieves the information from the database. The actual manipulation of the database is accomplished by another software package called the **database management system (DBMS).** This dichotomy has several benefits. One is that the division of duties simplifies the design process. Just as the end user's task would be complicated by the requirement to consider computer concepts along with the task of solving a problem in the application world, the application programmer's task would be more complex if the actual data manipulation were a part of the application software. This is exemplified in the context of a **distributed database** (a database spread over several machines in a network). Without the services of a database management system, the application program must contain routines for keeping up with the actual location of the various portions of the database. With a well-designed database management system, the application software can be written as though the database were stored on a single machine.

A second advantage of separating the application software from the database management system is that such an organization provides a means for controlling access to the database. By dictating that all access to the database be performed by a central database management system, that system is placed in a position to enforce the restrictions imposed by the various subschemas. In particular, the database management system can use the entire database schema for its internal needs but require that each user remain within the bounds described by that user's subschema.

Still another reason for separating the user interface and actual data manipulation into two different software packages is to achieve **data independence.** This refers to the ability to change the organization of the database itself without changing the application software. For example, the personnel department might need to add an additional field to each employee's record to indicate whether or not the corresponding employee chose to participate in the company's new health insurance program. If the application software dealt directly with the database, such a change in the data's format would require modifications to all application programs dealing with the same database. Thus, the change instigated by the personnel department would cause changes to the payroll program as well as to the program for printing mailing labels for the company's newsletter.

The distinction between application software and the database management system removes the need for such reprogramming. To implement a change required by a single user, one needs to change only the schema used by the central system and the subschemas of those users involved in the change. All other subschemas remain the same, so the corresponding application software executes as though no changes were made.

One final advantage of the separation of application software and the database management system is that it allows the application software to be written in terms of a simplified, conceptual view of the database rather than the actual, complex structure involving disk tracks, pointers, and overflow areas. Recall that in our discussion of data structures, we saw that software routines could be used to translate requests (such as push and pop) in terms of a conceptual structure (a stack) into the proper activities in the actual storage organization. In a similar manner, a database management system contains routines that can be used as subprograms in the application software to convert commands in terms of a conceptual view of the database, called the *database model,* into terms of the actual database storage.

More precisely, application software is often written in general-purpose programming languages, such as those discussed in Chapter 5. These languages provide the basic ingredients for algorithm expression but lack the operations that make manipulation of the database convenient. The routines provided by the database management system in effect extend the capabilities of the language being used (as we will see in the following sections) in a manner that supports the conceptual image of the database model. This concept of the general-purpose language being the original system to which the capabilities of the database management system are added results in the original language being referred to as the *host language.* (Many commercial database management system packages today are actually combinations of the traditional database system and a host language. This tends to disguise the two as one, although the distinction still exists within.)

In summary, a database system is constructed from layers in much the same manner as an operating system, with each layer providing abstract tools to be used by other layers. In fact, the onion-skin diagram used to describe the architecture of an operating system is also quite applicable here (Figure 9-3, on the following page). We envision the outer layer in a database system as consisting of the application software, because this software unit communicates with the user in much the same manner as an operating system's command processor. Within this layer is the database management system, which in turn communicates with the database itself.

To develop application software for a database installation, a programmer must understand the abstract tools provided by the database management system being used. This is the subject of the next two sections. We look through the eyes of the application programmer at the database models available from popular database management systems. One of these models, called the relational model, allows the application software to be written as though the data in the database were stored in tables with rows and columns. The other model, called the network model, produces

Figure 9-3 An onion-skin diagram of a database system

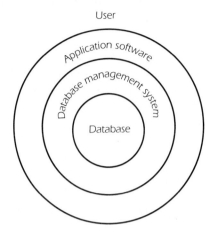

the image of those data items having common characteristics being linked in ring structures that can be traversed in a circular fashion.

The search for better database models is an ongoing process. The goal is to find models that allow complex data systems to be conceptualized easily, lead to concise ways of expressing requests for information, and can be implemented efficiently through database management systems to provide abstract tools for use in application programming.

Questions/Exercises

1. Does the use of a common indexed file for both payroll processing and interactive data retrieval provide data independence?
2. In a form similar to Figure 9-2, draw a diagram representing the machine language, high-level language, and end-user views of a computer.
3. Summarize the roles of the application software, the database management system, and the actual data-manipulating routines in retrieving information from a database.

9-3   The Relational Model

The first database model we discuss is the relational model, which is the most popular model today. Its popularity stems from the simplicity of its structure. It portrays data as being stored in tables called *relations.* As an example, the relational model allows information regarding the employees of a firm to be represented by a relation such as that in Figure 9-4.

Figure 9-4 A relation containing employee information

Emplld	Name	Address	SSNum
25X15	Joe E. Baker	33 Nowhere St.	111223333
34Y70	Cheryl H. Clark	563 Downtown Ave.	999009999
23Y34	G. Jerry Smith	1555 Circle Dr.	111005555
.	.	.	.
.	.	.	.
.	.	.	.

A row in a relation is called a *tuple.* Thus, in the relation of Figure 9-4, tuples consist of the information about a particular employee. Columns in a relation are referred to as *attributes* because each entry in a column describes some characteristic, or attribute, of the entity represented by the corresponding tuple.

Relational Design

The design of a database in terms of the relational model centers around the design of the relations making up the database. Although this may appear to be a simple task, many subtleties are waiting to trap the unwary designer.

Suppose that, in addition to the information contained in the relation of Figure 9-4, we want to include information about the jobs held by the employees. Associated with each employee, we may want to include a job history, consisting of such attributes as job title (secretary, office manager, floor supervisor), a job identification code (unique to each job), the skill code associated with each job, the department in which the job exists, and the period during which the employee held the job in terms of a starting date and termination date. (We use an asterisk as the termination date if the job represents the employee's current position.)

One approach to this problem is to extend the relation in Figure 9-4 to include these attributes as additional columns in the table, as shown in Figure 9-5, on the following page. However, close examination of the result reveals several problems. One is a lack of efficiency. Indeed, the relation no longer contains one tuple for each employee but rather one tuple for each assignment of an employee to a job. Thus, if an employee has advanced in the company through a sequence of several jobs, several tuples in the new relation are dedicated to that single employee. The problem with this is that the information contained in the original relation (each employee's name, address, identification number, and Social Security number) must be repeated. Moreover, if a particular job has been held by numerous employees, the department associated with that job along with the appropriate skill code must be identified in each tuple representing an assignment of the job. Of course, this repetition of data need not be present in the actual storage system because it can be simulated from a single source by the database management system. But if the need for this repetition is avoided in the first place, the overall database system is more efficient.

Figure 9-5 A relation containing redundancy
(Note: The personal information about Baker and Smith is repeated because
they have held more than one job. Also duplicated is the description of the
floor manager job because it has been held by more than one person.)

EmpIId	Name	Address	SSN	JobId	JobTitle	SkillCode	Dept	StartDate	TermDate
25X15	Joe E. Baker	33 Nowhere St.	111223333	F5	Floor manager	FM3	Sales	9-1-81	9-30-83
25X15	Joe E. Baker	33 Nowhere St.	111223333	D7	Dept. head	D2	Sales	10-1-83	*
34Y70	Cheryl H. Clark	563 Downtown Ave.	999009999	F5	Floor manager	FM3	Sales	10-1-83	*
23Y34	G. Jerry Smith	1555 Circle Dr.	111005555	S25X	Secretary	T5	Personnnel	3-1-81	4-30-82
23Y34	G. Jerry Smith	1555 Circle Dr.	111005555	S25Z	Secretary	T6	Accounting	5-1-82	*
.	.	.	.	.	.	.	.	.	.
.	.	.	.	.	.	.	.	.	.
.	.	.	.	.	.	.	.	.	.

Another, perhaps more serious problem with our extended relation surfaces when we consider deleting information from the database. Suppose, for example, that Joe E. Baker is the only employee to hold the job identified as D7. If he were to leave the company and be deleted from the database represented in Figure 9-5, we would lose the information about job D7. Indeed, the only tuple containing the fact that job D7 requires a skill level of D2 is the tuple relating to Joe Baker. Thus, if we were to delete all references to Joe Baker and then return to the database to retrieve information about the job D7, we would not find the needed data.

You might argue that the ability to erase only a portion of a tuple could solve the problem, but this would in turn introduce other complications. (Should the information relating to job F5 also be retained in a partial tuple, or does this data reside elsewhere in the relation?) Moreover, the temptation to use partial tuples is a strong indication that the design of the relation is not compatible with the application.

The source of these problems is that we are trying to combine more than one concept into a single relation. As it is proposed, the extended relation contains information dealing directly with employees (name, identification number, address, Social Security number), information about the jobs available in the company (job identification, job title, department, skill code), and information regarding the relationship between employees and jobs (start date, termination date). Having made this observation, we find that our problems can be solved by redesigning the system using three relations—one for each of the preceding topics. Thus, we can keep the original relation (which we now call the EMPLOYEE relation) as it is and insert the additional information in the form of the two new relations called JOB and ASSIGNMENT, which produces the database in Figure 9-6.

Figure 9-6 An employee database consisting of three relations

EMPLOYEE relation

EmplId	Name	Address	SSNum
25X15	Joe E. Baker	33 Nowhere St.	111223333
34Y70	Cheryl H. Clark	563 Downtown Ave.	999009999
23Y34	G. Jerry Smith	1555 Circle Dr.	111005555
.	.	.	.
.	.	.	.
.	.	.	.

JOB relation

JobId	JobTitle	SkillCode	Dept
S25X	Secretary	T5	Personnel
S26Z	Secretary	T6	Accounting
F5	Floor manager	FM3	Sales
.	.	.	.
.	.	.	.
.	.	.	.

ASSIGNMENT relation

EmplId	JobID	StartDate	TermDate
23Y34	S25X	3-1-91	5-1-92
34Y70	F5	10-1-93	*
23Y34	S26Z	5-1-93	*
.	.	.	.
.	.	.	.
.	.	.	.

A database consisting of these three relations contains the pertinent information about employees through the EMPLOYEE relation, about available jobs through the JOB relation, and about job history through the ASSIGNMENT relation. Additional information is implicitly available by combining the information from different relations. For instance, we can find the departments in which a given employee has worked by first finding all the jobs that employee has held using the ASSIGNMENT relation and then finding the departments associated with those jobs by means of the JOB relation. Through processes such as this, any information that could be obtained from the single large relation can be obtained from the three smaller relations without the problems previously cited.

Unfortunately, dividing information into various relations is not always as trouble-free as in the preceding example. For instance, compare the relation in Figure

Figure 9-7 A three-attribute relation of employes, jobs, and departments

9-7, having attributes EmplId, JobTitle, and Dept, to its decomposition into two relations in Figure 9-8.

At first glance, the two-relation system may appear to contain the same information as the single-relation system, but in fact it does not. Consider, for example, the problem of finding the department in which a given employee works. This is easily done in the single-relation system by interrogating the tuple containing the employee identification number of the target employee and extracting the corresponding department. However, in the two-relation system, the desired information is not necessarily available. We can find the job title of the target employee and a department having such a job, but this does not necessarily mean that the target employee works in that particular department because several departments may have jobs with the same title.

Thus, in some cases, a relation can be decomposed into smaller relations without losing information (called a ***nonloss decomposition***), and at other times, information is lost. The classification of such characteristics has been, and still is, a concern in computer science. Such questions concerning the properties of relations have resulted in a hierarchy of relation classes called first normal form, second normal form, third normal form, and so on, with the relations in each class being more conducive to use in a database than those in the preceding class.

Relational Operations

Now that you have a basic understanding of the structure involved in the relational model, it is time to see how such an organization can be used from a programmer's point of view. We begin with a look at some operations that we may want to perform on relations.

At times we need to select certain tuples from a relation. To retrieve the information about an employee, we must select the tuple with the appropriate identification attribute value from the EMPLOYEE relation, or to obtain a list of the job titles in a certain department, we must select the tuples from the JOB relation having that department as their department attribute. The result of this selection is another

Figure 9-8 Two relations containing information about employees, jobs, and departments

EmplId	JobTitle		JobTitle	Dept

relation (another table) consisting of the tuples selected from the parent relation. (The outcome of selecting information about a particular employee results in a relation containing only one tuple from the EMPLOYEE relation. The outcome of selecting the tuples associated with a certain department probably results in several tuples from the JOB relation.)

Consequently, one operation we may want to perform on a relation is to select from one relation tuples possessing certain characteristics and to place these selected tuples in a new relation. To express this operation, we adopt the syntax

NEW ← SELECT from EMPLOYEE where EmplId = "34Y70"

The semantics of this statement is to create a new relation called NEW containing those tuples (there should be only one in this case) from the relation EMPLOYEE whose EmplId attribute equals 34Y70 (see Figure 9-9).

In contrast to the SELECT operation that extracts rows from a relation is the PROJECT operation that extracts columns. Suppose, for example, that in searching for the job titles in a certain department, we had already SELECTed the tuples from the JOB relation that pertained to the target department and placed these tuples in a new relation called NEW1. The list we are seeking is the JobTitle column within this new relation. The PROJECT operation allows us to extract this column (or columns if required) and place the result in a new relation. We express such an operation as

NEW2 ← PROJECT JobTitle from NEW1

The result is the creation of another new relation (called NEW2) that contains the single column of values from the JobTitle column of relation NEW1.

Figure 9-9 The SELECT operation

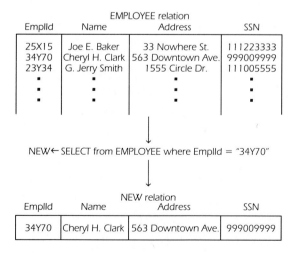

As another example of the PROJECT operation, the statement

MAIL ← PROJECT Name, Address from EMPLOYEE

can be used to obtain a listing of the names and addresses of all employees. This list is in the newly created (two-column) relation called MAIL (see Figure 9-10.)

The third operation we introduce is the JOIN operation. It is used to combine different relations into one. The JOIN of two relations produces a new relation whose attributes consist of the attributes from the original relations (see Figure 9-11). The names of these attributes are the same as those in the original relations except that each is prefixed by the relation of its origin. (If relation A containing attributes V and W is JOINed with relation B containing attributes X, Y, and Z, then the result has five attributes named A.V, A.W, B.X, B.Y, and B.Z.) This naming convention ensures that the attributes in the new relation have unique names, even though the original relations may have attribute names in common.

The tuples (rows) of the new relation are produced by concatenating tuples from the two original relations (Figure 9-11). Which tuples are actually joined to form tuples in the new relation is determined by the condition under which the JOIN is constructed. One such condition is that designated attributes have the same value. This, in fact, is the case represented in Figure 9-11, where we demonstrate the result of executing the statement

C ← JOIN A and B where A.W = B.X

Figure 9-10 The PROJECT operation

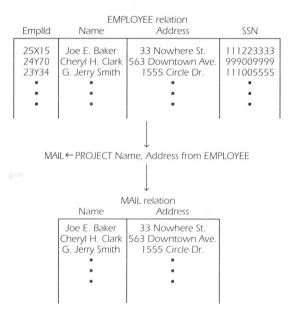

In particular, a tuple from relation A should be concatenated with a tuple from relation B if and only if the attributes W and X in the two tuples are equal. Thus, the concatenation of the tuple (r, 2) from relation A with the tuple (2, m, q) from relation B appears in the result because the value of attribute W in the first equals the value of attribute X in the second. On the other hand, the result of concatenating the tuple (r, 2) from relation A with the tuple (5, g, p) from relation B does not appear in the final relation because these tuples do not share common values in attributes W and X.

As another example, Figure 9-12 (on the following page) represents the result of executing the statement

$$C \leftarrow \text{JOIN A and B where A.W} < \text{B.X}$$

Note that the tuples in the result are exactly those in which attribute W in relation A is less than attribute X in relation B.

Let us now see how the JOIN operation can be used in the database of Figure 9-6 to obtain a listing of all employee identification numbers along with the department in which each employee works. Our first observation is that the data required are distributed over more than one relation, and thus the process of retrieving the

Figure 9-11 The JOIN operation

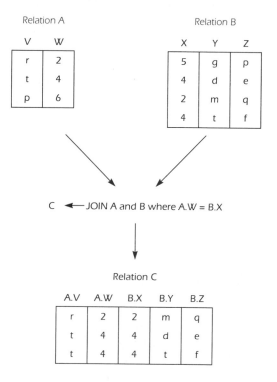

Figure 9-12 Another example of the JOIN operation

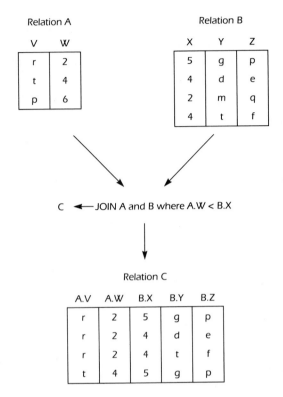

information must entail more than SELECTions and PROJECTions. In fact, the weapon we need is the statement

NEW1 ← JOIN ASSIGNMENT and JOB where ASSIGNMENT.JobId = JOB.JobId

that produces the relation NEW1, as shown in Figure 9-13. From this relation, our problem can be solved by first SELECTing those tuples in which ASSIGNMENT.TermDate equals "*" and then PROJECTing the attributes ASSIGNMENT.EmpIId and JOB.Dept. In short, the information we need can be obtained from the database in Figure 9-6 by executing the statements

NEW1 ← JOIN ASSIGNMENT and JOB
    where ASSIGNMENT.JobId = JOB.JobId
NEW2 ← SELECT from NEW1 where ASSIGNMENT.TermDate = "*"
    LIST ← PROJECT ASSIGNMENT.EmpIId, JOB.Dept from NEW2

Before closing this section, we return to the overall picture of a database system to see where the relational model fits. Remember that the data in a database are actually stored in terms of a mass storage system. To relieve the application

Figure 9-13 An application of the JOIN operation

ASSIGNMENT relation

Empl Id	Job Id	Start Date	Term Date
23Y34	S25X	3-1-81	5-1-82
34Y70	F5	10-1-83	*
25X15	S26Z	5-1-82	*
...	...	...	...

JOB relation

Job Id	Job Title	Skill Code	Dept
S25X	Secretary	T5	Personnel
S26Z	Secretary	T6	Accounting
F5	Floor manager	FM3	Sales
...	...	...	...

NEW1 ← JOIN ASSIGNMENT and JOB where ASSIGNMENT.JobId = JOB.JobId

NEW1 relation

ASSIGNMENT.EmplId	ASSIGNMENT.JobId	ASSIGNMENT.StartDate	ASSIGNMENT.TermDate	JOB.JobId	JOB.JobTitle	JOB.SkillCode	JOB.Dept
23Y34	S25X	3-1-81	5-1-82	S25X	Secretary	T5	Personnel
24Y70	F5	10-1-83	*	F5	Floor manager	FM3	Accounting
25X15	S26Z	5-1-82	*	S26Z	Secretary	T6	Sales
...	...	...	...	...	...	...	...

programmer from these concerns as well as for other reasons, a database management system is provided that allows the application software to be written in terms of a database model, such as the relational system we have been discussing. It is the duty of the database management system to accept commands in terms of the relational model and convert them into actions relative to the actual storage structure. This is done by providing a collection of subprograms that can be used within the application software. Normally, one subprogram is provided for each operation that may need to be performed on the model. Thus, a database management system using the relational model includes routines to perform the SELECT, PROJECT, and JOIN operations, which can then be called from the application software using a syntactic structure compatible with the host language. In this manner, the application software can be written as though the data were actually stored in the simple tabular form of the relational model.

Questions/Exercises

1. Answer the following questions based on the partial information given in the EMPLOYEE, JOB, and ASSIGNMENT relations in Figure 9-6:
   a. Who is the secretary in the accounting department with experience in the personnel department?
   b. Who is the floor manager in the sales department?
   c. What job does G. Jerry Smith currently hold?
2. Based on the EMPLOYEE, JOB, and ASSIGNMENT relations presented in Figure 9-6, write a sequence of relational operations to obtain a list of all job titles within the personnel department.
3. Based on the EMPLOYEE, JOB, and ASSIGNMENT relations presented in Figure 9-6, write a sequence of relational operations to obtain a list of employee names along with the employees' departments.
4. How does the relational model provide for data independence?
5. How are the different relations in a relational database tied together?

9-4 The Network Model

Another database model for consideration is the network model, which, having undergone extensive standardization efforts, probably shows more consistency among its implementations than the other models available in commercial database management systems. Most of the terminology introduced in this section is a result of this standardization effort as it originates in the proposals of the Data Base Task Group (DBTG) of the Conference on Data Systems Languages (CODASYL). Many refer to the database model presented here as the DBTG model.

The basic building block in a network database is the structure referred to as a *set*, which consists of a collection of information called the *owner* of the set and a varying number of other collections called *members* of the set. These member collections are attached to the owner via a linkage system similar to that of a linked list. Set structures are used to represent such relationships as found between a magazine (owner) and its subscribers (members), a business (owner) and its departments (members), or a course (owner) and its prerequisites (members).

In contrast to the structure of a simple linked list in which the last pointer is NIL, the last pointer in a set structure points back to the owner of the set, where the head pointer is stored. Thus, after beginning at a set's owner and visiting each member of a set, one is naturally repositioned at the owner.

The result of this set structure is a database that contains a network of paths that can be followed by the user to find the information required at the time. Such a model closely reflects the way data are actually stored in mass storage, which is, no doubt, why the network model was developed well before the more conceptual relational model.

Network Design

As in Section 9-3, we will discuss the network model in the context of constructing a database containing information about employees and their job histories within a company. Our first task is to identify the items of information about employees (name, address, identification number, Social Security number) that we want to have in the database. If we were going to store this information on paper in a traditional filing cabinet, we might at this point design a form, called the EMPLOYEE form, with a space in which to record each of these items and have the print shop print several copies of it. As each employee joined the company, we could fill out an EMPLOYEE form and file it in the cabinet.

The process when creating a network database is quite similar, except that a form is called a *group*, and it is not an organization on paper but rather an organization in a machine's mass storage. We distinguish between this mere organization (or a blank form) and a collection of data having this organization (a filled-in form) by referring to the latter as an occurrence of the group or sometimes a *group occurrence*.

At this point, our concept of the database is that of several occurrences of the EMPLOYEE group (one for each employee) scattered over mass storage. At times we will need to interrogate each of these group occurrences systematically so we link them together as a linked list, except that we adjust the last pointer to point back to the head pointer rather than being NIL. The result is an example of the set structure described earlier, with the head pointer playing the role of the set owner and the occurrences of the EMPLOYEE group being the members. This example of a set owner is a special case because it does not constitute a collection of data in the same sense as the EMPLOYEE group occurrences. However, we will see in a moment that this special case serves as an entry point to the database. For now, we note that the network model allows for such a special set owner and refers to it (or to collections of them) as *area.*

The database as designed thus far is represented in Figure 9-14. Rectangles represent group occurrences (with the group name nearby) and arrows represent the pointers. (The dots indicate that the picture is not complete.) Note that we have named the set EMPLOYEE–SET and placed this name in the diagram.

Our next step might be to incorporate each employee's job history in the database. One approach to this would be to design another group called JOB–ASSIGNMENT to contain information about a job and its assignment (job identification number, job title, skill code, department, start date, termination date), store one occurrence of this group for each job assignment made in the company, and link the occurrences with the appropriate EMPLOYEE to form several ASSIGNMENT–SETs, each consisting of an EMPLOYEE as owner and JOB–ASSIGNMENTs as members. The result would be the structure shown in Figure 9-15.

This arrangement, however, has serious disadvantages. If a job has been assigned to several employees over the years, information about it appears in the job history of each of these employees. Even worse, if we delete all the employees who have held a given job, we lose the information about that job as well.

Consequently, designers of network databases never adopt this approach. Rather, they divide the JOB–ASSIGNMENT group into two groups, called perhaps JOB and ASSIGNMENT, with the JOB group containing information relating only to the job (job identification, job title, skill code, department) and the ASSIGNMENT group containing information relating to the assignment of an employee to a job (start date, termination date). An occurrence of the JOB group is stored for each job in the company, and these group occurrences are linked together forming a set called JOB–SET owned by the area. At this point, the database has the structure shown in Figure 9-16.

With this arrangement established, EMPLOYEEs and JOBs are associated by means of the ASSIGNMENT group. This is done by allowing each EMPLOYEE to own a set of

Figure 9-14 Employees as members of a set

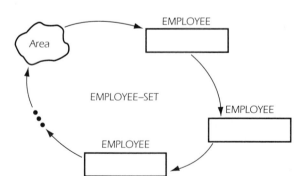

ASSIGNMENTs via a set structure we call the WORK–HISTORY set, while at the same time each JOB is given ownership to a set of ASSIGNMENTs through a set structure we call the FILLED–BY set. Each time an employee is assigned a job, a new occurrence of the ASSIGNMENT group is stored with the appropriate date information. This new group occurrence is then placed in the WORK–HISTORY set owned by the EMPLOYEE involved and in the FILLED–BY set owned by the JOB being assigned. The result is a database with the structure shown in Figure 9-17, on the following page.

Figure 9-15 Employees as members of the EMPLOYEE-SET and owners of ASSIGNMENT-SETs

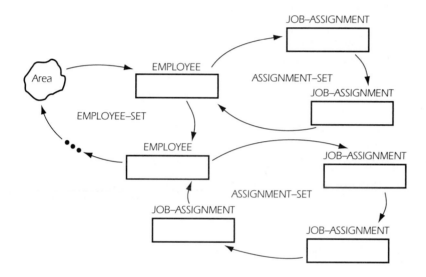

Figure 9-16 A database containing employees and jobs

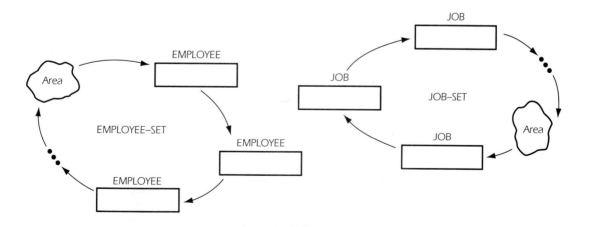

Figure 9-17 The structure of the complete database

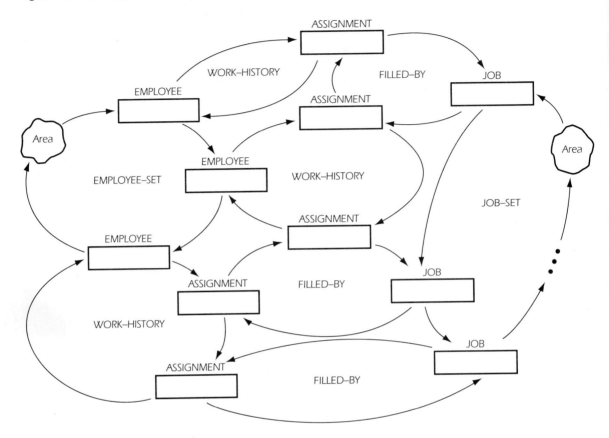

Network Operations

To gain an understanding of the operations required to interrogate a network database, consider the question of finding the job history of the second EMPLOYEE in the EMPLOYEE–SET of Figure 9-17. We begin by noting that this EMPLOYEE has held two positions in the company, as indicated by the fact that two ASSIGNMENTs are in its WORK–HISTORY set. We can also see that these JOBs are the first and second JOBs in the JOB–SET, because these are the JOBs that own those ASSIGNMENTs also owned by the target EMPLOYEE. Intuitively, we find this information by traversing the WORK–HISTORY set owned by the EMPLOYEE in question while stopping at each member to find the owner of that corresponding FILLED–BY set. This suggests that the operations we need to interrogate a network database include the ability to move to the next entry in a set and the ability to move directly to the owner of a set.

These operations are traditionally implemented in the form of two commands called FIND–NEXT and FIND–OWNER. The first is used to advance one entry in the identified set. In particular, we use the syntax

FIND–NEXT *set name*

where in place of *set name* we insert the actual name of the set in question.

The second operation is used to advance directly to the owner of the target set. We use the syntax

FIND–OWNER *set name*

where again an actual name of a set takes the place of *set name.*

To understand how these two commands can actually be used to maneuver within a database, it is important to realize that both commands request action relative to a previously established position. A request to find the next entry in a set implies the existence of a current entry (which may be the owner or a member). Moreover, a request to find the owner of a set requires more specification than just the set name. For example, the command FIND–OWNER FILLED–BY alone is ambiguous in the database of Figure 9-17, because there are several instances of the FILLED–BY set.

To resolve these problems, one's position in a database is initially considered to be at the areas that we recognized earlier as being special examples of set owners. Thus, any initial request is interpreted relative to this position. Later, any command referring to a set is interpreted relative to the last position established in a set occurrence of that name.

To demonstrate these ideas, let us use the FIND–NEXT and FIND–OWNER commands to retrieve the job history of the second employee in the example database of Figure 9-17. We begin with our current position established at the areas in the database, as shown by the bold arrows in Figure 9-18, on the following page.

From this starting configuration, we see that executing the sequence

FIND–NEXT EMPLOYEE–SET
FIND–NEXT EMPLOYEE–SET

moves our position in the EMPLOYEE–SET to the second EMPLOYEE. Having done this, our position within the network is as shown in Figure 9-19, on the following page. Note that the current EMPLOYEE group occurrence, being associated with a WORK–HISTORY set, provides a reference from which motion in this latter set can now be made. Thus, we can find the first ASSIGNMENT for this EMPLOYEE by executing the command

FIND–NEXT WORK–HISTORY

which shifts our reference positions in the database to the configuration in Figure 9-20, on p. 359.

At this point, the dates stored in the current ASSIGNMENT group occurrence are available to us, but the information about the job itself is stored in the JOB group

Figure 9-18

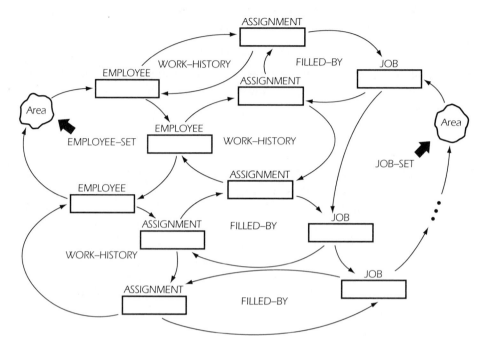

Figure 9-19

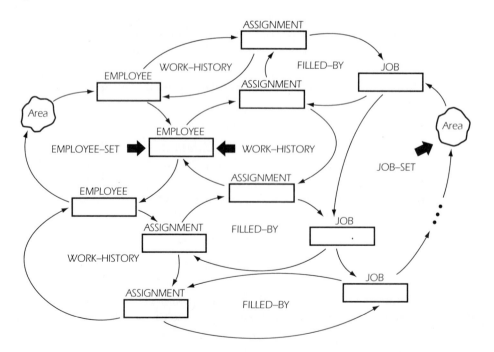

Figure 9-20

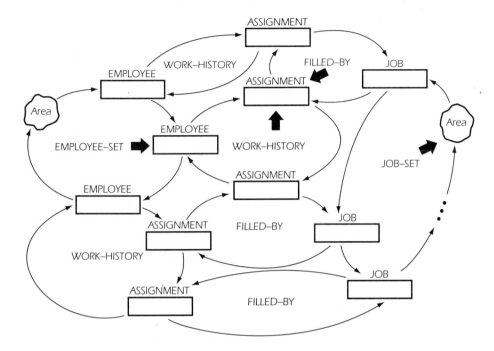

occurrence owning the current ASSIGNMENT. To reach this JOB, we can use the command

FIND–OWNER FILLED–BY

which establishes a position at the owner of the current FILLED–BY set. (Note that this command would have been ambiguous before we reached an ASSIGNMENT group occurrence.) Following this command, our situation is as in Figure 9-21 on page 360.

The next step is to move on to the next ASSIGNMENT owned by the EMPLOYEE in question. You may have noticed that, as we shift attention from one set to another, we leave bold arrows in the diagrams marking the last entry visited in each type of set. These arrows mark our current position in each of the appropriate sets. Consequently, we can move to the next ASSIGNMENT owned by the EMPLOYEE in question with the command

FIND–NEXT WORK–HISTORY

which produces the situation represented by Figure 9-22 on page 360.

It is important to note that the new ASSIGNMENT is a member of another FILLED–BY set, and moving to it has shifted our position from the old FILLED–BY set to the new one. Consequently, executing the command

FIND–OWNER FILLED–BY

Figure 9-21

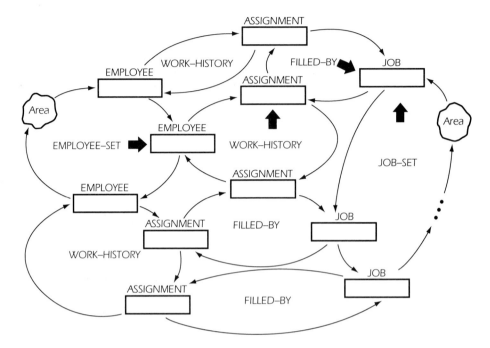

Figure 9-22

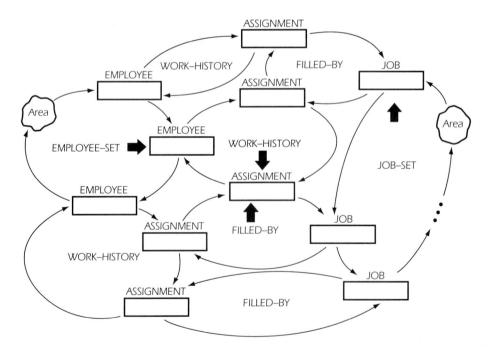

Figure 9-23

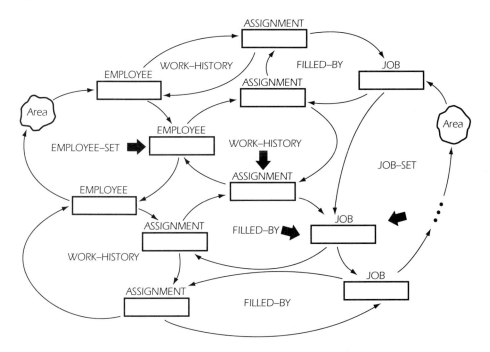

leads us to the JOB that owns this other FILLED–BY set (Figure 9-23). At this point, we can extract information about the second and final job in the target employee's job history. (We can detect that this is the final job by executing the instruction

FIND–NEXT WORK–HISTORY

and discovering that we are back to the owner of the WORK–HISTORY set.)

In closing, we should note that operations such as FIND–NEXT and FIND–OWNER are provided as a part of a network database management system in the form of subprograms that can be called by the application software when needed. Consequently, the application programmer is allowed to pretend that the data in the database are actually stored in the network structure rather than being scattered over the tracks of a disk.

Questions/Exercises

1. How does retrieving information from a set in a network database compare with reading records from a sequential file?
2. Write a sequence of steps to direct the printing of the names of those employees who have held the second job represented in the database of Figure 9-17.

3. Could the first operation after opening the database of Figure 9-17 be FIND–NEXT WORK–HISTORY?

4. If information stored in the middle of a large network database is needed, is it necessary to start from the area and "walk" all the way into the structure using FIND–NEXT and FIND–OWNER commands?

5. Would you expect an airline representative at the airport counter to be able to tell you whether the database being used for reservations is based on either the relational or network model?

9-5   Object-Oriented Databases

One of the newer areas in database research involves applying the object-oriented paradigm to the construction of a database, resulting in what is called an **object-oriented database.** The motivation behind this movement is at least fourfold. First, data independence can be achieved by means of encapsulation. Second, the concepts of classes and inheritance appear ready-made for describing schemas and subschemas of databases. Third, the image of a database consisting of intelligent data objects that can answer questions themselves rather than being interrogated by a supervisory program is inviting. Fourth, early research indicates that the object-oriented approach may overcome some of the restrictions inherent in other database models.[1]

Let us consider an object-oriented implementation of the employee database from the previous sections. We have three classes (types of objects): EMPLOYEE, JOB, and ASSIGNMENT. An object from the EMPLOYEE class contains storage structures for such entries as EmpId, Name, Address, and SSNum; an object from the class JOB contains storage structures for the items JobId, JobTitle, SkillCode, and Dept; and each object from the class ASSIGNMENT contains structures for StartDate and TermDate.

In addition to these storage structures, each object encompasses a collection of methods (internal routines) defining how that object responds to requests for information and commands to update data. For example, each object from the class EMPLOYEE might have a method for reporting that employee's job history and perhaps a method for changing that employee's job assignment. Likewise, each object from the JOB class might have a method for reporting those employees who have held that

---

[1]For example, if a person's entire name is stored as a single attribute in a relational database, then inquiries regarding only last names are awkward. However, if the name is stored as three separate attributes (FirstName, MiddleName, LastName), then it becomes awkward to deal with people who do not have exactly three names. An object, however, can store a person's name in an internal linked list and have the ability to report the entire name as one long string, only the last name, or even how many names the person has.

particular job. Retrieving an employee's job history would not require a procedure involving such operators as SELECT, PROJECT, or FIND–NEXT. Instead, we would merely ask the appropriate employee object to report its job history.

For the methods within objects to perform their tasks in an efficient manner, some form of linkage between different objects must be maintained. How, for example, does an object from the EMPLOYEE class know which objects from the ASSIGNMENT class represent assignments pertaining to its employee?

One approach toward providing this linkage is to extend the composition of objects beyond that found in traditional object-oriented environments. Traditional objects are composed of data structures and methods. For the purposes of constructing an object-oriented database, this composition can be extended to include a third kind of component, a list of other objects. Objects in such a system therefore consist of data structures, methods, and lists of objects.

If such an approach is applied to our employee database, an object from the class EMPLOYEE can encompass and maintain a list of those objects from the class ASSIGNMENT that relate to the pertinent employee. Methods within the object then can use this list when responding to inquiries about the object's job history. The result is a database consisting of objects that maintain records about the existence of other objects and are, therefore, able to identify the appropriate objects and communicate with them when responding to requests for information.

Questions/Exercises

1. What methods can be contained in an instance of an object from the ASSIGNMENT class in the employee database discussed in this section?
2. Identify some classes, as well as some of their internal characteristics, that can be used in an object-oriented database dealing with a warehouse inventory.
3. Identify an advantage that an object-oriented database can have over a relational database.

9-6   Concurrency Control

We turn now to the problem of coordinating access to a database in a multiuser environment.

Problems in Concurrency Control

Imagine a database residing on one of the machines in a computer network. From there, the database receives requests generated by the users working on other machines in the network. (The machine holding the database is often called a *server,* while the others are called *clients.*) Each request is for the execution of a single transaction, examples of which may include transferring $100 from one checking account to another, making a deposit of $200 to a savings account, and computing the sum of all overdue loans.

As long as these requests are spaced with adequate time intervals between them, the database management system has no problems with coordinating the required activities; it merely executes each of the transactions as they are received. But if several users make requests at the same time, it is likely that requests will begin to pile up in a queue.

One approach to avoiding this log jam is to interweave the steps from different transactions so that several requests can be served at the same time. Indeed, if two transactions involve withdrawals from different accounts, the system can retrieve the balance of the first account and then request the balance of the other to be read from disk storage while the new balance of the original account is being calculated.

Of course, we cannot always allow transactions to be interwoven in an arbitrary fashion. Suppose, for example, two separate transactions request the withdrawal of $100 from the same account, which has an initial balance of $400. The correct result should be a balance of $200, but if the steps in the transactions (retrieve the original balance, subtract $100, and store the new balance) are interwoven, the erroneous balance of $300 is obtained. (The database starts the first transaction by retrieving the initial balance, and then, while computing the new balance, it starts the other transaction by again retrieving the initial balance. The result is that each transaction is applied to a balance of $400, and thus the final balance is recorded as $300 rather than $200.)

To avoid such erroneous results, the database management system needs a software package, called a scheduler, to control the concurrent execution of transactions. Such a scheduler allows the steps of different transactions to be interwoven when it is safe to do so, but delays the execution of other transactions when concurrent execution causes conflicts. Part of this scheduler, then, must include an algorithm for determining whether or not a certain interweaving of transactions is safe.

To develop the basics for such an algorithm, let us denote the step of reading a single item x from the database by $R(x)$ and writing the item x as $W(x)$. Then, we can summarize the database activity within the transaction for withdrawing $100 from an account as follows:

$$R(x) \; W(x)$$

where x represents the data item within the database containing the balance of the target account. In other words, the transaction must first read the value of x and later write a value to x.

With this notation, we can represent a possible schedule for transactions T1 and T2 as follows:

```
T1:   R(x)          R(y)   W(y)
T2:          R(z)                W(z)
```

In particular, T1 consists of the steps R*(x)*, R*(y)*, and W*(y)*; T2 consists of R*(z)* and W*(z)*; and these steps are interwoven to form the sequence:

> T1 reads item *x*
> T2 reads item *z*
> T1 reads item *y*
> T1 writes item *y*
> T2 writes item *z*

Clearly, this schedule represents a safe interweaving of steps because the transactions deal with different data items. However, as we have seen in the case of making withdrawals from a common account, the schedule

```
T3:   R(x)          W(x)
T4:          R(x)           W(x)
```

is not safe.

Conflict Serializable Schedules

Now consider the schedule

```
T5:                              R(x)   W(x)
T6:   R(x)          W(x)                        W(y)
T7:          R(x)          W(y)
```

We might be inclined to say that it is not safe because it interweaves read and write steps involving the same data items. However, this conclusion is incorrect. The schedule is, in fact, safe.

To justify this claim, we first define two steps in different transactions to be in conflict if they involve the same data item and at least one of the steps is a write step. [The step R*(x)* in T7 in the previous schedule conflicts with step W*(x)* in T6 as well as with W*(x)* in T5. Moreover, W*(x)* in T6 conflicts with the step W*(x)* in T5.] In turn, two schedules for the same transaction are **conflict equivalent** if each pair of conflicting steps in one schedule occurs in the same order as in the other schedule. Thus, if we allow the step R*(x)* in T5 of the above schedule to precede W*(y)* in T7, we obtain the schedule

```
T5:                        R(x)          W(x)
T6:   R(x)          W(x)                        W(y)
T7:          R(x)                  W(y)
```

which is conflict equivalent to the original one because we have not reversed the order of any conflicting steps. On the other hand, we cannot allow W*(x)* in T6 to precede R*(x)* in T7 and maintain conflict equivalence.

Note that two conflict equivalent schedules produce the same effect on a database. (The fact that they are conflict equivalent means that any interaction between the transactions in one schedule must be mirrored in the other schedule.) Thus, if a transaction schedule is conflict equivalent to a schedule that is known to be safe, the original schedule itself must be safe.

Moreover, we know that a schedule in which each transaction is allowed to execute entirely before another transaction is permitted to start is always safe. Such a schedule is called a *serial schedule.* Thus, serial schedules can serve as test schedules. In particular, any schedule that is conflict equivalent to a serial schedule is safe. This type of schedule is called a *conflict serializable schedule.*

Now compare the pattern of conflicting steps of our original schedule for T5, T6, and T7 to those in the following serial schedule:

> T5:   R*(x)*   W*(x)*
> T6:   R*(x)*   W*(x)*   W*(y)*
> T7:   R*(x)*   W*(y)*

As seen in Figure 9-24, these patterns are identical. Hence, the original schedule is conflict serializable and therefore represents a safe interweaving of steps.

Testing for Conflict Serializability

We might suspect that a scheduler for a multiuser database should allow conflict serializable schedules to proceed but should block schedules that are not conflict serializable. But how can a scheduler test a potential schedule for conflict serializability?

Figure 9-24 Our original schedule and a conflict equivalent serial schedule

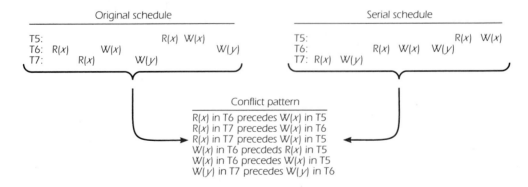

Figure 9-25 *The conflict graph for the schedules in Figure 9-24*

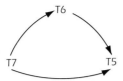

Based on the conflict pattern of a transaction schedule, we can construct what is known as the schedule's conflict graph. This graph is obtained by representing each transaction in the schedule by a single point and then, for each pair of transactions containing conflicting steps, drawing an arrow from the point representing one transaction to the other if the first transaction has a step preceding (in time) a conflicting step in the other transaction. For example, the transaction graph for the preceding schedule appears in Figure 9-25. The arrow from T7 to T5 represents the fact that a step in T7 [namely R(x)] conflicts with and precedes a step in T5 [namely W(x)]. Likewise, the arrow from T7 to T6 reflects the fact that some step in T7 occurs before a conflicting step in T6.

Given a schedule's conflict graph, a simple test determines if the schedule is serializable. One merely checks that no loops appear in the graph. Indeed, the absence of loops indicates that there is a serial arrangement of the transactions in which all conflicts occur in the same order as the original schedule. For example, the graph in Figure 9-25 indicates that the underlying schedule is conflict equivalent to the serial schedule in which the transactions are executed in the order T7, T6, and T5.

In contrast, the conflict graph of the schedule

```
T5:                              R(x)   W(x)
T6:   R(x)          W(x)   W(y)
T7:          R(x)                              W(y)
```

is shown in Figure 9-26. The arrows in this graph readily show that any conflict equivalent schedule must have transaction T7 preceding T6 and T6 preceding T7,

Figure 9-26 *The conflict pattern of a transaction schedule and that schedule's conflict graph*

Conflict pattern	Conflict graph
R(x) in T6 precedes W(x) in T5 R(x) in T7 precedes W(x) in T6 W(x) in T6 precdeds R(x) in T5 W(x) in T6 precedes W(x) in T5 W(y) in T6 precedes W(y) in T7	(graph: T7 → T6 → T5, with loop between T7 and T6)

which is a set of restrictions that no serial schedule can meet. Thus, the schedule above is not conflict serializable and is not considered safe for execution.

In short, we can determine that a given schedule of interwoven transactions is safe by checking to see if it is conflict serializable. But this is merely the task of determining if loops occur in the schedule's conflict graph, a process that turns out to be easily testable. In turn, a scheduler for a multiuser database can quickly test potential transaction schedules for conflict serializability, allowing those producing affirmative results to proceed while delaying other transactions until they can be executed safely.

Questions/Exercises

1. Give an example of two actual transactions T1 and T2 of the form $R(x)$ $R(y)$ $W(x)$ $W(y)$ and $R(x)$ $R(y)$ $W(z)$, respectively. Then, explain what can go wrong in the case of those transactions if they are executed according to the following schedule:

   T1: $R(x)$ $R(y)$ $W(x)$ $W(y)$
   T2: $R(x)$ $R(y)$ $W(z)$

2. Which of the following schedules are conflict serializable?

   a. T1: $R(x)$ $W(x)$
      T2: $R(x)$ $W(y)$

   b. T1: $R(x)$ $R(y)$ $W(x)$ $W(y)$
      T2: $R(x)$ $W(x)$

   c. T1: $R(x)$ $W(x)$
      T2: $R(x)$ $W(y)$
      T3: $R(x)$ $W(y)$

3. Draw the conflict graph for each of the schedules in exercise 2.

Chapter 9 Review Problems

1. Summarize the distinction between a simple file and a database.

2. What is meant by data independence?

3. What is the role of a database management system in the layered approach to a database implementation?

4. What is the difference between a schema and a subschema?

5. Identify two benefits of separating application-software from the database management system.

6. Identify the level within a database system (end user, programmer of application software, designer of the database management system software) at which each of the following concerns or activities occur:

   a. How should the data be stored on a disk to maximize efficiency?

b. Is there a vacancy on flight 243?

c. Should the owner of the set be found through consecutive FIND–NEXT commands or should a FIND–OWNER be used?

d. Should set owners be stored close to the set members on the disk?

e. Could a relation be stored as a sequential file?

f. How many times should a user be allowed to mistype a password before the conversation is terminated?

g. Should the user/machine interface be menu driven?

h. How can the PROJECT operation be implemented?

i. How many packages of sardines were accidentally shipped without ice?

7. For each of the database models we have discussed, draw a diagram representing the conceptual image of the following information about airlines, flights (for a particular day), and passengers:

Airlines: Clear Sky, Long Hop, and Tree Top
Flights for Clear Sky: CS205, CS37, and CS102
Flights for Long Hop: LH67 and LH89
Flights for Tree Top: TT331 and TT809
Smith has reservations on CS205 (seat 12B), CS37 (seat 18C), and LH89 (seat 14A).
Baker has reservations on CS37 (seat 18B) and LH89 (seat 14B).
Clark has reservations on LH67 (seat 5A) and TT331 (seat 4B).

8. In terms of the following relations, what is the appearance of the relation RESULT after executing each of these instructions:

X relation

U	V	W
A	Z	5
B	D	3
C	Q	5

Y relation

R	S
3	J
4	K

a. RESULT ← PROJECT W from X
b. RESULT ← SELECT from X where W = 5
c. RESULT ← PROJECT S from Y
d. RESULT ← JOIN X and Y where X.W ≥ Y.R

9. Using the commands SELECT, PROJECT, and JOIN, write a sequence of instructions to answer each of the following questions about parts and their manufacturers in terms of the database shown below:

PART relation

PartName	Weight
Bolt 2X	1
Bolt 2Z	1.5
Nut V5	0.5

MANUFACTURER relation

CompanyName	PartName	Cost
Company X	Bolt 2Z	.03
Company X	Nut V5	.01
Company Y	Bolt 2X	.02
Company Y	Nut V5	.01
Company Y	Bolt 2Z	.04
Company Z	Nut V5	.01

a. Which companies make Bolt 2Z?

b. Obtain a list of the parts made by Company X along with each part's cost.

c. What companies make a part with weight 1?

10. What redundancy is introduced if the information in the PART and MANUFACTURER relations in problem 9 are combined into one single relation?

11. Using commands such as SELECT, PROJECT, and JOIN, write sequences to answer the following questions about the information in the EMPLOYEE, JOB, and ASSIGNMENT relations in Figure 9-6:

a. Obtain a list of the names and addresses of the company's employees.

b. Obtain a list of the names and addresses of those who have worked or are working in the personnel department.

c. Obtain a list of the names and addresses of those who are working in the personnel department.

12. Design a relational database containing information about publishers, magazines, and subscribers, in which the relationships between these entities are represented by the following entity-relationship diagram.

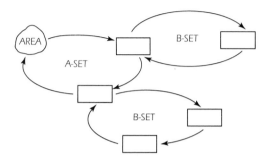

13. Solve the previous problem using the network model.

14. Design a relational database containing information about parts, suppliers, and customers. Each part may be supplied by several suppliers and ordered by many customers. Each supplier may supply many parts and have many customers. Each customer may order many parts from many suppliers; in fact, the same part may be ordered from more than one supplier.

15. Solve the previous problem using the network model.

16. What changes are required in the design of the relational database shown in Figure 9-6 to allow one to obtain a list of all employees with the last name Smith using only the SELECT operation?

17. What inconvenience may arise because of our decision to combine the month, day, and year into a single attribute in the relational database in Figure 9-6?

18. Write a sequence of instructions (using the operations SELECT, PROJECT, and JOIN) to retrieve the JobId, StartDate, and TermDate for each job in the accounting department from the relational database described in Figure 9-6.

19. Write a sequence of instructions (using the operations SELECT, PROJECT, and JOIN) to retrieve the Name, Address, JobTitle, and Dept of every current employee from the relational database described in Figure 9-6.

20. Write a sequence of instructions (using the operations SELECT, PROJECT, and JOIN) to retrieve the Name and JobTitle of each current employee from the relational database described in Figure 9-6.

21. What is the difference in the information supplied by the single relation

Name	Department	TelephoneNumber
Jones	Sales	111-2222
Smith	Sales	111-3333
Baker	Personnel	111-4444

and the two relations

Name	Department
Jones	Sales
Smith	Sales
Baker	Personnel

Department	TelephoneNumber
Sales	111-2222
Sales	111-3333
Personnel	111-4444

22. In terms of the relational model, design a database containing information about automobile parts and their subparts. Be sure to allow for the fact that one part may contain smaller parts and at the same time be contained in still larger parts.

23. Based on the database represented in Figure 9-6, state the question that is answered by the following program segment:

TEMP ← SELECT from ASSIGNMENT
      where TermDate = "*"
RESULT ← PROJECT JobId, StartDate from TEMP

24. Based on the database represented in Figure 9-6, state the question that is answered by the following program segment:

```
TEMP1 ← JOIN EMPLOYEE and ASSIGNMENT
        where EMPLOYEE.EmplId =
        ASSIGNMENT.EmplId
TEMP2 ← SELECT from TEMP1
        where TermDate = "*"
RESULT ← PROJECT Name, StartDate
        from TEMP2
```

25. Based on the database represented in Figure 9-6, state the question that is answered by the following program segment:

```
TEMP1 ← JOIN EMPLOYEE and JOB
        where EMPLOYEE.EmplId =
        JOB.EmplId
TEMP2 ← SELECT from TEMP1
        where Dept = "SALES"
RESULT ← PROJECT Name from TEMP2
```

26. Redesign the database in problem 22 using the network model.

27. In the setting of the network database model, what is the difference between the commands FIND–NEXT and FIND–OWNER?

28. In the following network database, what ambiguity exists if we start a query with the command FIND–NEXT B–SET:

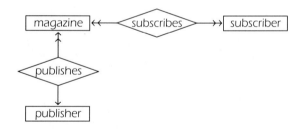

29. Draw a diagram representing the current positions in the database of problem 28 after executing the following sequence of commands:

```
FIND–NEXT A–SET
FIND–NEXT B–SET
FIND–NEXT A–SET
FIND–NEXT B–SET
```

30. If we start from the areas in the employee/job database of Figure 9-17 and execute the following sequence of commands

```
FIND–NEXT EMPLOYEE–SET
FIND–NEXT EMPLOYEE–SET
FIND–NEXT EMPLOYEE–SET
FIND–NEXT WORK–HISTORY
FIND–OWNER FILLED–BY
```

which JOB group occurrence is the current one?

31. If we start from the areas in the employee/job database of Figure 9-17 and execute the following sequence of commands

```
FIND–NEXT JOB–SET
FIND–NEXT FILLED–BY
FIND–OWNER WORK–HISTORY
FIND–NEXT EMPLOYEE–SET
```

which EMPLOYEE group occurrence is the current one?

32. Using the commands FIND–NEXT and FIND–OWNER, write a sequence of instructions that lead to the EMPLOYEEs who have held the second JOB in the employee/job database of Figure 9-17.

33. Based on the database represented in Figure 9-17, state the question that is answered by the following program segment:

```
repeat (FIND–NEXT JOB
        print job identification)
until (there are no more jobs)
```

34. Based on the database represented in Figure 9-17, state the question that is answered by the following program segment:

```
repeat FIND–NEXT JOB
    until (name = "plant supervisor")
repeat (FIND–NEXT FILLED–BY
        FIND–OWNER WORK–HISTORY
        print employee name)
until (there are no more assignments)
```

35. Based on the database represented in Figure 9-17, state the question that is answered by the following program segment:

```
repeat FIND–NEXT EMPLOYEE
    until (name = "John Doe")
repeat (FIND–NEXT WORK–HISTORY
        FIND–OWNER FILLED–BY
        print job identification)
until (there are no more assignments)
```

36. Which of the following schedules are conflict serializable?

```
a. T1:  R(x)           W(x)
   T2:        R(x)  W(x)

b. T1:  R(x)       W(x)
   T2:        R(x)        W(x)
```

c. T1:   R(x)   W(x)
   T2:   R(x)   R(y)   W(y)
   T3:   R(x)   W(y)

37. Draw the conflict graph for the following schedule:

   T1:   R(x)   W(x)
   T2:   R(y)   W(y)
   T3:   R(x)   W(x)
   T4:   R(y)   W(y)

38. Which of the following conflict graphs correspond to conflict serializable schedules?

a.

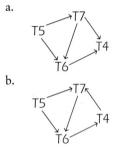

b.

39. List all the schedules that can be constructed from the transitions T1, consisting of R(x) W(x), and T2, consisting of R(x) W(x). Which ones are conflict serializable?

40. What incorrect information is generated by the following schedule of transactions T1 and T2?

    T1 is designed to compute the sum of accounts A and B; T2 is designed to transfer $100 from account A to account B. T1 begins by retrieving the balance of account A; then, T2 performs its transfer; and finally, T1 retrieves the balance of account B and reports the sum of the values it has retrieved.

41. Show that the schedule in the preceding problem is not conflict serializable.

d.

e.

Problems for the Programmer

1. Using sequential files to represent relations with each record representing one tuple, write a system of subprograms to perform the operations of SELECT, PROJECT, and JOIN appearing in the relational model.

2. Using the routines developed in programming problem 1, write a program to answer a specific question about the information in the database. What part of this complete software system is classified as part of a database management system? What part is classified as application software?

3. Write an application software package that understands a limited number of questions (from a user) about the information in the network employee database of Figure 9-17 and activates the appropriate sequence of FIND–NEXT and FIND–OWNER commands to generate the answer to each. Use stubs for the FIND–NEXT and FIND–OWNER routines.

4. Write a program to test transaction schedules for conflict serializability.

Additional Reading

Bernstein, P. A., Hadzilacos, V., and Goodman, N. *Concurrency Control and Recovery in Database Systems.* Reading, Mass.: Addison-Wesley, 1987.

Cattell, R. G. G. *Object Data Management.* Reading, Mass.: Addison-Wesley, 1991.

Date, C. J. *An Introduction to Database Systems,* 5th ed. Reading, Mass.: Addison-Wesley, 1990.

Desai, B. C. *An Introduction to Database Systems.* St. Paul, Minn.: West, 1990.

Elmasri, R., and Navathe, S. B. *Fundamentals of Database Systems*, 2nd ed., Redwood City, Calif.: Benjamin/Cummings, 1994.

Korth, H. F., and Silberschatz, A. *Database System Concepts.* New York: McGraw-Hill, 1986.

Loomis, M. E. S. *The Database Book.* New York: Macmillan, 1987.

Papadimitriou, C. *The Theory of Database Concurrency Control.* Rockville, Md.: Computer Science Press, 1986.

Teorey, T. J. *Database Modeling and Design: An Entity-Relationship Approach.* San Mateo, Calif.: Morgan Kaufmann, 1990.

Ullman, J. D. *Principles of Database and Knowledge-Base Systems,* Rockville, Md.: Computer Science Press, 1988.

PART FOUR

THE POTENTIAL OF ALGORITHMIC MACHINES

In Part Four, we conclude our introduction to computer science by considering the potential of algorithmic machines. We begin by investigating the subject of artificial intelligence in Chapter 10. There we find that major advances are being made in the production of machines that mimic the activities of humans and thus project the image of intelligent behavior. This raises the question as to what, if any, are the limitations of machines.

We address this question in Chapter 11, where we study the theory of computation. There we learn that there are, in fact, bounds on the tasks that algorithmic machines can accomplish. Moreover, we find that issues of practicality limit these tasks even further. That is, we find that there are tasks that, although within the theoretical powers of computers, would require so much time that they are infeasible in reality, even with advances in technology.

CHAPTER TEN

ARTIFICIAL INTELLIGENCE

A major goal among computer scientists is the development of machines that communicate with their environments through traditionally human sensory means and proceed intelligently without human intervention. Such a goal often requires that the machine "understand," or perceive, the input received and be able to draw conclusions through some form of a reasoning process.

Both perception and reasoning fall within the category of common-sense activities that, although natural for the human mind, are apparently quite difficult for machines. The result is that the area of research associated with this pursuit, known as artificial intelligence, is still in its infancy when compared to its goals and expectations. This is not to say that successes have not been achieved. The efforts of many have resulted in well-founded theories and techniques.

In this chapter, we look at some of these theories in the context of designing a puzzle-solving machine that possesses elementary perception and reasoning abilities. As a side effect, we have an opportunity to see how such concepts as trees and stacks are used as tools in actual applications.

10–1 Some Philosophical Issues

Perhaps one of the more difficult tasks for a beginner in computer science involves the separation of science fiction from science, and nowhere is this distinction more clouded than in the area of artificial intelligence. Although the major thrust behind the subject is merely to build machines that are able to forge ahead in uncontrolled environments without relying on human backup (and thus better serve the human race), the popular press would have us believe that computer scientists are striving to build mechanical humans.[1] Of course, the aura of mystery is only enhanced by calling the subject artificial intelligence. Let us begin then by considering the distinction between today's algorithmic machines and human minds.

Machines Versus Humans

Although the computer is often personified, an important distinction exists between its properties and the properties of the human mind. Algorithmic machines are designed to perform precisely defined tasks with speed and accuracy, and they do this extremely well; however, machines are not gifted with common sense. When faced with a situation not foreseen by the programmer, a machine's performance is likely to deteriorate rapidly. The human mind, although often floundering on complex computations, is capable of understanding and reasoning. Thus, whereas a machine might outperform a human in computing solutions to problems in nuclear physics, the human is much more likely to understand the problem and to comprehend the meaning of the results.

---

[1]There are those, of course, who dream of building models of the human mind. Early researchers such as John von Neumann often thought along these lines and even discussed the components of early machines in terms of organs. However, major breakthroughs must still be made before such dreams have a chance of becoming realities.

We see, then, that if we are to build machines that are able to continue when faced with unforeseen or unpredictable situations, the machines must become more humanlike in the sense that they must possess (or at least simulate) the ability to reason. Recognizing this requirement, computer scientists have turned to psychologists and their models of the human mind in hopes of finding principles that can be applied to the construction of more flexible machines and programs. The result is that it is often difficult to distinguish between the research of a psychologist and that of a computer scientist. The distinction is not in what they do but rather in their goals. The psychologist is trying to learn more about the human mind; the computer scientist is trying to build more useful machines.

Performance Versus Simulation

Suppose that a mathematician and a psychologist each embark independently on projects to develop a poker-playing program. The mathematician would most likely design a program based on the foundations of probability and statistics. The result would be a program that would play the odds, bluff at random, show no emotion, and consequently maximize its chances of winning. The psychologist, on the other hand, would probably develop a program based on theories of human thought and behavior. The project might even result in the production of several different programs; one might play aggressively while another might be easily intimidated. In contrast to the mathematician's program, the psychologist's program might become "emotionally involved" in the game and lose everything it owned.

Reconsidering, we hypothesize that the mathematician's main concern while developing the program would be the program's final performance. Such an approach is said to be *performance oriented.* In contrast, the psychologist would be more interested in understanding the processes of natural intelligence; thus, the project would be approached as an opportunity to test theories by building computer models based on those theories. From this point of view, the development of the "intelligent" program is actually a side effect of another pursuit—progress in understanding human thought and behavior. This approach is said to be *simulation oriented.*

Both approaches are sound and make significant contributions to the field of artificial intelligence. However, they also raise elusive philosophical questions within the discipline. Consider, for example, the discussion that might ensue if a group is asked to decide if the programs possess intelligence and if so which program is more intelligent. (Is intelligence measured by the ability to win or the ability to be humanlike?)

Intelligence as an Interior Characteristic

The difficulty in determining whether or not a program possesses intelligence is rooted in the difficulty of distinguishing between the mere appearance of intelligence and its actual existence. In the final analysis, intelligence is an interior characteristic whose existence is detected from the outside only indirectly in the context of a stimulus/reaction dialogue.

This illusive nature of intelligence was recognized by Alan Turing in 1950 when he proposed a test (now known as the *Turing test*) for detecting intelligence within a machine. Turing's proposal was to allow a human, whom we call the interrogator, to communicate with a test subject by means of a typewriter system, without being told whether the test subject was a human or a machine. In this environment, a machine would be declared intelligent in the event that the interrogator was not able to distinguish it from a human. As yet, machines have not been able to pass the Turing test, although surprising results have been achieved.

A well-known example arose as a result of the program DOCTOR (a version of the more general system called ELIZA) developed by Joseph Weizenbaum in the mid-1960s. This interactive program was designed to project the image of a Rogerian analyst conducting a psychological interview; the computer played the role of analyst while the user played the patient. Internally, all that DOCTOR did was restructure the statements made by the patient according to some well-defined rules and direct them back to the terminal screen. For example, in response to a statement such as "I am tired today," DOCTOR might have replied with "Why do you think you're tired today?" If DOCTOR was unable to recognize the sentence structure, it merely responded with something like "Go on" or "That's very interesting."

Weizenbaum's purpose in developing DOCTOR dealt with the study of natural language communication. From this point of view, the subject of psychotherapy played the secondary role of providing an environment (or a domain of discourse) in which the program could function. To Weizenbaum's dismay, however, several psychologists proposed using the program for actual psychotherapy. (The Rogerian thesis is that the patient, not the analyst, should lead the discussion during the therapeutic session, and thus, they argued, a computer could possibly conduct a discussion as well as a therapist could.) Moreover, DOCTOR projected the image of comprehension so strongly that many who "communicated" with it found themselves relating intimate thoughts and feelings and, in many cases, actually becoming subservient to the machine's question-and-answer dialogue. The result was that moral, as well as technical, issues were raised.

An "Intelligent" Machine

With such philosophical questions residing at the very foundation of artificial intelligence, it is not surprising that much of the subject is accompanied by an aura of mystery often exploited by both the news media and fiction writers. In an effort to get our feet firmly on the ground, let us consider the design of a machine having elementary, "intelligence" properties.

Our machine takes the form of a metal box equipped with a gripper, a video camera, and a finger with a rubber end so that it does not slip when pushing something (see Figure 10-1).

Figure 10-1 Our puzzle-solving machine

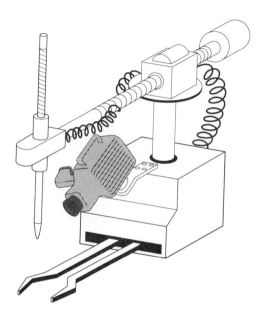

Imagine such a machine next to a table on which an 8-puzzle is placed. This is a puzzle consisting of eight square tiles labeled 1 through 8 mounted in a frame capable of holding a total of nine such tiles in three rows and three columns. Thus, among the tiles in the frame is a vacancy into which any of the adjacent tiles can be pushed. The tiles are currently arranged as shown in Figure 10-2.

We begin by picking up the puzzle and rearranging it by repeatedly pushing arbitrarily chosen tiles into the vacancy. We then turn on the machine, and the gripper begins to open and close as if asking for the puzzle. We place the puzzle in the gripper, and the gripper closes on the puzzle. After a short time the finger lowers and begins pushing the tiles around in the frame (in an orderly fashion) until they are back in their original order. At this point the machine places the puzzle back on the table and turns

Figure 10-2 The 8-puzzle in its solved configuration

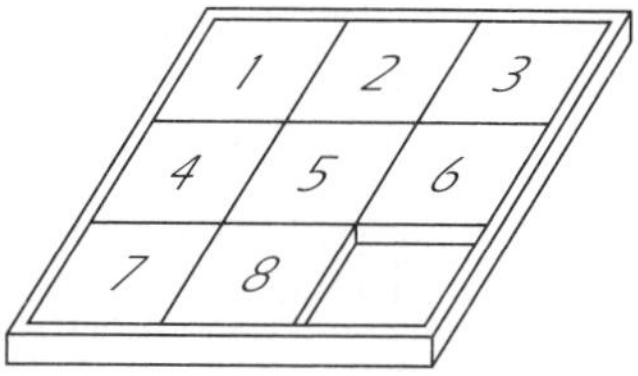

itself off. Because such a machine involves elementary perception as well as reasoning abilities, its design provides a basis for presenting the topics of the following four sections.

Questions/Exercises

1. A plant placed in a dark room with a single light source grows toward the light. Is this an intelligent response? Does the plant possess intelligence?
2. Suppose a vending machine is designed to dispense various products depending on which lever is pulled. Would you say that such a machine is "aware" of which lever is pulled?

10–2 Image Analysis

The opening and closing of the gripper on our machine presents no serious problem, and the ability to detect the presence of the puzzle in the gripper during this process is straightforward because our application requires very little precision. (Automatic garage door openers are able to detect and react to the presence of an obstacle in the doorway when closing.) Even the problem of focusing the camera on the puzzle can be handled simply by designing the arm to position the puzzle at a particular predetermined position for viewing. Thus, the first intelligent behavior required by our puzzle-solving machine is the extraction of information through a visual medium.

It is important to realize that the problem faced by our machine when looking at the puzzle is not that of merely producing and storing an image. Technology has been able to do this for years as in the case of traditional photography and tele-vision systems. Rather, the problem is to understand the image in order to ex-tract the current status of the puzzle (and later to monitor the movement of the tiles). This is a significant distinction from the activity of a television receiver that simply transforms the image from one medium to another with no conceptual understanding of the image. In short, our machine must demonstrate the ability to perceive.

In the case of our puzzle-solving machine, the options as to what the images might be are relatively limited. We can assume that what appears is always an image of the puzzle containing the digits 1 through 8 in a well-organized pattern. The problem is merely to extract the arrangement of these digits. For this, we imagine that the picture of the puzzle has been coded in terms of 1s and 0s in the computer's memory, with each bit representing the brightness level of a particular part of the picture called a *pixel* (short for picture element). Assuming a uniform size of the image (the machine holds the puzzle at a predetermined location in front of the camera), we can detect which tile is in which position by comparing the different sections of the picture to prerecorded templates consisting of the bit patterns produced by the individual digits used in the puzzle. As matches are found, the condition of the puzzle is revealed.

This technique of recognizing images is one method used in optical character readers. It has the drawback, however, of requiring a certain degree of uniformity among the style, size, and orientation of the symbols being read. In particular, the bit pattern produced by a physically large character does not match the template for a smaller version of the same symbol, even though the shapes are the same, and you can imagine how such problems increase when trying to process handwritten material.

Another approach to the problem of character recognition is based on matching the geometric characteristics rather than the exact appearance of the symbols. In such cases the digit 1 might be characterized as a single vertical line, 2 might be an opened curved line joined with a horizontal straight line across the bottom, and so on. Thus, recognition of the symbols turns out to be the process of extracting the features from the image being processed (called *feature extraction*) and comparing them to those of known symbols (*feature evaluation*). This technique is not foolproof either, because minor errors in the image can produce a set of entirely different geometric features, as in the case of distinguishing between an O and a C or, in the case of the 8-puzzle, a 3 and an 8.

We are fortunate in our puzzle application that we do not need to recognize and understand images of general three-dimensional scenes. Consider, for example, the advantage we have by being assured that the shapes to be recognized (the digits 1 through 8) are isolated in different parts of the picture rather than appearing as overlapping images, as is common in more general settings. In a general photograph, for instance, one is faced not only with the problem of recognizing an object from different angles but also with the fact that some portions of the object may be hidden from view.

In short, the problems associated with general image analysis are enormous. Tasks that are performed quickly and apparently easily by the human mind continue to lie beyond the capabilities of machines. On the other hand, there are indications that alternative machine architectures may someday overcome the problems that elude us today (see Section 10-6).

Questions/Exercises

1. How do the requirements of a video system on a robot differ if the pictures are used by the robot itself to control its activities as opposed to being relayed to a human who controls the robot remotely?

2. What tells you that the following drawing is nonsense? How can this insight be programmed into a machine?

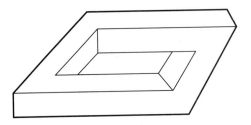

10–3 Reasoning

Once our puzzle-solving machine has deciphered the positions of the tiles from the visual image, its task becomes that of actually solving the puzzle. One technique that might come to mind is to preprogram the machine with solutions to all possible arrangements of the tiles. Then, the machine's task is merely to select and execute the proper program. However, because even this simple puzzle provides a total of 181,440 different configurations, the idea of providing an explicit solution for each is certainly not inviting and probably not even possible when time and storage constraints are considered.

We are thus forced to approach the problem in terms of programming our machine to solve the problem itself. Consequently, the program we develop must provide the machine with the ability to make decisions, draw conclusions, and in short, perform elementary reasoning activities.

Production Systems

The development of reasoning abilities within a machine is a current topic of research, and as with any subject of current research, a high degree of debate exists over which technique or theory is the correct one to pursue. For our purposes, we approach the subject in the context of production systems. A **production system** consists of three main components:

1. *A collection of states.* Each **state** is a situation that might occur in the application environment. The beginning state is called the **start** (or initial) **state;** the desired state (or states) is called the **goal state.** (In our case, the start state is the configuration of the puzzle when handed to the machine; the goal state is the configuration of the solved puzzle, as shown in Figure 10-2.)

2. *A collection of productions (or rules).* A **production** is an operation that can be performed in the application environment to move from one state to another. Each production may be associated with preconditions; that is, conditions may

exist that must be present in the environment before a production can be applied. (Productions in our case are the movements of tiles. Each movement of a tile has the precondition that the vacancy must be next to the tile in question.)

3.   A *control system.* The **control system** consists of the logic that solves the problem of moving from the start state to the goal state. At each step in the process, the control system must decide which of those productions whose preconditions are satisfied should be applied next. (Given a particular state in our 8-puzzle example, there would be several tiles next to the vacancy and therefore several applicable productions. The control system must decide which tile to move.)

From the point of view of production systems, the task of developing an intelligent machine is to implement the control system as a program stored in the machine. This program inspects the current state of the target system, identifies a sequence of productions that leads to the goal state, and executes this sequence. Thus, the control system constructs an algorithm to solve the initial problem using productions as building blocks. The main obstacle to designing our puzzle-solving machine is the development of this control program. This we do in the following sections.

For now we should present the concept of a *state graph,* which is a convenient way of representing, or at least conceptualizing, all the states, productions, and preconditions in a production system. Here we use the term *graph* in its mathematical sense, meaning a collection of locations called *nodes* connected by arrows called *arcs.* A state graph consists of a collection of nodes representing the states in the system connected by arcs representing the productions that produce movement from one state to another. Thus, two nodes can be connected by an arc in the state graph if and only if a production is in the system that can be used to transform the system from the state at the origin of the arc to the state at the destination of the arc. Preconditions are implicitly represented by the absence of arcs between certain nodes.

We might emphasize here that just as the number of possible states prevented us from explicitly providing predesigned solutions to the 8-puzzle, the problem of magnitude prevents us from explicitly representing the entire state graph. Thus, a state graph is a way of conceptualizing the problem at hand but not something that we would consider expressing in its entirety. Nonetheless, you may find it helpful to consider (and possibly extend) the portion of the state graph for the 8-puzzle actually displayed in Figure 10-3, on the following page.

Note that in terms of the state graph, the problem faced by the control system becomes one of finding a sequence of arcs that leads from the start state to the goal state, because this sequence of arcs represents a sequence of productions that solve the original problem. This is the context in which our control system functions. Moreover, observe that there is nothing unique about the 8-puzzle that allows us to conceptualize the production system in terms of a state graph. Such a representation is applicable in any production system, and thus the formulation of problems in terms of production systems provides a uniform approach to the problem-solving process.

Figure 10-3 A small portion of the 8-puzzle's state graph

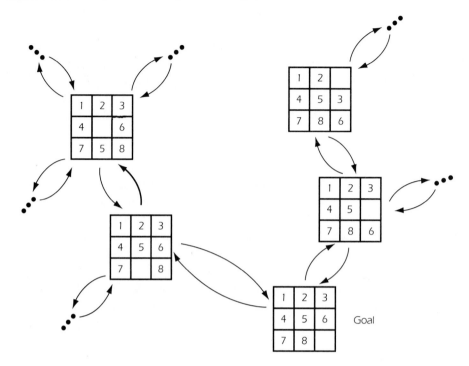

That is, regardless of the application, the control system involved always reduces to the problem of finding a path through a state graph. To emphasize this point we close this section by observing how some popular tasks can be formulated in terms of production systems and thus of state graphs.

Other Applications

One of the old standbys in the area of artificial intelligence is the playing of games such as chess. Such games involve moderate complexity in a well-defined context and hence provide an ideal environment for testing theories. In chess, the states are the possible board configurations, the productions are the moves of the pieces, and the control system is embodied in the players (human or otherwise). The start node of the state graph represents the board with the pieces in their initial positions. Branching from this node are arcs leading to those board configurations that can be reached after the first move in a game; branching from each of these nodes one finds those configurations reachable by the next move; and so on. With this formulation, we can imagine a game of chess as consisting of two players, each trying to find a path through a large state graph to a goal node of his or her own choosing.

Figure 10-4 Deductive reasoning in the context of a production system

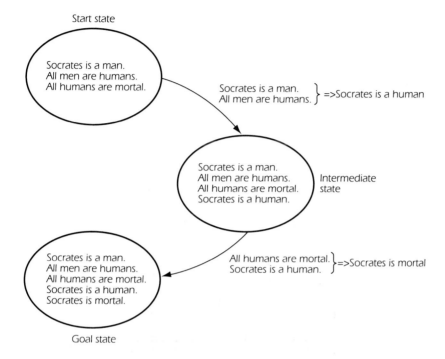

Perhaps a less obvious example of a production system is the problem of drawing logical conclusions from given facts. The productions in this context are the rules of logic that allow new statements to be formed from old ones. For example, the statements "All students work hard" and "John is a student" can be combined to produce "John works hard." Similarly, "Mary and George are smart" can be reworded as "Neither Mary nor George is not smart." States in such a system consist of collections of statements known to be true at particular points in the deduction process: The start state is the collection of given statements (often called axioms), and a goal state is any collection of statements that contains the proposed conclusion.

As an example, Figure 10-4 shows the portion of a state graph that might be traversed when the conclusion "Socrates is mortal" is drawn from the collection of statements "Socrates is a man," "All men are humans," and "All humans are mortal." There we see the body of knowledge shifting from one state to another as the reasoning process applies appropriate productions to generate additional statements.

Questions/Exercises

1. What is the significance of production systems in artificial intelligence?

2. Draw a portion of the state graph for the 8-puzzle surrounding the node representing the following state:

4	1	3
	2	6
7	5	8

3. Formulate the problem of traversing the following maze in terms of a production system:

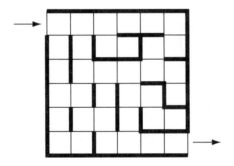

10–4 Control System Activities

A major point of Section 10-3 is that the problem of finding the proper sequence of productions in a production system can always be formulated in terms of finding a path through a state graph. This is important to computer scientists because it means that any knowledge gained about finding paths through graphs has immediate application to a multitude of problems. Thus, by designing control systems from the state-graph point of view, one is effectively working on numerous applications at the same time.

Our consideration of control systems therefore centers around the problem of graph traversals along with a look at how paths in a state graph (or actually in what we call the search tree) can be converted into solutions to the original problem. In terms of the graph traversal problem, we present in this section a rather brute-force technique and see in the next section how a degree of intuition can be added to provide a more efficient (or more intelligent) system.

Figure 10-5 An unsolved 8-puzzle

1	3	5
4	2	
7	8	6

Search Trees

The major part of the control system's job of developing a solution to the target problem requires little more than an algorithm for searching the state graph to find a path from the start node to the goal. A common method of performing this search is to traverse each of the arcs leading from the start state and in each case record the destination state, then traverse the arcs leaving these new states and again record the results, and so on. (Our search for the goal spreads out from the start state like a drop of dye in water.) This process continues until one of the new states is the goal, at which point a solution has been found. The control system needs merely to apply the productions along the discovered path from the start state to the goal.

Observe that the effect of this strategy is to build a tree called a *search tree,* with the root node being the start state and the children of each node being those states reachable by applying one production. Each arc between nodes in a search tree represents the application of a single production, and each path from the root to a leaf in the search tree represents a path between the corresponding states in the state graph. In particular, if the 8-puzzle were originally configured as in Figure 10-5, the tree of Figure 10-6 (p. 390) would represent the search tree that might result.

The leftmost branch of this tree represents an attempt to solve the problem by first moving the 6 tile up, the center branch represents the approach of moving the 2 tile to the right, and the rightmost branch represents moving the 5 tile down. Furthermore, the search tree shows that if we do begin by moving the 6 tile up, the only production allowable next is to move the 8 tile to the right. (Actually, at that point we could also move the 6 tile down but that would return us to the state represented by the root node and thus be an extraneous move.)

The goal state occurs in the last level of the search tree of Figure 10-6. Since this represents the completion of the search, the control system does not need to construct additional levels of the tree once this point is reached. As soon as this node is discovered, the control system can terminate its search procedure and begin constructing the instruction sequence that will be used to solve the puzzle in the external environment. This turns out to be the simple process of walking up the search tree from the location of the goal node while pushing the productions represented by the tree arcs on a stack as they are encountered. Applying this technique to the search tree in Figure 10-6 produces the stack of productions in Figure 10-7 (p. 391). Note that the control system can now solve the puzzle in the outside world by executing the instructions as they are popped from this stack.

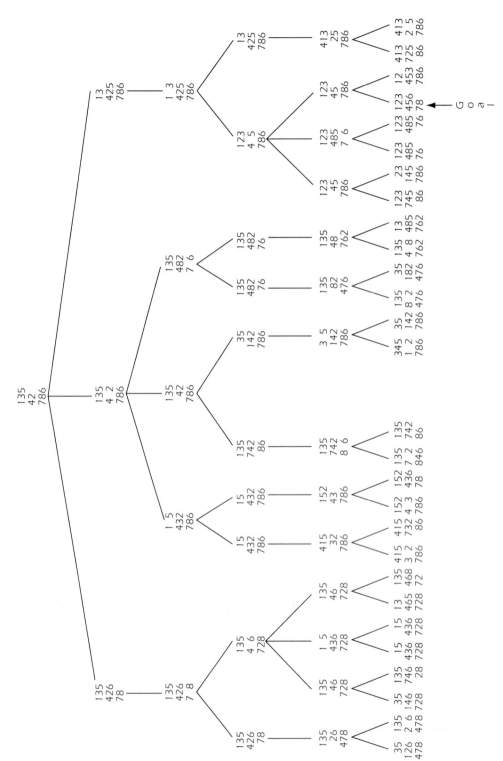

Figure 10-6 A sample search tree

Figure 10-7 Productions stacked for later execution

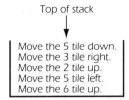

Top of stack

Move the 5 tile down.
Move the 3 tile right.
Move the 2 tile up.
Move the 5 tile left.
Move the 6 tile up.

One point remains. Recall that the trees we discussed earlier use a pointer system that points down the tree, thereby allowing us to move from a parent node to its children. In the case of a search tree, however, the control system must be able to move from a child to its parent as it moves up the tree from the goal state to the start state. Such trees are constructed with their pointer systems pointing up rather than down (or in some cases, with two sets of pointers that allow movement in the tree in both directions).

Problems of Efficiency

We pointed out earlier that the size of the state graph normally precludes its actual representation in a machine's memory. Thus, while analyzing the available productions, the control system usually stores only the search tree as it is created. After all, the search tree represents that part of the state graph considered pertinent to the task at hand and is therefore all that is required by the control system.

For our example in this section, we have chosen a problem that produces a manageable search tree. In contrast, you can imagine that the search tree generated in an attempt to solve a more complex problem would grow much larger than the preceding one because of a larger number of options at each stage and the greater depth required in the tree before the goal is found. For example, consider a game of chess that has 20 possible first moves: The root node of the search tree in such a case has 20 children rather than the 3 in the case of the 8-puzzle; and a game of chess can easily consist of 30 to 35 pairs of moves rather than the 5 straightforward ones in our example. Even in the 8-puzzle example, the search tree can become quite large if the goal is not quickly reached. Thus, it is not surprising that developing a full search tree can be as impractical as representing the entire state graph in terms of both time and memory space. In these cases, more economical methods of manipulating the search tree are required.

One approach is to change the order in which the search tree is constructed. Rather than building it in a **breadth-first** manner (meaning that the tree is constructed layer by layer), we can pursue the more promising paths to greater depths and consider the other options only if these original choices turn out to be false leads. This results in a **depth-first** construction of the search tree, meaning that the tree is constructed by building vertical paths rather than horizontal layers. This approach is the subject of the next section.

An additional approach to reducing the size of a search tree is to avoid redundancy. For example, the same state need not have multiple occurrences in the tree, because the occurrence of a node in the search tree indicates that the search process has discovered a path in the state graph leading to that node, and little is gained by maintaining records of several ways to reach the same state. Yet, had we not reached the goal in our example early in the search process, we would have soon found many duplications in the tree, and ultimately the search tree would have become plagued with repetitions. Thus, we should consider changing our search procedure so that the search tree retains records of only one path to each node.

In the case of the 8-puzzle this can be accomplished simply by adopting the policy of not attaching a new node to the tree if that state is already represented elsewhere. This certainly removes the chance for repeated entries but is too simplistic as a general rule in other applications. For instance, in other problems, it might well be the case that the new occurrence of the node in some way represents a more advantageous or efficient solution than the previous one and consequently should be added while the older occurrence is removed. In a game of chess, for example, trying to reach a certain board configuration via one path of moves may rely on the opponent's overlooking an opportunity to take control of the game, whereas pursuing another (perhaps longer) path might assure that the advantage remains at home. Thus, the more conservative path should be kept in the search tree, regardless of whether or not it was the first one discovered.

Consequently, many control systems use more complex methods for eliminating redundancy in the search tree than the simple technique previously proposed. These systems normally associate a cost to the various paths represented in the tree and pursue the paths with the smallest cost. Redundancy in the search tree is eliminated because, as repetitions of states are encountered, only the occurrence associated with the smallest cost is retained.

We can adopt this cost-evaluating approach in the 8-puzzle by considering the cost of any path to be the number of moves in the path. As repetitions of states occur in the search tree, we always keep the occurrence on the less expensive path. Of course, the less expensive path is the shorter one, so we always keep the occurrence of the state appearing highest in the tree. If we develop the tree level by level, as previously discussed, the node retained is always the older one, and the effect of adopting this cost system for our application is the same as applying the rule of always retaining the older node.

Questions/Exercises

1. Using a breadth-first approach, draw the search tree that is constructed by a control system when solving the 8-puzzle from the following start state:

1	2	3
4	8	5
7	6	

2. In what way can a depth-first approach to the construction of a search tree prove more efficient than a breadth-first approach?

3. Use pencil, paper, and the breadth-first approach to try to construct the search tree that is produced when solving the 8-puzzle from the following start state. (You do not have to finish.) What problems do you encounter?

4	3	
2	1	8
7	6	5

4. From the point of view of constructing our puzzle-solving machine, why is it better to express the productions on the stack as shown below rather than with the method used in the text:

Move the tile in the upper right corner down. (Top of stack)
Move the tile in the center of the top row right.
Move the tile in the center up.
Move the tile in the center of the right column left.
Move the tile in the bottom left corner up.

10–5 Using Heuristics

We closed Section 10-4 by briefly discussing ways in which the size of a search tree can be controlled through the use of elementary techniques. In this section, we look at this problem in more detail and discover that the equivalent of intuition can be added to our system to increase efficiency.

We might begin by considering how we as humans would proceed when faced with the 8-puzzle. We would rarely pursue several options at the same time, as our previous control system did. Instead, we probably would select the option that appeared most promising and follow it. Note that we said "appeared" most promising. After all, we usually do not know for sure which option is best at a particular point but follow our intuition, which may, of course, lead us into a trap.

Nonetheless, the use of such intuitive information seems to give humans an advantage over the brute-force methods of Section 10-4, where each option was given equal attention.

In this section, we alter the search procedure (or the way in which we construct the search tree) to take advantage of intuition in the hopes of obtaining a system that spends less time developing nonproductive branches in the search tree. Unfortunately, the term *intuition* introduces personified images and preconceived impressions to our discussion, and although coveted by the popular press, such extraneous connotations are not desirable for our purposes. It is therefore customary to refer to such untested and empirical information (which humans gain by the use of intuition) as heuristic information. More specifically, we define a heuristic policy as one that leads in a direction that appears to be the best but offers no assurance that it will turn out to be the correct direction. Thus, whereas a human might follow a rule of thumb, we speak of a program applying a heuristic policy.

Designing Heuristics

The first step is to identify those characteristics for which we as humans look when deciding which option to pursue. In general, we can argue that humans tend to keep the goal state in mind and pick the option that appears to lead toward that state. In the case of the 8-puzzle, this means that a human, when given a choice, tends to select the option that moves a tile in the direction of its final position.

To apply this technique in a programming environment, we must first develop a quantitative measure by which a program can determine which of several states is considered closest to the goal. Such a measure is called a ***heuristic.*** One heuristic might be to associate with each state the value equal to the number of tiles out of position and consider the state with the smallest value to be closest to the goal. However, this value does not take into account how far out of position the tiles are. Thus, we might want to adopt a slightly more complicated measure that accounts for this distance as well. One technique is to measure the distance each tile is from its destination and add these values to obtain a single quantity. The distance in this case can be taken as the minimum number of moves a tile must make to reach its goal position, disregarding any complexities introduced by the location of the other tiles. Thus, a tile immediately adjacent to its final destination is associated with a distance of one, whereas a tile whose corner touches the square of its final destination is associated with a distance of two (because it must move at least one position vertically and another position horizontally).

Adopting this system, we observe that the quantity associated with each state is actually an approximation of the number of moves required to reach the goal from that state, which we refer to as the projected cost. For instance, the total projected cost associated with the configuration in Figure 10-8 is seven (because tiles 2, 5, and 8 are each a distance of one from their final destinations while tiles 3 and 6 are each a

Figure 10-8 An unsolved 8-puzzle

1	5	2
4	8	
7	6	3

distance of two from home). In fact, it actually takes seven moves to return this puzzle configuration to the solved configuration.

The projected cost has two important characteristics. First, as just noted, it constitutes a reasonable estimate of the amount of work remaining in the solution if that state were reached. This means that it should be helpful in decision making. Second, it can be calculated easily. This means that its use has a chance of benefiting the search process rather than of becoming a burden. (In contrast, although the actual number of moves required to reach the goal from the given state is an excellent piece of information to have when making decisions, computing this information involves finding the actual solution first.)

Applying Heuristics

Now that we have a heuristic for the 8-puzzle, the next step is to incorporate it into our decision-making process. To this end, we recall that a human faced with a decision tends to select the option that appears closest to the goal. Thus, we alter our search procedure of Section 10-4 to consider the projected cost of each leaf node in the tree and pursue the search from a leaf node associated with the smallest such cost. Based on this principle, we present the algorithm of Figure 10-9 for developing a search tree and executing the solution obtained.

Let us walk through this algorithm as it applies to the 8-puzzle, starting from the initial configuration in Figure 10-5. First, we establish this initial state as the root node

Figure 10-9 An algorithm for a control system using heuristics

Establish the start node of the state graph as the root of the
    search tree and record its projected cost.
while (the goal node has not been reached) **do**
    [Select the leftmost leaf node with the smallest projected
        cost of all leaf nodes, and attach as children to the
        selected node those nodes that can be reached by a
        single production from the selected node.
    Record the projected cost of each of these new nodes next
        to the node in the search tree.]
Traverse the search tree from the goal node up to the root,
    pushing the production associated with each arc traversed onto a stack.
Solve the original problem by executing the productions as they
    are popped off the stack.

and record its projected cost, which is five. Then, the first pass through the body of the **while** structure instructs the addition of the three nodes, as in Figure 10-10. Note that we have recorded in parentheses the projected cost of each leaf node beneath it.

The goal node has not been reached, so we again pass through the body of the **while** structure, this time extending our search from the leftmost node ("the leftmost leaf node with the smallest projected cost"). After this, the search tree has taken the form displayed in Figure 10-11.

Note that the projected cost of the leftmost leaf node is now five, indicating that this is perhaps not a good choice to pursue after all. The algorithm picks up on this and in the next pass through the loop instructs us to expand the tree from the rightmost node (which now is the "leftmost leaf node with the smallest projected cost"). Having been expanded in this fashion, the search tree appears as in Figure 10-12.

At this point the algorithm seems to be on the right track. Because the projected cost of this last node is only three, the **while** structure instructs us to continue pursuing this path, and the search finally arrives at the goal, with the search tree appearing as in Figure 10-13 (p. 398). Comparing this with the tree in Figure 10-6 shows that, even with the temporary wrong turn taken early on by the new algorithm, the use of heuristic information has greatly decreased the size of the search tree and produced a much more efficient process.

After reaching the goal state, the **while** structure terminates, and we move on to traverse the tree from the goal node up to the root, pushing the productions encountered onto a stack as we go. Thus, the stack appears as depicted earlier in Figure 10-7.

Figure 10-10 The beginning of our heuristic search

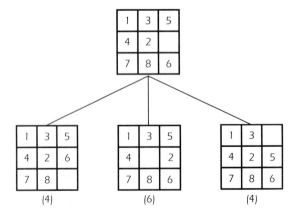

Figure 10-11

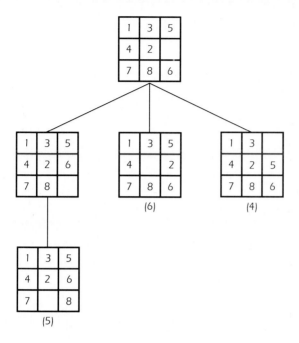

Figure 10-12

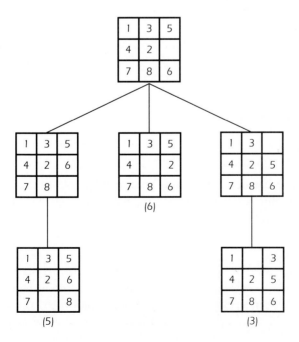

Figure 10-13 The search tree formed by our heuristic system

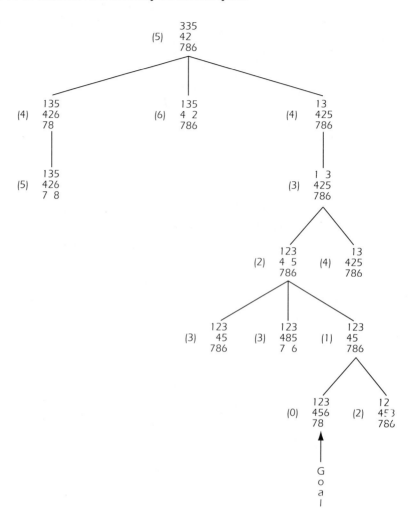

Finally, we are instructed to execute these productions as they are popped from the stack. At this point, we would observe the puzzle-solving machine lower its finger and begin to move the tiles.

Questions/Exercises

1. What analogy can be drawn between our heuristic system for solving the 8-puzzle and a mountain climber who attempts to reach the peak by considering only the local terrain and always proceeding in the direction of steepest ascent?

2. Using the heuristic information as presented in this section, apply the control-system algorithm of Figure 10-9 to the problem of solving the 8-puzzle configured as shown below:

1	2	3
4		8
7	6	5

3. Refine our method of computing the projected cost for a state so that the search algorithm of Figure 10-9 does not make the wrong choice, as it did in the example in this section. Can you find an example in which your system still causes the search to go astray?
4. What would be the shape of the search tree produced by the algorithm in Figure 10-9 if the projected cost of all states is the same?

10–6 Artificial Neural Networks

With all the progress that has been made in artificial intelligence, many problems in the field continue to tax the abilities of today's traditional computers. Central processing units that execute single sequences of instructions do not seem capable of perceiving and reasoning at levels comparable to those of the multiprocessor human mind. For this reason, many researchers are turning to machines with multiprocessing architectures. One of these is the artificial neural network.

As introduced in Chapter 2, artificial neural networks are constructed from many individual processors, which we will call processing units (or just units for short), in a manner that models networks of neurons in living biological systems. Each processing unit is a simple device that produces an output of 1 or 0, depending on whether or not the effective input of that unit exceeds a given threshold value. This effective input is a weighted sum of the actual inputs, as represented in Figure 10-14. In this figure, the outputs of three processing units (denoted by v_1, v_2, and v_3) are used as inputs to another unit. The inputs to this fourth unit are associated with values called weights (denoted by w_1, w_2, and w_3). The receiving unit multiplies each of its input values by the weight associated with that particular input position and then adds these products to form the effective input ($v_1w_1 + v_2w_2 + v_3w_3$). If this sum exceeds the processing unit's threshold value, the unit produces an output of 1, otherwise the unit produces a 0 as its output.

Figure 10-14 The activities within a processing unit

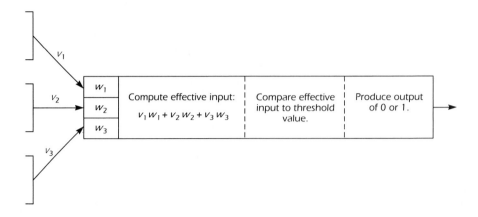

Following the lead of Figure 10-14, we adopt the convention of representing processing units as rectangles. At the input end of the unit, we place a smaller rectangle for each input, and in this rectangle, we write the weight associated with that input. Finally, we write the unit's threshold value in the middle of the large rectangle. As an example, Figure 10-15 represents a processing unit with three inputs and a threshold value of 1.5. The first input is weighted by the value -2, the second is weighted by 3, and the third is weighted by -1. Therefore, if the unit receives the inputs 1, 1, and 0, its effective input is $(1)(-2) + (1)(3) + (0)(-1) = 1$, and thus its output is 0. But, if the unit receives 0, 1, and 1, its effective input is $(0)(-2) + (1)(3) + (1)(-1) = 2$, which exceeds the threshold value, and thus the unit's output is 1.

The fact that a weight can be positive or negative means that the corresponding input can have either an inhibiting or exciting effect on the receiving unit. (If the weight is negative, then a 1 at that input position reduces the weighted sum and thus tends to hold the effective input below the threshold value. In contrast, a positive weight causes the associated input to have an increasing effect on the weighted sum and thus increase the chances of that sum exceeding the threshold value.) Moreover, the actual size of the weight controls the degree to which the corresponding input is

Figure 10-15 Representation of a processing unit

allowed to inhibit or excite the receiving unit. Thus, by adjusting the values of the weights throughout an artificial neural network, we can program the network to respond to different inputs in a predetermined manner.

As an example, the simple network presented in Figure 10-16a is programmed to produce an output of 1 if its two inputs differ and an output of 0 otherwise. If, however, we change the weights to those shown in Figure 10-16b, we obtain a network that responds with a 1 if both of its inputs are 1s and with a 0 otherwise.

To appreciate the power of artificial neural networks, let us return to the problem of character recognition. In particular, consider the problem of distinguishing between the uppercase letters C and T, as represented in Figure 10-17 on the following page. The problem is to identify either letter when it is placed in the field of vision, regardless of its orientation. Thus, all of the patterns in the top row of Figure 10-18 (on the following page) should be identified as Cs, while all of those in the lower row should be recognized as Ts.

We have already alluded to the complexities involved when trying to solve such a problem in the traditional procedural paradigm, in which template matching techniques or feature extraction and evaluation are used. Indeed, the list of special cases we must foresee when designing such a system seems to go on forever. We are

Figure 10-16 A neural network with two different programs

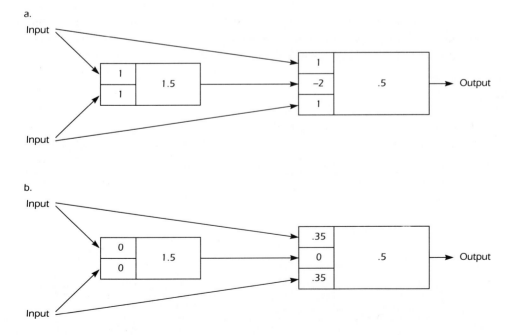

Figure 10-17 Uppercase C and uppercase T

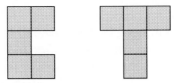

about to see, however, that the problem has a rather simple and elegant solution in terms of artificial neural networks.

We begin by assuming that each rectangle (each pixel) in the field of vision is attached to a detector that produces a 1 if that rectangle is covered by the letter being viewed and produces a 0 otherwise. We then use the outputs from these detectors as the inputs to our artificial neural network. This network itself contains two levels of processing units. The first level consists of a unit for each three-by-three block of rectangles in the field of view (see Figure 10-19). Each of these units has nine inputs, to which the detectors associated with that unit's three-by-three block are attached. (Note that each detector provides input to nine of the processing units at the first level.)

The second level of our network consists of a single processing unit, with a separate input for each of the units in the first level. This processing unit has a threshold value of .5, and each of its inputs is associated with a weight of 1. Thus, this top-level unit produces an output of 1 if and only if at least one of its inputs is 1.

Each lower-level processing unit has the threshold value of .5. Each input is given a weight of -1, except for the input associated with that unit's middle square, which is given a weight of 2. Thus, each unit can produce an output of 1 if and only if it

Figure 10-18 Various orientations of the letters C and T

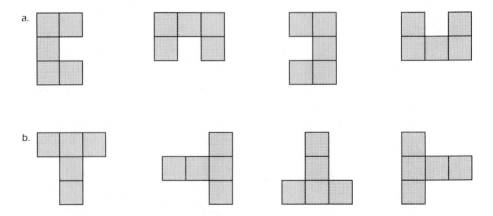

Figure 10-19 Two lower-level processing units and their three-by-three blocks in the field of view

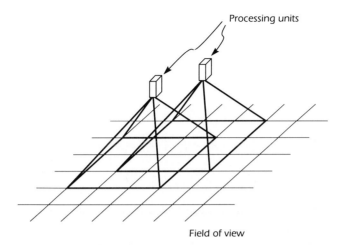

Processing units

Field of view

receives a 1 from at most two of its detectors, one of which must be associated with the square in the center of the unit's three-by-three block.

Note that if a portion of the uppercase C covers the middle square of any three-by-three block, then the letter must also cover two or more additional squares in the block. Therefore, if the uppercase C is the letter in the field of view, all of the lower-level processing units produce an output of 0, and hence the upper-level unit also produces an output of 0.

In contrast, suppose the letter in the field of view is the uppercase T, and consider the three-by-three block whose center is the square covered by the bottom of the T's stem (see Figure 10-20 on the following page). The processing unit assigned to this square receives an effective input of 1 (2 from the center pixel and -1 from the other pixel covered by the stem). This exceeds the unit's threshold, and thus the unit sends an output of 1 to the upper-level unit. This, then, causes the upper-level unit to produce an output of 1.

In summary, we have an artificial neural network that distinguishes between the letters C and T, regardless of the letter's orientation in the field of view: If the letter is a C, the network produces a 0 as its output; if the letter is a T, the network outputs a 1.

Of course, the ability to distinguish between just two letters is a far cry from the image-processing capabilities of the human mind. But, the elegance of the solutions obtained using artificial neural networks, especially when compared to those obtained through more traditional approaches, indicates that further research in the area is justified.

Major effort is being applied toward solving the problems associated with designing and programming artificial neural networks. Typical goals relating to

Figure 10-20 The three-by-three block whose center square contains the bottom of the T's stem

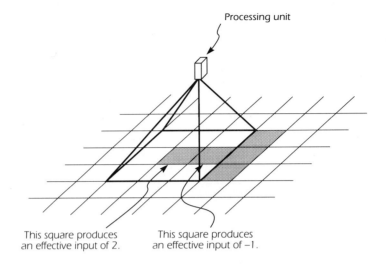

Processing unit

This square produces an effective input of 2.

This square produces an effective input of −1.

network design include determining how many processing units and how many levels of units are required to solve certain problems and what patterns of connections between these units are most productive. As for the subject of network programming, we have already mentioned that the task of programming an artificial neural network is that of assigning the proper weights to the various processing unit inputs throughout the system. The most popular way of doing this at the present is to perform a repetitive training process, in which sample inputs are applied to the network and then the weights are adjusted by small increments so that the actual output of the network approaches the desired output. As this process is repeated among the sample inputs, one hopes that the weights require less and less adjusting until the network begins to perform correctly over the entire range of sample data. Current research is aimed at determining how the weights can be adjusted during this training process so that each new adjustment leads toward the overall goal rather than destroying the progress made on the previous samples.

Questions/Exercises

1. What is the output of the following processing unit when both its inputs are 1s? What about the input patterns 0, 0; 0, 1; and 1, 0?

2. Adjust the weights and threshold value of the following processing unit so that its output is 1 if and only if at least two of its inputs are 1s.

3. Design an artificial neural network that can detect which of the following two patterns is in its field of view.

4. Design an artificial neural network that can detect which of the following two patterns is in its field of view.

10–7 Applications of Artificial Intelligence

Having considered some of the techniques used in artificial intelligence, we turn now to the areas in which such techniques have found or are finding applications.

Language Processing

We begin with the task of translating statements from one language to another. Here, we find either traditional or artificial intelligence systems being used, depending on the languages involved. The distinction centers around whether or not the semantics of a statement must be considered to produce the translation. For instance, traditional programming languages are designed so that they can be translated through the rather straightforward process of essentially finding the original statement (or statement part) in a table in which it is stored along with its translated equivalent. Thus, the machine is never called upon to understand the statements being translated; it must merely recognize their syntax. We therefore classify such applications as being in the range of traditional computer applications.

The problem of translating natural languages such as English, German, and Latin, however, usually requires an understanding of a sentence before a correct translation can be made. For example, the task of translating the sentences

John fired the gun.

and

John fired the employee.

cannot be accomplished by merely translating each word. Instead, the correct translation of *fired* requires that the translator display the ability to understand the sentences.

Developing computers that can understand natural language has become a major research area in artificial intelligence. It is also an area that demonstrates how challenging research in artificial intelligence can become. The major problem in natural language processing is that people do not seem to conform to rules when they speak. In fact, in some cases, they do not even say what they mean. For example,

Do you know what time it is?

often means "Please tell me what time it is," or if the speaker has been waiting for a long time, it may mean "You are very late."

To unravel the meaning of a statement in a natural language, then, requires several levels of analysis. The first of these is the parsing process. It is here that the subject of the sentence

Mary gave John a black eye.

is recognized as *Mary* while the subject of

John got a black eye from Mary.

is found to be *John*.

Another level of analysis is called semantic analysis. In contrast to the parsing process, which merely identifies the grammatical role of each word, semantic analysis is charged with the task of identifying the semantic role of each word in the statement. Semantic analysis seeks to identify such things as the action described, the agent of that action (which may or may not be the subject of the sentence), and the object of the action. Thus, it is through semantic analysis that the sentences "Mary gave John a black eye" and "John got a black eye from Mary" would be recognized as saying the same thing.

A third level of analysis is contextual analysis. It is at this level that the context of the sentence is brought into the understanding process. For example, it is easy to identify the grammatical role of each word in the sentence

The bat slipped from his hand.

We can even perform semantic analysis by identifying the action involved as *slipping,* the agent as *bat,* and so on. But it is not until we consider the context of the statement that its meaning becomes clear. Indeed, it has a different meaning in the context of a baseball game than it does in the context of exploring a cave.

Finally, we should note that understanding natural language is further complicated by the fact that the various levels of analysis are not independent. The subject of the sentence

Stampeding cattle can be dangerous.

is the noun *cattle* (modified by the adjective *stampeding*) if we envision the cattle stampeding on their own. But, the subject is the gerund *stampeding* (with object *cattle*) in the context of a troublemaker whose entertainment consists of starting stampedes.

Robotics

Another application of artificial intelligence is found in the area of robotics or, from a less flamboyant perspective, machinery control. Consider the use of computer-controlled systems in factory assembly lines. In this setting, a machine is often asked to repeat a task over and over in an atmosphere where each execution of the task is exactly the same (or at least any variations can be handled in a straightforward manner). The important point is that the machine performs its task in a controlled environment; if the task is to pick up assemblies and place them in boxes, the assemblies arrive on a conveyer belt at regular intervals, and full boxes are consistently replaced by empty ones in the same location. Thus, the machine does not really pick up an assembly but merely closes its gripper at a particular time at a particular location and moves its arm to another location where, rather than placing the assembly in a box, it merely opens its gripper. Most would agree, then, that intelligence is not embedded in such an application.

A major difference arises if the machine must perform its task in an uncontrolled environment. Prominent examples occur in uninhabitable and unknown environments, as found in such exotic pursuits as space exploration, or even in our factory assembly lines. Indeed, slight modifications of the task of picking up assemblies previously cited can result in the machine's being required to exhibit significant intelligent characteristics. For example, suppose the assemblies are delivered in a box containing an assortment of other parts rather than being isolated on a conveyer belt. The machine's task includes recognizing the correct assemblies, moving other parts out of the way, and picking up the correct objects. Assuming that the objects are placed in the box in an arbitrary manner, the retrieval of each assembly requires a unique sequence of steps that must be developed within the machine itself. Moreover, the machine must monitor and comprehend the situation constantly because parts in the box might shift, which would cause the required activities to change.

Such concerns fall within the scope of artificial intelligence and comprise much of the subject of robotics. Since successes in this area can readily result in financial gain, it is not surprising that this subject has attracted major attention from the industrial sector of our society and that corresponding progress has been made in recent years.

Database Systems

Next we consider data storage and retrieval systems. These systems represent a major application of natural language processing systems. The goal is to be able to request information from these systems by means of a natural language rather than requiring the human using the system to conform to a special and somewhat technical query language. However, artificial intelligence techniques are also used in the process of actually answering the question posed by the user.

Along these lines, traditional systems can merely retrieve facts that are explicitly requested and previously stored, whereas the goal of artificial intelligence systems is to provide for the retrieval of both information that is related although not directly requested and information not explicitly stored. A need for the former capabilities is found in legal searches. A lawyer might need to retrieve information about all previous cases relating to the present litigation; however, whether or not a case relates to the current one is a vague concept requiring judgment. A common approach to this problem taken by today's computer systems is to request the searcher to identify key words and phrases that should appear in any relevant case. The system then searches through all the case histories and retrieves those cases containing these words and phrases. Of course, such a system is really merely a sieve that reduces the number of cases that must be reviewed by the lawyer and may even overlook the most important case because it deals with "minors" rather than with "infants." A truly intelligent system, however, would produce a more reliable selection.

With regard to the ability to reply with information not explicitly stored, consider a database consisting of information about the presidents of the United States of America. When asked if there has ever been a president who was 10 feet tall, a traditional system would not be able to reply with the answer unless the height of each president was actually stored in the database. On the other hand, an intelligent system could reply correctly without knowing each president's height. The line of reasoning might go like this: If there had been a president who was 10 feet tall, that would have been significant and would be stored in the database. Therefore, since no president is recorded as being 10 feet tall, there have been no such presidents.

The conclusion that there have not been presidents who were 10 feet tall involves an important concept in database design—the distinction between closed-world databases and open-world databases. A closed-world database is one that is assumed to contain all true facts about the topic involved, whereas an open-world database does not encompass this assumption. Thus, the ability to reject the hypothesis of a

10-foot president in the previous example was based on the closed-world assumption that if the fact is not recorded then it must be false.

Although the closed-world assumption appears innocent enough on the surface, its application can lead to subtle complications. Consider, for example, a database consisting of the single statement

Item A is overstocked, or item B is overstocked.

From this statement alone we cannot conclude that item A is in fact overstocked. Thus, the closed-world assumption forces us to conclude that

Item A is not overstocked.

In a similar manner, the closed-world assumption forces us to conclude that

Item B is not overstocked.

We see, then, that the closed-world assumption has led us to the contradictory conclusion that although item A or item B is overstocked, neither of them is overstocked. Understanding the limitations of such innocent-looking reasoning techniques is a goal of current research in artificial intelligence.

Still another goal of artificial intelligence research within the database environment deals with the problem of figuring out what the user of the system really wants to know or should be told instead of literally answering the question posed. Suppose we have a database consisting of the courses taught by the professors at a university along with the grades they awarded the students. Consider the following sequence of events: We ask the database for the number of A grades awarded by Professor Johnson last semester. The database replies, "none." We conclude that Professor Johnson was a rather demanding instructor and ask for the number of F grades awarded by Professor Johnson last semester. Again, the database replies, "none." We decide that Professor Johnson considers all students to be average except in extreme cases. Thus, we ask for the number of C grades awarded by Professor Johnson last semester. The database again replies, "none." At this point we begin to get suspicious and ask whether Professor Johnson taught a course last semester. The database replies, "no." If only it had said so in the first place!

Expert Systems

An important and increasingly popular extension of the intelligent database concept is the development of *expert systems*—software packages designed to assist humans in situations in which an expert in a specific area is required. These systems are designed to simulate the cause-and-effect reasoning that experts would do if confronted with the same situations. Thus, a medical expert system will propose the same procedure as a medical expert who knows that a biopsy should be performed if an abnormality is noticed and an X ray shows the presence of mass in that location.

It follows that a major task in constructing an expert system is to obtain the required knowledge from an expert. How this can be done has become an important area of research. The problem is actually twofold. One task is to procure and maintain the expert's cooperation—an undertaking that may not be easy because the questioning involved is likely to be long and frustrating, and the expert may not wish to relinquish knowledge to a system that might ultimately take the expert's place. The other complicating factor is that most experts have never considered what reasoning process they use in reaching their conclusions. When asked, "How did you know to do that?" they often reply, "I don't know."

Once these acquisition problems are overcome, the knowledge gained from the expert must be organized into a format compatible with a software system. This organization is normally done by expressing the knowledge as a collection of rules in the form of **if-then** statements. For instance, the rule that an abnormality, confirmed by X rays, leads to the performance of a biopsy can be expressed as

> **if** abnormality noticed and
> X ray shows presence of mass
> **then** perform biopsy

(Those who read the optional section on declarative programming in Chapter 5 will recognize the similarity between the structure of an expert system and that of a Prolog program. This similarity is a major reason for the popularity of Prolog in the field of artificial intelligence. Indeed, Prolog is an excellent language in which to develop an expert system.)

Notice the similarity between the rules of an expert system and the productions of a production system. The "if" portion of the rule essentially states the preconditions for performing or concluding the statement found in the "then" portion. Indeed, many expert systems are essentially production systems, with the rules obtained from the human expert being the productions and the underlying reasoning based on these rules being simulated by the control system. In this context, the collection of productions is often called the system's knowledge base, and the control system is sometimes referred to as an inference engine.

Do not be misled, however, into thinking that an expert system is merely a large version of the puzzle-solving system discussed earlier. Some expert systems are organized as collections of production systems that combine their efforts to solve problems. Examples include expert systems that are based on the blackboard model in which several problem-solving systems, called knowledge sources, share a common storage area called the blackboard. This blackboard contains the current state of the problem being solved and, since it is shared by all the knowledge sources, provides a medium through which the knowledge sources can contribute to the problem's solution. To coordinate the activities of the knowledge sources, a control module is provided that is given the task of activating the appropriate knowledge source at the appropriate time. In the terminology of the blackboard model, this control module is said to determine the "focus of attention" of the system.

Another distinction between an expert system and a simple production system is that an expert system is not necessarily charged with reaching a predetermined goal but is more likely to be charged with deriving well-founded advice. This means that the heuristics used are not measurements of closeness to a goal, because no precise goal is actually present. Rather, heuristics used in expert systems tend to be the rules of thumb used by the human expert.

Our claim that no precise goal may exist in the setting of an expert system may bother you, so let us consider this claim a bit further. Suppose either an expert or an expert system is charged with the problem of diagnosing diseases. Ideally, one would like both systems to conclude with a definitive statement of the form "The disease is X," where in place of X the statement gives the name of the disease present. Unfortunately, such precision may not be possible. Instead, the best answer might be "The disease is most likely X" or perhaps "The disease is either X or Y. Please perform the following test to determine which is more likely." Because of this ambiguity, the control system within an expert system may choose to follow several paths through the system's state graph and report on the results of each. Indeed, if the production applied at some state is

if rheumatoid factor present and
patient has pain in joints
then 80% chance of rheumatoid arthritis

then any further reasoning based on the fact that the disease is rheumatoid arthritis has the potential of being invalid.

As in other research areas, early applications of expert systems were limited to only a few areas. Today, however, the number of areas in which expert systems are finding applications is rapidly increasing. One catalyst for this expansion is the realization that an expert system can be separated into its reasoning component and its knowledge component. By removing the knowledge base from an existing expert system, one is left with a system of reasoning routines that is likely to be applicable in other settings as well. Thus, new expert systems in other areas can be constructed merely by attaching a new knowledge base to this already existing reasoning system. Indeed, this is essentially the observation that the control system we developed for solving the 8-puzzle can be applied to other problems merely by replacing the 8-puzzle productions with the productions representing those other problems.

Questions/Exercises

1. Identify the ambiguities involved when translating the sentence "They are racing horses."

2.   Compare the results of parsing the following two sentences. Then, explain how the sentences differ semantically.

> The farmer built the fence in the field.
> The farmer built the fence in the winter.

3.   A database about magazine subscribers typically contains a list of subscribers to each magazine but does not contain a list of those who do not subscribe. How, then, does such a database determine that a person does not subscribe to a particular magazine?

4.   What is the difference between a traditional database and a knowledge base for an expert system?

Chapter 10 Review Problems

1. Sometimes the ability to answer a question depends as much on knowing what facts are known as on the facts themselves. For example, suppose databases A and B both contain a complete list of employees who belong to the company's health insurance program, but only database A is aware that the list is complete. What could database A conclude about a member who was not on its list that database B could not?

2. In the text, we briefly discussed the problems of understanding natural languages as opposed to formal programming languages. As an example of the complexities involved in the case of natural languages, identify two situations in which the question "Do you know what time it is?" has different meanings.

3. As demonstrated by problem 2, humans may use a question for a purpose other than asking. An example is "Do you know that your tire is flat?" which is used to inform rather than to ask. Give examples of questions used to reassure, to warn, and to criticize.

4. Compare the roles of the prepositional phrases in the following two sentences (that differ by only one word):

> The pigpen was built by the barn.
> The pigpen was built by the farmer.

5. If a researcher uses computer models for studying the memorization capabilities and processes of the human mind, do the programs developed for the machine necessarily memorize to the best of the machine's abilities? Explain.

6. Which of the following activities do you expect to be performance oriented and which are simulation oriented:
    a. The design of a flight simulator.
    b. The design of an automatic pilot system.
    c. The design of a database dealing with library materials.
    d. The design of a model of a nation's economy for testing theories.
    e. The design of a program for monitoring a patient's vital signs.

7. Identify a small set of geometric properties that can be used to distinguish between the symbols O, G, C, and Q.

8. Describe the similarities between the technique of identifying characteristics by comparing them to templates and the error-correcting codes discussed in Chapter 1.

9. Describe two interpretations of the following line drawing based on whether the "corner" marked A is convex or concave:

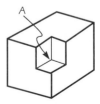

10. In the setting of a production system, what is the difference between a state graph and a search tree?

11. Characterize the task of solving the Rubik's cube as a production system. (What are the states, the productions, and so on?)

12. Characterize the task of developing a software system in terms of a production system.

13. In the text, we mentioned that a production system is often used as a technique for drawing conclusions from known facts. The states of the system are the facts known to be true at each stage of the reasoning process, and the productions are the rules of logic for manipulating the known facts. Identify some rules of logic that allow the conclusion "John is tall" to be obtained from the facts that "John is a basketball player," "Basketball players are not short," and "John is either short or tall."

14. The following tree represents possible moves in a competitive game, showing that player X currently has a choice between move A and move B. Following the move of player X, player Y is allowed to select a move, and then player X is allowed to select the last move of the game. The leaf nodes of the tree are labeled W, L, or T, depending on whether that ending represents a win, loss, or tie for player X. Should player X select move A or move B? Why? How does selecting a "production" in a competitive atmosphere differ from a one-person game such as the 8-puzzle?

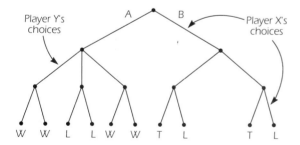

15. By considering the manipulation rules of algebra as productions, problems involving the simplification of algebraic expression can be solved in the setting of a production system. Identify a set of

algebraic productions that allow the equation $3/(2x + 1) = 2/(2x - 2)$ to be reduced to the form $x = 4$. What are some rules of thumb (that is, heuristic rules) used when performing such algebraic simplifications?

16. Draw the search tree that is generated by a breadth-first search in an attempt to solve the 8-puzzle from the start state shown below without using the assistance of any heuristic information.

	1	3
4	2	5
7	8	6

17. Draw the search tree that is generated by the algorithm of Figure 10-9 in an attempt to solve the 8-puzzle from the start state in problem 16 if the number of tiles out of place is used as a heuristic.

18. Draw the search tree that is generated by the algorithm of Figure 10-9 in an attempt to solve the 8-puzzle from the start state shown below, assuming the heuristic used is the same as that developed in Section 10-5.

1	2	3
5	7	6
4		8

19. What is the distinction between the technique of deciding which way to go when applying the binary search to a list stored as a tree (Chapter 8) and the use of a heuristic when searching for a goal state in the context of a production system?

20. Note that if a state in the state graph of a production system has an extremely low heuristic value in comparison to the other states and if there is a production from that state to itself, the algorithm in Figure 10-9 can get caught in the loop of considering that state over and over

again. Show that if the cost of executing any production in the system is at least one, then by computing the projected cost to be the sum of the heuristic value plus the cost of reaching the state along the path being traversed, this endless looping process will be avoided.

21. What heuristic do you use when searching for a route between two cities on a large road map?

22. List two properties that a heuristic should have if it is to be useful in a production system.

23. Suppose you have two buckets. One has a capacity of exactly 3 liters; the other has a capacity of 5 liters. You can pour water from one bucket to another, empty a bucket, or fill a bucket at any time. Your problem is to place exactly 4 liters of water in the 5-liter bucket. Formulate this problem as a production system.

24. Suppose your job is to supervise the loading of two trucks, each of which can carry at most 14 tons. The cargo is a variety of crates whose total weight is 28 tons but whose individual weights vary from crate to crate. The weight of each crate is marked on its side. What heuristic would you use for dividing the crates between the two trucks?

25. Design an artificial neural network that can tell which of the following two patterns is in its field of view.

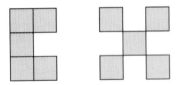

26. Design an artificial neural network that can tell which of the following two patterns is in its field of view.

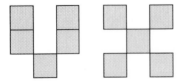

27. Design an artificial neural network that can tell which of the following four patterns is in its field of view.

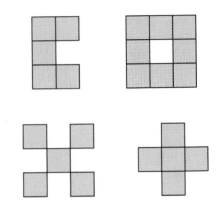

28. How do the results of parsing the two sentences below differ? How do the results of semantic analysis differ?

Theodore rode the zebra.

The zebra was ridden by Theodore.

29. How do the results of parsing the two sentences below differ? How do the results of semantic analysis differ?

If X = 5 then add 1 to X else subtract 1 from X.
If X ≠ 5 then subtract 1 from X else add 1 to X.

30. Give an example in which the closed-world assumption leads to a contradiction.

31. Give two examples where the closed-world assumption is commonly used.

32. Adjust the weights and threshold values in the artificial neural network in Figure 10-17 so that its output is 1 when both inputs are the same (both 0 or both 1) and 0 when the inputs are different (one being 0 while the other is 1).

33. Draw a diagram similar to Figure 10-4 representing the process of simplifying the algebraic expression $7x + 3 = 3x - 5$ to the expression $x = -2$.

34. Expand your answer to the previous problem to show other paths that a control system might pursue when attempting to solve the problem.

35. Draw a diagram similar to Figure 10-4 representing the reasoning process involved when con-

cluding that "Polly can fly" from the initial facts "Polly is a parrot," "A parrot is a bird," and "All birds can fly."

36. In contrast to the statement in the preceding problem, some birds, such as an ostrich or a robin with a broken wing, cannot fly. Indeed, it would not seem reasonable to construct a deductive reasoning system in which all the exceptions to the statement "All birds can fly" are explicitly listed. How then do we as humans decide whether or not a particular bird can or cannot fly?

37. Explain how the semantics of the sentence "I met the fat lady's husband" depend on the context.

38. Formulate the problem of traveling from one city to another as a production system. What are the states? What are the productions?

39. Suppose you must perform three tasks A, B, and C that can be performed in any order (but not simultaneously). Formulate your problem as a production system and draw its state graph.

40. How does the state graph in the previous problem change if task C must be performed before task A?

Problems for the Programmer

1. Write a program that matches input symbols to predefined templates and reports on its findings. Input the symbols in the form of a matrix of 0s and 1s, where 0s represent white pixels of the input image and 1s represent black pixels. Design your program so that it does not require an exact match but allows for slight imperfections. Experiment with the problem of distinguishing between the symbols O, Q, and C.

2. Implement the puzzle-solving algorithm in Figure 10-9. Design your system to accept the initial puzzle state in the form of a three-by-three matrix and to display the solution as a series of such matrices. You may want to experiment with different heuristics for determining the projected cost. (How can you design your program to make such experimentation as easy as possible?)

3. Write a program that changes simple statements of the form "I am . . ." into questions of the form "Why are you . . . ?" Does your program correctly handle the statement "I am your friend"? (It should change "your" to "my" to produce "Why are you my friend?") What character-manipulating features are available in your programming language that simplify your programming task?

4. Write two programs, one performance oriented and the other simulation oriented, to play tic-tac-toe.

5. Implement your solutions to review problems 25, 26, and 27.

Additional Reading

Allen, J. *Natural Language Understanding.* Redwood City, Calif.: Benjamin/Cummings, 1987.

Genesereth, M. R., and Nilsson, N. J. *Logical Foundations of Artificial Intelligence.* Los Altos, Calif.: Morgan Kaufmann, 1987.

Luger, G. F., and Stubblefield, W. A. *Artificial Intelligence and the Design of Expert Systems,* 2nd ed. Redwood City, Calif.: Benjamin/Cummings, 1993.

McCorduck, P. *Machines Who Think.* New York: W. H. Freeman and Co., 1979.

Nilsson, N. J. *Principles of Artificial Intelligence.* Los Altos, Calif.: Tioga, 1980.

Pearl, J. *Heuristics.* Reading, Mass.: Addison-Wesley, 1984.

Penrose, R. *The Emperor's New Mind.* New York: Oxford University Press, 1989.

Rich, E., and Knight, K. *Artificial Intelligence,* 2nd ed. New York: McGraw-Hill, 1991.

Rumelhart, D. E., and McClelland, J. L. *Parallel Distributed Processing.* Cambridge, Mass.: MIT Press, 1986.

Tanimoto, S. L. *The Elements of Artificial Intelligence.* New York: W. H. Freeman and Co., 1990.

Weizenbaum, J. *Computer Power and Human Reason.* New York: W. H. Freeman and Co., 1979.

Zurada, J. M. *Introduction to Artificial Neural Systems.* St. Paul, Minn.: West, 1992.

CHAPTER ELEVEN

THEORY OF COMPUTATION

In this chapter we discuss some theoretical ideas founded on the question of what algorithmic computers can and cannot do. We start by introducing a very simple programming language. Next, we see that any problem that can be solved on a modern computer has a solution that can be expressed in that language. (If a programming language is designed to encompass the features of this simple language, it is guaranteed to provide a means of expressing a solution to any problem that the machine is capable of solving.) Using this language, we then discover that there are problems that today's machines cannot solve and that apparently no future algorithmic machine will be able to solve. Finally, we find that even among the machine-solvable problems, there are problems whose solutions are so complex that they are apparently unsolvable from any practical point of view.

Many of the results in this chapter were originally obtained in the early 20th century by mathematicians working in the area of mathematics known as logic and foundations. Thus, many of the points about the problem-solving ability of modern machines summarized here were known well before today's technology evolved. Today, the subject is known as the theory of computation, and although born within mathematics, it is now classified by many as computer science.

Regardless of its classification, the subject presents a truly fascinating study of the power and limitations of mathematical reasoning. Paramount in the subject is the paper published by the German mathematician Kurt Gödel in 1931 that essentially shows that within any mathematical system encompassing the system of natural numbers (0, 1, 2, 3, . . .) and the arithmetic operations of addition and multiplication, statements exist that can be neither proven nor disproven. This startling result implies that a complete understanding of even our "simple" arithmetic system lies beyond the capabilities of algorithmic machines.

11–1 A Bare Bones Programming Language

Let us assume that we have been asked to design a new procedural programming language that can serve as a general-purpose programming language well into the future. Our task is complicated by the fact that we cannot foresee the particular applications that the future will bring. How, then, can we guarantee that our language will contain those features required to express solutions to any problems future programmers may encounter?

Our answer is to design our language to encompass the power of algorithmic processes themselves. That is, we want to ensure that if a problem can be solved algorithmicly, then an algorithm for solving that problem can be expressed in our language. Hence, if a future programmer finds that a problem cannot be solved using our language, then the reason will not be a fault of our language. Instead, it will be that there is not an algorithm for solving the problem.

Let us also assume that considerations of expense dictate that we not provide an abundance of features that merely enhance convenience. Our task is to design a powerful yet concise programming language.

In this section, we describe a procedural programming language that fulfills these requirements. Because our language has few of the conveniences found in other languages, it is fitting that we refer to it as Bare Bones. Indeed, our language isolates the minimum requirements of a general-purpose programming language.

Our description of Bare Bones follows the format of the discussion of programming languages in Chapter 5. We first present the language features for data description, followed by the assignment statements, and then we discuss the control statements in the language.

Data Description Statements

As we have seen, the data description statements found in high-level programming languages allow programmers the luxury of thinking in terms of arrays of numeric values and strings of alphabetic characters, even though the machine itself does not associate interpretations to the bit patterns representing these objects. The machine merely manipulates the patterns as directed by the instructions being executed. Before being presented to a machine for execution, a high-level instruction directing that two characters in a string be interchanged must be translated into machine-level instructions to interchange two bit patterns.

In turn, the design of a programming language can be simplified by forcing the programmer to express all operations in terms of bit patterns in the first place. Such a language has a single data type and structure, so it does not need data description statements.

For simplicity sake, our Bare Bones language adopts this approach. All variables are considered to be of type "bit pattern of any length." Thus, in a Bare Bones program, we do not need a declarative part in which variable names and their associated properties are described; we can simply begin using the names as they are required in the procedural part of the program.

Of course, a translator for our Bare Bones language must be able to distinguish variable names from the other terms. This is done by designing the syntax of Bare Bones so that the role of any term can be identified by its context. For this purpose, we adopt the policy of terminating each statement with a semicolon so that a translator can easily separate statements. Furthermore, we specify that variable names consist only of letters from the traditional alphabet. Thus, the strings XYZ, Bill, and abcdefghi can be used as variable names, whereas G25, %o, or x.y cannot.

Process Description Statements

Bare Bones contains only three assignment statements, each of which takes the form of modifying the contents of the variable identified in the statement. The first allows us to associate a string of zeros with a variable name. Its syntax is

clear *name*;

where *name* can be any legal variable name.

The other assignment statements are essentially opposites of each other:

incr *name*;

and

decr *name*;

Again, *name* represents any legal variable name. The first of these statements increments the value associated with the identified variable. Here the term *increment* refers to the interpretation of bit patterns as representing numeric values in base two notation. From the purely bit manipulative point of view, *increment* means to advance the binary odometer one position. Thus, if the pattern 101 is associated with the variable Y before the statement

incr Y;

is executed, the pattern 110 is associated with Y afterward. That is, 1 is added to the value assigned to Y.

In contrast, the statement decr *name*; is used to decrement the value associated with the identified variable or, in other words, to roll the binary odometer backward one position. An exception is when the identified variable is already associated with zero, in which case this statement leaves the value unaltered. Therefore, if the value associated with Y is 101 before the statement

decr Y;

is executed, the pattern 100 is associated with Y afterward. However, if the value of Y had been zero before executing the statement, the value would remain zero after execution.

Bare Bones contains only one control structure represented by a while-end statement pair. The statement sequence

while *name* not 0 do;

.

.

.

end;

(where *name* represents any legal variable name) causes any statement or statement sequence positioned between the while and end statements to be repeated as long as the value of the variable *name* is not zero. To be more precise, when a while-end structure is encountered during program execution, the value of the identified variable is first compared to zero. If it is zero, the structure is skipped and execution continues with the statement following the end statement. If, however, the variable's value is not zero, the statement sequence within the while-end structure is executed and control is returned to the while statement, whereupon the comparison is conducted again. Note that the burden of loop control is partially placed on the programmer, who must explicitly request that the variable's value be altered within the loop body to avoid an infinite loop. For instance, the sequence

```
incr X;
while X not 0 do;
    incr Z;
end;
```

results in an infinite process because the value associated with X can never be zero, whereas the sequence

```
clear Z;
while X not 0 do;
    incr Z;
    decr X;
end;
```

ultimately terminates with the effect of transferring the value associated with X to the variable Z.

Observe that while and end statements must appear in pairs with the while statement appearing first. However, a while-end statement pair may appear within the instructions being repeated by another while-end pair. In such a case, the pairing of while and end statements is accomplished by scanning the program in its written form from beginning to end while associating each end statement with the nearest preceding while statement not yet paired. Although not syntactically necessary, we often use indentation to enhance the readability of such structures.

As a closing example, the instruction sequence in Figure 11-1 results in the product of the values associated with X and Y being associated with Z (although it has the side effect of destroying any nonzero value that may have been associated with X). (The while-end structure controlled by the variable W has the effect of restoring the original value of Y.)

Figure 11-1 A Bare Bones program for computing X × Y

```
clear Z;
while X not 0 do;
    clear W;
    while Y not 0 do;
        incr Z;
        incr W;
        decr Y;
    end;
    while W not 0 do;
        incr Y;
        decr W;
    end;
    decr X;
end;
```

Finally, we note that a Bare Bones program terminates when the end of the list of instructions is reached.

The Scope of Bare Bones

Keep in mind that although we set the stage for this section with a proposal for a usable programming language, our goal is actually to investigate what is possible, not what is practical. Bare Bones would probably prove to be more awkward than most machine languages if used in an applied setting. On the other hand, in Sections 11-2 and 11-3, we argue that this simple language fulfills our goal of providing a no-frills language.

Although not practical in an application programming environment, languages such as Bare Bones find use within theoretical computer science. For example, in Appendix E, we use Bare Bones as a tool to settle the question regarding the equivalence of iterative and recursive structures raised in Chapter 4. There we find that our suspicion of equivalence was, in fact, justified.

For now, we support our claims regarding the power of Bare Bones by demonstrating how its use allows the expression of some elementary operations. We first note that with a combination of the assignment statements, any value (any bit pattern) can be associated with a given name. For example, the following sequence assigns the bit pattern 11 (the binary representation for 3) to the name X by first clearing any previous association and then incrementing its value three times:

```
clear X;
incr X;
incr X;
incr X;
```

Another common activity in programs is to move data from one location to another. In terms of Bare Bones, this means that we need to be able to assign to one name a bit pattern previously assigned to another name. This can be accomplished by first clearing the destination and then incrementing it an appropriate number of times. In fact, we have already observed that the sequence

```
clear Z;
while X not 0 do;
    incr Z;
    decr X;
end;
```

transfers the value associated with X to Z. On the other hand, this sequence has the side effect of destroying the original value of X. To correct for this, we can introduce an auxiliary variable to which we first transfer the subject value from its initial location. We then use this auxiliary variable as the data source from which we restore the original variable while placing the subject value in the desired destination. In this manner, the movement of Tax to Extra can be accomplished by the sequence shown in Figure 11-2.

We adopt the syntax

move name1 to name2;

(where *name1* and *name2* represent variable names) as a shorthand notation for a statement structure of the form in Figure 11-2. Thus, although Bare Bones itself does not have an explicit move instruction, we often write programs as though it did, with the understanding that to convert such informal programs into real Bare Bones programs, one must replace the move statements with their equivalent while-end structures using an auxiliary variable whose name does not clash with a name already used elsewhere in the program.

Questions/Exercises

1. Show that the statement Invert X; (whose action is to convert the value of X to zero if its initial value is nonzero and to 1 if its initial value is zero) can be simulated by a Bare Bones program segment.

2. Show that even our simple Bare Bones language contains more statements than necessary by showing that the clear statement can be replaced with combinations of other statements in the language.

3. Show that the if-then-else structure can be simulated using Bare Bones. That is, write a program sequence in Bare Bones that simulates the action of the statement

if X not 0 then S1 else S2;

where S1 and S2 represent arbitrary statement sequences.

4. Show that each of the Bare Bones statements can be expressed in terms of the machine language of Appendix B. (Thus, Bare Bones can be used as a programming language for such a machine.)

5. How can negative numbers be dealt with in Bare Bones?

Figure 11-2 A Bare Bones implementation of the instruction "move Tax to Extra"

```
clear Aux;
clear Extra;
while Tax not 0 do;
   incr Aux;
   decr Tax;
end;
while Aux not 0 do;
   incr Tax;
   incr Extra;
   decr Aux;
end;
```

11–2 Turing Machines

In Section 11-1, we claimed that with Bare Bones we could express a solution for any problem that algorithmic machines are capable of solving. We discuss this claim in more detail in Section 11-3, but first we must develop a better understanding of the capabilities of algorithmic machines themselves.

Turing Machine Fundamentals

We now consider the class of computing machines known as **_Turing machines._** These machines were introduced by Alan M. Turing in 1936 as a tool for studying the power of algorithmic processes and are still used for that purpose today. Keep in mind that Turing "invented" these machines before technology could produce them. Thus, a Turing machine is a conceptual device rather than an actual machine. Although today we often think of a Turing machine as an electronic device, Turing originally envisioned these machines in terms of a human performing a calculation with pencil and paper.

A Turing machine consists of a control unit that can read and write symbols on a tape by means of a read/write head (Figure 11-3). The tape extends indefinitely at both ends and is divided into cells, each of which can contain any one of a finite set of symbols. This set is called the machine's alphabet.

At any time during a Turing machine's computation, the machine must be in one of a finite number of conditions, called states. A Turing machine's computation begins in a special state called the start state and ceases when the machine reaches another special state known as the halt state.

A Turing machine's computation consists of a sequence of steps that are executed by the machine's control unit. Each step consists of observing the symbol in the current tape cell (the one under the read/write head), writing a symbol in that cell, possibly moving the read/write head one cell to the left or right, and then shifting

Figure 11-3 The components of a Turing machine

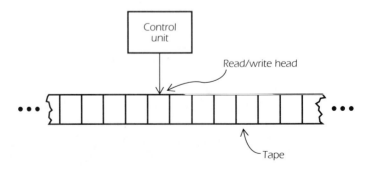

states. The exact action to be performed is determined by a program that tells the control unit what to do based on the machine's state and the contents of the current tape cell.

Being conceptual in nature, a Turing machine can be implemented in a variety of forms. In fact, today's computers are actually Turing machines (except that their memories are finite, whereas an abstract Turing machine has an unlimited supply of tape). The CPU is the control unit, whose states are the various bit patterns that can be assigned to the registers; the machine's memory takes the place of the traditional tape storage system; and the alphabet consists of the symbols 0 and 1.

This similarity between Turing machines and the machines of today is not completely coincidental. It was Turing's objective to design an abstract machine that captured the essence of computational processes. It is fitting, then, for the machines of today to incorporate the basic features identified by Turing.

The significance of Turing machines in theoretical computer science lies in the conjecture that (according to the Church–Turing thesis, which we will discuss later) the computational power of Turing machines is as great as any algorithmic system. That is, if a problem cannot be solved by a Turing machine, then it cannot be solved by any algorithmic system. Thus, Turing machines are simple in design yet represent a theoretical bound on the capabilities of actual machines. In turn, Turing machines are useful as tools for investigating the limitations of algorithmic machines and of algorithmic processes themselves.

A Specific Example

We now consider an example of a specific Turing machine. For this purpose, we represent the machine's tape as a horizontal strip divided into cells in which we can record symbols from the machine's alphabet. We indicate the machine's current position on the tape by placing a pointer under the current cell. The alphabet for our example consists of the symbols 0, 1, and *. Thus, the tape of our machine might appear as follows:

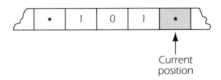

Current
position

By interpreting a string of symbols on the tape as representing binary numbers separated by asterisks, we recognize that this particular tape contains the value 5. Our Turing machine is designed to increment such a value on the tape by 1. More precisely, it assumes that the starting position is at an asterisk marking the right end of a string of 0s and 1s, and it proceeds by rolling the binary odometer one notch.

Figure 11-4 A Turing machine for incrementing a value

Current state	Current cell content	Value to write	Direction to move	New state to enter
START	*	*	Left	ADD
ADD	0	1	Left	NO CARRY
ADD	1	0	Left	CARRY
ADD	*	*	Right	HALT
CARRY	0	1	Left	NO CARRY
CARRY	1	0	Left	CARRY
CARRY	*	1	Left	OVERFLOW
NO CARRY	0	0	Left	NO CARRY
NO CARRY	1	1	Left	NO CARRY
NO CARRY	*	*	Right	RETURN
OVERFLOW	(ignored)	*	Right	RETURN
RETURN	0	0	Right	RETURN
RETURN	1	1	Right	RETURN
RETURN	*	*	No move	HALT

The states for our machine are START, ADD, CARRY, NO CARRY, OVERFLOW, RETURN, and HALT. The actions corresponding to each of these states and the content of the current cell are described in the table in Figure 11-4. We assume that the machine always begins in the START state.

Let us apply this machine to the tape pictured earlier that contains the value 5. Observe that when in the START state with the current cell containing * (as is our case), we are instructed by the table to rewrite the *, move our position one cell to the left, and enter the ADD state. Having done this, our situation can be described as follows:

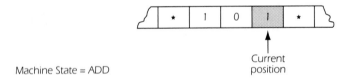

Machine State = ADD

Current position

To proceed, we look at the table to see what to do when in the ADD state with the current cell containing 1. The table tells us to replace the 1 in the current cell with 0, move one cell to the left, and enter the CARRY state. Our situation can then be described by the following:

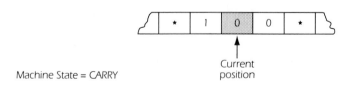

Machine State = CARRY

Current position

We again refer to the table to see what to do next and find that when in the CARRY state with the current cell containing 0, we should replace the 0 with 1, move one cell to the left, and enter the NO CARRY state. After doing this our situation is as follows:

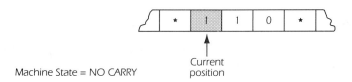

Machine State = NO CARRY   Current position

From this situation, the table instructs us to proceed by replacing the 1 in the current cell with another 1, move one cell to the left, and remain in the NO CARRY state. Consequently, we find our machine in the following condition:

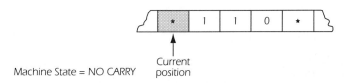

Machine State = NO CARRY   Current position

Now the table tells us to rewrite the asterisk in the current cell, move one position to the right, and enter the RETURN state. Continuing in this fashion, we remain in the RETURN state as we move back to the right cell by cell until we finally arrive at the condition as follows:

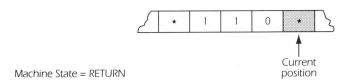

Machine State = RETURN   Current position

At this point, we see that the table instructs us to rewrite the asterisk in the current cell and HALT. The machine thus stops in the following configuration (the symbols on the tape now represent the value 6 as desired):

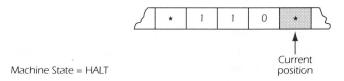

Machine State = HALT   Current position

In closing, we note that this example has shown how a Turing machine might perform the action described by the statement

incr X;

in the Bare Bones language of Section 11-1.

Questions/Exercises

1. Apply the Turing machine described in this section, starting with the following initial status:

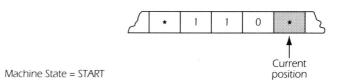

Machine State = START

Current position

2. Describe a Turing machine that replaces a string of zeros and ones with a single zero.
3. Describe a Turing machine that decrements the value on the tape if it is greater than zero or leaves the value unaltered if it is zero.
4. Identify an everyday situation in which calculating takes place. How is that situation analogous to a Turing machine?

11–3 Computable Functions

Our goal is to use Turing machines to investigate the power of our Bare Bones language. But first we need a method of measuring computing power.

Functions and Their Computation

The measure we need is available in the concept of computable functions. To explain, let us first return to the example in Section 11-2 of a Turing machine that increments a value. We can consider this as a machine that accepts a value as an input and, based on that value, produces another value as an output. Such an association between input values and output values is called a *function.* Many functions are so common that they have been given names, such as addition, which with each input pair associates an output value equal to the sum of the inputs; multiplication, which again accepts an input pair but outputs a value equal to the product of the inputs; and the successor function, which with each input value associates an output that is one greater than the input.

Numerous techniques have been used to display or otherwise represent the associations of a given function. One is to present a table displaying the possible input values along with their corresponding output values. However, the table in Figure 11-5 that attempts to describe the successor function points out a problem with such a technique. Since there is no limit to the list of possible input/output pairs, the table is destined to be incomplete.

Another way of describing a function that avoids the size limitations of tables is to describe (in an algorithmic style) how the output is obtained from the input. You have most likely seen this technique in the form of an algebraic formula. For example, to describe the function whose input values consist of temperatures measured in Celsius and whose outputs consist of the Fahrenheit equivalences, we would write

$$F = (9/5)C + 32$$

which describes how the conversion is done rather than presenting the results of the conversion in tabular form.

(We note that the addition function is traditionally handled with a combination of the tabular and algorithmic techniques. That is, students are taught to memorize the first part of the incomplete table in the form of addition facts and then to calculate the output in the case of more complex inputs.)

If there is a way of "calculating" the output of a function, we say that the function is **computable.** We have placed calculating within quotation marks because it proves to have a rather nebulous meaning. Intuitively, to calculate means to go through a well-defined, step-by-step process such as that described by the temperature conversion formula or perhaps the process of looking up the result in a table.

The vastness in the number of functions that exists is enough to allow mathematical arguments that show that for any reasonable definition of "to calculate," there remain functions that are not computable. Thus, just as there are functions that cannot be displayed in tabular form, there are functions that cannot be

Figure 11-5 The successor function

Input	Output
0	1
1	10
10	11
11	100
100	101
101	110
110	111
111	1000
1000	1001
.	.
.	.
.	.

represented by any algorithmic technique. In turn, the output values of these functions cannot be determined by any computer.

To actually identify a noncomputable function requires a more precise definition of the concepts involved. We continue, then, by giving a definition for computability that is widely accepted as encompassing the intuitive meaning of "to calculate" and that links the computing power of Turing machines with that of our simple Bare Bones language.

The Equivalence of Turing Machines and Bare Bones

We again return to the Turing machine example of Section 11-2. This machine can be used to find the output values for the successor function by placing the input value in its binary form on the tape, running the machine until it halts, and reading the output value from the tape. In other words, the Turing machine previously described actually calculates, or computes, the successor function outputs for us. We therefore say that the successor function is Turing machine computable. Following this lead, we consider a function to be **Turing machine computable** if a Turing machine can be designed that, given any input to the function, can calculate the function's corresponding output.

In the previous paragraph, we ignored the fact that some Turing machines may never reach their halt state. Consider, for example, the machine with only one state, START, in which it always writes the symbol 0 in the current position on the tape, moves left one position, and reenters the START state. Such a machine, regardless of the input value, can never halt but continues writing 0s and stepping to the left forever. Other Turing machines may halt for some input values but not for others. To allow for such cases we say that a machine computes a **partial function,** meaning that the function may have undefined outputs associated with some or all of its inputs. A major result in computer science is that the collection of all the partial functions that are Turing machine computable has been identified and is known as the class of **partial recursive functions.**

Turning now to the Bare Bones programming language, we observe that any program written in Bare Bones can be considered as computing a function by considering the initial values of certain variables called input variables (including all those with nonzero initial values) as the function's input and the values of certain variables called output variables (which may or may not be the same as the variables used for input) when the program halts as the function's output. Under these conditions the program

incr X;

can be considered as computing the successor function as clearly as the Turing machine example of Section 11-2. Moreover, some of the programs written in our language compute functions (partial functions) that are undefined for some input values, as seen by the following example. (The program halts with X equal to 0 if X started as 0. However, for any other starting value of X, the program becomes caught in an infinite loop.)

```
while X not 0 do;
end;
```

At this point we have identified two ways of "calculating" functions. One uses Turing machines and the other uses programs written in our Bare Bones programming language. The important point is that researchers have shown that the two are equivalent. That is, any partial function that can be computed by a Turing machine can be computed by a program in Bare Bones, and any partial function that can be computed by a program written in Bare Bones can be computed by some Turing machine. Thus, the computational power of Turing machines is equivalent to the expressive power of our Bare Bones programming language.

This equivalence allows us to solve the problem posed in Section 11-1 of developing a simple yet powerful programming language. Indeed, by combining this equivalence with the Church–Turing thesis, which states that the computational power of Turing machines encompasses that of any algorithmic process, we must conclude that Bare Bones also encompass the power of any algorithmic process. Thus, if an algorithm exists for solving a problem, then that problem can be solved by some Bare Bones program. In turn, Bare Bones could theoretically serve as a general-purpose programming language.

We say *theoretically* because such a language is certainly not as convenient as the high-level languages introduced in Chapter 5. On the other hand, each of those languages essentially contains the features of Bare Bones as its core. It is, in fact, this core that ensures the universality of each language; all the other features are included for the convenience of the programmer.

Questions/Exercises

1. Describe a Turing machine that ultimately halts for some inputs but never halts for others.
2. Identify other functions whose output can be described as an algebraic expression involving its input.
3. Identify a function that cannot be described in terms of an algebraic formula. Is your function nonetheless computable?
4. Describe the function computed by the following Bare Bones program, assuming the function's input is represented by X and its output by Z:

```
clear Z;
while X not 0 do;
    incr Z;
    incr Z;
    decr X;
end;
```

11–4 A Noncomputable Function

At this stage, we have acquired two definitions for the term *computable*. The first definition refers to the intuitive meaning of "to calculate." The second definition is in reference to the computing power of Turing machines or, equivalently, the Bare Bones programming language. A widely accepted conjecture known as the **Church–Turing thesis** is that the two definitions are actually the same. That is, no algorithmic process exists for calculating a function that is not also Turing machine computable. It is therefore common practice in computer science to drop the prefix "Turing machine" from the phrase "Turing machine computable." We follow this practice in this section. Thus, the noncomputable function presented here is in reality a function that is not Turing machine computable and is thus widely believed to be noncomputable in the general sense.

Some Preliminaries

Our presentation of a noncomputable function requires the understanding of two additional concepts. The first is Gödel numbering, which refers to a technique initially used by Kurt Gödel for assigning a unique positive integer to each object in a collection. The objects in Gödel's case were such things as formulas and proofs. In our case, they are programs written in Bare Bones. Gödel's system was built around the properties of prime numbers and consisted of a more complex process than we need here. For our purpose, the process summarized in Figure 11-6 suffices. We first consider any program written in Bare Bones as one single long string of characters (in which the instructions are separated by semicolons). We then code each character of this string into a bit pattern using the ASCII code. After this, any program appears as a long string of 0s and 1s that can be interpreted as representing a (rather large) number in binary notation. Thus, we see that it is possible to associate any program written in Bare Bones with a unique positive integer.

It is not important in our case whether the positive integers associated with the programs in Bare Bones are obtained by the process just described or by Gödel's original technique. The important point is that such an association is possible. Having established this possibility, we continue by assuming such an association has been

Figure 11-6 Computing the Gödel number of a Bare Bones program

C	l	e	a	r		X	;	(Program in Bare Bones)
1100011	1101100	1100101	1100001	1110010	0100000	1011000	0111011	(Program coded in ASCII)

56,210,531,013,334,459   (Equivalent value in base ten notation)

carried out. Moreover, we call the number associated with a given program that program's *Gödel number.*

The second concept is that of a self-terminating program. Observe that any program written in Bare Bones must contain at least one variable name, and since each such variable consists of a string of letters, the names in a given program can be placed in alphabetical order. In terms of this order, we can speak of the first variable of a program. We say that a program is *self-terminating* if the program halts after being started with its first variable initialized to the program's own Gödel number and its other variables being set to 0. (Note that this use of the program probably has no relation to the purpose for which the program was originally written.) Any program written in Bare Bones either is self-terminating or is not.

Essentially, a program is self-terminating if and only if it ultimately halts if started with itself as its input. Thus, the concept of a self-terminating program involves self-reference—the idea of an object referring to itself. This ploy has repeatedly led to amazing results in mathematics from such informal curiosities as the statement "This statement is false" to the more serious paradox represented by the question "Does the set of all sets contain itself?" What we have done, then, in defining the concept of a self-terminating program, is to set the stage for a line of reasoning similar to "If it does, then it doesn't; but, if it doesn't, then it does," as we see shortly.

The Halting Problem

We are now in position to define a function that is not computable. It associates with each Gödel number of a program in Bare Bones (the function's input) a 1 or a 0 (the function's output) depending on whether or not the program in question is self-terminating. More precisely we will define the function so that Gödel numbers of self-terminating programs produce the output value 1 and Gödel numbers of non-self-terminating programs produce the output value 0.

The problem of computing this function is actually the problem of calculating whether or not programs ultimately halt after being started from a particular initial state; it is therefore commonly referred to as the *halting problem.*

Our task now is to show that the preceding function is not computable. To this end, we show that the assumption that it is computable leads to an impossible situation. Consequently, we are forced to conclude that the function is not computable.

Referring to Figure 11-7 on the following two pages, we proceed with the assumption that the function is computable. This means that there must be a program in Bare Bones that computes the function. In other words, there is a program that halts with its output either equal to 1 if its input variable was the Gödel number of a self-terminating program or equal to a 0 if not. We can assume that the variables in this program are named so that the input variable is the first in alphabetical order; otherwise we could simply rename them to have this property. Likewise, we may assume that the program's output variable is named X.

Figure 11-7 Proving the unsolvability of the halting program

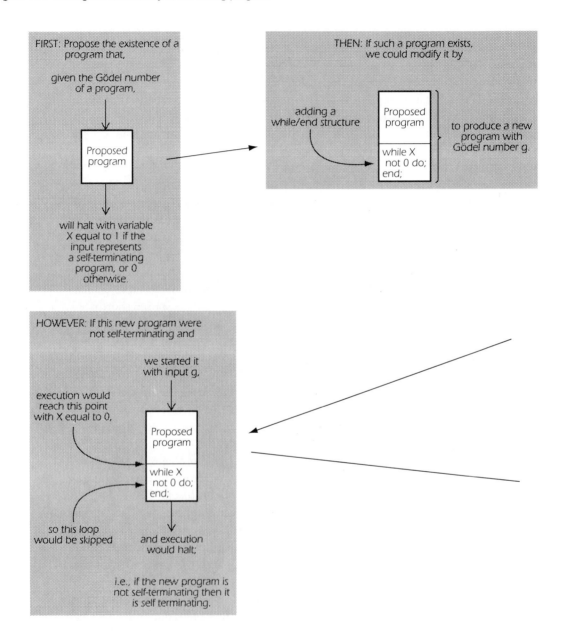

Figure 11-7 (Continued)

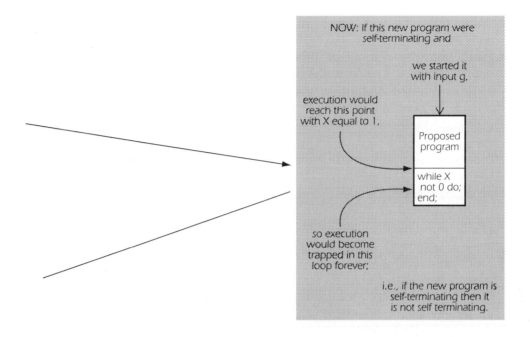

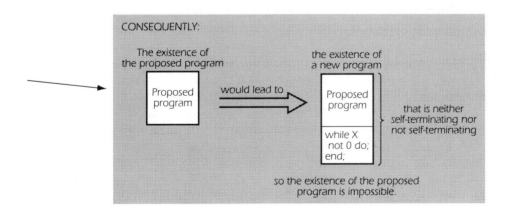

We could then modify the program by attaching the statements:

```
while X not 0 do;
end;
```

at its end. This new program must be either self-terminating or not. However, we are about to see that it can be neither! In particular, if this new program were self-terminating and we ran it with its input being equal to its own Gödel number, then when its execution reached the while statement that we added, the variable X would contain a 1. (To this point the new program is identical to the original program that produced a 1 if its input was the Gödel number of a self-terminating program.) At this point, the program's execution would be caught forever in the while-end structure because we made no provisions for X to be decremented within the loop. But, this contradicts our assumption that the new program is self-terminating. Therefore, we must conclude that the new program is not self-terminating.

If, however, this new program were not self-terminating and we executed it with its input being its own Gödel number, it would reach the added while statement with X being assigned the value zero. (This occurs because the statements preceding the while statement constitute the original program that produces an output of 0 when its input represents a program that is not self-terminating.) In this case, the loop in the while-end structure would be avoided and the program would halt. But this is the property of a self-terminating program, so we are forced to conclude that the new program is self-terminating, just as we were forced to conclude earlier that it is not self-terminating.

In summary, we see that we have the impossible situation of a program that on the one hand must be either self-terminating or not and on the other hand can be neither. Consequently, the assumption that led to this dilemma must be false. In other words, the function in question is not computable.

With this conclusion, we have arrived at perhaps the most fascinating result within computer science (and mathematics as well): There is a limit to the power of algorithmic processes (or, in mathematics, there is a limit to the power of logical deduction).

Earlier we agreed to substitute the single word *computable* for the phrase "Turing machine computable." Similarly, it is customary to drop the term *algorithmicly* from the phrase "algorithmicly solvable." A problem having an algorithmic solution is called a **solvable** problem, whereas a problem without an algorithmic solution, such as the halting problem, is called an unsolvable problem.

Finally, we should relate what we have just discussed to the ideas in Chapter 10. There, a major underlying question was whether or not the powers of computing machines include those required for intelligence itself. We have now seen that there are limits to the abilities of machines that technology cannot overcome. They can solve only problems with algorithmic solutions. The question, then, is whether or not natural intelligence embodies more than the execution of algorithmic processes. Needless to say, this is a highly debatable and sometimes emotional issue.

Questions/Exercises

1. Complete the following sentence:

   Turing machines were designed in an attempt to . . . .

2. What value would our Gödel numbering technique associate with the following simple Bare Bones program:

   decr X;

3. Is the program "incr X; decr Y;" self-terminating?
4. What is wrong with the following scenario:

   In a certain community, everyone owns his or her own house. The house painter of the community claims to paint all those and only those houses that are not painted by their owners.

   (Hint: Who paints the house painter's house?)

11–5 Complexity and Its Measure

In Section 11-4, we investigated problems in terms of their solvability. In this section and in Section 11-6, we are interested in the more down-to-earth issue of whether or not a solvable problem has a practical solution.

The tool used for our investigation is a measure of the **complexity** of a problem. Here again we are using a term whose meaning should be clarified, because *complexity* means different things to different people. One interpretation deals with the amount of branching and decision making involved in a problem's solution. Intuition tells us that following a twisted and entwined list of directions is more complicated than following instructions in the sequential order in which they are listed. This is complexity from a software engineer's point of view. However, such an interpretation does not capture the concept of complexity from a machine's point of view. A machine does not really make any decisions when selecting the next instruction for execution but merely executes the instruction that is indicated by the program counter. Consequently, a machine can execute a set of tangled instructions as easily as it can execute a list of instructions in the order they are listed. Our intuitive interpretation, therefore, tends to measure the complexity of a solution's representation rather than the solution itself.

An interpretation that more accurately reflects the complexity of a solution is based on the number of steps that must be performed when executing the solution. Note that this is not the same as the number of instructions appearing in the written program. For example, a loop whose body consists of a single print statement but whose control requests the body's execution 100 times is equivalent to 100 print statements when executed. Such a routine is considered more complex than a list of 50 similar print statements, even though the latter appears longer in written form. The point to remember is that our meaning of *complexity* is ultimately concerned with the time it takes a machine to execute an algorithm and not with the size of the algorithm in its written form. In a sense, then, our measure of complexity can be considered a measure of efficiency.

Keep in mind that what we are measuring with this concept is actually a property of a solution and not the problem directly. Different solutions to the same problem might well be associated with different degrees of complexity. To assign a level of complexity to a problem, we select the complexity of the simplest solution to the problem in question. Unfortunately, finding the simplest solution to a problem and knowing that it is the simplest is often a difficult problem in itself. In fact, mathematicians have shown that many problems do not have a simplest solution. That is, regardless of what algorithm we use to solve these problems, there is always a more efficient method waiting to be discovered. It is not surprising then that the exact complexity of many problems is still unknown.

In reality, when calculating the complexity of a solution, we do not try to count every step in the algorithm's execution. Rather, we concentrate on the significant or time-consuming steps. In defense of this looseness, we note that the major use of a complexity measure is in making comparisons in which only a relative measure is actually required. This might be in the form of comparing different solutions to the same problem (as we are about to do) or comparing different problems (as in Section 11-6).

Observe that we have already used these ideas to compare the sequential and binary search algorithms in Section 4-6. There we found that when faced with a sorted list of 30,000 entries, the sequential search would interrogate an average of 15,000 entries, whereas the binary search would consider at most 15.

Let us now consider the complexities of the insertion and quick sort algorithms. In each case, it suffices to count the number of times two names are compared because this activity dominates both algorithms. Of course, the number of such comparisons depends on the number of names in the list. Thus, it is convenient to express the number of comparisons required in terms of the length of the list being sorted. For this purpose, we use the letter n in the following discussion to represent the number of names in the list.

Complexity of the Insertion Sort

We begin with the insertion sort (summarized in Figure 4-12). Recall that the process involves selecting a list entry, called the pivot, comparing this entry to those preceding it until its proper place is found, and then inserting the pivot in this place. The first pivot chosen is the second list entry, the second chosen is the third entry, the third is the fourth entry, and so on. In the best possible case, each pivot is already in its proper place and thus needs to be compared to only a single name before this is discovered. Thus, in the best case, sorting a list with n entries requires $n - 1$ comparisons. (The second entry is compared to one name, the third entry to one name, and so on.)

In contrast, the worst scenario is that each pivot is compared to all the preceding entries before its proper location can be found. This occurs if the original list is in reverse order. In this case, the first pivot (the second list entry) is compared to one name, the second pivot (the third list entry) is compared to two names, and so on (Figure 11-8). Thus, the total number of comparisons when sorting a list of n entries is $1 + 2 + 3 + \ldots + n - 1$, which is equivalent to $n(n - 1)/2$ or $(1/2)(n^2 - n)$. In particular, if the list contained 10 entries, the sort process requires 45 comparisons.

Having analyzed the insertion sort in both the best and worst possible cases, we might also consider what we expect the average performance to be. In short, we expect each pivot to be compared to half of the entries preceding it. This results in half as many comparisons as were performed in the worst case, or a total of $n(n - 1)/4$ comparisons to sort a list of n names. Thus, if we use the insertion sort to sort a variety of lists of length 10, we expect the average number of comparisons per sort to be 22.5.

Complexity of the Quick Sort

Let us now analyze the quick sort algorithm (summarized in Figure 4-18). We first consider the task of sorting a list that is already in the desired order. For example, consider the list Alice, Bob, Carol, David, and Elaine. In this case, the quick sort algorithm designates the first name as the pivot entry, compares it to each of the other names (performing $n - 1$ comparisons), and finally exchanges the pivot with itself. It then proceeds by sorting first the sublist in front of the pivot entry (a list of length 0) and then the sublist following the pivot entry (a list of length $n - 1$). This process is shown in Figure 11-9 on the following page.

The list of length 0 requires no comparisons, but the list of length $n - 1$ requires $n - 2$ comparisons before further divisions take place. In particular, its first entry

Figure 11-8 Applying the insertion sort in a worst-case situation

Initial list					Sorted list
	\multicolumn{4}{c	}{Comparisons made for each pivot}	
	1	2	3	4	
Elaine	Elaine	David	Carol	Barbara	Alfred
David	David	Elaine	David	Carol	Barbara
Carol	Carol	Carol	Elaine	David	Carol
Barbara	Barbara	Barbara	Barbara	Elaine	David
Alfred	Alfred	Alfred	ALfred	Alfred	Elaine

Figure 11-9 The action of the quick sort algorithm when the pivot belongs at the first of the list

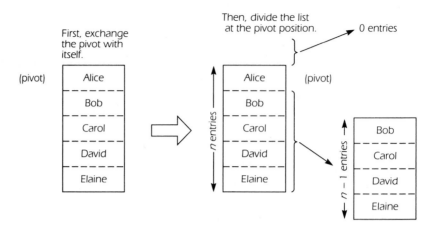

is designated as the pivot entry, then compared to each of the other entries (of which there are $n - 2$), and finally switched with itself. Note that this results in the creation of two new lists to be sorted (one of length $n - 2$ and the other of length 0) in a manner similar to the previous step that produced two lists (of length $n - 1$ and 0).

This process continues, with additional recursive activations of the algorithm being applied to shorter and shorter lists. Observe that each such activation operates on a list whose length is 1 less than the previous activation and compares the first name of its list to the other names in its list before calling the next activation. Consequently, the first activation of the algorithm in the chain performs $n - 1$ comparisons, the next $n - 2$, the next $n - 3$, and so on. Thus, the total number of comparisons required is

$$(n - 1) + (n - 2) + \ldots + 1 = (1/2)(n^2 - n)$$

The quick sort technique is designed to divide the original list into shorter lists, each of which should be easier to sort. Such a technique performs best when the lists produced from the division are both the same size and thus half the size of the original but is at a disadvantage if the division results in "smaller" tasks almost as large as the original. This, however, is exactly what happens in the previous example. Thus, the preceding discussion constitutes a worst-case analysis of the quick sort algorithm.

We now turn to a best-case analysis. For this we assume that the original list is arranged so that each list division results in two lists as nearly equal in size as possible.

Figure 11-10 The hierarchy of problems generated by the quick sort algorithm

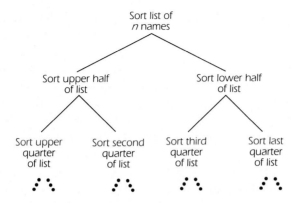

In turn, the divide-and-conquer approach of the quick sort algorithm has its optimal effect.

Under these conditions the algorithm will first attack the list of n names in such a way that the initial sorting problem is reduced to two smaller problems of sorting lists, each of length approximately $n/2$. These two problems in turn are reduced to a total of four problems of sorting lists of length approximately $n/4$. This division process can be analyzed in terms of the tree structure in Figure 11-10, where we use each node of the tree to represent a single problem in the recursive process and the branches below each node to represent the smaller problems resulting from the division. Hence, we can find the total number of comparisons that occur when sorting the initial list by adding together the number of comparisons that occur at each node.

Our first task is to determine the number of comparisons performed at each level of the tree. However, to avoid complications, we settle for a rough approximation. Observe that each node appearing across any level of the tree requests the sorting of a unique segment of the list. This sorting process is accomplished by dividing the node's segment into two shorter segments that are ultimately sorted by the nodes below. To perform this division requires no more comparisons than there are names in the segment. (The first name in the segment is compared to each of the other names.) Hence, each level of the tree requires no more comparisons than the total number of names in its list segments, and since the segments across a given level consist of disjoint portions of the original list, this total is no greater than the length of the original list. Consequently, each level of the tree requires no more than n comparisons. (Note that the bottom level is composed entirely of nodes representing the sorting of list segments of length 1 or 0 and thus requires no comparisons.)

Next we need to determine the number of levels (or the depth) of the tree. For this, observe that the division process continues until lists of length no greater than 1 are obtained. Thus, the depth of the tree is equal to the number of times (starting with the number n) that we can repeatedly divide by 2 until the result is no larger than 1. This is nothing more than the logarithm of n (base two), which we write as $\lg n$.

Figure 11-11 is a table of base two logarithms of values from 10 to 1000. Note that the entries in the table do not have integer values, whereas the depth of a tree is an integer. Thus, to get the actual depth of the tree obtained from sorting a list of n names, we round the value of $\lg n$ up to the nearest integer. However, since the bottom level of the tree involves no comparisons, we can more accurately estimate the number of levels contributing to our comparison count by rounding the value of $\lg n$ down to the nearest integer. We denote this rounded value with the notation $\lfloor \lg n \rfloor$. Thus, we estimate that if the list in question contained 10 names, the tree would contain $\lfloor \lg 10 \rfloor = 3$ levels that involve comparisons.

Finally, by multiplying the number of contributing levels ($\lfloor \lg n \rfloor$) by the maximum number of comparisons in each level (n), we obtain $n \lfloor \lg n \rfloor$ as our best-case estimate of the number of comparisons required by the quick sort algorithm.

In summary, given an arbitrary list of n names, we expect quick sort to require between $n(\lfloor \lg n \rfloor)$ (best case) and $(1/2)(n^2 - n)$ (worst case) comparisons to sort it. In particular, when sorting a list of 10 names we would expect the quick sort to require between 30 and 45 comparisons.

(If you compare this projected performance to that of the insertion sort, you may wonder how the quick sort got its name. The answer is that the average performance of the quick sort algorithm tends to be closer to its best-case performance, which for large lists proves to be more efficient than the average performance of the insertion sort. For example, given a collection of arbitrary lists containing 100 entries each, the average number of comparisons required by the insertion sort tends to be $(100)(99)/4 = 2475$, whereas the average performance of the quick sort is closer to $100 (\lfloor \lg 100 \rfloor) = 700$.)

Orders of Complexity

Although we may have made some approximations when computing the complexities of the insertion sort and quick sort algorithms, we were actually more precise than many situations require as well as being more precise than other situations may justify.

Figure 11-11 Logarithms (base two)

n	$\lg n$	n	$\lg n$
10	3.322	200	7.644
20	4.322	300	8.229
30	4.907	400	8.644
40	5.322	500	8.966
50	5.644	600	9.229
60	5.907	700	9.451
70	6.129	800	9.644
80	6.322	900	9.814
90	6.492	1000	9.966
100	6.644		

For instance, we measured the average complexity of the insertion sort to be $n(n - 1)/4 = (1/4)(n^2 - n)$, but for large values of n, the difference between $(1/4)(n^2 - n)$ and simply $(1/4)(n^2)$ becomes insignificant when compared to the size of the numbers involved. (When n is 100, the difference between the two expressions is 25, whereas the two expressions themselves are on the order of 2500.) Furthermore, for small values of n, the time required to execute the statements that we did not count (we counted only the number of times names were compared) could easily be significant in comparison to the computed complexity. In short, our claim that the average complexity of the insertion sort is $(1/4)(n^2 - n)$ is probably no more accurate than another's claim that the complexity is $(1/4)(n^2)$.

Moreover, if we use our complexity measure to estimate the actual time required to execute an algorithm, we find that differences between complexities such as $(1/4)n^2$ and simply n^2 have little significance. After all, distinctions determined by constant factors can be mitigated merely by executing the algorithm on different machines. On one machine, an algorithm may appear to have a complexity of $(1/4)n^2$, while on another, slower machine, the complexity might appear to be n^2. We see then that any constant coefficient involved in the computation of the complexity of an algorithm is more likely to be a property of the environment in which the algorithm is executed than of the algorithm itself.

Because of such uncertainties and variations, one rarely distinguishes between such expressions as $(1/4)(n^2 - n)$ and n^2 when determining the complexity of an algorithm. Instead, one tends to isolate the dominant term in the expression of the complexity while dropping any constant coefficients. Thus, although we computed the average complexity of the insertion sort to be $(1/4)(n^2 - n)$, we actually claim no more than that the insertion sort should be expected to require a time period proportional to n^2 or, using other terminology, that the complexity of the insertion sort is on the order of n^2.

Computer scientists use O-notation (read "big oh notation") to represent such approximate measures. For example, the complexity of the insertion sort is considered to be $O(n^2)$ (read "big oh of n squared" or "on the order of n squared"). Thus, after all is said and done, two algorithms whose complexities are computed to be $(1/2)(n^2 - 5n + 2)$ and $(2/3)(n^2 + 2n - 3)$ are considered to have essentially the same complexities, because both fall in the class of algorithms having complexity $O(n^2)$. In turn, both algorithms are considered more efficient than an algorithm in the class $O(n^3)$.

Questions/Exercises

1. Suppose we find that a machine programmed with our insertion sort algorithm requires an average of one second to sort a list of 100 names. How long do you estimate it takes to sort a list of 1000 names? How about 10,000?

2. If a machine required a minimum of one second to sort a list of 100 names using the quick sort algorithm, how long do you expect it to take to sort 1000 names?

3. How many comparisons does the quick sort algorithm require to sort a list of 10 names already in order?

4. Arrange the names Alice, Bill, Carol, David, Earl, Fred, and Gwen so as to require the least number of comparisons when sorted by the quick sort algorithm. How many comparisons would actually be required in this case?

11–6 Problem Classification

A *polynomial* (in x) is defined to be a mathematical expression of the form:

$$a_n x^n + a_n - {}_1 x^{n-1} + \ldots + a_1 x + a_0$$

where each subscripted a represents a constant numeric value, n represents a nonnegative integer, and x is called the polynomial's variable. Thus $3x^2 + 2x + 5$ is a polynomial (in x) and $w + 5$ is a polynomial (in w). Note that any polynomial describes a function by associating with each input an output value obtained by replacing the polynomial's variable with the input.

In contrast to polynomial expressions are the *exponential* expressions that have the form:

$$b^{ax}$$

where a and b represent constant numeric values and x again represents a variable. The actual letter used to represent the variable is arbitrary. Thus, examples of exponential expressions include 4^{2x} and 2^w. As with polynomials, each exponential expression describes a function obtained by substituting the input in place of the expression's variable and performing the indicated operations.

The significance of exponential expressions for our purpose is that if the constant b is greater than one and a is positive, the value of the expression is larger than the value of any given polynomial if the input values are large enough. That is, if we pick any polynomial and proceed to compare its outputs to those of any exponential for similar inputs, as the inputs become larger we find that the outputs of the exponential eventually increase more rapidly than those of the polynomial and ultimately leave the polynomial outputs far behind.

Although an example of this phenomenon does not constitute a proof of its certainty, it is nonetheless instructive to take a look at the example given in the graph in Figure 11-12. Here we compare the outputs of the polynomial x^2 to the exponential 2^x for input values in the range of 0 to 8. Note that although the exponential expression produces outputs smaller than those of the polynomial for some input values, its outputs overtake those of the polynomial as the inputs become larger.

Figure 11-12 The exponential 2^x compared to the polynomial x^2

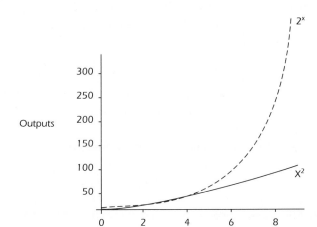

Polynomial Problems

Observe that the complexities obtained in Section 11-5 either were polynomials themselves (such as $(1/4)n^2 - (1/4)n$) or were bounded by a polynomial (such as $n \lfloor \lg n \rfloor$). (An expression is bounded by a polynomial if the expression's value for each possible input is always less than or equal to the polynomial's value for the same input. Thus, $n\lfloor \lg n \rfloor$ is bounded by the polynomial n^2.) As a result, the insertion and quick sort algorithms belong to the class known as ***polynomial algorithms,*** the class consisting of those algorithms whose complexity is bounded by a polynomial. Since our complexity is actually a measure of the time required to execute the algorithm, we often say that the algorithms in this class run in polynomial time.

This relationship between complexity and an algorithm's run time is the key to the importance of the class of polynomial algorithms. An algorithm that is not in this class is characterized by extremely long run times as the size of its input increases. For instance, the graph in Figure 11-12 shows that an algorithm of complexity 2^n becomes unbearably time-consuming when applied to large inputs. Consequently, such algorithms are seldom practical for routine use.

As mentioned earlier, problems are assigned degrees of complexity based on the complexity of their solutions. Thus, we find a class of problems (called ***polynomial problems***) defined as being those problems with polynomial time solutions. Determining whether a theoretically solvable problem is or is not in this class is of major importance because it is closely related to the question of whether or not the problem has a practical algorithmic solution.

Nonpolynomial Problems

Unfortunately, many solvable problems fall outside the class of polynomial problems. For example, consider the problem of listing all possible committees of size one or more that can be formed from a group of n people. Since there are $2^n - 1$ such committees (we allow a committee to consist of the entire group) any algorithm that solves this problem must have at least $2^n - 1$ steps and thus a complexity at least that large. In turn, this problem does not have a polynomial time solution, and hence any solution becomes enormously time consuming as the size of the group from which the committees are selected increases.

In contrast to our subcommittee problem, whose complexity is large merely because of the size of its output, problems exist whose complexities are large even though their ultimate output is merely a simple yes or no answer. An example involves the ability to answer questions about the truth of statements involving the addition of real numbers. For instance, we can easily recognize that the answer to the question "Is it true that there is a real number that when added to itself produces the value 6?" is yes, whereas the answer to "Is it true that there is a nonzero real number which when added to itself is 0?" is no. However, as such questions become more involved, our ability to answer them begins to fade. If we found ourselves faced with many such questions, we might be tempted to turn to a computer program for assistance. Unfortunately, the ability to answer these questions has been shown to require exponential time, thus even a computer ultimately fails to produce timely answers as the questions become more involved.

NP Problems

To this point we have insisted that algorithms be deterministic; that is, at each step in an algorithm's execution, the next instruction to be executed must be uniquely identified and unambiguously described. Our motivation for this restriction was that a set of instructions that did not uniquely identify which instruction was to be performed at each step or did not clearly describe the action required by each instruction would not constitute our intuitive concept of valid directions. (The purpose of an algorithm is to communicate the steps to be performed, not merely to propose options.)

It is time now to relax this condition by considering what can be accomplished if we allow "algorithms" that propose options from which we are allowed to pick in a nondeterministic manner. For instance, we now allow instructions such as

> When you reach the third traffic light,
> follow one of the roads leaving that intersection.

without providing any insight as to which of the options might be the better choice. (In contrast, a true algorithm must explain how the choice is made so that at the time of the decision, only one option is selectable.) We refer to the "algorithms" that can be obtained when such choices are allowed as ***nondeterministic algorithms.***

You may wonder why computer scientists want to consider nondeterministic algorithms. After all, algorithms with nondeterministic behavior do not seem to be useful in practical settings. One answer is that by studying the power of these more general algorithms, we can gain a better understanding of the power and limitations of deterministic algorithms. (If we as humans could experience a sixth sense, we would better understand the power and limitations of having only five senses.)

Let us now consider the *traveling salesman problem.* This problem involves a traveling salesman who must visit each of his clients in different cities without exceeding his travel budget. His problem, then, is to find a path (starting from his home, connecting the cities involved, and returning to his home) whose total length does not exceed his allowed mileage.

The traditional solution to this problem is to consider each potential path in a systematic manner, comparing the length of each path to the mileage limit until either an acceptable path is found or all possibilities have been considered. This approach, however, does not produce a polynomial algorithm. As the number of cities increases, the number of paths that may require testing grows more rapidly than any polynomial. In turn, solving the traveling salesman problem in this manner is impractical for cases involving large numbers of cities.

Now consider the following nondeterministic solution to the traveling salesman problem:

> Pick one of the possible paths, and compute its total distance.
> **If** this distance is no greater than the allowable mileage,
>   **then** declare a success
>   **else** declare nothing.

Note that whether or not following these directions leads to a solution depends on the choice we make. If we choose the right path, the problem is solved quickly; if we choose a wrong one, we learn nothing.

We define the time complexity of a nondeterministic algorithm as the time required to execute the algorithm if we make the correct choice at each point of nondeterminism. By "the correct choice" we mean the choice that leads to the solution to the problem at hand in the optimal amount of time. We can consider this definition as an attempt to measure how good the algorithm is rather than how good our choices are; our point of view is that if we make the wrong choice, it is our fault, not that of the algorithm.

According to this definition, our nondeterministic solution to the traveling salesman problem has a polynomial time complexity. Indeed, the time required to compute the total distance along the chosen path is proportional to the number of cities to be visited, and the time required to compare this total to the mileage limit is independent of the number of cities. Thus, the time required to apply this solution to a problem involving n cities is bounded by some polynomial expression of the form $an + b$, where a and b are constants.

Figure 11-13 A graphic summation of problem classification

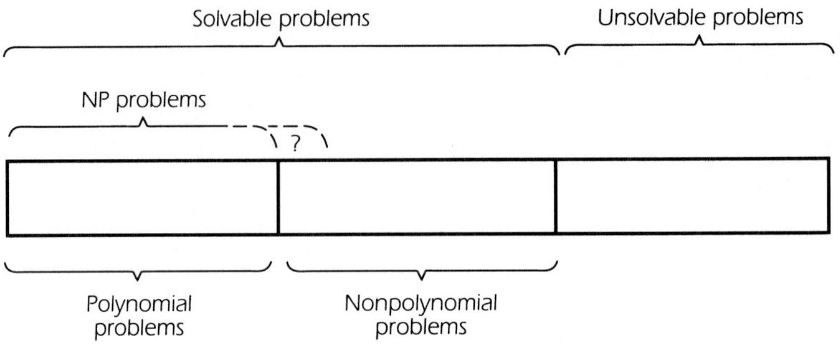

We call a problem that can be solved in polynomial time by a nondeterministic algorithm a ***nondeterministic polynomial problem,*** or an ***NP problem*** for short. Of course, the class of NP problems contains the truly polynomial problems, because if a problem can be solved by a (deterministic) algorithm in polynomial time, then it certainly can be solved in polynomial time by a nondeterministic algorithm. Moreover, the traveling salesman problem suggests that there are NP problems that are not polynomial problems. That is, there appear to be problems that can be solved in polynomial time by nondeterministic algorithms but that require nonpolynomial time under any deterministic algorithm—although no one has been able to prove this. In particular, no one has been able to show that there does not exist a strictly polynomial time algorithm for solving the traveling salesman problem. Thus, the classification of the NP problems constitutes one of the mysteries in computer science today.

In summary, we have found that problems can be classified as either solvable (having an algorithmic solution) or unsolvable (not having an algorithmic solution), as depicted in Figure 11-13. Moreover, within the class of solvable problems are two subclasses. One is the collection of polynomial problems considered to have practical solutions. The second is the collection of nonpolynomial problems whose solutions are considered to be practical for only relatively small or carefully selected inputs. Finally, there are the mysterious NP problems that thus far have evaded precise classification. They are contained in the class of solvable problems and contain the polynomial problems. Whether there are true polynomial solutions to all the NP problems remains an open question.

Questions/Exercises

1. For the same input value, does a polynomial expression always produce a value less than a given exponential?

2. List all of the subcommittees that can be formed from a committee consisting of the two members Alice and Bill. List all the subcommittees that can be formed from the committee consisting of Alice, Bill, and Carol. What about the subcommittees from Alice, Bill, Carol, and David?

3. Give an example of a problem in each of the following classes:

> polynomial problems
> nonpolynomial problems

Give an example of an NP problem that as yet has not been shown to be a polynomial problem.

Chapter 11 Review Problems

1. Show how a structure of the form:

    while X equals 0 do;

    .

    .

    .

    end;

    can be simulated with Bare Bones.

2. Write a Bare Bones program that places a 1 in the variable Z if the variable X is less than or equal to the variable Y and places a 0 in the variable Z if it is greater.

3. Write a Bare Bones program that places the Xth power of 2 in the variable Z.

4. In each of the following cases, write a program sequence in Bare Bones that performs the indicated activity:
    a. Associate 0 with Z if the value of X is even; otherwise associate 1 with Z.
    b. Calculate the sum of the integers from 0 to X.

5. Write a Bare Bones routine that divides the value of X by the value of Y. Disregard any remainder; that is, 1 divided by 2 produces 0, and 5 divided by 3 produces 1.

6. The example of a Turing machine that never halts given in the text used the fact that the tape was infinitely long. Design a Turing machine that never halts but uses no more than a single cell on its tape.

7. Design a Turing machine that places 0s in all the cells to the left of the current cell until it reaches a cell containing an asterisk.

8. Suppose a pattern of 0s and 1s on the tape of a Turing machine is delimited by asterisks at either end. Design a Turing machine that rotates this pattern one cell to the left, assuming that the machine starts with the current cell being the asterisk at the right end of the pattern.

9. Design a Turing machine that reverses the pattern of 0s and 1s that it finds between the current cell (which contains an asterisk) and the first asterisk to the left.

10. Summarize the Church–Turing thesis.

11. What value does our Gödel numbering technique associate with the program: "incr A;"?

12. What Bare Bones program is represented by the number

    167,003,256,847,376,500,260,297,734,958,
    162,681,576,272,443

    when using our Gödel numbering system described in this chapter?

13. Is the following Bare Bones program self-terminating?

    while X not 0 do;
    end;

14. Analyze the validity of the following two statements:

    The next statement is true.
    The above statement is false.

15. Analyze the validity of the statement "The cook on a ship cooks for all those and only those who do not cook for themselves."

16. Summarize the significance of the halting problem in the field of theoretical computer science.

17. Is the problem of searching through a list for a particular entry a polynomial problem? Justify your answer.

18. Compute the complexity of the traditional grade school algorithms for addition and multiplication. That is, if asked to add two numbers each having n digits, how many individual additions must be performed, and if requested to multiply two n-digit numbers, how many individual multiplications are required?

19. Is a polynomial solution to a problem always better than an exponential solution? Explain.

20. Does the fact that a problem has a polynomial solution mean that it can always be solved in a practical amount of time? Explain.

21. Given the problem of dividing a group (of an even number of people) into two disjoint subgroups of equal size so that the difference between the total ages of each subgroup is as large as possible, Charlie Programmer proposes the solution of forming all possible subgroup pairs, computing the difference between the age totals of each pair, and selecting the pair with the largest difference. Mary Programmer, on the other hand, proposes that the original group first be sorted by age and then divided into two subgroups by forming one subgroup from the younger half of the sorted group and the other from the older half. What is the complexity of each of these solutions? Is the problem itself of polynomial, NP, or nonpolynomial complexity?

22. Sometimes a slight change in a problem can significantly alter the form of its solution. For example, find a simple solution to the following problem and determine its complexity class:

Divide a group of people into two disjoint subgroups (of arbitrary size) such that the difference in the total ages of the members of the two subgroups is as large as possible.

Now change the problem so that the desired difference is as small as possible. What is the complexity of your solution?

23. From the following list, extract a collection of numbers whose sum is 3165:

26, 39, 104, 195, 403, 504, 793, 995, 1156, 1673

What is the complexity of your technique for solving this problem? Does this appear to be a polynomial problem or a nonpolynomial problem?

24. Is the following algorithm deterministic? Explain your answer.

procedure mystery (Number)
if (Number > 5)
    then (answer "yes")
    else (pick a value less than 5 and
           give this number as the answer)

25. Is the following algorithm deterministic? Explain your answer.

Drive straight ahead.
At the third intersection, ask the person standing on the corner if you should turn right or left.
Turn according to that person's directions.
Drive two more blocks and stop there.

26. Identify the points of nondeterminism in the following algorithm:

Select three numbers between 1 and 100.
If (the sum of the selected numbers is greater than 150)
    then (answer "yes")
    else (select one of the chosen numbers and
           give that number as the answer)

27. Does the following algorithm have a polynomial or nonpolynomial time complexity? Explain your answer.

procedure mystery (ListOfNumbers)
Pick a collection of numbers from ListOfNumbers.
if (the numbers in that collection add to 125)
    then (answer "yes")
    else (do not give an answer)

28. Which of the following problems are in the class P?
    a. a problem with complexity n^2
    b. a problem with complexity 3^n
    c. a problem with complexity $n^2 + 2^n$
    d. a problem with complexity $n!$

29. Summarize the distinction between stating that a problem is a polynomial problem and stating that it is a nondeterministic polynomial problem.

30. Give an example of a problem that is in both the class P and the class NP.

31. Suppose you are given two algorithms for solving the same problem. One algorithm has time complexity n^4 and the other has time complexity 4^n. For what size inputs is the former more efficient than the latter?

32. Summarize the significance of Turing machines in the field of theoretical computer science.

33. Summarize the Church–Turing thesis.

34. How many comparisons between names are made if the quick sort algorithm (Figure 4-18) is applied to the list Alice, Bob, Carol, and David? How many are required if the list was Alice, Bob, Carol, David, and Elaine?

35. Give an example of a problem in each of the categories represented in Figure 11-13.

36. Arrange the names Brenda, Doris, Raymond, Steve, Timothy, and William in an order that requires the least number of comparisons when sorted by the quick sort algorithm (Figure 4-18).

37. What is the largest number of entries that are interrogated if the binary search algorithm (Figure 4-14) is applied to a list of 4000 names? How does this compare to the sequential search (Figure 4-7)?

38. Design an algorithm for finding integer solutions for equations of the form $x^2 + y^2 = n$, where n is some given positive integer. Determine the time complexity of your algorithm.

39. Design an algorithm for determining whether a given positive integer (the input value) is prime. How does the time required by your algorithm depend on the input value?

40. The following algorithm for sorting a list is called the bubble sort. How many comparisons between list entries does the bubble sort require when applied to a list of n entries?

```
procedure BubbleSort (List)
Assign Counter the value 1;
while (Counter < number of entries in List) do
    [Assign n the number of entries in List;
    while (n > 1) do
        (if (the nth List entry is less than the
            entry preceding it)
            then (interchange the nth entry
                with the preceding entry)
        Subtract 1 from n)]
```

Problems for the Programmer

1. Identify a small collection of instructions in a programming language you know that collectively provide all the features of Bare Bones. Show how each Bare Bones statement can be simulated with the instructions you picked.

2. Using only those instructions identified in programming problem 1 together with any I/O instructions you may need, write a program that displays a 0 at your terminal if a positive integer is typed and a 1 if 0 is typed.

3. Write a program to list all the numbers that can be obtained by rearranging the various groupings of digits appearing in a given number. Why would you not want to execute this program for large input values?

4. Rewrite the program of programming problem 3 to print only those rearrangements whose digits total a particular value. What techniques can you apply to increase the efficiency of your solution?

5. Write a program to simulate a Turing machine.

6. Write a program for computing the Gödel numbers of Bare Bones programs using the numbering system adopted in the text.

7. Write an interpreter for our Bare Bones language.

Additional Reading

Arbib, M. A. *Brains, Machines, and Mathematics,* 2nd ed. New York: Springer-Verlag, 1987.

Brookshear, J. G. *Theory of Computation.* Redwood City, Calif.: Benjamin Cummings, 1989.

Cohen, D. I. A. *Introduction to Computer Theory,* revised ed. New York: John Wiley and Sons, 1991.

Garey, M. R., and Johnson, D. S. *Computers and Intractability.* New York: W. H. Freeman and Co., 1979.

Hofstadter, D. R. *Gödel, Escher, Bach: An Eternal Golden Braid.* St. Paul, Minn.: Vintage Book Co., 1980.

Lewis, H. R., and Papadimitriou, C. H. *Elements of the Theory of Computation.* Englewood Cliffs, N.J.: Prentice-Hall, 1981.

Appendices

A. Popular Codes

The following is a partial listing of the ASCII and EBCDIC codes:

Symbol	ASCII	EBCDIC
(space)	0100000	01000000
!	0100001	01011010
"	0100010	01111111
#	0100011	01111011
$	0100100	01011011
%	0100101	01101100
&	0100110	01010000
'	0100111	01111101
(	0101000	01001101
)	0101001	01011101
*	0101010	01011100
+	0101011	01001110
,	0101100	01101011
-	0101101	01100000
.	0101110	01001011
/	0101111	01100001
0	0110000	11110000
1	0110001	11110001
2	0110010	11110010
3	0110011	11110011
4	0110100	11110100
5	0110101	11110101
6	0110110	11110110
7	0110111	11110111
8	0111000	11111000
9	0111001	11111001
:	0111010	01111010
;	0111011	01011110
<	0111100	01001100
=	0111101	01111110
>	0111110	01101110
?	0111111	01101111
@	1000000	01111100
A	1000001	11000001
B	1000010	11000010
C	1000011	11000011
D	1000100	11000100
E	1000101	11000101
F	1000110	11000110
G	1000111	11000111
H	1001000	11001000
I	1001001	11001001
J	1001010	11010001
K	1001011	11010010
L	1001100	11010011
M	1001101	11010100

Symbol	ASCII	EBCDIC
N	1001110	11010101
O	1001111	11010110
P	1010000	11010111
Q	1010001	11011000
R	1010010	11011001
S	1010011	11100010
T	1010100	11100011
U	1010101	11100100
V	1010110	11100101
W	1010111	11100110
X	1011000	11100111
Y	1011001	11101000
Z	1011010	11101001
[	1011011	01001010
\	1011100	
]	1011101	01011010
^	1011110	
_	1011111	
a	1100001	10000001
b	1100010	10000010
c	1100011	10000011
d	1100100	10000100
e	1100101	10000101
f	1100110	10000110
g	1100111	10000111
h	1101000	10001000
i	1101001	10001001
j	1101010	10010001
k	1101011	10010010
l	1101100	10010011
m	1101101	10010100
n	1101110	10010101
o	1101111	10010110
p	1110000	10010111
q	1110001	10011000
r	1110010	10011001
s	1110011	10100010
t	1110100	10100011
u	1110101	10100100
v	1110110	10100101
w	1110111	10100110
x	1111000	10100111
y	1111001	10101000
z	1111010	10101001
{	1111011	
}	1111101	

B. A Typical Machine Language

Machine Architecture

The machine has 16 general purpose registers named R0 through R15 (or R0 through RF in hexadecimal). Each register is 1 byte (8 bits) long. For identifying registers within instructions, each register is assigned the unique 4-bit pattern that represents its register number. Thus, R0 is identified by 0000 (hexadecimal 0), R1 is identified by 0001 (hexadecimal 1), and R15 is identified by 1111 (hexadecimal F).

Main memory consists of 256 cells. Each cell contains 8 bits (or 1 byte) of data. Since there are 256 cells in memory, each cell is assigned a unique address consisting of an integer in the range of 0 to 255. An address can therefore be represented by a pattern of 8 bits ranging from 00000000 to 11111111 (or a hexadecimal value in the range of 00 to FF).

Floating-point values are assumed to be stored in the format shown as follows.

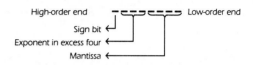

Machine Language

Each machine instruction is 2 bytes long. The first 4 bits consist of the op-code; the last 12 bits make up the operand field. The following table lists the instructions in hexadecimal notation together with a short description of each. The letters R, S, and T are used in place of hexadecimal digits in those fields representing a register identifier that varies depending on the particular application of the instruction. The letters X and Y are used in lieu of hexadecimal digits in variable fields not representing a register.

Op-code	Operand	Description
1	RXY	LOAD the register R with the bit pattern found in the memory cell whose address is XY. *Example:* 14A3 would cause the contents of the memory cell located at address A3 to be placed in register R4.
2	RXY	LOAD the register R with the bit pattern XY. *Example:* 20A3 would cause the value A3 to be placed in register R0.
3	RXY	STORE the bit pattern found in register R in the memory cell whose address is XY. *Example:* 35B1 would cause the contents of register R5 to be placed in the memory cell whose address is B1.
4	0RS	MOVE the bit pattern found in register R to register S. *Example:* 40A4 would cause the contents of register R10 to be copied into register R4.
5	RST	ADD the bit patterns in registers S and T as though they were two's complement representations and leave the result in register R. *Example:* 5726 would cause the binary values in registers R2 and R6 to be added and the sum placed in register R7.
6	RST	ADD the bit patterns in registers S and T as though they represented values in floating-point notation and leave the floating-point result in register R. *Example:* 634E would cause the values in registers R4 and R14 to be added as floating-point values and the result to be placed in register R3.
7	RST	OR the bit patterns in registers S and T and place the result in register R. *Example:* 7CB4 would cause the result of ORing the contents of registers R11 and R4 to be placed in register R12.

8	RST	AND the bit patterns in registers S and T and place the result in register R.
		Example: 8045 would cause the result of ANDing the contents of registers R4 and R5 to be placed in register R0.
9	RST	EXCLUSIVE OR the bit patterns in registers S and T and place the result in register R.
		Example: 95F3 would cause the result of EXCLUSIVE ORing the contents of registers R15 and R3 to be placed in register R5.
A	ROX	ROTATE the bit pattern in register R one bit to the right X times. Each time place the bit that started at the low order end at the high order end.
		Example: A403 would cause the contents of register R4 to be rotated 3 bits to the right in a circular fashion.
B	RXY	JUMP to the instruction located in the memory cell at address XY if the bit pattern in register R is equal to the bit pattern in register number 0. Otherwise, continue with the normal sequence of execution.
		Example: B43C would first compare the contents of register R4 with the contents of register R0. If the two were equal, the execution sequence would be altered so that the next instruction executed would be the one located at memory address 3C. Otherwise, program execution would continue in its normal sequence.
C	000	HALT execution.
		Example: C000 would cause program execution to stop.

C. Insertion Sort in Assembly Language

```
        .TITLE INSERT - - SORTS A LIST USING INSERTION SORT ALGORITHM
        .IDENT *VAX-11/8600*
;
;— — — — — — — —
; DATA SECTION
;— — — — — — — —
;       CHANGE LSIZE BELOW TO SORT LISTS OF DIFFERENT SIZES.
;
        .PSECT DATA, NOEXE, WRT
TERMFB: $FAB        FNM = SYS$INPUT,—    ; FILE ACCESS BLOCK
                    RAT = CR, —          ;     FOR TERMINAL.
                    FAC = < GET, PUT >
TERMRB: $RAB        FAB = TERMFB, —      ; RECORD ACCESS BLOCK.
                    UBF = CRTBUF, —      ; USER BUFFER FOR $GET.
                    USZ = BFSIZE         ; BUFFER SIZE.
;
INSIZE: .BLKW       1
;
CRTBUF: .BLKB       80                   ; TERMINAL LINE BUFFER.
BFSIZE =            .—CRTBUF
;
LSIZE    = 10                      ; LSIZE IS THE NUMBER OF NAMES IN LIST.
;
NAME:   .BLKQ       LSIZE           ; SPACE FOR ARRAY OF NAMES.
TEMP:   .BLKQ       1               ; FOR INTERCHANGING NAMES.
;
;

;— — — — — — — —
; LOGIC SECTION
;— — — — — — — —
;
        .PSECT LOGIC, EXE, NOWRT
;
        .ENTRY START,0
        $OPEN    FAB-TERMFB              ; PREPARE
        BLBS     R0,CONT                 ;    FOR
        BRW      ERROR                   ;      I/O
CONT:   $CONNECT RAB-TERMRB              ; OPERATIONS.
        BLBS     R0,CONT1
        BRW      ERROR
;
```

```
;          READ IN THE NAMES
;
CONT1:  MOVL         #0,R6                           ; R6 = INDEX TO NAMES ARRAY.
RD_NM:  $GET         RAB=TERMB                       ; GET NAME FROM TERMINAL.
        BLBS         R0,CONT2
        BRW          ERROR
CONT2:  MOVW         TERMRB+RAB$W_RSZ,INSIZE         ; SAVE LENGTH.
        MOVC5        INSIZE, CRTBUF,#^A/ /,-
                     #8, CRTBUF                      ; FILL OR TRUNCATE.
        MOVQ         CRTBUF,NAME[R6]
        AOBLSS  #    LSIZE,R6, RD_NM                 ; REPEAT LSIZE TIMES.
;
; SORT THE LIST
;
; REGISTER USAGE:   R6 = INDEX OF PIVOT ENTRY
;                   R5 = INDEX OF HOLE
;                   R4 = INDEX OF NAME TO BE COMPARED WITH PIVOT
;                        (ADVANCES THROUGH SORTED PART)
;
;
;                   R7, R8    HOLD ADDRESSES OF NAMES FOR COMPARISON
;
        MOVL         #1, R6                          ; R6 POINTS TO SECOND NAME IN LIST.
REPEAT: MOVQ         NAME[R6], TEMP
        MOVL         R6, R5
        MOVL         R6, R4
WHILE:  SOBGEQ       R4, GO_ON                       ; MOVE R4 UP ONE NAME.
        BRB          ENDWH                           ; GO TO ENDWH IF PAST TOP OF LIST.
GO_ON:  MOVAQ        NAME[R4],R7
        MOVAQ        TEMP,R8
        CMPC3        #8, (R7), (R8)                  ; COMPARE NAME [R4] AND PIVOT NAM
        BLEQ         ENDWH                           ; GO TO ENDWH IF NAME[R4] < =
                                                     PIVOT NAME.
        MOVQ         NAME[R4],NAME[R5]               ; MOVE NAME DOWN.
        MOVL         R4,R5                           ; MARK NEW POSITION OF HOLE.
        BRB          WHILE                           ; BACK UP TO WHILE.
ENDWH:  MOVQ         TEMP,NAME[R5]                   ; MOVE PIVOT ENTRY INTO HOLE.
        AOBLSS       #LSIZ,R6,REPEAT                 ; MOVE DOWN A NAME AND
                                                     ;   GO BACK TO REPEAT.
;
; WRITE NAMES
;
        MOVL         #0,R6                           ; R6 = INDEX TO ARRAY OF NAMES
WRT_N:  MOVAQ        NAME[R6],-
                     TERMRB+RAB$L_RBF                ; SET POSITION.
        MOVW         #8,TERMRB+RAB$W_RSZ             ; SET LENGTH.
        $PUT         RAB=TERMRB                      ; WRITE NAME.
        BLBS         R0,CONT3
        BRW          ERROR
CONT3:  AOBLSS       #LSIZE,R6,WRT_N                 ; REPEAT LSIZE TIMES.
;
        $CLOSE FAB=TERMFB
ERROR:  RET
;
        .END         START
```

D. Syntax Diagrams for Pascal

The following is a set of syntax diagrams for Pascal. The diagrams are arranged in a general to specific order. The first diagram describes the overall structure of a program as consisting of a program header followed by a declaration part that is in turn followed by a process part. The remaining diagrams further describe these components in a stepwise-refinement manner.

Components contained in rectangles are nonterminal in the sense that they are described in more detail by another diagram; symbols within ovals or circles are terminal in that no further definition is required for them. They are the symbols that actually appear in a program itself. The exceptions to this convention are the components called character, letter, and digit defined as follows:

Character—essentially any one of the symbols in the ASCII character set except the apostrophe

Letter—one of the alphabetic characters

Digit—one of the symbols 0, 1, 2, 3, 4, 5, 6, 7, 8, 9

These syntax diagrams do not describe the complete grammar of Pascal, because syntax diagrams are unable to describe context-sensitive features of a grammar. For example, the diagrams shown here do not specify that different variables cannot have the same name or that the + operation is not defined for Boolean operands. On the other hand, most of a language's grammatical structure can be efficiently and clearly described with such diagrams; thus, even with their shortcomings, they have become a popular tool for language description.

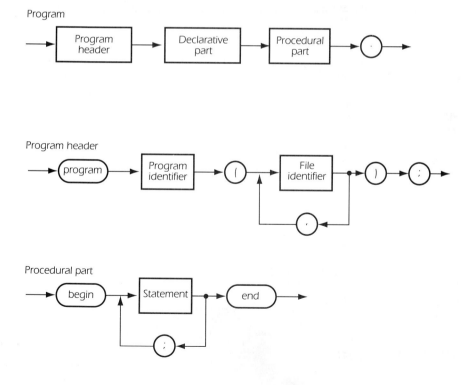

Declarative part

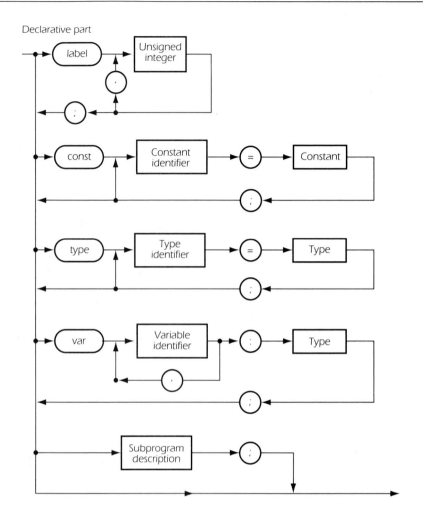

Subprogram description

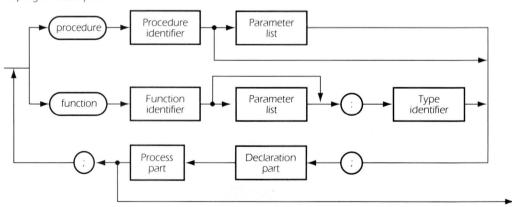

Statement

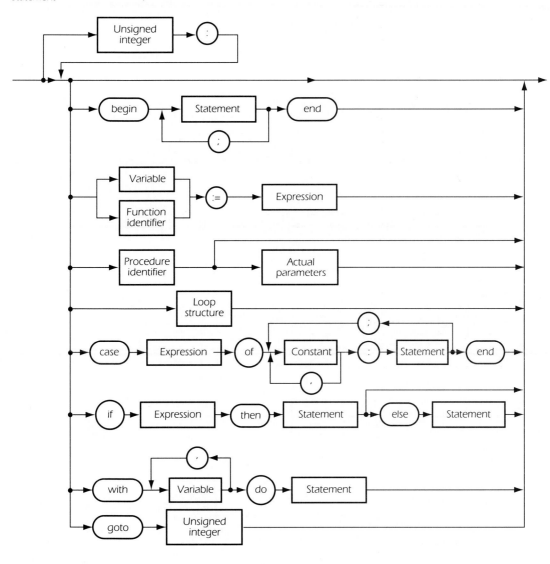

Loop structure

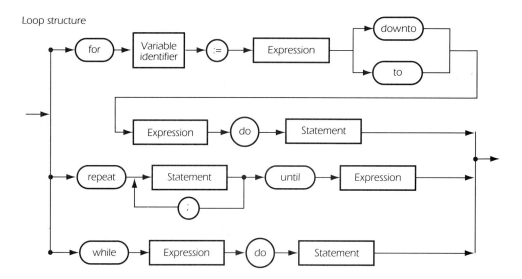

Field list

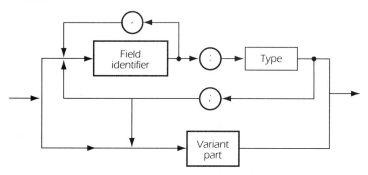

Variant part

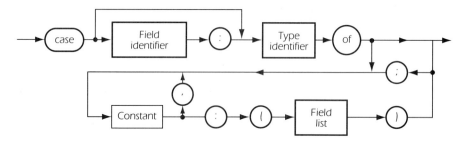

Parameter list

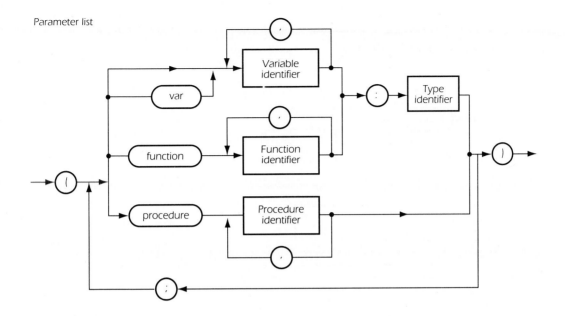

Actual parameters

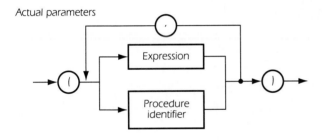

Type

Simple type

Structured type

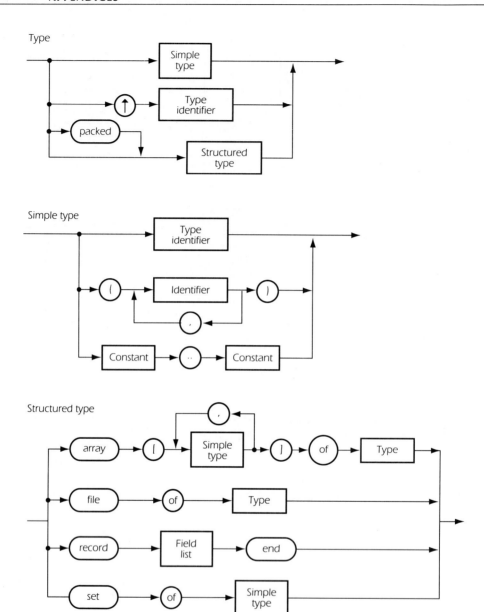

Variable

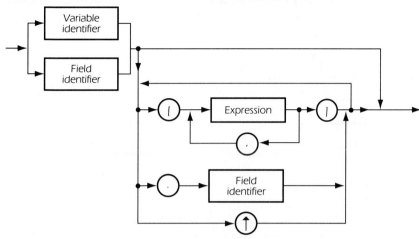

Constant

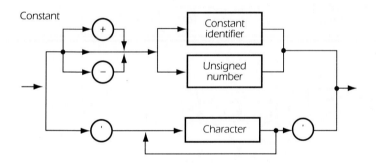

Expression

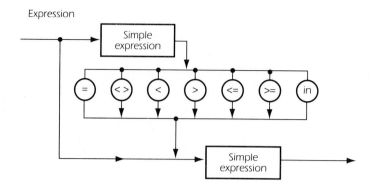

Simple expression

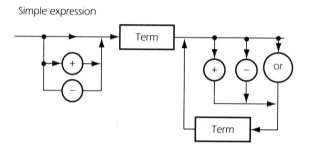

Term

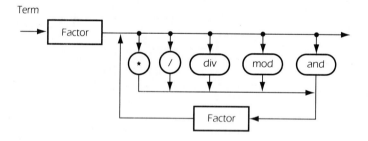

Factor

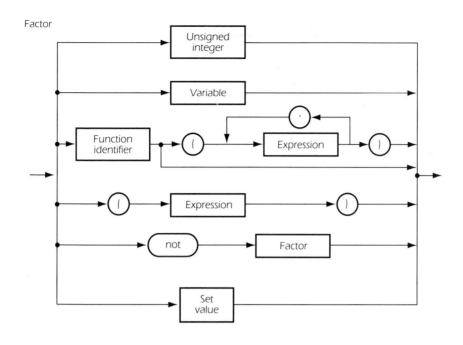

Set value

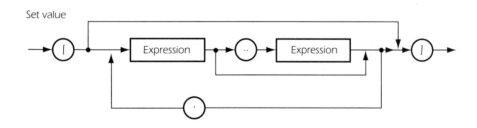

Unsigned constant

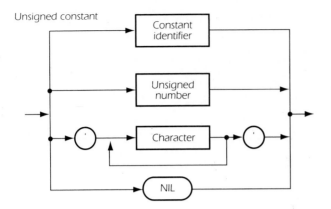

Unsigned number

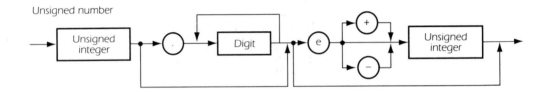

Unsigned integer

Identifier, field indentifier, function identifier, constant identifier,
procedure identifier, type identifier, variable identifier

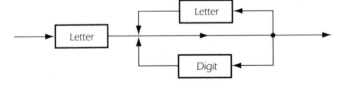

E. The Equivalence of Iterative and Recursive Structures

In this appendix, we use our Bare Bones language of Chapter 11 as a tool to answer the question posed in Chapter 4 regarding the relative power of iterative and recursive structures. Recall that Bare Bones contains only three assignment statements (clear, incr, and decr) and one control structure (constructed from a while/end statement pair). Moreover, this simple language has the same computing power as a Turing machine, and thus, if we accept the Church-Turing thesis, we may conclude that any problem with an algorithmic solution has a solution expressible in Bare Bones.

The first step in the comparison of iterative and recursive structures is to replace the iterative structure of Bare Bones with a recursive structure. We do this by removing the while and end statements from the language and in their place providing the ability to divide a Bare Bones program into units along with the ability to call one of these units from another location in the program. More precisely, we propose that each program in the modified language can consist of a number of syntactically disjoint program units. We suppose that each program must contain exactly one unit called MAIN having the syntactic structure of

MAIN: begin;
.
.
.
end;

(where the dots represent other Bare Bones statements) and perhaps other units (semantically subordinate to MAIN) that have the structure

unit: begin;
.
.
.
return;

(where unit represents the unit's name that has the same syntax as variable names). The semantics of this

unit system is that the program always begins execution at the beginning of the unit MAIN and halts when that unit's end statement is reached. Other program units can be called as subprograms by means of the conditional statement

if name not 0 perform unit;

(where name represents any variable name and unit represents any of the program unit names other than MAIN). Moreover, we allow the units other than MAIN to call themselves recursively.

With these added features, we can simulate the old while-end structure. For example, a Bare Bones program of the form

while X not 0 do;
S;
end;

(where S represents any sequence of Bare Bones statements) can be replaced by the unit structure

MAIN: begin;
if X not 0 perform unitA;
end;

unitA: begin;
S;
if X not 0 perform unitA;
return;

Consequently, we may conclude that the modified language has all the capabilities of the original Bare Bones.

It can also be shown that any problem that can be solved using the modified language can be solved using Bare Bones. One method of doing this is to show how any algorithm expressed in the modified language could be written in the original Bare Bones. However, this involves an explicit description of how recursive structures can be simulated with the while/end structure of Bare Bones, which in turn requires that we describe how the environments of the various

469

unit activations can be saved in a stack storage structure using Bare Bones.

For our purpose, it is simpler to rely on the Church-Turing thesis as presented in Chapter 11. In particular, the Church-Turing thesis, combined with the fact that Bare Bones has the same power as Turing machines, dictates that no language can be more powerful than our original Bare Bones. We can thus conclude immediately that any problem solvable in our modified language can also be solved using Bare Bones.

Thus, we see that the power of the modified language is the same as that of the original Bare Bones. Moreover, the only distinction between the two languages is that one provides an iterative control structure while the other provides recursion. We must therefore conclude that the two control structures are, in fact, equivalent in terms of computing power.

F. Answers to Questions/Exercises

Part One
Chapter 1

Section 1-1

1. In the first case, memory cell number 6 ends up containing the value 5. In the second case, it ends up with the value 8.

2. Step 1 erases the original value in cell number 3 when the new value is written there. Consequently, step 2 does not place the original value from cell number 3 in cell number 2. The result is that both cells end up with the value that was originally in cell number 2. A correct procedure is the following:

   Step 1. Move the contents of cell number 2 to cell number 1.

   Step 2. Move the contents of cell number 3 to cell number 2.

   Step 3. Move the contents of cell number 1 to cell number 3.

3. 32768 bits.

4. △ □ ○ ◇ ◇ ○ △

5. a. 6AF2 b. E85517 c. 48

6. a. 0101111111110110010111
   b. 0110000100001010
   c. 1010101111001101
   d. 0000000100000000

Section 1-2

1. Faster retrieval of data and higher transfer rates.

2. The point to remember here is that the slowness of mechanical motion compared with the speed of the internal functioning of the computer dictates that we minimize the number of times we must move the read/write heads. If we fill a complete surface before starting the next, we must move the read/write head each time we finish with a track. The number of moves therefore is approximately the same as the total number of tracks on the two surfaces. If, however, we alternate between surfaces by electronically switching between the read/write heads on the two surfaces, we must mechanically move the read/write heads only after each pair of tracks has been filled. This technique requires half the number of mechanical motions as the previous technique and is therefore preferred.

3. In this application, a constant expansion and shrinking takes place within the data. If the information were stored on tape, this would result in an endless rewriting process to accommodate the upheaval taking place within the data. (One envisions the last block of the data yo-yoing back and forth as reservations earlier on the tape are made, dropped, or become outdated.) When using disk storage, however, each change affects only the portion of the data stored on the track involved. Consequently, much less rewriting of data is required when updates are made.

4. a. The data can be written or read more quickly because the tape device does not have to change direction during the process.
   b. Individual portions of the data can be retrieved more quickly because the tape device does not have to read past all the data being skipped to reach the portion of the tape containing the desired data.

Section 1-3

1. Computer science.

2. The two patterns are the same, except that the second bit from the high-order end is always 0 for uppercase and 1 for lowercase.

3. a. 1001001 0100000 1101100 1101001
      1101011 1100101 0100000 1101101
      1101001 1101100 1101011 0101110

b. 1010111 1101000 1100101 1110010
  1100101 0100000 1100001 1110010
  1100101 0100000 1111001 1101111
  1110101 0111111

c. 0100010 1001000 1101111 1110111
  0111111 0100010 0100000 1000011
  1101000 1100101 1110010 1111001
  1101100 0100000 1100001 1110011
  1101011 1100101 1100100 0101110

d. 0110010 0101011 0110011 0111101
  0110101 0101110

4.

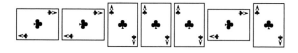

5. a. 5 b. 9 c. 11 d. 6 e. 16 f. 18

6. a. 110 b. 1101 c. 1011 d. 10010
  e. 11011 f. 100

7. In 21 bits, we can store 3 symbols using ASCII. Thus, we can store values as large as 999. However, if we use the bits as binary digits, we can store values up to 16,777,215.

Section 1-4

1. a. 42 b. 33 c. 23 d. 6 e. 31

2. a. 100000 b. 1000000 c. 1100000
  d. 1111 e. 11011

3. a. $3\frac{1}{4}$ b. $5\frac{7}{8}$ c. $2\frac{1}{2}$ d. $6\frac{3}{8}$ e. $\frac{5}{8}$

4. a. 100.1 b. 10.11 c. 1.001 d. 0.0101
  e. 101.101

5. a. 100111 b. 1011.110 c. 100000
  d. 1000.00

Section 1-5

1. a. 6 since $1110 \rightarrow 14 - 8$
  b. -1 since $0111 \rightarrow 7 - 8$
  c. 0 since $1000 \rightarrow 8 - 8$
  d. -6 since $0010 \rightarrow 2 - 8$
  e. -8 since $0000 \rightarrow 0 - 8$
  f. 1 since $1001 \rightarrow 9 - 8$

2. a. 1101 since $5 + 8 = 13 \rightarrow 1101$
  b. 0011 since $-5 + 8 = 3 \rightarrow 0011$
  c. 1011 since $3 + 8 = 11 \rightarrow 1011$
  d. 1000 since $0 + 8 = 8 \rightarrow 1000$

e. 1111 since $7 + 8 = 15 \rightarrow 1111$
f. 0000 since $-8 + 8 = 0 \rightarrow 0000$

3. No. The largest value that can be stored in excess eight notation is 7, represented by 1111. To represent a larger value, at least excess 16 (which uses patterns of 5 bits) must be used. Similarly, 6 cannot be represented in excess four notation. (The largest value that can be represented in excess four notation is 3.)

4. a. 3 b. 15 c. -4 d. -6 e. 0 f. -16

5. a. 00000110 b. 11111010 c. 11101111
  d. 00001101 e. 11111111 f. 00000000

6. a. 11111111 b. 10101011 c. 00000100
  d. 00000010 e. 00000000 f. 10000001

7. a. With 4 bits the largest value is 7 and the smallest is -8.
  b. With 6 bits the largest value is 31 and the smallest is -32.
  c. With 8 bits the largest value is 127 and the smallest is -128.

8. a.
$$\begin{array}{rr} 0101 & 5 \\ +\ 0010 \rightarrow & +\ 2 \\ \hline 0111 & 7 \end{array}$$
  b.
$$\begin{array}{rr} 0011 & 3 \\ +\ 0001 \rightarrow & +\ 1 \\ \hline 0100 & 4 \end{array}$$

c.
$$\begin{array}{rr} 0101 & 5 \\ +\ 1010 \rightarrow & +\ (-6) \\ \hline 1111 & -1 \end{array}$$
  d.
$$\begin{array}{rr} 1110 & (-2) \\ +\ 0011 \rightarrow & +\ \ 3 \\ \hline 0001 & 1 \end{array}$$

e.
$$\begin{array}{rr} 1010 & (-6) \\ +\ 1110 \rightarrow & +\ (-2) \\ \hline 1000 & (-8) \end{array}$$

9. a.
$$\begin{array}{rr} 0100 & 4 \\ +\ 0011 \rightarrow & +\ 3 \\ \hline 0111 \rightarrow & 7 \end{array}$$

b.
$$\begin{array}{rr} 0101 & 5 \\ +\ 0110 \rightarrow & +\ 6 \\ \hline 1011 \rightarrow & -5 \end{array}$$
(incorrect due to overflow)

c.
$$\begin{array}{rr} 1010 & (-6) \\ +\ 1010 \rightarrow & +\ (-6) \\ \hline 0100 \rightarrow & 4 \end{array}$$
(incorrect due to overflow)

d.
$$\begin{array}{rr} 1010 & (-6) \\ +\ 0111 \rightarrow & +\ 7 \\ \hline 0001 \rightarrow & 1 \end{array}$$

e. $\begin{array}{r} 0111 \\ + 0001 \rightarrow \\ \hline 1000 \rightarrow \end{array}$ $\begin{array}{r} 7 \\ + 1 \\ \hline -8 \end{array}$ (incorrect due to overflow)

10. a. $\begin{array}{r} 6 \\ + 1 \rightarrow \\ \hline \end{array}$ $\begin{array}{r} 0110 \\ + 0001 \\ \hline 0111 \end{array}$ $\rightarrow$ 7

b. $\begin{array}{r} 3 \\ - 2 \rightarrow \\ \hline \end{array}$ $\begin{array}{r} 0011 \\ - 0010 \\ \hline \end{array}$ $\rightarrow$ $\begin{array}{r} 0011 \\ + 1110 \\ \hline 0001 \rightarrow \end{array}$ 1

c. $\begin{array}{r} 4 \\ - 6 \\ \hline \end{array}$ $\rightarrow$ $\begin{array}{r} 0100 \\ 0110 \\ \hline \end{array}$ $\rightarrow$ $\begin{array}{r} 0100 \\ + 1010 \\ \hline 1110 \rightarrow \end{array}$ -2

d. $\begin{array}{r} 2 \\ + 4 \rightarrow \\ \hline \end{array}$ $\begin{array}{r} 0010 \\ + 0100 \\ \hline 0110 \end{array}$ $\rightarrow$ 6

e. $\begin{array}{r} 1 \\ - 5 \rightarrow \\ \hline \end{array}$ $\begin{array}{r} 0001 \\ - 0101 \\ \hline \end{array}$ $\rightarrow$ $\begin{array}{r} 0001 \\ + 1011 \\ \hline 1110 \rightarrow \end{array}$ -4

11. No. Overflow occurs when an attempt is made to store a number that is too large for the system being used. When adding a positive value to a negative value, the result must be between the values being added. Thus, if the original values are small enough to be stored, the result is also.

Section 1-6

1. a. $\frac{5}{8}$ b. $3\frac{1}{4}$ c. $\frac{9}{32}$ d. $-1\frac{1}{2}$ e. $-\frac{11}{64}$
2. a. 01101011 b. 01111010 (round-off error)
   c. 01001100 d. 11101110
   e. 11111000 (round-off error)
3. 01001001 (9/16) is larger than 00111101 (13/32). The following is a simple way of determining which of two patterns represents the larger value:
   Case 1. If the sign bits are different, the larger is the one with 0 sign bit.
   Case 2. If the sign bits are both 0, scan the remaining portions of the patterns from left to right until a bit position is found where the two patterns differ. The pattern containing the 1 in this position represents the larger value.
   Case 3. If the sign bits are both 1, scan the remaining portions of the patterns from left to right until a bit position is found where the two patterns differ. The pattern containing the 0 in this position represents the larger value.

The simplicity of this comparison process is one of the reasons for representing the exponent in floating-point systems with an excess notation rather than with two's complement.

4. The largest value would be 7½, which is represented by the pattern 01111111. As for the smallest positive value, you could argue that there are two "correct" answers. First, if you stick to the coding process described in the text, which requires the most significant bit of the mantissa to be 1 (called normalized form), the answer is 1/32, which is represented by the pattern 00001000. However, most machines do not impose this restriction for values close to 0. For such a machine, the correct answer is 1/256 represented by 00000001.

Section 1-7

1. b, c, and e.
2. Yes. If an even number of errors occurs in one byte, the parity technique does not detect them.
3. In this case, errors occur in bytes a and d of question 1. The answer to question 2 remains the same.
4. a. 01001001 00100000 11101100
      11101001 01101011 11100101
      00100000 01101101 11101001
      11101100 01101011 10101110
   b. 01010111 01101000 11100101
      11110010 11100101 10100000
      01100001 11110010 11100101
      00100000 01111001 11101111
      01110101 10111111
   c. 10100010 11001000 11101111
      11110111 10111111 10100010
      00100000 01000011 01101000
      11100101 11110010 01111001
      11101100 00100000 01100001
      01110011 01101011 11100101
      01100100 10101110
   d. 00110010 10101011 10110011
      00111101 10110101 10101110
5. a. BED b. CAB c. HEAD
6. One solution is the following:
   A 0 0 0 0 0
   B 1 1 1 0 0
   C 0 1 1 1 1
   D 1 0 0 1 1

Chapter 2

Section 2-1

1. On small machines this is often a two-step process consisting of first reading the contents from the first cell into a register and then writing it into the destination cell. On most large machines, this activity appears as one event.

2. The value to be written, the address of the cell in which to write, and the command to write.

3. The term *move* often carries the connotation of removing from one location and placing in another, thus leaving a hole behind. In most cases within a machine, this removal does not take place. Rather, the object being moved is most often copied (or cloned) into the new location.

4. A common technique, called relative addressing, is to state how far rather than where to jump. For example, an instruction might be to jump forward three instructions or jump backward two instructions. You should note, however, that such statements must be altered if additional instructions are later inserted between the origin and the destination of the jump.

5. This could be argued either way. The instruction is stated in the form of a conditional jump. However, because the condition that 0 be equal to 0 is always satisfied, the jump will always be made as if there were no condition stated at all. You will often find machines with such instructions in their repertoires because it provides an efficient design. For example, if a machine is designed to execute an instruction with a structure such as "If . . . jump to . . ." this instruction form can be used to express both conditional and unconditional jumps.

Section 2-2

1. a. STORE the contents of register 6 in memory cell number 8A.
   b. JUMP to location DE if the contents of R10 equals that of R0.
   c. AND the contents of registers 3 and 12, leaving the result in register 0.
   d. MOVE the contents of register 15 to register 4.

2. The instruction 15AB requires that the CPU query the memory circuitry for the contents of the memory cell at address AB. This value, when obtained from memory, is then placed in register 5. The instruction 25AB does not require such a request of memory. Rather, the value AB is placed in register 5.

3. a. 2356   b. A503   c. B7F3   d. 80A5

Section 2-3

1. Hexadecimal 34

2. a. 0F   b. C3

3. a. 00   b. 01   c. four times

4. It halts. This is an example of what is often called self-modifying code. That is, the program modifies itself. Note that the first two instructions place hexadecimal C0 at memory location F8, and the next two instructions place 00 at location F9. Thus, by the time the machine reaches the instruction at F8, the halt instruction (C000) has been placed there.

Section 2-4

1. One set of registers is used for fetching, decoding, and executing microinstructions, while the other set is used for fetching, decoding, and executing the machine language instructions as directed by the microprogram.

2. The pipe would contain the instructions B1B0 (being executed), 5002 (being decoded), and B0AA (being fetched). If the value in register 0 is equal to the value in register 1, the jump to location B0 is executed, and the effort expended on the last two of these instructions is wasted.

3. If no precautions are taken, the information at memory locations F8 and F9 is fetched as an instruction before the previous part of the program has had a chance to modify these cells.

4. a. The CPU that is trying to add 1 to the cell can first read the value in the cell. Following this the other CPU reads the cell's value. (Note that at this point both CPUs have retrieved the same value.) If the first CPU now finishes its addition and writes its result back in the cell before the second finishes its subtraction and writes its result, the final value in the cell reflects only the activity of the second CPU.
   b. The CPUs might read the data from the cell as before, but this time the second CPU might write its result before the first. Thus, only the activity of the first CPU is reflected in the cell's final value.

Section 2-5

1. a. 00001011 b. 10000000 c. 00101101
   d. 11101011 e. 11101111 f. 11111111
   g. 11100000 h. 01101111 i. 11010010

2. 0011100 with the AND operation

3. 0011100 with the EXCLUSIVE OR operation

4. a. The final result is 0 if the string contained an odd number of 1s. Otherwise it is 1.
   b. The result is the value of the parity bit for even parity.

5. The logical EXCLUSIVE OR operation mirrors addition except for the case where both operands are 1, in which case the EXCLUSIVE OR produces a 0, whereas the sum is 10. (Thus, the EXCLUSIVE OR operation can be considered an addition operation with no carry.)

6. Use AND with the mask 1011111 to change lowercase to uppercase. Use OR with 0100000 to change uppercase to lowercase.

7. a. 01001101 b. 11100001 c. 11101111

8. a. 57 b. B8 c. 6F d. 6A

9. 5

10. 00110110 in two's complement. 01011110 in floating-point. The point here is that the procedure used to add the values is different depending on the interpretation given the bit patterns.

11. One solution is:
    12A7 (LOAD register 2 with the contents of memory cell A7.)
    2380 (LOAD register 3 with the value 80 (= 10000000).)
    7023 (OR registers 2 and 3 leaving the result in register 0.)
    30A7 (STORE contents of register 0 in memory cell A7.)
    C000 (HALT.)

12. One solution is:
    15E0 (LOAD register 5 with the contents of memory cell E0.)

A502 (ROTATE 2 bits to the right the contents of register 5.)
260F (LOAD register 6 with the value 0F (= 00001111).)
8056 (AND registers 5 and 6 leaving the result in register 0.)
30E1 (STORE the contents of register 0 in memory cell E1.)
C000 (HALT.)

Section 2-6

1. Since each state communicated represents 3 bits, the measure of bps is three times the baud rate.

2. Examples of simplex communication include traditional radio and television broadcasting. The station talks to the audience, but the audience cannot talk back via the same communication channel.

   Half-duplex communication is found in citizens band and other shortwave radio systems. In these cases, one person talks while the other listens and then the roles are reversed. The coordination of this exchange of roles is the purpose of such terminology as "over" or "over and out."

   Full-duplex communication is found in telephone systems. Both parties can talk at the same time and still receive each other's voice.

3. a. 35FA (STORE the contents of register 5 in memory cell number FA.)
   b. 1,000,000 times.
   c. No way! A traditional page of text contains no more than 5,000 characters. Thus, the printer in question is capable of printing no more than 25,000 characters per minute, while the CPU can send more than this in a single second.

4. "Don't send more characters. I'm still busy with the previous ones."
   "I'm ready for more characters."
   "I'm out of paper."

Part Two
Chapter 3

Section 3-1

1. Hardware is to software as:
   a. CDs and tapes are to music

   b. television sets are to television programs
   c. books are to stories

2. In the case of microcomputers, access to the machine is normally controlled by controlling access to the room in which the machine is kept and is therefore of minor importance in their operating systems. Controlling data and its access, providing for efficient device access, and the management of resources remain important tasks on small machines as well as on large ones.

3. 1, 2, and 3.

Section 3-2

1. How many times have you waited in line for access to one of a bank's drive-in tellers and wondered why the lines moved so slowly? How many tellers do you think were actually inside serving the windows? How many virtual tellers were being simulated? As another example, how about an image in a mirror?

2. So long as the system is operating correctly and the user does not attempt to circumvent the system, the distinction between virtual and real characteristics should have no significance. However, in the case of the mail-order business, by knowing that the business is not really a big operation, a customer is able to guard against disappointment by placing Christmas orders earlier than is otherwise done. Similarly, understanding the distinction between virtual and real characteristics can increase a user's success with the system. For example, knowing that the separation between one user's data and another's is actually an illusion created by the operating system might have a significant influence on whether or not truly sensitive data is stored in the system.

3. How about the health care system. It provides a convenient user interface via doctors' offices, hospitals, clinics, and pharmacies, each of which relies on numerous layers of abstraction to present its final product.

4. Most operating systems provide a collection of routines for manipulating files (copy, delete, rename, append, and so on). Each of these is an abstract tool; another is the file directory system itself.

Section 3-3

1. Traffic in a congested area is supposed to move in a FIFO manner, but there always seems to be someone who tries to pass in the outside lane and then cut in ahead of everyone else.

2. Definitely, application a. (It would become quite confusing if the letters did not appear on the screen in a timely fashion as they are typed.)

   Not application b.

   Application c is an example of requirements changing as capabilities change. Several years ago customers' accounts were reconciled at the end of the day in a batch processing environment. The only real-world time coordination was for the job to be done by the next morning. Today, with automatic bank tellers, each balance can be updated by a machine as deposits and withdrawals are made; this real-time processing is becoming the expected procedure.

3. a and b. In these applications, all input data can be collected before the program package is submitted to the operating system for execution. On the other hand, the playing of a video game requires interaction with the user during execution and therefore is unsuitable for batch processing.

4. Time-sharing refers to the technique of alternating a CPU's attention between several processes so that they appear to be executed at the same time. The term *time-sharing* is usually used when the processes sharing time belong to different users. The term *multitasking* is normally used to refer to similar techniques applied to processes belonging to a single user.

5. By multitasking, the time that may have been wasted by one process (such as waiting for a peripheral device to complete a task) can be applied to other processes, creating a more efficient use of the machine's resources.

6. An open network is one whose specifications and protocols are public, allowing different vendors to produce compatible products.

Section 3-4

1. command processor: communicates with user
   scheduler: prepares jobs for execution
   file manager: maintains record of stored information
   resource allocator: coordinates the assignment of resources
   dispatcher: oversees execution of the scheduled activities
   utility software: removes programming burden from user

2. How about something like this?

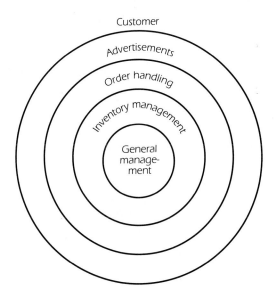

3. In most machines, each letter occupies 1 byte of memory. Thus, this cell size is conducive to character manipulation.

4. In the final analysis there isn't any difference. In fact, many operating systems are built on this observation. In such systems each user-written program automatically becomes a utility program.

Section 3-5

1. If the processes required no external resources, it takes longer to run them in a time-sharing system because of the overhead of swapping back and forth between the two. However, most processes involve I/O operations and often have to wait for slow peripheral devices. In such cases, a time-sharing system can run another process during this waiting period. Consequently, the total time required to run two processes in a time-sharing system may actually be less than the sum of the individual time requirements.

2. Give the high-priority processes longer time slices than the others or give time slices only to the processes of highest priority.

3. First: Stop executing the current process.
   Second: Save the state of the current process.
   Third: Begin executing the interrupt routine.

4. First: Decide which process should be next.
   Second: Reload that process' state.
   Third: Reset the timer.
   Fourth: Start the process.

5. Approximately 20. We say "approximately" because the swapping overhead tends to decrease this value, whereas the fact that some processes will not use their entire slice tends to increase it.

Section 3-6

1. This system guarantees that the resource is not used by more than one process at a time; however, it dictates that the resource be allocated in a strictly alternating fashion. Once a process has used and relinquished the resource, it must wait for the other process to use the resource before the original process can access it again. This is true even if the first process needs the resource right away and the other process won't need it for some time.

2. If two cars enter opposite ends of the tunnel at the same time, they will not be aware of the other's presence. The process of entering and turning on the lights is another example of a critical region, or in this case we might call it a critical process. In this terminology we could summarize the flaw by saying that cars at opposite ends of the tunnel could execute the critical process at the same time.

3. a. This guarantees that the nonshareable resource is not required and allocated on a partial basis; that is, a car is given the whole bridge or nothing at all.

   b. This means that the nonshareable resource can be forcibly retrieved.

   c. This makes the nonshareable resource shareable, which removes the competition.

4. A sequence of arrows that form a closed loop in the directed graph. It is on this observation that techniques have been developed, allowing some operating systems to recognize the existence of deadlock and consequently to take appropriate corrective action.

Section 3-7

1. Otherwise, the bootstrap could be overwritten and thus not available the next time the machine is turned on.

2. Just as the bootstrap routine is a small program used to start a larger one, a car's starter is a small motor used to start a larger one.

3. When turned on, the machine always starts fetching instructions from a predetermined area of main memory. This area of memory is constructed with nonvolatile cells in which is stored the bootstrap program. This program directs the loading of the general purpose operating system from mass storage and then transfers control to this system.

Section 3-8

1. A single break in the ring can disrupt the entire network.

2. A, E, D, C, A, E, C, A

3. One technique is to allow one of the machines in the ring to generate a new token if a certain amount of time passes without the token passing by.

4. The addressing system (name, street address, city, state, zip code) is standard throughout the United States. Thus, a package prepared for one shipper is acceptable to all others.

5. This is an ethical question for discussion. Can the repercussions of inserting the virus be controlled so that only the guilty party is damaged? To what extent is the software developer justified in punishing the pirate?

Chapter 4

Section 4-1

1. You will find that most algorithms used in everyday life fail to be algorithms from a rigorous point of view. This is sometimes true even when the term *algorithm* is used in identifying the process. For example, consider the long-division algorithm. To truly be an algorithm, this process must be combined with a stopping criterion. Otherwise, the repetitive process may continue forever, as when dividing 1 by 3.

2. The problem here is ambiguity. Natural languages developed as communication tools between intelligent beings and therefore lack the precision often required when expressing an algorithm. This is one of the main reasons that the high-level languages discussed in Chapter 5 use a well-defined subset of the English language rather than the complete florid system.

3. If you're thinking in terms of the ambiguity of which table or which pocket, you're missing the point here. The problem of termination is much more important. After all, once started, the process continues to request the removal of coins forever. You may argue that in reality the process must stop because of the lack of coins. This, however, is a property of the algorithm's environment and not of the algorithm itself. The lack of coins does not actually terminate the algorithm's execution; it introduces ambiguity. In light of this argument,

one way to modify the sequence to form an algorithm is the following:

Step 1. If there are no coins in your pocket, stop; otherwise, remove one of them and put it on the table.

Step 2. Return to step 1.

Section 4-2

1. One example is found in the composition of matter. At one level, the primitives are considered molecules, yet these particles are actually composites made up of atoms, which in turn are composed of electrons, protons, and neutrons. Today, we know that even these "primitives" are composites.

2. Once a program module is correctly constructed, it can be used as a building block for larger program structures without reconsidering the module's internal composition.

3. assign X the value of the larger input;
   assign Y the value of the smaller input;
   while (Y not zero) **do**
        (assign Remainder the value of the
            remainder after dividing X by Y;
        assign X the value of Y;
        assign Y the value of Remainder)
   assign GCD the value of X

4. All other colors of light can be produced by combining red, blue, and green. Thus, a television picture tube is designed to produce these three basic colors.

Section 4-3

1. a. Use 667 3s.
   b. Use as many 3s as possible and then no more than two 2s.

2. a. Yes. Hint: place the first tile in the center so that it avoids the quadrant containing the hole while covering one square from each of the other quadrants. Then, each quadrant represents a smaller version of the original problem.
   b. The board with a single hole contains $2^{2n} - 1$ squares, and each tile covers exactly three squares.
   c. Parts a and b of this question provide an excellent example of how knowing a solution to one problem helps solve another. See Polya's fourth phase.

3. It says, "This is the correct answer."

4. The algorithm consists of the single step
   1. Predict the sum to be 28.
   Because the opposing faces of a die always add to seven. Thus, the sum of the top and bottom faces of four dice must always be 28. The point here is that you would probably not find a solution to this problem by following a particular problem-solving methodology. Instead, one must get involved in the problem and do a little creative thinking. You may have gotten your foot in the door by looking at a die.

Section 4-4

1. Change the test in the while statement to read "target value not equal to current entry and there remain entries to be considered."

2. assign Z the value 0;
   assign X the value 1;
   repeat (assign Z the value Z + X;
              assign X the value X + 1)
   until (X = 6)

3.
Cheryl	Alice	Alice
George	Cheryl	Bob
Alice	George	Cheryl
Bob	Bob	George

4. It is a waste of time to insist on placing the pivot above an identical entry in the list. For instance, make the proposed change and then try the new program on a list in which all entries are the same.

Section 4-5

1. The first sublist consists of the names following Henry—that is, Irene, Joe, Darryl, Larry, Mary, Nancy, and Oliver. Next are the names from this list preceding Larry—that is, Irene, Joe, and Darryl. At this point, the search process would find the target Joe at the center of the sublist in question.

2. 8, 17

3.
Bob	Alice
Alice	Bob
Carol	Carol
Larry	Larry
John	John

4. This is an example of how unintelligent an algorithm can be. Rather than recognize that no work is needed, the algorithm ultimately picks each name as the pivot entry and ends up replacing it with itself.

   If the input list is in reverse order, the effect of the algorithm is to exchange the first name with the last, then exchange the new first name with itself, and then turn its attention to the portion of the list between the first and last entries.

5. The effect is that the first occurrence of the name is interchanged with the last, then the first with the next-to-the-last, and so on, until the first occurrence is exchanged with the second.

Section 4-6

1. No. The answer is not correct, although it may sound right. The truth is that two of the three cards are the same on both sides. Thus, the probability of picking such a card is two-thirds.

2. No. If the dividend is less than the divisor, such as in 3/7, the answer given is 1, although it should be 0.

3. No. If the value of X is zero and the value of Y is nonzero, the answer given will not be correct.

4. Each time the test for termination is conducted, the statement "Sum = 1 + 2 + ... + I and I less than or equal to N" is true. Combining this with the termination condition "I greater than or equal to N" produces the desired conclusion "Sum = 1 + 2 + ... + N." Since I is initialized at zero and incremented by one each time through the loop, its value must ultimately reach that of N.

Chapter 5

Section 5-1

1. A program in a third-generation language is machine independent in the sense that its steps are not stated in terms of the machine's attributes such as registers and memory cell addresses. On the other hand, it is machine dependent in the sense that arithmetic overflow and round-off errors will still occur.

2. The major distinction is that an assembler translates each instruction in the source program into a single machine instruction, whereas a compiler often produces many machine-language instructions to obtain the equivalent of a single source program instruction.

3. The declarative paradigm is based on developing a description of the problem to be solved. The functional paradigm forces the programmer to describe the problems solution in terms of solutions to smaller problems. The object-oriented paradigm places emphasis on describing the components in the problem's environment.

4. The later-generation languages allow the program to be expressed more in terms of the problem's environment and less in terms of computer gibberish than do the earlier-generation languages.

Section 5-2

1. First, through the process known as lexical analysis, individual symbols in the program are grouped into strings representing objects such as numbers or words. Then, the parsing process is used to recognize instructions and clauses within instructions. Finally, as the various clauses in the program are recognized, the code generation step produces the equivalent instructions in the target language.

2. a. A translator produces a copy of the source program in a different language but does not execute the program. An interpreter executes the program from its source form without producing a formal, translated version.

   b. To change a program that is being translated, one must first change the source version of the program and then translate, link, and load the altered version before finally executing the program. In contrast, if an interpreter is used, one needs only to change the source program

and then ask the interpreter to execute the new version.

3. The object version of a program usually contains many references to other program segments. These loose ends must be resolved by the linker before the program is ready to load into memory and be executed.

4. A relocatable module is a program segment in machine language that avoids references to explicit memory locations. Thus, the program executes correctly regardless of where it is placed in memory. This means that the loader need not be concerned with modifying the module to reflect its location in memory.

Section 5-3

1. Does the expression "X and Y or Z" mean that either both X and Y are true or Z is true, or does it mean that X is true as well as either Y or Z? This ambiguity can be resolved with parentheses by writing "(X and Y) or Z" in the first case and "X and (Y or Z)" in the second.

2. If the expression is evaluated from left to right, the result is 7. If it is evaluated from right to left, the result is 14. If it is evaluated according to the normal rules of arithmetic, the result is 11.

3. a, d, and e.

4. The definitions of terms in a natural language are not precise enough to avoid ambiguity. This is why many legal cases are argued in court on the basis of the meaning of a law, with opponents presenting different interpretations. In the case of programming languages, this potential problem of ambiguity is removed by restricting the language used to a few well-defined statement forms.

5. Did John chase the parade or did he wait for the parade to pass before going for his afternoon jog?

Section 5-4

1. Probably something of the form XYZ(3,5). Note that the row is identified before the column.

2. a. The fractional part must be dropped, leaving the value 26.

   b. Both the integer and the fractional part are stored; however, the fractional part probably is inaccurate since one-tenth cannot be represented exactly in binary notation.

c. The four characters (2, 6, ., and 1) that represent the value are stored in coded form.

3. a. A matrix with five rows (one for each employee) and seven columns (one for each day of the week).

b. Perhaps a three-dimensional array with the dimensions represented by employees, days of the week, and weeks of the year.

c. A vector of six entries (one for each game).

d. A heterogeneous vector because the entries are of different types: name (of type character), quantity (of type integer), and so on.

4. A constant in a program is a name that refers to a value that cannot change as the program executes. A variable is a name of a memory cell whose contents (and thus the value associated with the name) can vary during program execution.

5. In addition to moving the data, the data must be recoded to agree with the type associated with the new location.

6. Ada: at the first begin.
BASIC: at line number 200.
C: at the statement main.
FORTRAN: at the second comment line.
Pascal: at the second begin.

7. The ignored statements are:
those beginning with -- in Ada
those surrounded by /* and */ in C
those beginning with C in FORTRAN
those surrounded by brackets {} in Pascal
These statements are provided to assist a human, not the machine.

Section 5-5

1. Only c.

2. Start the critical region with an in statement to retrieve a tuple of a particular type from the tuple space and close the critical region with an out statement to replace the tuple. Then, place a single tuple of that type in the tuple space. Any process trying to enter the critical region must first retrieve the tuple, and because there is only one such tuple, only one process is allowed in the critical region at a time.

3. a. The process executing this statement is blocked because there is no tuple of the form (4, 2) in the tuple space to be retrieved.

b. A tuple of the form (8, 3.4) is placed in the tuple space.

c. The variable Value is assigned the value 5. The tuple (5, 7) remains in the tuple space.

d. The tuple (5, 7) is retrieved from the tuple space, and Value is given the value 5.

Section 5-6

1. R, T, and V. For instance, we can show that R is a consequence by adding its negation to the collection and showing that resolution can lead to the empty statement, as shown below:

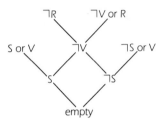

2. No. The collection is inconsistent since resolution can lead to the empty statement, as shown below:

3. a. smaller(sue, carol)
smaller(sue, john)

b. smaller(sue, carol)
smaller(bill, carol)

c. smaller(carol, john)
smaller(bill, sue)
smaller(sue, carol)
smaller(bill, sue)
smaller(sue, john)

Chapter 6

Section 6-1

1. A long sequence of assignment statements is not as complex in the context of program design as a few nested **if** statements.

2. One approach is to intentionally place some errors in the software when it is designed. Then, after the software has supposedly been debugged, check to see how many of the original errors are still present. If 5 of the 7 original errors have been removed, then conclude that only 5/7 of the total errors in the software have been removed.

3. How about the number of errors found after a fixed period of use? One problem here is that this value cannot be measured in advance.

Section 6-2

1. System requirements are stated in terms of the application environment, whereas the specifications are stated in technical terms and identify how the requirements will be met.

2. The analysis phase concentrates on what the proposed system must accomplish. The design phase concentrates on how the system accomplishes its goals. The implementation phase concentrates on the actual construction of the system. The testing phase concentrates on making sure that the system does what it is intended to do.

3. The traditional waterfall approach dictates that the analysis, design, implementation, and testing phases be performed in a linear manner. The prototyping model allows for a more relaxed trial-and-error approach.

Section 6-3

1. No.

2. The chapters of a novel build on one another, whereas the sections in an encyclopedia are largely independent. Hence, a novel has more coupling between its chapters than an encyclopedia has between its sections. However, the sections within an encyclopedia probably have a higher level of cohesion than the chapters in a novel.

3. Explicit coupling includes the identification of the trump suit, which hand is dummy, who will lead, and so on. Insights gained from the bidding process, such as who holds which cards, can be considered implicit coupling.

4. This is a tough one. From one point of view, we could start by placing everything in a single module. This would result in little cohesion and no coupling at all. If we then begin to divide this single module into smaller ones, the result would be an increase in coupling. We might therefore conclude that increasing cohesion tends to increase coupling.

   On the other hand, suppose the problem at hand naturally divides into three very cohesive modules, which we will call A, B, and C. If our original design did not observe this natural division (for example, half of task A might be placed with half of task B, and so on), we would expect the cohesion to be low and the coupling high. In this case, redesigning the system by isolating tasks A, B, and C into separate modules would most likely decrease intermodule coupling as intramodule cohesion increases.

5. a. The common goal or interest of the club members. As various club activities are undertaken, committees and subcommittees are often formed to organize them. This can be viewed as a natural tendency to maximize cohesion. The cohesion of the club as a whole is weak compared with the specific tasks of the committees. Also, the duties of the officers of a club are modularized according to function. For example, the president presides over meetings, the secretary maintains records, and the treasurer manages the finances.

   b. The marketing of merchandise. Here again we find a natural tendency to seek greater cohesion within the organization. In this case, it results in the formation of departments based on the type of merchandise being sold. In addition, we find the management divided according to function in a similar manner to the officers in a club.

   c. The registration of students. This activity is normally broken into its functional components to obtain a greater degree of cohesion. For example, one component might deal with confirming admission, another with selecting courses, still another with paying fees.

d. The conveying of information. Again observe the natural desire to increase cohesion by subdivision. Newspapers are divided into sections according to subject matter.

Section 6-4

1.

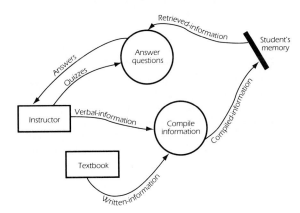

2.

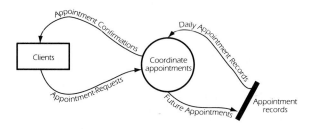

3. A dataflow diagram is a representation of the paths through which information flows through a system. An entity-relationship diagram is a pictorial representation of the various items of information in a system and how each item relates to the others. A data dictionary is a depository of information relating to the various data items in a software system.

4. The relationship between a company and its flights is one-to-many. The relationship between flights and passengers, as well as between companies and passengers, is many-to-many.

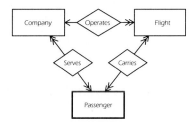

Section 6-5

1. In accompanying manuals, within the source program in the form of comments and well-written code, through interactive messages that the program itself writes at a terminal, through data dictionaries, and in the form of design documents such as structure charts, dataflow diagrams, and entity-relationship diagrams.

2. In both the development and modification phases. The point is that modifications must be documented as thoroughly as the original program. (It's also true that software is documented while in its use phase. For example, a user of the system might discover problems, which are then reported in the system user's manual. Moreover, books written on the use and design of popular software systems are common. These are often written by people other than the original designers and after the software has been in use for some time and has gained popularity.)

3. Different people will have different opinions on this one. Some will argue that the program is the point of the whole project and thus is naturally the more important. Others will argue that a program is worth nothing if it is not documented, because if you can't understand a program, you can't use it or modify it. Moreover, with good documentation, the task of creating the program can be "easily" recreated.

Part Three

Chapter 7

Section 7-1

1. 5 3 7 4 2 8 1 9 6

2. If R is the number of rows in the matrix, the formula is $R(J - 1) + (I - 1)$.

3. From the beginning address of 25, we must skip over $11(3 - 1) + (6 - 1) = 27$ entries in the matrix, each of which occupies two memory cells. Thus, we must skip over 54 memory cells. The final address can therefore be found by adding 54 to the address of the first entry, resulting in the address of 79.

4. $(C \times I) + J$

Section 7-2

1. As an example, to find the fifth entry in a dense list, multiply the number of cells in each entry by 4 and add the result to the address of the first entry. The situation is quite different in the case of the linked list because the address of the fifth entry is in no way related to the address of the first. Thus, to find the fifth entry, one must actually traverse each preceding entry.

2. The head pointer contains the NIL value.

3. assign Last the value of the last name to be printed
assign Finished the value false
assign Current Pointer the value in the head pointer;
while (Current Pointer not NIL and Finished = false) **do**
(print the entry pointed to by Current Pointer,
if (the name just printed = Last) **then**
(assign Finished the value true)
assign Current Pointer the value in the pointer cell in the entry pointed to by Current Pointer)

4. assign Current the value in the head pointer
assign Previous the value NIL
assign Found the value false
while (Current not NIL and Found is false) **do**
(**if** (the entry pointed to by Current is the target entry)
then (assign Found the value true)
else (assign Previous the value of Current;
assign Current the value in the pointer cell of the entry pointed to by Current))
if (Found is true) **then**
(**if** (Previous = NIL)

then (assign head pointer the value in the pointer cell of the entry pointed to by Current)
else (assign the pointer cell in the entry pointed to by Previous the value in the pointer cell in the entry pointed to by Current))

Section 7-3

1. One traditional example is the stack of trays in a cafeteria. Many of these are spring-loaded to keep the top tray at a convenient level. In this case, the term *push* is truly representative of the process of adding more entries to the stack.

2.

Activity	Stack Immediately Following Activity
Main program calls subprogram A.	Position in main
Subprogram A calls subprogram B.	Position in A Position in main
Subprogram B completes.	Position in main
Subprogram A calls subprogram C.	Position in A Position in main
Subprogram C completes.	Position in main
Subprogram A completes.	Stack empty

3. The stack pointer points to the cell immediately below the base of the stack.

4. **if** (the stack pointer points below the stack base)
then (exit with error message)
extract the stack entry pointed to by the stack pointer;
adjust the stack pointer to point to the next lower stack entry

5. Represent the stack as a one-dimensional array and the stack pointer as a variable of integer type. Then use this stack pointer to maintain a record of the position of the stack's top within the array rather than of the exact memory address.

Section 7-4

1.

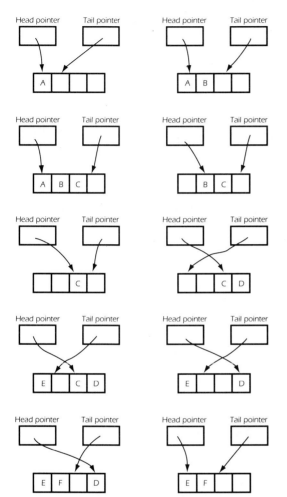

2. Both empty and full conditions are indicated by the equal head and tail pointers. Thus, additional information is required to distinguish between the two conditions.

3. **if** (Full is true) **then** (exit with error message)
Store the new entry in the location pointed to by the tail pointer;
advance the tail pointer;
if (the tail pointer points beyond the reserved block)

then (alter the tail pointer to point to the first cell of the reserved block)
if (head pointer = tail pointer)
then (assign Full the value true)

Section 7-5

1. The root is 11, the leaf nodes are 1, 2, 6, 3, and 4. There are four Qy subtrees below the node 9, with roots 5, 1, 2, and 6. The nodes 9 and 10 are siblings, as are 5 and 6, 1 and 2, and 7 and 8.

2. The root pointer is NIL.

3.

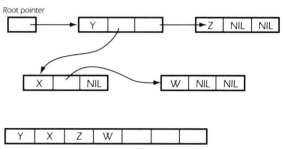

4.

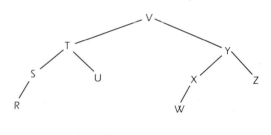

5. When searching for J:

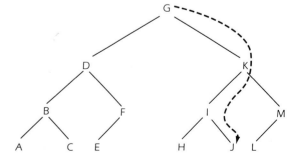

When searching for P:

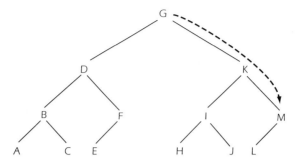

6.

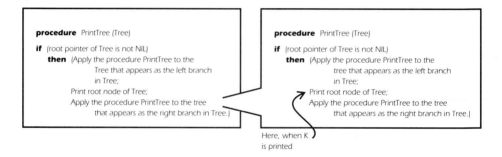

Here, when K
is printed

Section 7-6

1. Deposits and withdrawals to and from a checking account can be executed only through specific procedures that are supported by laws.

2. An abstract data type is a concept; an instance of that data type is an actual object of that type. For example, dog is a type of animal, whereas Lassie and Rex are instances of that type.

3. A traditional program module is normally designed to carry out a specific procedure and thus consists of a single routine. An instance of an abstract data type is designed to simulate the underlying type and thus may be capable of executing several procedures. For example, an instance of a stack is capable of pushing new entries on the stack as well as popping old entries from the stack.

4. A queue of integers might be implemented using either a dense or linked list as the underlying structure. Or, you may have answered as a circular queue restricted to a specific block of memory cells or a roaming block of cells, although this latter implementation would prove dangerous to the other data structures residing in memory.

Section 7-7

1. One might be an escalator that should be able to receive shoppers at one level and deposit them at another. Another might be an entrance that should be able to introduce new shoppers into the system while removing others from the system.

2. Each object package contains those routines used to simulate the abstract object being represented.

3. A single object often consists of separate routines for performing the various operations on the object. For example, a stack object would have routines for pushing and popping entries. Each of these routines could be implemented as a submodule of the object.

Chapter 8

Section 8-1

1. You should be led through these beginning stages:

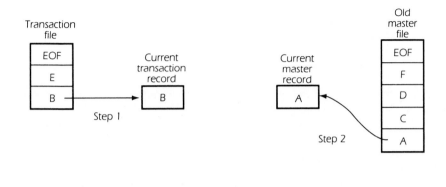

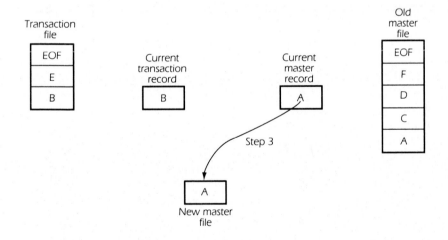

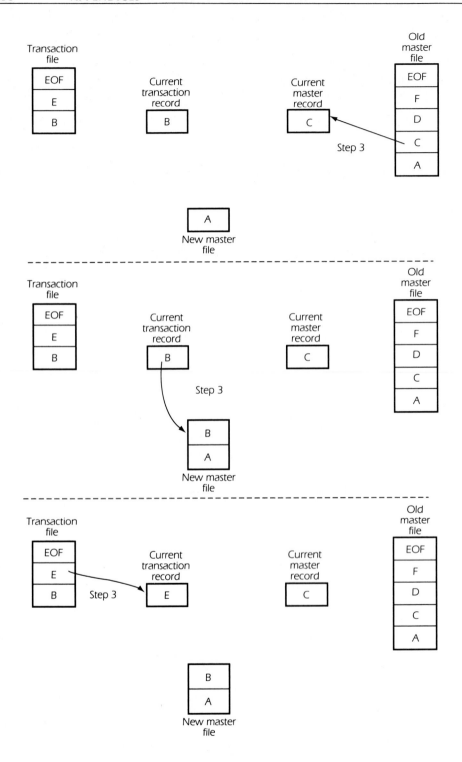

2. The idea is to first divide the file to be stored into many separate files containing one record each. Next, group the one-record files into pairs, and within each pair, designate one file as the transaction file and the other as the old master. Since each file is sorted (it has only one record), we can now apply the merge algorithm to each pair. This results in half as many files, each with two records. Furthermore, each of these two-record files is sorted. We can group them into pairs, call one member of each pair the transaction file and the other the old master file, and again apply the merge algorithm to the pairs. Again we find ourselves with fewer but larger files, each of which is sorted. Continuing in this fashion, we are ultimately left with only one file that consists of all the original records but in sorted order. (If an odd number of files occurs at any stage of this process, we need merely to set the odd one aside and pair it with one of the larger files in the next stage.)

3. First, sequentially read the tape until the position is reached where the new record belongs. Note that because a record is there now, we must read that record into main memory for safekeeping before writing the new one in its place. Having read this record, we are now beyond the "hole" on the tape, so we must rewind the tape and sequentially read back to the position of the hole. We can now write the new record into the hole. At this point we must place the record being held in memory back on the tape. It belongs at the current position (immediately after the record just inserted), but a record is already there. Therefore, we must read this record into main memory before writing in its place. Having read this record, we are beyond the required hole and must rewind the tape and sequentially . . . . (Note that if the records were not the same size we would not know that retrieving one record would provide a hole big enough to hold its replacement.)

Section 8-2

1. A text file is essentially a sequential file in which each record is a single symbol.

2. Documents processed by word processors (letters, manuscripts, memoranda, brochures) are normally stored as text files. Mail transferred via e-mail is also normally handled as text files.

3. Normally a large part of the document is held in main memory, allowing random access to that portion of the document. However, as the latter portion of the document is processed, the earlier portion may be placed in mass storage. If one then wanted to back up to this earlier portion, and that portion had been stored as a text file, then the processor would have to read from the beginning of the document to find the part to be updated.

Section 8-3

1. Suppose the entries in the index are the smallest key field values from each segment and we are looking for the record with key field value 7. If the first entry in the index is 5, we do not know whether or not the target record is in the segment represented by this entry. Thus, we must go on to the next entry. If this next entry is 11, we can conclude that the previous entry is the one we need, because our target key field, 7, is less than 11. Consequently, we must backtrack to the previous index entry to continue the search.

   In contrast, suppose the entries in the index are the largest key field value from each segment. When looking for the entry 7, we might first find the entry 10. Since 10 is larger than the target key field value, we can conclude immediately that this is the segment of interest, without going further in the index.

2. The purpose is to provide both direct and sequential access to the file. As pointed out in the section, sequential access is possible in an indexed file if the index is constructed so that it can be traversed sequentially, as we did in the tree structure in Chapter 7. On the other hand, if the file is designed as an indexed sequential file, sequential processing might well be carried out more efficiently.

3. A list, in some cases, is easier to update. On the other hand, searching for an entry can take significantly more time than in the case of a tree.

4. It depends on how generally you interpret "the technique presented in this section." The point is that the partial-index system we presented relies on each physical segment being a contiguous part of the overall sorted file. Since the file cannot be physically divided according to two different orders, the technique could not literally be applied to different key fields in the same file. On the other hand, approximations to the technique can be implemented using a pointer system to represent the second order. Since an index based on this additional system is less efficient than the one

based on the physical storage order, we normally use it for the key field that is used less frequently.

Section 8-4

1. This is a good example of the kinds of things that must be considered when selecting a hash algorithm. In this case, the first three digits of the Social Security numbers are a poor choice because these digits represent the area of the country in which the number was assigned. Consequently, citizens in one area of the country tend to have the same starting digits in their Social Security numbers, and this would result in more clustering than normal in the hashed file.

2. A poorly chosen hash algorithm results in more clustering than normal and thus in more overflow. Since the overflow from each section of mass storage is organized as a linked list, searching through the overflow records is essentially searching a sequential file.

3. The section assignments are as follows:
   a. 0   b. 0   c. 3   d. 0   e. 3
   f. 3   g. 3   h. 3   i. 3   j. 0
   Thus, all the records hash into buckets 0 and 3 leaving buckets 1, 2, 4, and 5 empty. The problem here is that the number of buckets being used (6) and the key field values have the common factor of 3. (You might try rehashing these key field values using 7 buckets and see what improvement you find.)

4. The point here is that we are essentially applying a hash algorithm to place the people in the group into one of 365 categories. The hash algorithm, of course, is the calculation of one's birthday. The amazing thing is that only 23 people are required before the probability is in favor of at least two of the birthdays being the same. In terms of a hashed file, this indicates that when hashing records into

365 available buckets of mass storage, clustering is likely to be present after only 23 records have been entered.

5. The buckets of mass storage identified by the hashing process are normally chosen to be tracks on the disk, with the overflow area as another one or more tracks.

Section 8-4

1. The operating system first searches the index to find which segment should be interrogated. Having established the desired segment number, the operating system might then check to see if that segment is already in main memory (it may be the same segment that was previously accessed). If it is already in main memory, the operating system searches it and relays the correct record to the program. Otherwise, the segment must be retrieved from mass storage and then searched.

2. The operating system in a time-sharing environment does its best to use all time efficiently. If the required storage segment is not already in main memory, the operating system asks the controller of the disk drive to retrieve the correct segment; but rather than wait for the data to arrive, the operating system terminates the original program's time slice and starts another program. After the controller has placed the requested segment in main memory, the operating system returns to the original program, gives it the record it needed, and allows it to continue execution in the normal sequence of time slices.

3. No. For some reason this is a common mistake made by beginning programmers. Keep in mind that an index for a file must be maintained as the file is initially constructed and later modified. The operating system cannot perform the magic of creating an index for a previously nonindexed file.

Chapter 9

Section 9-1

1. The purchasing department would be interested in inventory records to place orders for more raw goods, whereas the accounting department would need the information to balance the books.

2. Employee, student, alumni, finance, registration, equipment/supplies, and so on.

3. The subschema for the purchasing department would probably include the addresses of the

various manufacturers who supply the parts in inventory and perhaps the name of the sales representative for each of these companies. The subschema for the accounting department would probably not include this information.

Section 9-2

1. No. The use of file systems invariably dictates that the application program be expressed in terms of the actual organization of records in the file. Thus,

a change in the record structure would require changes in all programs accessing that file.

2.

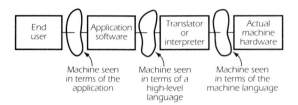

3. The application software translates the user's requests from the terminology of the application into terminology compatible with the database management system. The database management system in turn converts the requests into a form understood by the routines that actually manipulate the data in mass storage. These last routines perform the retrieval of data.

Section 9-3

1. a. G. Jerry Smith
   b. Cheryl H. Clark
   c. S26Z

2. One solution is
   TEMP ← SELECT from JOB
        where Dept = "PERSONNEL"
   LIST ← PROJECT JobTitle from TEMP
   In some systems this results in a list with a job title repeated, depending on how many times it occurred in the personnel department. That is, our list may contain numerous occurrences of the title secretary. It is more common, however, to design the PROJECT operation so that it removes duplicate tuples from the resulting relation.

3. One solution is
   TEMP1 ← JOIN JOB and ASSIGNMENT
        where JOB.Job =
        ASSIGNMENT.Job-Id
   TEMP2 ← SELECT from TEMP1
        where TermDate = "*"
   TEMP3 ← JOIN EMPLOYEE and TEMP2
        where EMPLOYEE.EmpId =
        TEMP2.EmpId
   RESULT ← PROJECT Name, Dept from TEMP3

4. The model itself does not provide data independence. This is a property of the data management system. Data independence is achieved by providing the data management system the ability to present a consistent relational organization to the application software even though the actual organization may change.

5. Through common attributes. For instance, the EMPLOYEE relation in this section is tied to the ASSIGNMENT relation via the attribute EmpId, and the ASSIGNMENT relation is tied to the JOB relation by the attribute JobId. Attributes used to connect relations like this are sometimes called connection attributes.

Section 9-4

1. The concept is almost identical except that the end of file is indicated in the set environment by returning to the owner rather than by finding a special mark. Another difference is that retrieval of a record from a sequential file is combined with the advancement of one's position in the file, whereas the network model normally separates these activities. Although we didn't mention it in the text, the FIND-NEXT and FIND-OWNER commands shift one's position in the database but do not actually retrieve data. An additional operation called GET is normally used for actual retrieval.

2. First open the database and then do the following:
   FIND-NEXT JOB-SET
   FIND-NEXT JOB-SET
   FIND-NEXT FILLED-BY
   FIND-OWNER WORK-HISTORY
   Retrieve the current EMPLOYEE group and print that employee's name.
   FIND-NEXT FILLED-BY
   FIND-OWNER WORK-HISTORY
   Retrieve the current EMPLOYEE group and print that employee's name.
   Stop

3. No. When the database is first opened, no position in a WORK-HISTORY set is yet established; thus an instruction to find the next entry in such a set is meaningless.

4. No. You wouldn't know this from the discussion in the text, however. Indexes are often maintained on certain groups to allow timely response to frequently asked questions, just as in indexed files. An example is in an airline reservation system, information about flights and their passenger lists are frequently interrogated. Here indexes allow the application software to reach information about "walking" to it step by step.

5. Most likely not. In fact you would probably be considered strange for asking. The point here is to emphasize again that the database models being discussed are of concern to the application software and not to the end user.

Section 9-5

1. There may be methods for assigning and retrieving the StartDate as well as the TermDate. Another method may be provided for reporting the total time in service.

2. One approach is to establish an object for each type of product in inventory. Each of these objects could maintain the total inventory of its product, the cost of the product, and links to the outstanding orders for the product.

3. As indicated at the beginning of this section, object-oriented databases appear to handle composite data types more easily than relational databases. Moreover, the fact that objects can contain methods that take an active role in answering questions promises to give object-oriented databases an advantage over relational databases whose relations merely hold the data.

Section 9-6

1. Suppose x is a person's checking account balance, y is that person's savings account balance, and z is

that person's total balance. Let T1 be the transaction of transferring funds from the savings account to the checking account and T2 be the transaction of updating the total of both accounts. Then, the proposed schedule produces a total based on the old checking account balance and the new savings account balance.

2. a. This schedule is conflict equivalent to
   T1: $R(x)$ $W(x)$
   T2: $R(x)W(y)$
   b. This schedule is not conflict serializable. In any conflict equivalent schedule the $R(x)$ step of T2 must precede the $W(x)$ of T1, and the $W(x)$ step of T1 must precede the $W(x)$ step of T2.
   c. This schedule is conflict equivalent to
   T1: $R(x)$ $W(x)$
   T2: $R(x)$ $W(y)$
   T3: $R(x)$ $W(y)$

3. a. T1 → T2
   b. T1 ⇄ T2
   c. T1 ← T2
      ↖   ↗
       T3

Part Four

Chapter 10

Section 10-1

1. Our purpose here is not to give a decisive answer to this issue but to use it to show how delicate the argument over the existence of intelligence really is.

2. Although most of us would probably say no, we would probably claim that if a human dispensed the same products in a similar atmosphere, awareness would be present even though we might not be able to explain the distinction.

Section 10-2

1. In the remote control case, the system needs only to relay the picture, whereas to use the picture for maneuvering, the robot must be able to "understand" the meaning of the picture.

2. The possible interpretations for one section of the drawing do not match any of those of another

section. To embed this insight into a program, one might isolate the interpretations allowable for various line junctions and then write a program that tries to find a set of compatible interpretations (one for each junction). In fact, if you stop and think about it, this is probably what your own senses did in trying to evaluate the drawing. Did you detect your eyes scanning back and forth between the two ends of the drawing as your senses tried to piece possible interpretations together? (If this subject interests you, you'll want to read about the work of people such as D. A. Huffman, M. B. Clowes, and D. Waltz.)

Section 10-3

1. Production systems provide a uniform approach to a variety of problems. That is, although apparently different in their original form, all problems

reformulated into terms of production systems become the problem of finding a path through a state graph.

2.

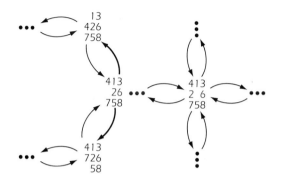

3. The states might include that of starting the maze, finishing the maze, deciding which way to go from the current position, or being stuck at a dead end. These individual states are so closely associated with particular positions in the maze that we can identify them by the positions labeled below. Thus, we can speak of being in state S (the starting state), state B (deciding which way to go from that position), or state G (having reached the goal).

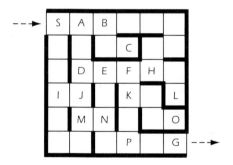

The productions consist of the movements from one location to another. Thus, the state graph has the following form:

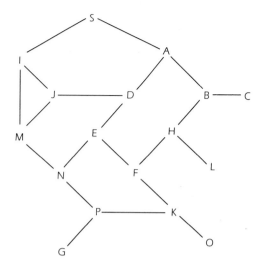

Section 10-4

1. The tree is four moves deep. The upper portion appears as follows:

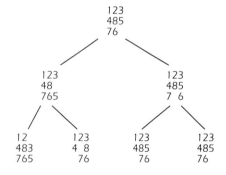

2. Less of the tree needs to be constructed, thus saving both time and storage space.

3. The task requires too much paper as well as too much time.

4. Remember that the control system must execute the productions as they are popped off the stack. At execution time, the instruction *move the tile in the upper right hand corner down* would be easier to execute than the instruction *move the 5 tile down*. The latter form requires the system to return to the puzzle image to find where the 5 tile is located at that time.

Section 10-5

1. Our heuristic system for solving the 8-puzzle is based on an analysis of the immediate situation, just as that of the mountain climber. This short-sightedness is what allowed our algorithm to proceed initially along the wrong path in the example of this section just as a mountain climber can be led into trouble by always plotting a course based only on the local terrain. (This analogy often causes heuristic systems based on local or immediate information to be called hill-climbing systems.)

2. The system rotates the 5, 6, and 8 tiles either clockwise or counterclockwise until the goal state is reached.

3. The problem here is that our heuristic scheme ignores the value of keeping the hole adjacent to the tiles that are out of place. If the hole is surrounded by tiles in their correct position, some of these tiles must be moved before those tiles still seeking their correct place can be moved. Thus, it is incorrect to consider all those tiles surrounding the hole as actually being correct. To fix this flaw, we might first observe that a tile in its correct position but blocking the hole from incorrectly positioned tiles must be moved away from its correct position and later moved back. Thus, each correctly positioned tile on a path between the hole and the nearest incorrectly positioned tile accounts for at least two moves in the remaining solution. We can therefore modify our projected cost calculation as follows:

First, calculate the projected cost as before. However, if the hole is totally isolated from the incorrectly positioned tiles, find a shortest path between the hole and an incorrectly positioned tile, multiply the number of tiles on this path by two, and add the resulting value to the previous projected cost.

With this system, the leaf nodes in Figure 10-10 have projected costs of 6, 6, and 4 (from left to right), and thus the correct branch is pursued initially.

Our new system is not foolproof. For example, consider the following configuration. The solution is to slide the 5 tile down, rotate the top two rows clockwise until those tiles are correct, move the 5 tile back up, and finally move the 8 tile to its correct position. However, our new heuristic system wants us to start by moving the 8 tile,

because the state obtained by this initial move has a projected cost of only 6 compared with the other options that have costs of 8.

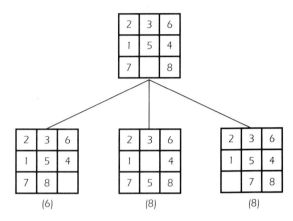

(6)   (8)   (8)

4. The search tree is little more than a linked list representing the result of depth-first search without a depth limit, because the "leftmost leaf node with the smallest projected cost" is always the leftmost leaf node. Thus, the search tree consists of only the leftmost possible path.

Section 10-6

1. All patterns produce an output of 0 except for the pattern 1, 0, which produces an output of 1.

2. Assign a weight of 1 to each input, and assign the unit a threshold value of 1.5.

3. Design a two-level network as described in the text. The lower-level units should assign each of their inputs the weight 1 and have a threshold of 7½. Thus, one of these units outputs a 1 if the pattern in the field of view is the circle; otherwise, all the lower-level units produce an output of 0. In turn, if the upper-level unit assigns each of its inputs the weight 1 and has a threshold of ½, then the entire network produces a 1 when the pattern is a circle and a 0 when the pattern is an X.

4. Design a two-level network as described in the text. Each lower-level unit should have a threshold of 2½, assign the weight of 0 to the corner squares in its field of view, and assign the weight of 1 to the other squares. The only way one of these units can produce a 1 as its output is to have the C pattern in its field of view. In fact,

if this is the pattern, two lower-level units produce an output of 1. Thus, if the upper-level unit assigns each of its inputs the weight 1 and has a threshold of 1, then it produces an output of 1 when the pattern in the field of view is the C and an output of 0 when the pattern is the V.

Section 10-7

1. Is the sentence describing what kind of horses they are, or is it telling what some people are doing?

2. The parsing process produces identical structures, but the semantic analysis recognizes that the prepositional phrase in the first sentence tells where the fence was built, whereas the phrase in the second sentence tells when the fence was built.

3. It uses the closed-world assumption.

4. In many ways, the two are the same. However, traditional databases tend to contain only facts such as an employee's name, address, and so on, whereas knowledge bases tend to include rules such as "if raining, check rain gauge" that can be used to direct the reasoning process.

Chapter 11

Section 11-1

1. clear AUX;
   incr AUX;
   end;
   while AUX not 0 do;
     incr X;
     clear AUX;
   end;

2. while X not 0 do;
     decr X;
   end;

3. move X to AUX;
   while AUX not 0 do;
     S1
     clear AUX;
   end;
   move X to AUX;
   invert AUX;
   while AUX not 0 do;
     S2
     clear AUX;
   end;
   while X not 0 do;
     clear AUX;
     clear X;

4. If we assume that X refers to the memory cell at address 40 and that each program segment starts at location 00, we have the following conversion table:

clear X;	Address	Contents
	00	20
	01	00
	02	30
	03	40

incr X;	Address	Contents
	00	11
	01	40
	02	20
	03	01
	04	50
	05	01
	06	30
	07	40

decr X;	Address	Contents
	00	20
	01	00
	02	11
	03	40
	04	22
	05	01
	06	40
	07	03
	08	50
	09	02
	0A	B1
	0B	06
	0C	33
	0D	40

while X not 0 do;	Address	Contents
	00	20
	01	00
.	02	11
.	03	40
.	04	B1
end;	05	WZ
.	.	.
.	.	.
	WX	B0
	WY	00

5. Just as in a real machine, negative numbers could be dealt with via a coding system. For example, the

rightmost bit in each string can be used as a sign but with the remaining bits used to represent the magnitude of the value.

Section 11-2

1. The result is the following diagram:

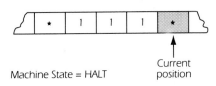

Machine State = HALT

Current position

2.

Current State	Cell Content	Value to Write	Direction to Move	New State to Enter
START	*	*	left	STATE 1
STATE 1	0	0	left	STATE 2
STATE 1	1	0	left	STATE 2
STATE 1	*	0	left	STATE 2
STATE 2	0	*	right	STATE 3
STATE 2	1	*	right	STATE 3
STATE 2	*	*	right	STATE 3
STATE 3	0	0	right	HALT
STATE 3	1	0	right	HALT

3.

Current State	Current Cell Content	Value to Write	Direction to Move	New State to Enter
START	*	*	left	SUBTRACT
SUBTRACT	0	1	left	BORROW
SUBTRACT	1	0	left	NO BORROW
BORROW	0	1	left	BORROW
BORROW	1	0	left	NO BORROW
BORROW	*	*	right	ZERO
NO BORROW	0	0	left	NO BORROW
NO BORROW	1	1	left	NO BORROW
NO BORROW	*	*	right	RETURN
ZERO	0	0	right	ZERO
ZERO	1	0	right	ZERO
ZERO	*	*	no move	HALT
RETURN	0	0	right	RETURN
RETURN	1	1	right	RETURN
RETURN	*	*	no move	HALT

4. The point here is that the concept of a Turing machine is supposed to capture the meaning of "to compute." That is, any time a situation occurs in which computing is taking place, the components and activities of a Turing machine should be present. For example, a person figuring income tax is doing a certain degree of computing. The computing machine is the person and the tape is represented by the paper on which values are recorded.

Section 11-3

1. The machine described by the following table halts if started with an even input but never halts if started with an odd input:

Current State	Current Cell Content	Value to Write	Direction to Move	New State to Enter
START	*	*	left	STATE 1
STATE 1	0	0	right	HALT
STATE 1	1	1	no move	STATE 1
STATE 1	*	*	no move	STATE 1

2. The computation of a loan payment, the area of a circle, or a car's mileage.

3. Mathematicians call such functions transcendental functions. Examples include the logarithmic and trigonometric functions. These particular examples can still be computed but not by algebraic means. For example, the trigonometric functions can be calculated by actually drawing the triangle involved, measuring its sides, and only then turning to the algebraic operation of dividing.

4. The function is multiplication by 2.

Section 11-4

1. ...capture the meaning of "to compute" or equivalently "to calculate."

decr X.   (program)
↓
11001001100101110001111100100100000101100001110011   (ASCII code)
↓
443,301,799,406,651   (Gödel number in base ten)

2. Yes. In fact, this program halts for any input value. Thus, it must halt if its input is its own Gödel number.

3. The point here is that the logic is the same as in our argument that the halting problem does not have an algorithmic solution. If the house painter paints his or her own house, he or she doesn't and vice versa.

Section 11-5

1. If the machine sorts 100 names in an average of one second, it can perform (1/4) (10,000 − 100) comparisons in one second. This means that each comparison takes approximately 0.0004 second. Consequently, sorting 1000 names [which requires an average of (1/4) (1,000,000 − 1000) comparisons] requires roughly 100 seconds or 1⅔ minutes.

2. To sort a list of 100 names using the quick sort algorithm requires at least 100 [lg 100] = 600

comparisons. Since it takes the machine one second to do this, it requires about 0.0016 second for each comparison. Because to sort a list of 1000 names requires at least 100 [lg 1000] = 9000 comparisons, at least 15 seconds is required.

3. Surprising as it may seem, this is a worst-case example for the quick sort algorithm. Thus, to sort 10 names requires 1/2(100 − 10) or 45 comparisons.

4. The list David, Carol, Alice, Bill, Gwen, Earl, Fred requires only 10 comparisons.

Section 11-6

1. No. Depending on which polynomial and exponential are compared, either may be small in comparison to the other for small inputs. In fact, it is true that exponential algorithms are sometimes preferred as opposed to polynomial ones when the application involves only small inputs.

2. From Alice and Bill we could form these three subcommittees:
   1. Alice
   2. Bill
   3. Alice, Bill

   From Alice, Bill, and Carol we could form these subcommittees:

   1. Alice
   2. Bill
   3. Carol
   4. Alice, Bill
   5. Alice, Carol
   6. Bill, Carol
   7. Alice, Bill, Carol

   From Alice, Bill, Carol, and David we could obtain 15 different subcommittees. The point here is that the number of subcommittees is growing exponentially, and from this point on, the job of listing all the possibilities becomes a laborious task.

3. Within the class of polynomial problems is the sorting problem, which can be solved by polynomial algorithms such as the insertion sort or the quick sort.

   Within the class of nonpolynomial problems is the task of listing all the subcommittees that could be formed from a given parent committee.

   Any polynomial problem is an NP problem, but the problem of finding a subcommittee whose age total is a given value is an example of an NP problem that has not been shown to be a polynomial problem.

Index